Getting Started With PowerPivot For Excel 2010

By Dr. Indera E. Murphy

Tolana Publishing
Teaneck, New Jersey

Getting Started With PowerPivot For Excel 2010

Published By:
Tolana Publishing
PO Box 719
Teaneck, NJ 07666 USA

Find us online at www.tolanapublishing.com
Inquiries may be sent to the publisher: tolanapub@yahoo.com

Our books are available online at www.barnesandnoble.com. They can also be ordered from Ingram and Baker & Taylor.

Quantity discounts are available for corporations, non-profit organizations and educational institutions for educational purposes, fundraising or resale. www.tolana.com/wholesale.html

ISBN-13: 978-1-935208-16-7
ISBN-10: 1-935208-16-0

Library of Congress Control Number: 2011920114

Printed and bound in the United States Of America

Cover by Mary Kramer, owner of Milkweed Graphics, www.milkweedgraphics.com

v1.0

About The Series

Getting Started With PowerPivot For Excel 2010, is part of the growing series of computer software books that are designed to be used in a classroom setting, an online class or as a self-paced learning tool. The books contain an abundance of step-by-step instructions and screen shots to help reduce the "stress" often associated with learning new software.

Titles In The Series

	ISBN
ACT! 2007	978-0-9773912-5-7
ACT! 2009	978-1-935208-07-5
ACT! 2010	978-1-935208-09-9
ACT! Pro 2011	978-1-935208-13-6
Using Crystal Reports 2008 With ACT! 2010 Databases	978-1-935208-10-5
Crystal Reports For Visual Studio 2005	978-0-9773912-6-4
Crystal Reports Basic For Visual Studio 2008	978-0-9773912-8-8
Crystal Reports For Visual Studio 2010	978-1-935208-12-9
Crystal Reports XI For Beginners (2nd Edition)	978-1-935208-00-6
What's New In Crystal Reports 2008	978-1-935208-01-3
Crystal Reports 2008 For Beginners (Revised)	978-0-9773912-9-5
Crystal Xcelsius 4.5	978-1-935208-02-0
Xcelsius 2008	978-1-935208-05-1
Microsoft Office Starter 2010 (Word & Excel)	978-1-935208-14-3
Microsoft PowerPivot For Excel 2010	978-1-935208-16-7
OpenOffice.org 2 Writer	978-0-9773912-4-0
OpenOffice.org 3 Writer	978-1-935208-08-2
Microsoft Works 7	978-0-9773912-2-6
Microsoft Works 8 & 8.5	978-0-9773912-1-9
Microsoft Works 9	978-0-9773912-7-1
Windows XP	978-0-9773912-0-2

About The Author

Dr. Indera E. Murphy is an author, educator and IT professional that has over 20 years of experience in the Information Technology field. She has held a variety of positions including technical writer, programmer, consultant, web designer, course developer and project leader. Indera has designed and developed software applications and web sites, as well as, manage technology driven projects in several industries. In addition to being an Executive Director and consultant, as an online adjunct professor, she has taught courses in a variety of areas including project management, technical writing, information processing, Access, HTML, Windows, Excel, Dreamweaver and critical thinking.

Thank you for purchasing this book!

Why A Beginners Book Specifically For PowerPivot For Excel 2010?

There are a few reasons that I decided to write a book for PowerPivot for Excel 2010. They are listed below.

⇒ I've never had the opportunity to write a book on the first version of a software package before. Never mind a free tool that I suspect will grow by leaps and bounds and become well known by a variety of Excel users. I'm excited and I hope that you are as well.

⇒ There is always a need for a beginners book for a software package.

⇒ I wrote this beginners guide for PowerPivot for Excel to show people that have created basic pivot tables or pivot charts or people that have never created a pivot table or pivot chart, what PowerPivot adds to Excel. As a beginner book, it does not cover every feature and function that PowerPivot has. If you go through all of the exercises, you will have a good foundation of how to use PowerPivot to create and enhance pivot tables and pivot charts.

⇒ After reading the descriptions of the four or five books that were already available for PowerPivot at the time this book went to print, I came to the conclusion that they were written for people that are heavy pivot table users. There are many people that are like me, who have created a few pivot tables over the years and are now curious about this new add-in for Excel.

⇒ With so many different groups of people interested in PowerPivot, I had a choice of audiences to write for. I decided to write for the beginner or novice Excel user to help level the playing field amount Excel users. I did not want this to be one of my usual 500 plus page beginner level books because I suspected that with PowerPivot, people wanted to kick the tires for a while first, before making a serious commitment to the tool.

Who This Book Is For

This book is primarily for people that have never used PowerPivot for Excel, but want to learn what functionality PowerPivot adds to pivot tables and pivot charts. Business Intelligence consultants and professionals will find this book helpful in terms of how they can incorporate PowerPivot into the projects that they work on. It is also for people that used the beta version of PowerPivot to see what the software was about and are now looking for step-by-step instructions.

Over the years, I have come to realize that many people only use a small percent of the features that software has to offer. One of the goals in all of the books that I write is to point out as many features as possible. My theory is that if more people knew about more than 10% of the features that a software package has, at the very least, they would try a few of them.

I know that many books claim to have "step-by-step instructions". If you have tried to follow books that make this claim and you got lost or could not complete a task as instructed, it may not have been your fault. When I decided to write computer books, I vowed to really have step-by-step instructions that actually included every step, even though some people claim that it is annoying. This includes steps like which file to open, which option to select, when to save a file and more. In my opinion, it is this level of detail that makes a computer book easy to follow. I hope that you feel the same way. If not, this is probably not the book for you.

CONTENTS

GETTING STARTED WITH MICROSOFT POWERPIVOT FOR EXCEL 2010

After reading this chapter and completing the exercises you will be able to:

- ☑ Know what PowerPivot is and what you can use it for
- ☑ Understand the difference between the 32 and 64-bit versions of Excel
- ☑ Understand the difference between the 32 and 64-bit versions of PowerPivot for Excel
- ☑ Download the sample files
- ☑ Understand terms related to PowerPivot
- ☑ Understand the difference between PowerPivot for Excel and PowerPivot for SharePoint

CHAPTER 1

Welcome To PowerPivot For Excel!

There are several types of people that have an interest in learning PowerPivot for Excel because it can be used across an organization. The fact that the software is free will definitely increase the number of users. When I first heard about PowerPivot, I was concerned about two things:

① How seriously would the software be taken because it was a free add-in? Not so long ago free software was not taken seriously and was often deemed inferior on one level or another. Thankfully, there have been some very successful open source software packages that have helped removed the stigma of free software being inferior.

② Would a large number of people want to take the time to learn how to use this tool, considering that there is not a lot of information and documentation about it that a novice user could take and run with, as they say.

What I did know was that traditional business intelligence tools, self-service or otherwise, are in demand, even if they have a steep learning curve. For a reason that I cannot explain, many people believe that free equals easy. I decided that a beginners book (meaning brief and to the point, with step-by-step instructions) would be needed because many people that wanted to learn more about PowerPivot for Excel would not want to have to sift through a 500 plus page book to figure out how to use free software. Hopefully, you feel that this book is the right fit for your introduction to PowerPivot.

There is a broad spectrum of people that could benefit from learning PowerPivot. There are regular Excel users like me and probably, you too. There are Excel power users that have spent countless hours pushing Excel past its intended limits <smile>. I suspect that business analysts will use it as a prototype tool for a business intelligence solution.

Because PowerPivot workbooks can be published on SharePoint servers, SharePoint users will be interested also because they will have a repository, if you will, of pivot table reports that they can use and share. Database Administrators will become more interested in PowerPivot over time when they understand that PowerPivot will not allow enterprise databases to become compromised and that PowerPivot does not write back to the database. DBA's can provide a link to the appropriate database and let the PowerPivot user handle it from there.

The goal of this book is to show novice users how to enhance pivot tables and pivot charts that they have been creating in Excel by using PowerPivot for Excel 2010. This book is a visual guide that has over 415 illustrations that practically eliminate the guess work. While you can jump to the section that covers something that you need to know right now, I hope that you go through the entire book because you will get more from the book that way.

Working through the exercises in the order that they are presented in this book will provide a better understanding of the concepts because you can see first hand what PowerPivot is capable of, instead of just reading about the concepts. I don't know about you, but it can be frustrating when you need to emulate something that you have read is possible for a software package to do and you try it on your own and it doesn't work! It is at that very moment that you realize how helpful it would be to have step-by-step instructions.

Learning tips and shortcuts will let you work faster and smarter, while also learning the boundaries and limitations of PowerPivot. The more that you know about PowerPivot for Excel 2010, the easier your day to day pivot table and pivot chart creation experiences will be, which will make you more productive. **So sit back and lets get started!**

How This Book Is Organized

Topics and exercises in one chapter build on ones covered in previous chapters. To get the most out of this book, it is not advised that you skip around. The first reason is because some of the workbooks used in later chapters are created in exercises earlier in the book. The other reason is that a topic or option may have been covered in more detail earlier in the book. If you decide to skip around and cannot complete an exercise because there is something that you do not understand, you will have to go back and find the section that covers the topic in question. Below is an overview of what is covered in each chapter.

Chapter 1, Getting Started With Microsoft PowerPivot For Excel 2010 covers background information on PowerPivot, different versions of Excel 2010, different versions of PowerPivot and PowerPivot terminology.

Chapter 2, Quick Tour Of PowerPivot walks you through the steps needed to connect to a database, import data into PowerPivot and use the PowerPivot Field List to create a pivot table using PowerPivot data.

Chapter 3, Exploring The PowerPivot Workspace covers options in the PowerPivot workspace, including the PowerPivot tab on the Excel ribbon and the PowerPivot window ribbon.

Chapter 4, The Table Import Wizard covers the Table Import Wizard and the types of data sources that PowerPivot can use to import data from.

Chapter 5, Importing Data From A Database Into PowerPivot covers importing data from databases, views and queries.

Chapter 6, Importing Other Types Of Data Into PowerPivot covers a variety of ways to import data into PowerPivot, including importing data from a text file, spreadsheet and a data feed.

Chapter 7, Linking Tables, Pasting And Appending Data covers linking tables in Excel spreadsheets to PowerPivot tables, pasting and appending data in PowerPivot tables.

Chapter 8, Filtering And Sorting Data covers filtering and sorting data in a PowerPivot table. Other topics covered are changing the data type of columns in a PowerPivot table, formatting PowerPivot data and creating custom filters.

Chapter 9, Creating Relationships covers creating relationships manually between PowerPivot tables. Auto detection of relationships and managing relationships is also covered.

Chapter 10, Creating Data Analysis Expressions (DAX) covers creating Data Analysis Expressions (DAX) formulas in PowerPivot tables to enhance the data in pivot tables and pivot charts. DAX language operators, row context, filter context and query context are also covered.

Chapter 11, Creating Pivot Tables covers building pivot tables using data in PowerPivot tables. The options on the Pivot Table Tools contextual tab and PowerPivot Field List are also covered.

Chapter 12, Creating Pivot Charts covers building pivot charts using data in PowerPivot tables. Chart types and the options on the Pivot Chart Tools contextual tab are also covered.

Chapter 13, Enhancing Pivot Tables And Pivot Charts covers creating and using DAX Measures, Names Sets and refreshing data in pivot tables.

Chapter 14, Using Slicers covers adding slicers to pivot table reports and creating dashboards.

Helpful, But Not Required

This book is written to be used for self-paced training, as well as, accommodate classroom and online training. While there are no required prerequisites to successfully complete the exercises in this book, having a general knowledge of any of the following would be helpful.

- ☑ Database structures
- ☑ Queries
- ☑ Data analysis
- ☑ Business intelligence
- ☑ Excel 2010
- ☑ Slicers
- ☑ PivotTables
- ☑ PivotCharts

Objectives Of The Book

This book takes a hands-on, performance based approach to teaching you how to use PowerPivot for Excel and provides the skills required to create pivot tables and pivot charts efficiently. While PowerPivot for Excel may be considered very technical or "geeky", I explain the terms and concepts in a manner that is hopefully easy to understand. Examples and screen shots are also provided to help make sure that you understand the concepts and are completing the exercises correctly. After completing the exercises in this book, you will be able to perform the following tasks and more:

- ☑ Understand the PowerPivot workspace
- ☑ Understand the options on the PowerPivot tab on the Excel ribbon
- ☑ Create calculated columns
- ☑ Import data into PowerPivot
- ☑ Rename columns of data in a PowerPivot table
- ☑ Create relationships between tables of data in the PowerPivot window
- ☑ Filter and sort data in the PowerPivot window
- ☑ Create pivot tables and pivot charts using PowerPivot data
- ☑ Add slicers to pivot tables and pivot charts
- ☑ Use Data Analysis Expressions (DAX) to create formulas that cannot be created in Excel

Conventions Used In This Book

I designed the following conventions to make it easier for you to follow the instructions in this book.

- ☑ The `Courier font` is used to indicate what you should type.
- ☑ **Drag** means to press and hold down the left mouse button while moving the mouse.
- ☑ **Click** means to press the left mouse button once, then release it immediately.
- ☑ **Right-click** means to press the right mouse button once, which will open a shortcut menu.
- ☑ Press **CTRL+SHIFT** means to press and hold down the CTRL (Control) key, then press the Shift key.
- ☑ Click **OK** means to click the OK button on the dialog box.
- ☑ Press **Enter** means to press the Enter key on your keyboard.

☑ **SMALL CAPS** are used to indicate an option to click on or to bring something to your attention.

☑ This icon indicates a shortcut or another way to complete the task. It can also indicate a tip or additional information about the topic being discussed.

☑ This icon indicates a warning, like a feature that has been removed or information that you need to be aware of.

☑ When you see the phrase "**YOU SHOULD HAVE THE OPTIONS SHOWN IN FIGURE X-X**", or something similar in the exercises, check to make sure that your screen does look like the figure. If it does, continue with the next set of instructions. If your screen does not look like the figure, redo the steps that you just completed so that your screen does match the figure. Not doing so may cause problems when trying to complete exercises later in the book.

☑ The section heading **EXERCISE X.Y:** (where X equals the chapter number and Y equals the exercise number) represents exercises that have step-by-step instructions that you should complete. You will also see sections that have step-by-step instructions that are not an exercise. Completing them as you go through the book is optional, but recommended.

☑ "E2.4 File Name" is the naming convention for the workbooks that you will create. E2.4 stands for Chapter 2, Exercise 4. You may consider some of the file names to be long. I did this on purpose, so that it is easier to know what topic the workbook covers. If you do not like to type or do not want to type the entire file name, you can just type the first part as the file name. That way when you have to find a workbook to complete another exercise, you will be able to find the correct workbook. For example, if the workbook name is E5.3 Import data from a .csv file, you can save the workbook as E5.3.

☑ **PAGE LAYOUT TAB ⇒ PAGE SETUP GROUP ⇒ ORIENTATION**, means to click on the **PAGE LAYOUT** tab, look in the **PAGE SETUP** group on the Page Layout tab, to select the **ORIENTATION** button shown in Figure 1-1.

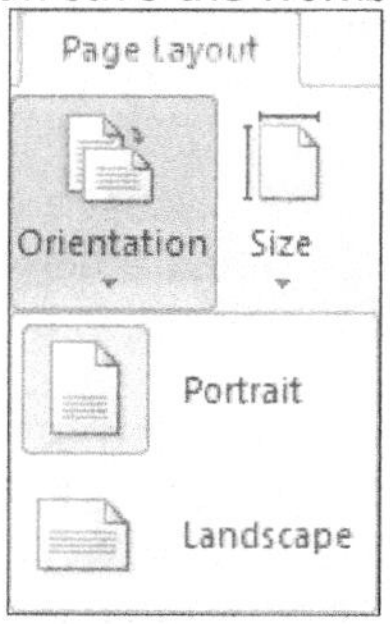

Figure 1-1 Ribbon navigation technique

Assumptions

Yes, I know one should never assume anything, but the following assumptions have been made. It is assumed that . . . .

☑ You have Excel 2010 for Windows (32 or 64-bit) installed on your computer. (1) PowerPivot does not work with **EXCEL STARTER 2010** or the **EXCEL WEB APP**. (3) If you are not sure which version of Excel to install, read the section, "What Is The Difference Between The 32 And 64-Bit Versions Of Excel 2010", later in this chapter.

☑ You are familiar with the Windows environment including Windows Explorer and are comfortable using a mouse.

☑ You have PowerPivot for Excel installed. If not, download it from www.powerpivot.com. The version of PowerPivot that you install has to match the version of Excel 2010 that you have installed. For example, if you have the 32-bit version of Excel 2010 installed, you have install the 32-bit version of PowerPivot.

☑ You know that the operating system used to write this book is Windows 7. If you are using a different version of Windows, some of the screen shots may have a slightly different look.

☑ You know that PowerPivot requires 100MB of disk space for the installation and uses an additional 33MB of disk space when the first pivot table is added to a worksheet.

☑ You know that the minimum amount of RAM needed to run PowerPivot for Excel and the Office 2010 components is 2GB. I tested some of the million plus record tables on a laptop with 2GB of RAM and on a laptop with 4GB of RAM. I did notice a performance increase on the laptop with 4GB of RAM. Importing large amounts of data did not take as long with 4GB of RAM. When working with large files, as will be the case in this book, it is possible that your computer could run out of memory. Sometimes closing other applications that are open on the computer or closing applications that are running in the background will free up enough memory. (4)

☑ You know that the phrase "end user" refers to the person that will use the pivot tables that you create. If you will create and use the pivot tables, in the context of this book you are also the end user. When designing reports for other people to use, a primary goal should be to make the product as user friendly as possible . . . without going over budget.

☑ For a reason that I can't explain, I use the words "spreadsheet" and "worksheet" interchangeably when referring to the data on a tab in Excel. I also use the words "field" and "column" interchangeably because the data is in a field in the database that you import data from and then it's called a column in Excel and PowerPivot.

☑ When you see <smile>, that signifies my attempt of adding humor to the learning process.

☑ You understand that some topics or concepts are repeated in this book because they are important and I want you to remember them when you are creating pivot tables on your own.

☑ You know that when I discuss a topic and reference pivot tables, the topic also applies to pivot charts, unless stated otherwise. The reason pivot charts are not generally referenced as much as pivot tables are, is because pivot charts require data from a pivot table to be created.

☑ You have access to the Internet to download the practice files that come with this book and to download any updates to PowerPivot that are available.

☑ You know the difference between **SAVE** (saves the file with the same file name) and **SAVE AS** (is used to save the file with a different file name or the same file name in a different folder). Excel has buttons for both save options above the ribbon on the Quick Access toolbar, as illustrated in Figure 1-2. Many exercises instruct you to save an existing workbook with a new file name. This is when you would use the Save As button. If you want to use the Save As button, but it is not currently displayed on your toolbar, you will learn how to add it to the toolbar in Chapter 3, "Customize The Quick Access Toolbar In Excel".

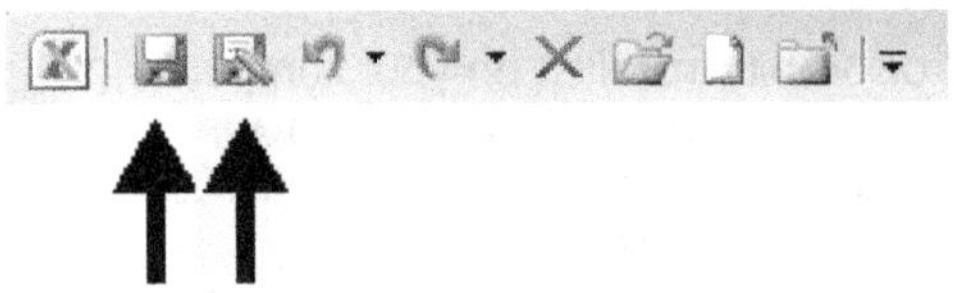

Figure 1-2 Excel Save options illustrated

(1)

Order To Install The Software

If you have not installed PowerPivot yet, below is the order that the software has to be installed in.

1. **.NET 3.5 SP1**. If your computer has Windows 7, this software is already installed because it is now part of Windows. If your computers operating system, is Windows Vista or Windows XP, you have to install this framework if it is not already installed. (2)
2. **OFFICE SHARED FEATURES**. This component has to be installed because it contains the Visual Studio Tools For Office (VSTO) run-time module. If you are only installing Excel 2010, you have to install the Office Shared Features component separately. If you are installing Office 2010, select the Office Shared Features component during the setup before the installation starts.
3. **EXCEL 2010**. If you already installed Excel, but did not install the Office Shared Features component first, you have to uninstall Excel, install the Office Shared Features component, then reinstall Excel.
4. **POWERPIVOT FOR EXCEL**. 100MB of hard drive space is required just for PowerPivot. This is in addition to the hard drive space required for all of the other required software listed above.

(2) Windows Minimum Requirements

Table 1-1 lists the requirements for older operating systems that your computer must have in order to install PowerPivot. Windows 7 and Windows Server 2008 R2 already meet the requirements.

Operating System	Minimum Requirement
Windows Vista	SP2
Windows XP	SP3, 32-bit only
Windows Server 2008	SP2

Table 1-1 Windows minimum requirements

Attention Windows XP Users

In Windows Vista and Windows 7, the PowerPivot options are available on a ribbon.
In Windows XP, the PowerPivot options are available on a set of menus. The link below shows the correlation between the options on the ribbon in Windows Vista and Windows 7 and their menu counterparts in Windows XP.
http://technet.microsoft.com/en-us/library/ff452230.aspx

(3) The Excel Web App can be used to view a workbook that has PowerPivot data, but the workbook cannot be edited in the Excel Web App.

(4)

Try ReadyBoost For Better Computer Performance

If you find that your computer is running slow or you see the low memory warning message, you can try using Microsoft's ReadyBoost feature, instead of buying more RAM right now. ReadyBoost works with Windows XP, Vista and Windows 7. This tool lets you use an external USB 2.0 drive as external RAM. The rule of thumb is to use an external USB drive that has twice the amount of RAM that the computer has. For example, if your computer has 4GB of RAM, using an 8GB or larger external USB drive (up to 32GB per removable device) will provide the most performance improvement. For more information and instructions on using ReadyBoost, go to www.microsoft.com and type `ReadyBoost` in the Search field.

ReadyBoost (Continued)
Below are some tips for using ReadyBoost.
① The external drive should be directly plugged into the computer.
② The external drive will perform better if it is not formatted in FAT32 format.
③ While you can store files on the external drive that you will ReadyBoost enable, for the best performance you should dedicate the drive to ReadyBoost.
④ When you first plug the external drive into your computer and start ReadyBoost, you may see a message saying that the drive is not ReadyBoost compliant. If so, click the **TEST AGAIN** button.
⑤ ReadyBoost will work with a 1GB external drive, but the larger the external drive, the better the performance will be.

What Is The Difference Between The 32 And 64-Bit Versions Of Excel 2010?

The list below provides an overview of the differences between the versions of Excel 2010.

① The 32 and 64-bit versions of Excel 2010 cannot be installed on the same hard drive on a computer.
② The 32-bit version of Excel 2010 can be installed on a computer that has an older version of Excel and will not modify the older version of Excel. The 64-bit version of Excel 2010 does not allow prior versions of Excel to be installed on the same hard drive.
③ Currently, add-ins for Excel 2010 are 32-bit and will not run in a 64-bit environment.
④ The 64-bit version of Excel can handle larger file sizes.

If you know that you will be working with large data sets (millions of records in a table, you should consider installing the 64-bit version of Excel 2010.

What Is The Difference Between The 32 And 64-Bit Versions Of PowerPivot?

The version of PowerPivot that you install must match the version of Excel 2010 that is installed. The difference between these versions is that the 32-bit version only supports up to 2GB of data in memory. The 64-bit version supports up to 4GB of data in memory.

How To Verify That PowerPivot Is Installed Correctly

After you have installed all of the components and PowerPivot for Excel, open Excel. On the Excel splash screen you should see the message shown in Figure 1-3 indicating that the PowerPivot add-in is being loaded.

Once Excel is open, you should see the PowerPivot tab on the Excel ribbon. Click on this tab, then click the PowerPivot Window button. An empty PowerPivot window will open. Seeing this window lets you know that PowerPivot is installed correctly.

Figure 1-3 Excel splash screen showing the PowerPivot add-in loading

Interactive Message Symbols

Like many other software packages, Excel and PowerPivot will display interactive messages that require a response from you to confirm an action. Table 1-2 explains the three types of interactive message symbols and what they mean.

Symbol	Name	This Interactive Message Type . . .
	Information	Provides information about an action that you just performed.
	Warning	Usually requires you to make a decision.
	Critical	Requires you to make a decision before moving on to the next step.

Table 1-2 Interactive message symbols explained

Getting Help

As discussed below, there are four primary ways to get help if you have a question on how to use a feature or option in PowerPivot.

① Read this book from cover to cover and complete the exercises. Many of the basic questions that you may have are probably covered in this book.
② The Online Help file. It is helpful for the basic definitions of features.
③ PowerPivot forum. You can post questions and learn how other people are using the software. The forum is also a great way to keep current on the latest PowerPivot trends and for getting ideas on how to enhance your pivot table and pivot chart reports. The name of the forum is SQL Server PowerPivot For Excel. The web site is http://social.msdn.microsoft.com/forums/en/sqlkjpowerpivotforexcel/threads.
④ Hire an Excel consultant. Need I say that this is the most expensive option and you probably will not get an answer to your question as fast as you would like.

Excel Pivot Tables

Excel pivot tables have been part of Excel for as long as I can remember. As great as they are and as easy as they are to use, there are some limitations in pivot tables being created in Excel that there is no work around for. Some of these limitations are briefly explained below.

① Creating the queries to get the data from a data source requires a skill set that many Excel users do not have. This is because the data needed for the pivot table is usually stored in multiple tables in a database or stored in multiple data sources. For example, some data may be stored in a database and other data that is needed to create the pivot table is stored on a worksheet in Excel.
② Pivot tables in Excel can only be created from one table on a worksheet.
③ If the data needs to be analyzed several ways, multiple queries may be needed to get the data in a format that can be used to create a pivot table for each way the data needs to be analyzed.
④ Excel worksheets have a row limitation. If the data source has more than one million rows, all of the query writing in the world will not let you add more rows of data to the worksheet.

What Is PowerPivot And What Can I Use It For?

PowerPivot is a tool that is used to pull data from multiple sources into one PowerPivot database that is part of an Excel 2010 workbook. This functionality is used to enhance data analysis done in pivot tables and pivot charts in Excel. PowerPivot workbooks, as I call them, can also be shared with other users if the workbook is published on a SharePoint server. PowerPivot is Microsoft's first self-service business intelligence tool. Business Intelligence (also known as BI) tools and analysts are in great demand in companies of all sizes, in all types of industries.

The standard business intelligence approach to data is to place the data in a data warehouse for staging and then import the data into an Online Analytical Processing (OLAP) database. PowerPivot allows the data to bypass the data warehouse staging area step and be imported directly into the software that will be used to process the data.

PowerPivot for Excel is a Visual Studio Tools for Office (VSTO) free add-in. Specifically, PowerPivot is an add-in for the pivot table and pivot chart functionality in Excel. While you will see the software referred to as PowerPivot for Excel, its official name is **MICROSOFT SQL SERVER POWERPIVOT FOR EXCEL**. This is because PowerPivot is included in SQL Server 2008 R2, which includes major enhancements for business intelligence.

PowerPivot is used to import millions and millions of rows of data that will be used to create pivot tables. In addition to spreadsheet data, data can be imported from a variety of sources including databases, like Access, text files, Oracle, Atom data feeds and more. PowerPivot has a database that is embedded in the workbook. Once the data is imported into PowerPivot, it can be analyzed by creating pivot tables in Excel. PowerPivot puts the data into OLAP format behind the scenes. To take PowerPivot to the next level, which includes enterprise collaboration, PowerPivot for SharePoint can be used.

One reason that PowerPivot will grow in popularity at a rapid rate is because it will empower an Excel user to create and analyze data in pivot tables that was not available before. For business analysts, PowerPivot will become an asset because they can connect to external data sources and import data into PowerPivot, without having to get the IT staff to help, once access has been granted.

Unlike pivot tables created from data in an Excel spreadsheet, pivot tables created with data from PowerPivot tables can use data from multiple sources and support a lot more data. In my opinion, the primary reasons to use PowerPivot are discussed below.

① You need the ability to create a pivot table with data from more than one data source.

② You need to create pivot tables that currently cannot be created in Excel.

③ You need to analyze data in a pivot table that has more than 1,048,575 rows of data, which the maximum number of rows that an Excel worksheet supports.

The purpose of PowerPivot for Excel is to help Excel end users access data in multi-dimensional databases without having extensive training and knowledge of this type of data modeling. Usually, only IT professionals have data modeling knowledge.

Additionally, PowerPivot has a new programming language called Data Analysis Expressions (DAX). This language adds data manipulation functionality to Excel formulas, including analysis and complex grouping that is above the formula capabilities that are available in Excel. DAX takes the formulas that you are use to creating for pivot tables and pivot charts in Excel to a whole new level.

The DAX programming language was created based on the formulas and functions that are already available in Excel, in hopes of making it easier for Excel users to create more advanced formulas to help resolve business intelligence needs. PowerPivot for Excel allows non programmers to access enterprise data to perform a higher level of analysis in one of Excels most popular analysis tools - PivotTables, then is available in Excel.

The primary functionality that PowerPivot adds to Excel is that it brings self-service business intelligence to the desktop. This means that the data that you use to create pivot tables in Excel, that are based on data in PowerPivot tables, can actually be saved on your computers hard drive, opposed to being saved on a server.

As I mentioned earlier, PowerPivot can be used to analyze millions of records. The Table Import Wizard is the primary tool used to import data into PowerPivot. The data is imported as tables and stored on separate tabs in the PowerPivot window. Believe it or not, data can also be pasted into a PowerPivot table. Really? That's what I thought when I first found that out. PowerPivot stores the data that is imported in a database that is saved in the Excel workbook. The local (database) engine is used to load, query and update the database in the Excel workbook.

This data analysis tool adds a lot of functionality to Excel pivot tables. Once the data is imported into PowerPivot, relationships between the tables of data can be created, very similar to how relationships between tables in a database are created, without using **VLOOKUP**.

Use Multiple Data Sources Data from a variety of sources from a text file to a large corporate database can be imported into PowerPivot, including, but not limited to the following:

- ☑ Access databases
- ☑ SQL Server databases
- ☑ Text files
- ☑ Other PowerPivot workbooks that are stored on a SharePoint Server
- ☑ Excel spreadsheets
- ☑ Data feeds
- ☑ Sybase
- ☑ Oracle

PowerPivot Workbooks vs Excel Workbooks

In addition to how PowerPivot and Excel handle data differently, there are other differences between these types of workbooks that you should be aware of, as discussed below.

① The biggest difference between these workbooks is that a PowerPivot workbook stores data in a database that is embedded in the workbook. Keep in mind that PowerPivot is an add-in application for Excel, not a stand alone application, which means that PowerPivot cannot run on its own.

② The second biggest difference is that PowerPivot tables can store more than one million rows of data, which is the maximum in Excel. While one million rows may sound like a lot of data, in BI analysis, one is often working with tens of millions of rows of data. Two scenarios that come to mind are the number of tests run on patients in a hospital over the last five years or the number of transactions for a major credit card company over the last year. In Chapter 6, you will import more than two millions rows of data into one PowerPivot table.

③ PowerPivot does not support **VISUAL BASIC FOR APPLICATIONS (VBA)**, but VBA can be used on the Excel side of a PowerPivot workbook to enhance pivot tables if needed.

④ PowerPivot lets you build the data model that you need, whether the data comes from one database or 20 databases.
⑤ PowerPivot data can only be saved in the following types of Excel workbook files: **.XLSX** (Excel workbook), **.XLSM** (Macro enabled workbook) and **.XLSB** (Excel Binary workbook).
⑥ The **GROUP** option in Excel pivot tables is not available in pivot tables that use PowerPivot data. The calculated columns feature in PowerPivot provides similar functionality.
⑦ PowerPivot supports moving and copying spreadsheets in an existing workbook, but does not support moving and copying spreadsheets that have pivot tables or pivot charts to a different workbook.
⑧ PowerPivot workbooks can save up to 2GB of data and can support up to 4GB of data in memory.

2GB File Size
While 2GB may not seem like a lot of space for a single workbook, keep in mind that .xlsx workbook files are really zip files. This means that it can store more than 2GB of raw data because of the data compression that zip files have and the **COLUMNAR DATABASE** that PowerPivot uses.

Using Excel 2007
Excel 2007 can be used to open a PowerPivot workbook to change the formatting and style of a pivot table in the PowerPivot workbook. Excel 2007 cannot be used to interact with pivot tables and pivot charts that use PowerPivot data or change the data.

Benefits Of Using PowerPivot For Excel

Below are some of the benefits of using PowerPivot to access enterprise data to create business intelligence solutions.

① Data from several sources can be imported into one PowerPivot workbook.
② Linking to data sources allows you to refresh the data in the PowerPivot workbook very easily.
③ PowerPivot allows you to use Excel, which you are already familiar with to create enhanced pivot tables and pivot charts.

Exercise 1.1: Create A Folder For Your Files

Many of the topics discussed in this book have step-by-step instructions. If you want to follow along, there are practice files that you can download and use. Some of the files used in this book are in a zip file named powerpivot2010.zip on our web site. Obtaining the remaining files used in this book are covered in Exercise 1.2.

1. To obtain the zip file, send an email to powerpivot2010@tolanapublishing.com. If you do not receive an email in a few minutes with the subject line PowerPivot For Excel 2010 Book Files, check the spam folder in your email software. When you receive the email, follow the steps below.

2. Open Windows Explorer, then click on the C drive or the primary drive that you save files on.

3. File ⇒ New ⇒ Folder.

4. Type `PowerPivot For Excel Practice Files` as the folder name, then press Enter. I will refer to this folder as **YOUR FOLDER** throughout this book.

5. Open the web page listed in the email that you received and download the zip file into the folder that you just created.

6. In Windows Explorer, click on the folder that you just created.

   Right-click on the zip file and select **EXTRACT TO HERE**, as illustrated in Figure 1-4 (if you are using WinZip). The files will be extracted (copied) to the folder.

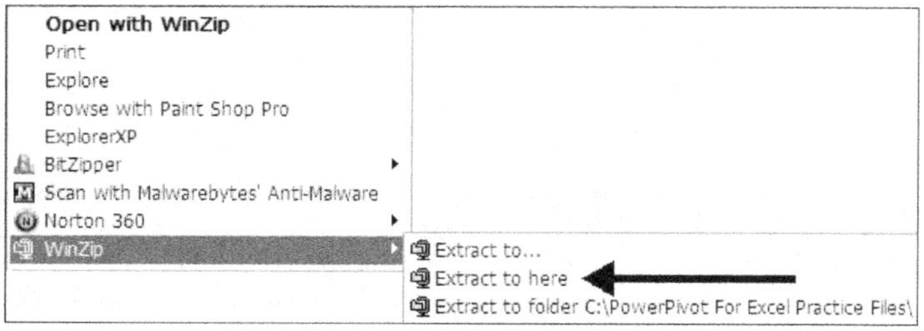

Figure 1-4 How to extract the files

Change The Default Folder Location

The folder that you just created will also be used to save the workbooks in that you create in this book. Therefore, it may be useful to set it as the default folder that Excel uses. If you want to change the default folder, follow the steps below. Doing this is optional. When you are finished working on the exercises in this book, you can change the default folder to the one that you will use most.

1. Open Excel, then File tab ⇒ Options ⇒ Save button.

2. Type `C:\PowerPivot For Excel Practice Files\` in the **DEFAULT FILE LOCATION** field shown at the bottom of Figure 1-5, then click OK.

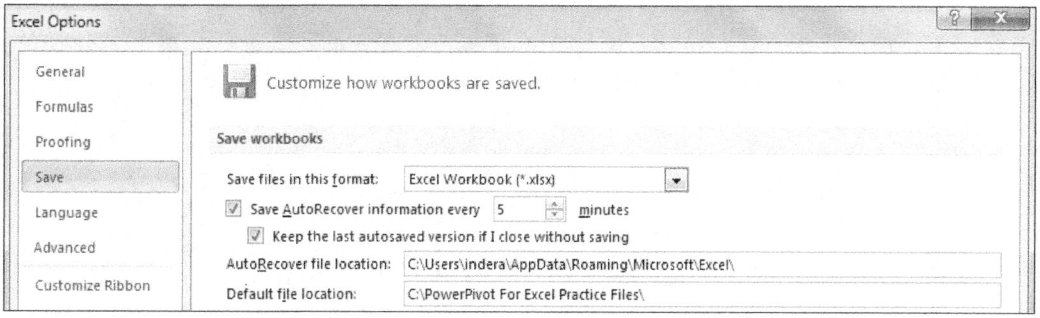

Figure 1-5 Excel Save options

Exercise 1.2: Download Sample Data

In addition to the practice files that you downloaded from our web site in the previous exercise, there are more sample files that are used as the basis for exercises in this book. The steps below show you where to get the files from.

Contoso Sample Data These sample files are for a fictitious company named Contoso. They sell a variety of products in their stores around the world. The zip file has the files explained in Table 1-3. To download the zip file, follow the steps below.

1. Go to http://powerpivotsampledata.codeplex.com.
2. Click the Downloads button. You should see a link for the **CONTOSO V2** file. The file date is June 10, 2010.
3. Download this file to your folder, then extract the files to the folder.

File	Description
Contoso Sales	This Access database contains tables for company store locations, products, product subcategories, promotions that stores have and sales information.
Geography	This spreadsheet contains information about the continents and countries that the company does business in.
Product Categories	This Access database has one table that lists the categories of products that the company has.
SQL Query	This text file contains a query that is used to select the records that will be imported from the database.
Stores	This spreadsheet contains contact information for all of the stores.

Table 1-3 Contoso sample data files explained

Viewing Microsoft Access Databases
If you have the need to open a database listed above in Table 1-3, you will see the security warning shown in Figure 1-6. If you want to edit the data, click the **ENABLE CONTENT** button illustrated in the figure. Opening a database in Microsoft Access is not needed to complete the exercises in this book.

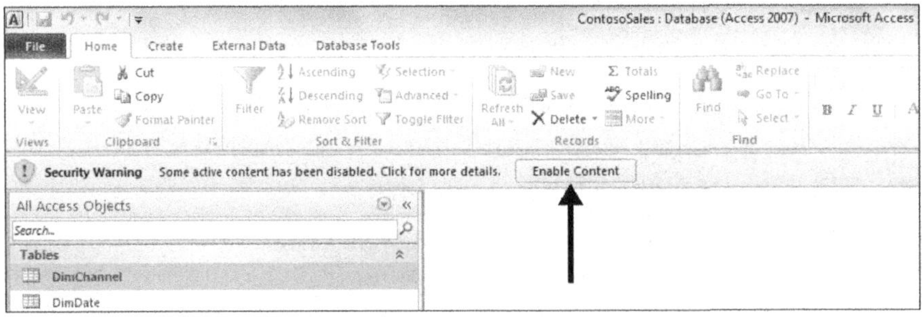

Figure 1-6 Access database security warning

Adventure Works Database This database is for a fictitious company named Adventure Works. The company makes and sells bicycles globally. This is the Microsoft Access version of the popular SQL database by the same name, that has been around for years. The database has 67 tables.

I decided to use the Access version of the database for this book because I did not want people to have to download and install SQL Server or upgrade the version that they may already have installed. If something went wrong with that installation or your computer is not powerful enough to support it, you would be stuck. The Access version does not require you to install any other software, not even Microsoft Access.

1. Go to http://adventureworksaccess.codeplex.com/releases/view/44496.
2. Click on the **ADVENTURE WORKS IN ACCESS 2010 FORMAT (ZIPPED)** link.
3. Download this file to your folder, then extract the database to the folder.

Northwind Database This database is for a fictitious company called Northwind Traders. The database contains the sales data for the companies imports and specialty foods. If you have Microsoft Access 2007 or Access 2010 already installed on your computer, you may already have this database (northwind.accdb). If not, follow the steps below.

1. Go to http://office.microsoft.com/en-us/templates/CT010142865.aspx.
2. Click on the Northwind 2007 link, then click on the Download link on the page that has the details for the database.
3. Download the database to your folder.

Additional Sample Databases

The databases discussed below are not used in this book. They are listed in case you want more PowerPivot samples to look at.

Microsoft PowerPivot For Excel Sample Files To download the zip file, follow the steps below. The spreadsheets are explained in Table 1-4.

1. Go to www.microsoft.com. Type `PowerPivot samples` in the Search field, then press Enter.
2. On the Search Results page, you should see a link for PowerPivot For Excel 2010 Samples. Click on the link.
3. The top of the page should have the heading, "Microsoft PowerPivot For Excel 2010 Samples". Download the **POWERPIVOTSAMPLES.EXE** file to your folder.
4. Double-click on the file. Select your folder as the folder to unzip the files to.

File	This Workbook Contains . . .
LCA BI - Financial Report Usage	A financial usage tracking report that uses data from four PowerPivot tables.
PowerPivot Healthcare Audit	Data from an SQL database. It contains several pivot tables and pivot charts, as well as a dashboard.
PowerPivot Tutorial Sample	A sales by channel report that contains data from two databases and a linked Excel table.

Table 1-4 Microsoft PowerPivot For Excel sample workbook files explained

PowerPivot For Excel 2010 Data Analysis Expressions Sample v1.0 To download the zip file, follow the steps below. The file is explained in Table 1-5.

1. Go to www.microsoft.com. Type `DAX samples` in the Search field, then press Enter.

2. Click on the PowerPivot DAX Samples link, then download the **POWERPIVOTDAXSAMPLES.EXE** file to your folder.

3. Double-click on the file. Select your folder as the folder to unzip the file to.

File	Description
Contoso Sample DAX Formulas	This workbook has several pivot tables that were created using DAX calculated fields created in the PowerPivot tables in the workbook. In Chapter 11, you will learn how to create a pivot table similar to the one on the Sales By Period tab in this workbook.

Table 1-5 PowerPivot For Excel 2010 Data Analysis Expressions sample workbook explained

Displaying File Extensions

Going through this book you will open a variety of file types. Some of the file names are the same, even though they have different file extensions, as illustrated in Figure 1-7. The arrows point to the file extensions. If you do not see these file extensions on your computer in Windows Explorer, but want to, follow the steps below.

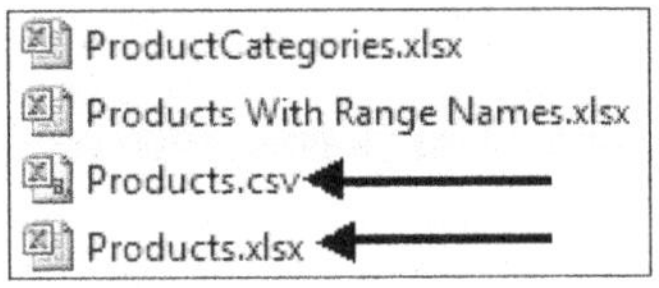

Figure 1-7 File extensions illustrated

1. Open the Control Panel in Windows, then double-click on the **FOLDER OPTIONS** option.

2. On the View tab, clear the check mark for the **HIDE EXTENSIONS FOR KNOWN FILE TYPES** option, illustrated in Figure 1-8.

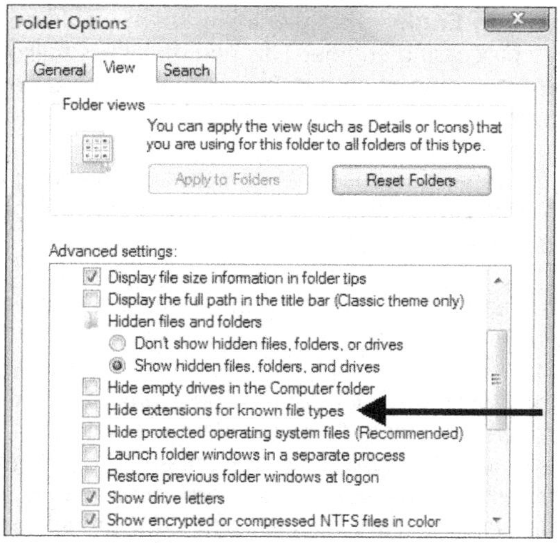

Figure 1-8 View tab on the Folder Options dialog box

3. Click the Apply button, then click OK.

PowerPivot Terminology

Before you go any further, there are some terms that you need to understand to get a better idea of how PowerPivot can aid in the decision making process, display trends in data and much more. You will also start to understand how powerful PowerPivot is.

These are terms that you may have heard before, but are not exactly sure what they mean, including: Relationship, Primary Keys, Data Refresh and Data Source Connection. The goal of this section is to briefly explain the terms and their relationship to PowerPivot.

PowerPivot Table can only contain data from one source. A table is one tab of data in the PowerPivot workbook. A PowerPivot workbook can have as many tables as needed.

PowerPivot Data is data that has been imported, appended or added to a PowerPivot table.

Relationship A relationship is a connection between two PowerPivot tables. It is how two or more tables are joined (linked). This relationship is based on a field (column) in each table that has the same value. PowerPivot tables can have more than one relationship. Tables can be joined when they have at least one field that is the same in each table. For example, an invoice table can be joined to a products table because each invoice will have at least one item from the products table. PowerPivot has a **AUTO DETECTION** feature that will automatically try to create relationships by joining tables that have related information.

Data Source Connection is information that PowerPivot uses to connect to a data source.

Slicers are a new feature in Excel 2010. They are used to filter data horizontally and vertically in pivot tables and pivot charts. PowerPivot for Excel has enhancements to slicers that are not available in the slicer functionality in Excel.

In-Memory Processing Engine In my opinion, there would be no PowerPivot without the VERTIPAQ in-memory processing engine. This engine allows millions of rows of data to be processed quickly because the processing of data in PowerPivot tables is done in memory instead of processing data from a hard drive.

PowerPivot uses a columnar database that compresses the data, thus using less space then Excel tables would use for the same amount of data. This is why millions and millions of rows of data can be imported into PowerPivot tables.

Data Refresh This feature is used to bring in the most recent version of data into a PowerPivot table from the original data source.

Data Analysis Expressions (DAX) is a new programming language that contains a collection of functions that are used to create formulas. Formulas are used to manipulate data in a PowerPivot table. The DAX programming language greatly enhances the formula capabilities that Excel provides. This allows for more calculations, analysis and grouping options to be used. If you are already familiar with the formula syntax in Excel, learning DAX should come easy.

Database Terminology

Below are key terms that you need to understand about databases in order to work with them effectively.

Field A field contains one piece of information and is stored in a record. Examples of fields include customer name and customer address. A column in a PowerPivot table is the same as a field in a database.

Record A record has one or more fields. Each of the fields in a record are related. A record looks like a row of data in a spreadsheet.

Table A table is stored in a database and is a collection of records. Most databases have more than one table. Tables are linked on fields. Tables may remind you of a spreadsheet, because SQL databases have rows and columns. Each table contains information about a specific topic. For example, a well designed customer table would only contain information about customers. The customer table would not contain information about products.

Database A database is a collection of information that is stored in one or more tables in the database. It is important to note that there are different types of physical database structures.

Relational Database A relational database is a collection of RELATED information that is stored in one or more tables in the database.

Primary Key is a unique identifier for each row of data in the table. Primary keys are usually numeric and system generated sequentially. They are often used to create relationships between tables.

Database Concepts

There are some database concepts that you need to be aware of. Having an understanding of these concepts is helpful to create pivot tables and pivot charts effectively.

Data Dictionary A data dictionary contains detailed information about the database and includes the following types of information: Database and table names, field names, field types, field sizes, indexes and related files. A data dictionary can be handwritten or typed. It can also be generated by some database software packages. When using PowerPivot, this document or file is very helpful when you are not familiar with the data that will be used to create pivot tables.

Data Source A data source is what the data is stored in. Examples of data sources are databases, tables, text files, OLAP cubes and spreadsheets.

PowerPivot For SharePoint Overview

Once you have created the PowerPivot workbook you can share it with other people like you have done in the past with Excel workbooks. While PowerPivot for SharePoint is not covered in this book, this section provides an overview of it, which will hopefully provide enough information for you to be able to make a decision whether or not the PowerPivot for SharePoint component will be helpful for your business intelligence applications and reports.

As I mentioned earlier, PowerPivot for SharePoint is used to store PowerPivot workbooks on a SharePoint server for the purpose of sharing them and for collaboration purposes. Unlike PowerPivot for Excel, PowerPivot for SharePoint will probably require the IT departments help to configure the server and install the software. If set up, PowerPivot workbooks on a SharePoint server can also be accessed from the Internet using a Web browser, in addition to viewing the workbook in Excel.

PowerPivot for SharePoint is like PowerPivot for Excel because both are add-ins. PowerPivot for SharePoint is an add-in for Microsoft SharePoint. PowerPivot for SharePoint is available as part of Microsoft SQL Server 2008 R2 and provides the following features.

① **REFRESHING DATA CAN BE SCHEDULED** This feature allows the data for PowerPivot published workbooks to be refreshed automatically, based on the schedule that you set up.
② **USE A WEB BROWSER TO VIEW POWERPIVOT WORKBOOKS** This feature allows PowerPivot workbooks to be viewed from virtually any location. When viewing the data or pivot tables in a web browser, the data is refreshed when it is filtered or sliced.
③ **MONITOR POWERPIVOT OPERATIONS** PowerPivot for SharePoint also has a set of management tools to help keep the SharePoint server and process running smoothly. Other tools are used to monitor the usage of PowerPivot workbooks. When PowerPivot for SharePoint is installed, the PowerPivot Management Dashboard is added to SharePoint. This dashboard tool allows administrators to view PowerPivot workbook usage reports, the data refresh usage and more.
④ **POWERPIVOT GALLERY** This feature is a SharePoint library that is used to view and store PowerPivot workbooks. The gallery is helpful because you do not have to know the name of the application. The PowerPivot Gallery requires Silver Light to view the PowerPivot workbooks in a Web browser. (www.microsoft.com/silverlight) The gallery has options for creating new workbooks and reports that are based on workbooks that have already been published to the PowerPivot Gallery. The gallery can also be used to create and display thumbnail images of worksheets.

PowerPivot For Excel vs PowerPivot For SharePoint

There are differences between the Excel and SharePoint versions of PowerPivot. Some of the differences are listed below.

① PowerPivot for Excel is free and does not require any additional hardware.
② PowerPivot for SharePoint is often referred to as the "server side" of PowerPivot because it requires a SharePoint server or farm.

③ PowerPivot for SharePoint adds more functionality to SharePoint 2010 by incorporating collaboration and document management for PowerPivot workbooks that are published. It also allows PowerPivot workbooks to be shared and applications can be monitored.

④ PowerPivot for SharePoint can be set up to automatically refresh the data.

QUICK TOUR OF POWERPIVOT

In this chapter you will take a quick tour of PowerPivot by creating a basic pivot table using data that you import into a PowerPivot workbook. This will provide an overview of the features and steps used to create pivot tables using data from PowerPivot tables.

CHAPTER 2

Overview

Since the 1990's when pivot table and pivot chart functionality was added to Excel, they have been used to analyze data. Hopefully as you go through the quick tour of PowerPivot in this chapter, you will see the benefit of being able to work with data from multiple external (to Excel) data sources seamlessly.

Once the data is imported, some relationships between the tables are automatically created. You have the ability to create additional relationships as needed. After the data is imported and the relationships have been created, you can create formulas that may be needed for each row of data in a PowerPivot table. Formulas that are needed to aggregate data in a pivot table are created from the PowerPivot Field List or by clicking the New Measure button on the PowerPivot tab on the Excel ribbon. You may have the need to create DAX measures to evaluate data in the pivot table.

Excel is used to create pivot tables with data that is stored in the PowerPivot database. Data can be imported into PowerPivot tables from a variety of sources including text files, databases, other workbooks and more.

As you will see, PowerPivot for Excel has two components, as explained below.

① The **POWERPIVOT WINDOW** is primarily used to import the data into PowerPivot, create relationships and to create calculated columns.

② The **POWERPIVOT FIELD LIST** is used to select the fields to create a pivot table, as well as create DAX measures.

Exercise 2.1: Let Me See What PowerPivot Can Do

In this exercise you will learn the basic steps of creating a pivot table that uses PowerPivot data. By the end of this exercise you will have used many of the core features of PowerPivot.

Step 1: Open The PowerPivot Window

This step covers opening the PowerPivot window and selecting a data source to connect to.

1. Open a new Excel workbook.

2. PowerPivot tab ⇒ PowerPivot Window button.

Welcome To PowerPivot! As you can see, PowerPivot has its own window, separate from the Excel window. Behind the scenes, the PowerPivot window is connected to the Excel workbook. If you have several Excel workbooks open, some with PowerPivot windows open and others not, Excel still knows which workbooks have PowerPivot windows open. It can get confusing looking at the Windows taskbar if you have multiple Excel workbooks and PowerPivot windows open, so you may find it helpful to close all open windows before starting an exercise, but that is up to you.

3. Home tab ⇒ Get External Data group ⇒ From Database button ⇒ From Access, as shown in Figure 2-1.

   The **TABLE IMPORT WIZARD** dialog box will open.

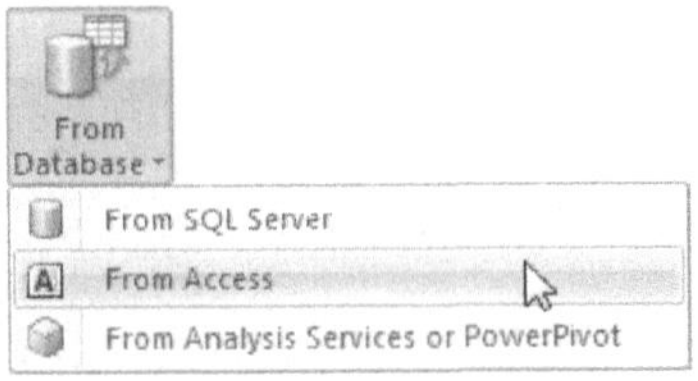

Figure 2-1 Options to select a Microsoft database

Step 2: Select The Data Source

This step covers selecting the data source and connecting to it. As you will learn, data from different sources including text files, spreadsheets, data feeds, as well as enterprise databases can be used to get the data for your analysis needs. This process is known as establishing a connection to a data source. Regardless of the data source, all data is imported as a table. Each table is placed on a different tab in the PowerPivot window, like worksheets in an Excel workbook.

1. On the Table Import Wizard dialog box, in the Friendly connection name field type `First PowerPivot Project.`

Using The Friendly Connection Name Field
It is not a requirement to use this field. By default, the type of database and database file name will automatically be filled in once data is imported from the database. It will be helpful to enter a name for the connection if you are going to import data from more than one data source into the same PowerPivot workbook. For example, if you are going to import data from different databases of the same type (like SQL or Access), using a descriptive name in this field will help you know which types or tables of data came from which database. PowerPivot has an option to display all of the connections in the workbook. The name entered in the Friendly connection field is also displayed, as illustrated in bold in Figure 2-2. All of the databases in the figure are Access databases. What helps to distinguish them is the Friendly connection name.

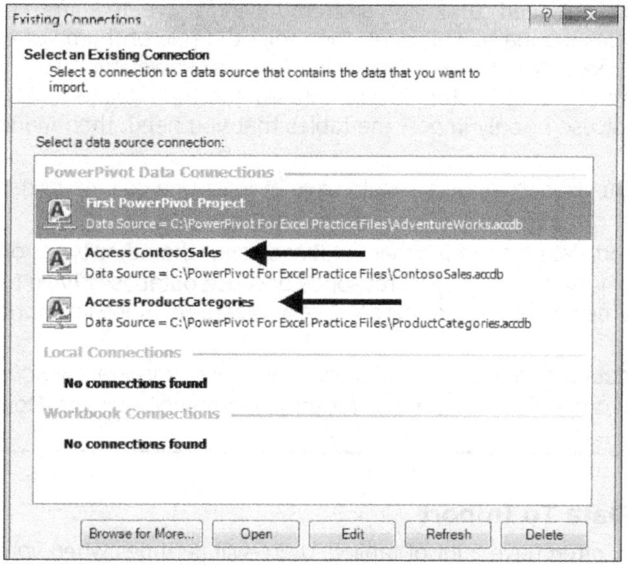

Figure 2-2 Existing Connections dialog box

2. Click the Browse button. Navigate to your folder, then double-click on the Adventure Works database. You should have the options shown in Figure 2-3. Click Next.

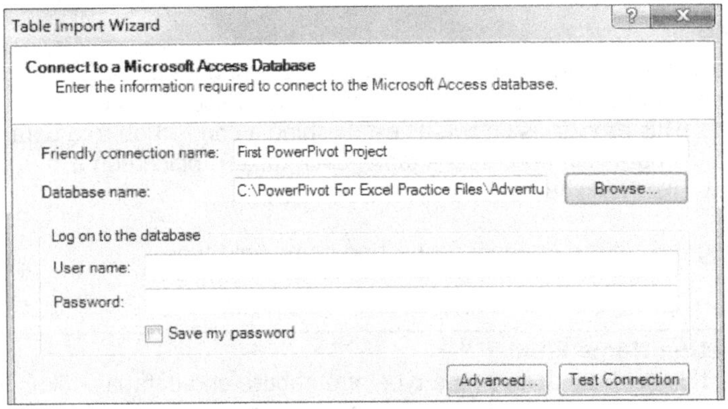

Figure 2-3 Microsoft Access database connection options

> **Importing Tips**
> Below are some tips that will help you import data better.
>
> ① In Chapter 4 you will read about database providers. Using the OLE DB provider for the data source can provide faster performance, especially for large databases.
> ② Importing multiple tables of data from the same database into PowerPivot and then deleting the tables that you do not need can keep you from having to create some relationships between the tables manually. This does contradict the rule of thumb of only importing the tables that you need. You have to determine for each PowerPivot workbook which is best, to have more relationships automatically created and then delete tables in the workbook that you will not use or only import the tables that you need, then manually create relationships.
> ③ The tables of data that you select to import should have at least one column of data in common so that relationships can automatically be created between the tables.
> ④ As much as possible, import data from relational databases over the other types of data sources because it will save you some steps. The reason is because databases have foreign keys in the tables. These key fields are used to automatically create relationships during the import process.
> ⑤ The order that tables of data are imported into PowerPivot is only important if you have really large tables. Large tables should be imported first for performance reasons. Doing this is optional.

Step 3: Select The Tables Of Data To Import

Data sources, in particular databases, often have a lot of tables. There will be times when you will not need all of the tables in a database. The steps below show you how to select the tables that you need. All of the tables and views in the database are displayed on the Select Tables and Views screen on the Table Import Wizard dialog box. Only importing the tables and data in the tables that you will use will keep the size of the PowerPivot workbook small.

For example, if a database has tables in the following categories; employees, products, financial, orders, car leases and retail stores and your goal is to create pivot charts on product sales, you can skip importing the financial and car leases tables. Remember that there is a workbook file size limitation.

1. Select the first option on the screen shown in Figure 2-4, then click Next.

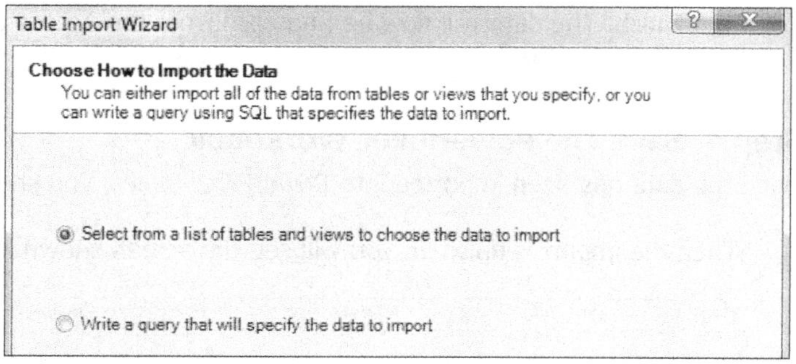

Figure 2-4 Import options

2. On the Select Tables and Views screen, click in the box in front of the following tables to select them: HumanResources_Employee, Person_Contact, Sales_SalesOrderHeader, Sales_SalesPerson and Sales_SalesTerritory, as shown in Figure 2-5.

Resizing Columns
If you need to see more of the Source Table name then is visible, the columns on the Table Import Wizard dialog box can be resized by placing the mouse pointer on the vertical line after the column that you need to resize and dragging the line to the right.

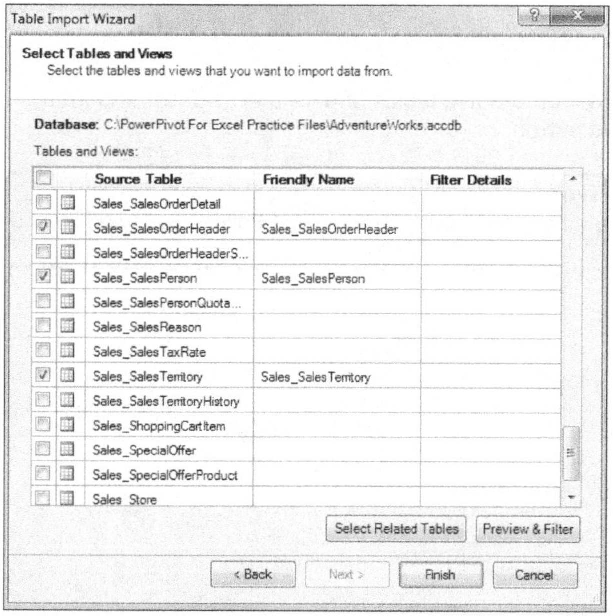

Figure 2-5 Tables selected to import

Selecting Records To Import
If you do not need to import all of the records and fields in a table, click the **PREVIEW & FILTER** button on the screen shown above in Figure 2-5. This is where you would create a filter to select the records and fields that you do not want to import.

3. Click Finish. The data will now be imported from the Access database into tables in the PowerPivot window.

Step 4: Save The PowerPivot Workbook

Once the data has been imported into PowerPivot tables, you should save it before modifying it.

1. When the import is finished, you will see the screen shown in Figure 2-6. Click the Close button.

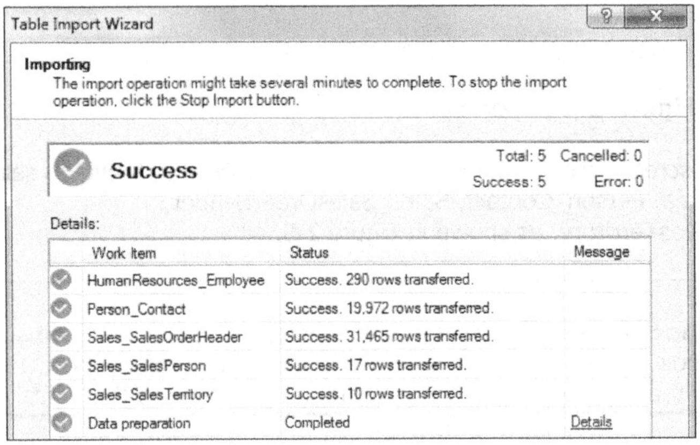

Figure 2-6 Importing screen

2. When you see the PowerPivot window with the five tables of data that you just imported, as shown in Figure 2-7, click the Save button.

Creating Formulas In PowerPivot
If you needed to create formulas, you would create them in the PowerPivot window shown in Figure 2-7.

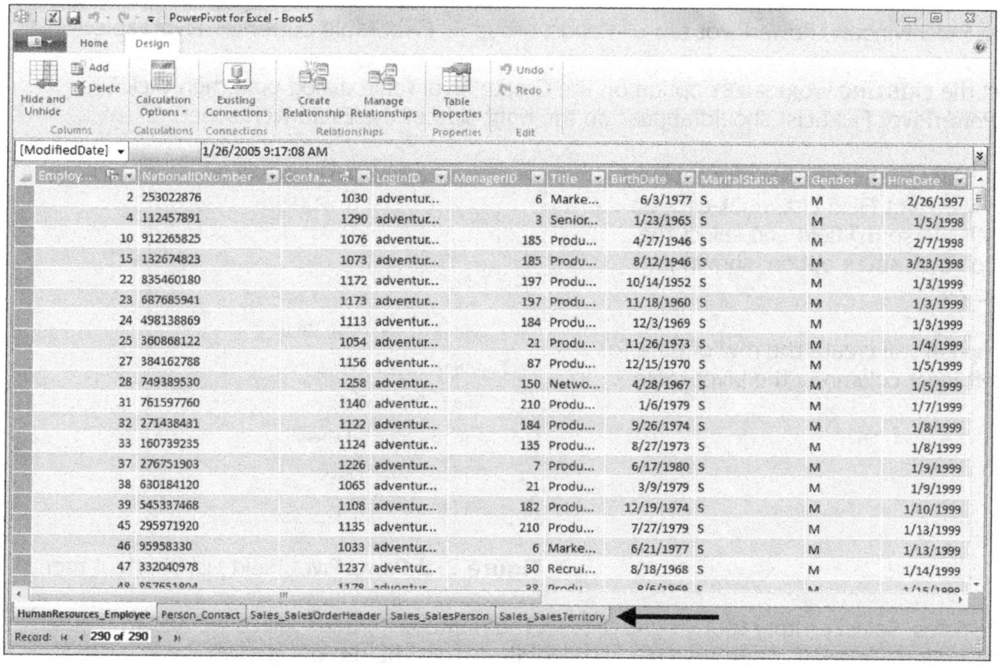

Figure 2-7 PowerPivot window with five tabs of data

3. Navigate to your folder if necessary, then type `E2.1 First PowerPivot Workbook` as the file name, then press Enter.

Using The PowerPivot Field List

When you select the type of pivot table or pivot chart that you want to create, you will see the Create PivotTable or Create PivotChart dialog box. This is how you select where on the worksheet the pivot table or pivot chart will be placed. You can move the pivot table or pivot chart later if necessary.

You will also see the PowerPivot Field List. The top section lists all of the tables and fields that are in the PowerPivot window. This section is used to select and add the fields to the pivot table. You can also use the top section to rename fields for the pivot table.

The bottom section of the PowerPivot Field List is the **DROP ZONE** section. It is used to select where the fields are placed on the pivot table.

> **Excel PivotTable Option**
> Excel has options on the Insert tab to create pivot tables and pivot charts. You cannot use these options because they are not connected to the PowerPivot data.

Step 5: Create The Pivot Table

In this step you will learn how to create a pivot table using the data that you imported into PowerPivot. The pivot table that you create will show the total sales amount by region for each sales rep.

1. In the Excel window, PowerPivot tab ⇒ Report group ⇒ PivotTable button ⇒ PivotTable.

2. Select the **EXISTING WORKSHEET** option on the Create PivotTable dialog box, then click OK. The PowerPivot Field List should appear on the right side of the Excel worksheet.

3. In the Sales_SalesOrderHeader table in the PowerPivot Field List, right-click on the SalesPersonID field and select the **ADD TO ROW LABELS** option, shown in Figure 2-8.

   This option will create the row of data for the left most column in the pivot table.

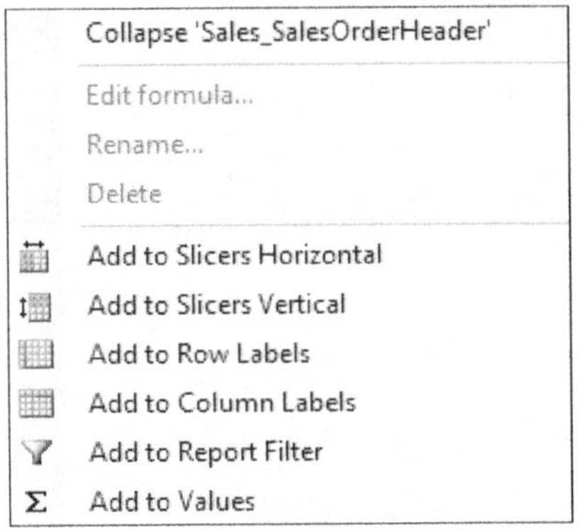

Figure 2-8 PowerPivot Field List shortcut menu

4. In the Sales_SalesTerritory table, right-click on the Name field, then select the Add to Column Labels option. This will create the column headings across the top of the pivot table.

5. In the Sales_SalesOrderHeader table, right-click on the SubTotal field, then select the Add to Values option. This will calculate the values that will be displayed in the middle of the pivot table.

6. The drop zone section of the PowerPivot Field List should look like the one shown in Figure 2-9.

   The pivot table should look like the one shown in Figure 2-10.

   Save the changes.

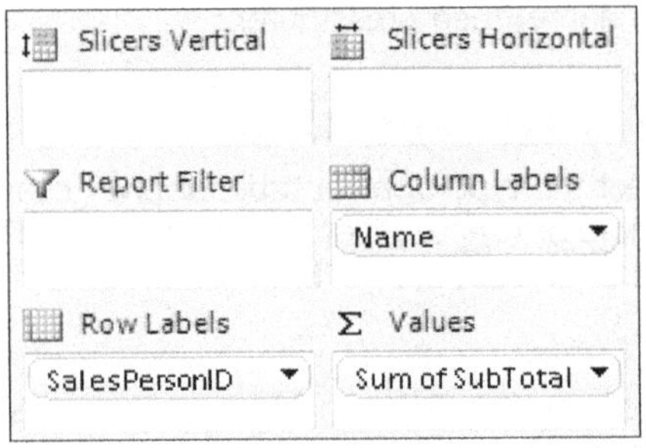

Figure 2-9 PowerPivot Field List drop zone options

Did you notice that you used fields from more than one table to create the pivot table without writing a formula or selecting any additional options? That is one of the features that makes PowerPivot rock in my opinion.

	A	B	C	D	E	F	G	H	I	J	K	L
1	Sum of SubTotal	Column Labels										
2	Row Labels	Australia	Canada	Central	France	Germany	Northeast	Northwest	Southeast	Southwest	United Kingdom	Grand Total
3		9061000.584	1977844.862	3000.8296	2644017.714	2894312.338	6532.4682	3649866.551	12238.8496	5718150.812	3391712.211	29358677.22
4	268		264867.0069	43824.0227			100165.0377	279997.5919	181804.2136	498966.7766		1369624.649
5	275			3127053.025			3547034.396		347730.2939	4230221.05		11252038.77
6	276			2225871.149				2562534.431		7859324.248		12647729.83
7	277			3543660.984			4735174.261		309496.8021	3569595.145		12157927.19
8	278		4380714.255									4380714.255
9	279								8714865.97			8714865.97
10	280							4029938.356				4029938.356
11	281			621258.9399				936689.47		6371216.557		7929164.967
12	282		2532500.913								4678149.585	7210650.498
13	283							4551897.661				4551897.661
14	284				118890.3863	239835.1362					533258.121	891983.6435
15	285		10302726.69									10302726.69
16	286				5505602.675							5505602.675
17	287							2814958.894				2814958.894
18	288	219088.8836										219088.8836
19	289					2241204.042						2241204.042
20	290	1758385.926										1758385.926
21	Grand Total	11038475.39	19458653.72	9564668.951	8268510.775	5375351.517	8388906.163	18825882.96	9566136.129	28247474.59	8603119.917	127337180.1

Figure 2-10 PowerPivot pivot table

Using The Pivot Table

At this point, PowerPivots job is finished, unless more data needs to be added to the pivot table or you need to create more calculated columns.

From this point on, you primarily use the PowerPivot Field List and the options on the PowerPivot tab to add pivot table and pivot chart functionality.

As shown above in Figure 2-10, the pivot table that is using data from PowerPivot can be used just like the pivot tables that are created from data in an Excel worksheet. That means that you can use the Excel filter options shown in Figure 2-11.

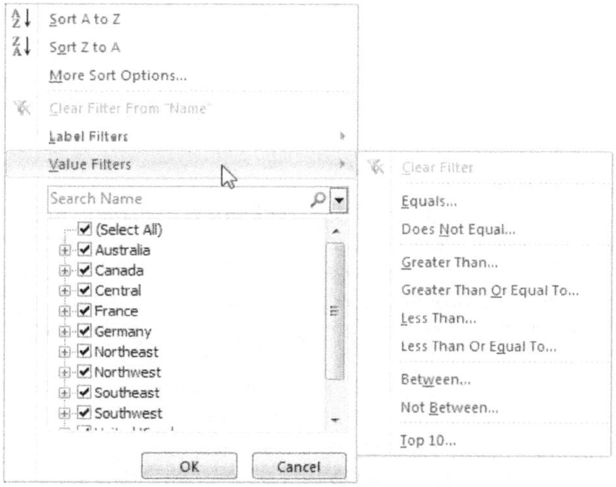

Figure 2-11 Excel filter options

If you find that you are using the same filter options over and over, you can add the field or fields to the **REPORT FILTER** drop zone on the PowerPivot Field List. That is what you will do in the next exercise.

Exercise 2.2: Modify A Pivot Table

In this exercise you will modify the pivot table that you created in the previous exercise to have a report filter. The filter that you add will let the pivot table display the sales data by shipping method.

If you look in the Sales_SalesOrderHeader table, you will see the ShipMethodID field. While you can use the ID field (which is a number) for the shipping method filter, it may be difficult to remember what each number means. None of the tables that you imported in Exercise 2.1 have the field with the shipping method names. These values are stored in the Purchasing_ShipMethod table. This is when it would be helpful to have the data dictionary that I discussed in Chapter 1 or a print out of all of the fields in each table in the database. Having that would make it easier to find the field that you need. As you read in Chapter 1, the Adventure Works database has 67 tables. Aren't you happy that this book has step-by-step instructions? <smile>

Step 1: Add Another Table Of Data To The PowerPivot Workbook

In this step you will import the data from the table that has the shipping method names that you will use for the report filter.

1. Save the E2.1 workbook as `E2.2 Modify pivot table.`
2. PowerPivot tab ⇒ PowerPivot Window button.
3. Design tab ⇒ Existing Connections button.
4. Select the Adventure Works database, then click the Open button.
5. Click Next on the Import Data screen.
6. Select the Purchasing_ShipMethod table, then click Finish. The table will now be imported into PowerPivot.
7. Click Close after the data has been imported, then save the changes.

Refreshing Data

PowerPivot pivot tables and PowerPivot pivot charts are based on the data in PowerPivot tables at the time that the pivot table or pivot chart was created. After the pivot tables and pivot charts are created, more than likely the data in PowerPivot tables will be updated. This means that the data in the underlying tables of the pivot table or pivot chart are out of sync, which causes the data displayed in the pivot table or pivot chart to not be current.

When the data is updated in the PowerPivot window, you will see the message shown below in Figure 2-12 at the top of the PowerPivot Field list. Click the **REFRESH** button to update the data in the pivot table or pivot chart, as well as, update the tables in the PowerPivot Field List if you imported more tables, appended data to an existing PowerPivot table or created more calculated fields.

If you created a pivot table and then create a measure or relationship, the message shown in Figure 2-12 will also be displayed in the PowerPivot Field List.

Step 2: Create The Report Filter

1. Display the pivot table.

At the top of the PowerPivot Field List you should see the message shown in Figure 2-12.

This message lets you know that data in the PowerPivot workbook has changed. In this case, the change was that a table was added to the workbook.

Figure 2-12 PowerPivot data was modified message

2. Click the Refresh button shown above in Figure 2-12.

3. Scroll to the bottom of the list of tables in the PowerPivot Field List pane. You will see the Purchasing_ShipMethod table. Add the Name field from this table to the Report Filter drop zone.

4. When you see the message at the top of the PowerPivot Field List that a relationship may be needed, as shown in Figure 2-13, click the Create button. You will see the dialog box shown in Figure 2-14.

Figure 2-13 PowerPivot relationship message

Relationship Detection And Creation

PowerPivot displayed the message shown above in Figure 2-13 because there may be a relationship that needs to be created between tables, based on the data that was modified in the workbook.

In the previous section you imported data after the pivot table was created and are now adding a field from the new PowerPivot table to the pivot table. Clicking the Create button tells PowerPivot to look for and create any relationships that it thinks should be created. The result of the search for new relationships is what is displayed in Figure 2-14. In this case, PowerPivot found at least one relationship that needed to be created and created it. This is not always the case. Sometimes when you see this message and click the Create button, the dialog box in Figure 2-14 will display a message indicating that no relationships were detected.

If you click on the **DETAILS** link across from the Relationship detection item, you will see the dialog box shown in Figure 2-15. This lets you know how many relationships PowerPivot found that could be created. If you click on the Details link across from the Relationship creation item, you will see the dialog box shown in Figure 2-16. You will see the relationships that were created.

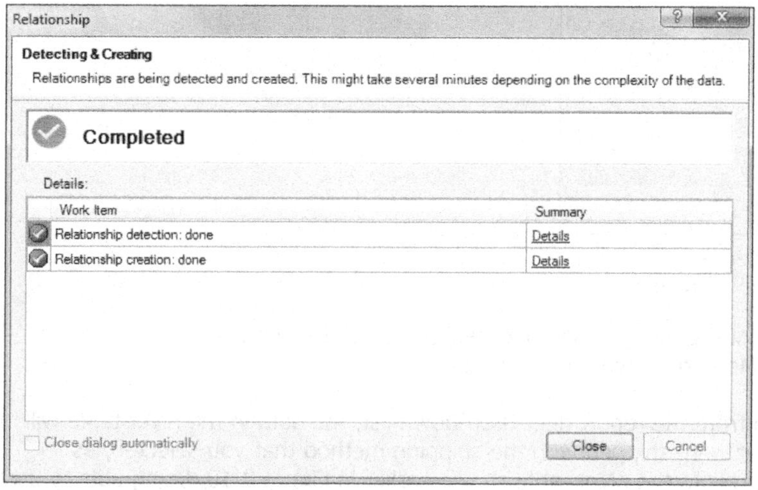

Figure 2-14 Relationship dialog box

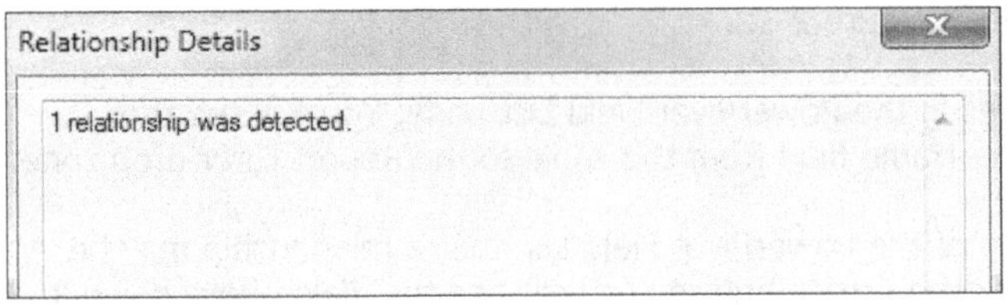

Figure 2-15 Relationship Details dialog box for the relationship detection option

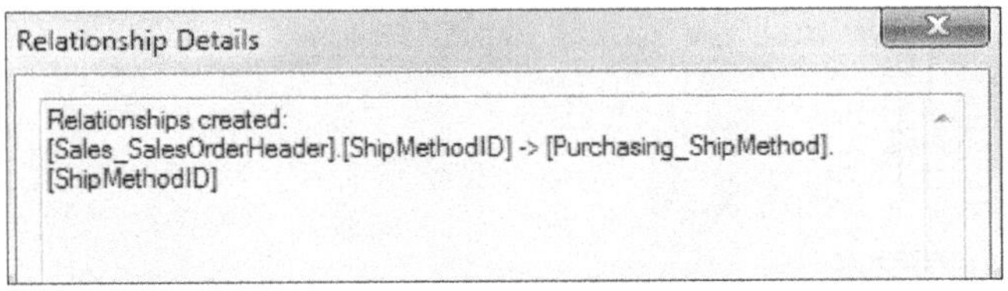

Figure 2-16 Relationship Details dialog box for the relationship creation option

5. Click the Close button on the Relationship dialog box shown earlier in Figure 2-14. If the relationship that was needed for the field that you selected was created, the field will be added to the drop zone.

How To Rename A Report Filter

By default when a field is added to the Report Filter drop zone or any drop zone for that matter, the field name is displayed for the filter above the pivot table or pivot chart. Sometimes, this name is not the best option to be displayed with the pivot table. When that is the case, you can rename the Report Filter. The steps below show you how.

6. Click on the Name field in the Report Filter drop zone, then select the Field Settings option on the shortcut menu.

7. In the Custom Name field type `Shipping Method`, as shown in Figure 2-17, then click OK.

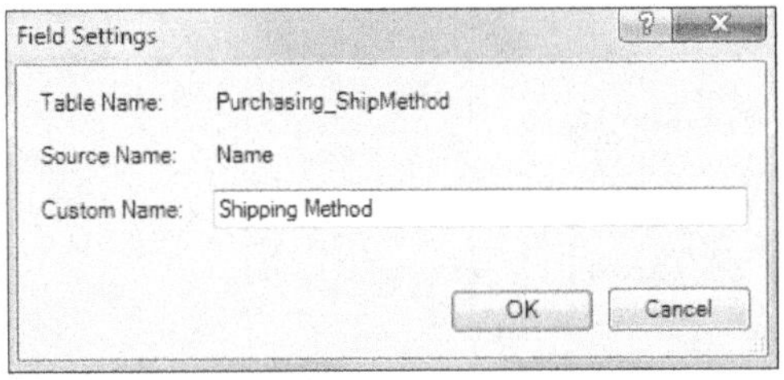

Figure 2-17 Field Settings dialog box

8. You will see that the name of the filter in the upper left corner of the worksheet has changed from "Name" to "Shipping Method". Save the changes.

If you select a shipping method from the report filter drop-down list, the data in the pivot table will only display totals for orders that were shipped with the shipping method that you selected, as shown in Figure 2-18. Compare this to the pivot table shown earlier in Figure 2-10. Being able to use a field in one table as the filter for data in multiple other tables should demonstrate how powerful PowerPivot is.

Shipping Method	CARGO TRANSPORT 5										
Sum of SubTotal	Column Labels										
Row Labels	Australia	Canada	Central	France	Germany	Northeast	Northwest	Southeast	Southwest	United Kingdom	Grand Total
268		264867.0069	43824.0227			100165.0377	279997.5919	181804.2136	498966.7766		1369624.649
275			3127053.025			3547034.396		347730.2939	4230221.05		11252038.77
276			2225871.149				2562534.431		7859324.248		12647729.83
277			3543660.984			4735174.261		309496.8021	3569595.145		12157927.19
278		4380714.255									4380714.255
279								8714865.97			8714865.97
280							4029938.356				4029938.356
281			621258.9399				936689.47		6371216.557		7929164.967
282		2532500.913								4678149.585	7210650.498
283							4551897.661				4551897.661
284				118890.3863	239835.1362					533258.121	891983.6435
285		10302726.69									10302726.69
286				5505602.675							5505602.675
287							2814958.894				2814958.894
288	219088.8836										219088.8836
289					2241204.042						2241204.042
290	1758385.926										1758385.926
Grand Total	1977474.81	17480808.86	9561668.121	5624493.061	2481039.179	8382373.695	15176016.4	9553897.279	22529323.78	5211407.706	97978502.89

Figure 2-18 Pivot table with filtered data

Quick Tour Wrap Up

Yes, I realize that you probably feel that you were rushed through the exercises in this chapter with all of the "Do this" and "Click that" instructions, without a lot of explanation of why. Lengthy explanations are not the goal of this chapter because that is what is covered in the rest of the book. The goal of this chapter was to briefly demonstrate some of the functionality that PowerPivot adds to Excel, in particular, what PowerPivot adds to pivot tables.

As I stated at the beginning of this chapter, PowerPivot can be used to import data from multiple databases or other data sources. Once the data is imported into tables in PowerPivot, all of the data can be used to create a single pivot table or pivot chart, as well as multiple pivot tables on multiple worksheets in the workbook. You are not limited to only using one worksheet in the workbook to create pivot tables.

As you saw in the exercises in this chapter, you used data from different PowerPivot tables to create one pivot table. This alone is worth the price of admission, as some people say. If you stick with it and learn how to use the DAX programming language and pivot table functionality that comes with PowerPivot, you will be able to create extensive and elaborate pivot tables and pivot charts for business intelligence analysis without needing IT people to help you. That is what this self-service business intelligence tool was designed to do.

The PowerPivot Field List Will Not Always Display Automatically
From time to time while I was writing this book, I would add a pivot table or pivot chart object to a worksheet and expected the PowerPivot Field List to display automatically. Sometimes that did not happen. I tried using the Field List button on the PowerPivot tab, but it was not always enabled. When that was the case, the only solution that I found was to exit Excel and then re-open it. I just wanted to let you know, in case you experience the same thing.

Viewing Relationships

In Exercise 2.1 you used data from two tables in the PowerPivot window to create the pivot table. In Exercise 2.2 you added data from a third table to enhance the pivot table, as shown above in Figure 2-18. The reason that you are able to do that is because there are relationships between these three tables. These relationships are stored in the columnar database that PowerPivot uses.

Figure 2-19 shows the relationships between the tables in the Adventure Works database that you used. This figure was taken in Microsoft Access, not Excel or PowerPivot because Access has a built-in relationship viewer, if you will, that is easy to understand. The lines indicate that relationships between the tables.

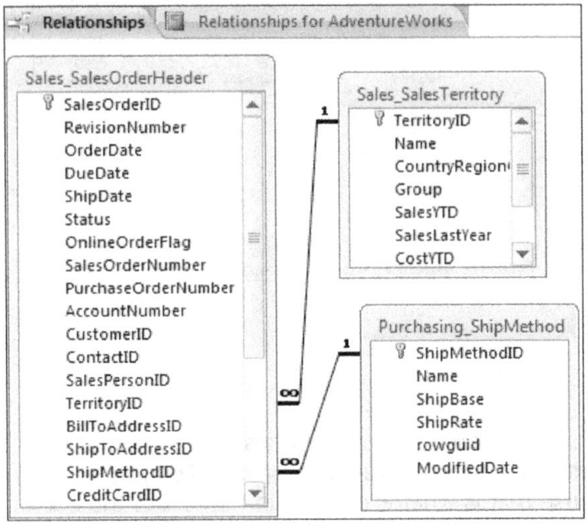

Figure 2-19 Some of the relationships in the Adventure Works database

If you look closely, you will see that each line is actually pointing to a specific field in the table. It is the data in those fields that allow you to be able to select fields from different tables in the PowerPivot Field List to create pivot tables and pivot charts.

These relationships are imported into PowerPivot when the tables from a database are imported, as long as the auto detection feature in PowerPivot is enabled. If these tables did not have relationships created between them, you could still use the same fields to create a pivot table. PowerPivot would prompt you to create the relationships.

Interestingly enough, if you do not create the relationships, PowerPivot will create the pivot table anyway. However, it will not display the data correctly, as shown in Figure 2-20. This happens because without relationships, PowerPivot has no way of knowing which territory each order is from.

Hopefully, the difference between the pivot tables in Figure 2-18 and Figure 2-20 do two things:

① Demonstrate how powerful PowerPivot is and how much more you can do with pivot tables.
② Convinces you to complete the exercises in this book.

	A	B	C	D	E	F	G	H	I	J	K	L
1	Shipping Method	All										
2												
3	Sum of SubTotal	Column Labels										
4	Row Labels	Australia	Canada	Central	France	Germany	Northeast	Northwest	Southeast	Southwest	United Kingdom	Grand Total
5		29358677.22	29358677.22	29358677.22	29358677.22	29358677.22	29358677.22	29358677.22	29358677.22	29358677.22	29358677.22	29358677.22
6	268	1369624.649	1369624.649	1369624.649	1369624.649	1369624.649	1369624.649	1369624.649	1369624.649	1369624.649	1369624.649	1369624.649
7	275	11252038.77	11252038.77	11252038.77	11252038.77	11252038.77	11252038.77	11252038.77	11252038.77	11252038.77	11252038.77	11252038.77
8	276	12647729.83	12647729.83	12647729.83	12647729.83	12647729.83	12647729.83	12647729.83	12647729.83	12647729.83	12647729.83	12647729.83
9	277	12157927.19	12157927.19	12157927.19	12157927.19	12157927.19	12157927.19	12157927.19	12157927.19	12157927.19	12157927.19	12157927.19
10	278	4380714.255	4380714.255	4380714.255	4380714.255	4380714.255	4380714.255	4380714.255	4380714.255	4380714.255	4380714.255	4380714.255
11	279	8714865.97	8714865.97	8714865.97	8714865.97	8714865.97	8714865.97	8714865.97	8714865.97	8714865.97	8714865.97	8714865.97
12	280	4029938.356	4029938.356	4029938.356	4029938.356	4029938.356	4029938.356	4029938.356	4029938.356	4029938.356	4029938.356	4029938.356
13	281	7929164.967	7929164.967	7929164.967	7929164.967	7929164.967	7929164.967	7929164.967	7929164.967	7929164.967	7929164.967	7929164.967
14	282	7210650.498	7210650.498	7210650.498	7210650.498	7210650.498	7210650.498	7210650.498	7210650.498	7210650.498	7210650.498	7210650.498
15	283	4551897.661	4551897.661	4551897.661	4551897.661	4551897.661	4551897.661	4551897.661	4551897.661	4551897.661	4551897.661	4551897.661
16	284	891983.6435	891983.6435	891983.6435	891983.6435	891983.6435	891983.6435	891983.6435	891983.6435	891983.6435	891983.6435	891983.6435
17	285	10302726.69	10302726.69	10302726.69	10302726.69	10302726.69	10302726.69	10302726.69	10302726.69	10302726.69	10302726.69	10302726.69
18	286	5505602.675	5505602.675	5505602.675	5505602.675	5505602.675	5505602.675	5505602.675	5505602.675	5505602.675	5505602.675	5505602.675
19	287	2814958.894	2814958.894	2814958.894	2814958.894	2814958.894	2814958.894	2814958.894	2814958.894	2814958.894	2814958.894	2814958.894
20	288	219088.8836	219088.8836	219088.8836	219088.8836	219088.8836	219088.8836	219088.8836	219088.8836	219088.8836	219088.8836	219088.8836
21	289	2241204.042	2241204.042	2241204.042	2241204.042	2241204.042	2241204.042	2241204.042	2241204.042	2241204.042	2241204.042	2241204.042
22	290	1758385.926	1758385.926	1758385.926	1758385.926	1758385.926	1758385.926	1758385.926	1758385.926	1758385.926	1758385.926	1758385.926
23	**Grand Total**	**127337180.1**	**127337180.1**	**127337180.1**	**127337180.1**	**127337180.1**	**127337180.1**	**127337180.1**	**127337180.1**	**127337180.1**	**127337180.1**	**127337180.1**

Figure 2-20 Pivot table without relationships

Make Nice Nice With The IT Department

If you know now that the data that you need to use to create pivot tables is on corporate servers, the best advice that I can give you is to learn as much about the data as you can now and to start making friends with someone in the IT Department that can help you gain access to the databases that you need.

Why am I telling you this, you ask. The answer is simple. I refer to myself as a retired IT person. I spent 20 plus years in one IT position or another. One of our biggest pet peeves is people calling or emailing and asking for help but really don't know what they need help with. Before you slam this book shut, hear me out.

We are not sitting in your office and have no idea what you need to do, so telling us that you need to get access to sales data for example, is not specific enough. Saying that you need sales data from 2005 to the present for the camera and camcorder product lines is something that we better understand.

If you are shaking your head, keep in mind that many companies have hundreds, if not thousands of databases. You will be hard pressed to find any one IT person that knows about every database that the company has, never mind which server it is on.

I can tell you that in most cases, IT's role in the company is not what all other departments think that it is, nor does every person in IT have the same skill set. Take from this what you will.

EXPLORING THE POWERPIVOT WORKSPACE

In this chapter you will learn about the PowerPivot workspace. This includes the options on the PowerPivot tab on the Excel ribbon and the options on the PowerPivot window ribbon.

CHAPTER 3

Overview

The topics covered in this chapter explain the PowerPivot options in Excel and the PowerPivot window. The PowerPivot tab on the Excel ribbon is used to interact with the data in the PowerPivot table. The PowerPivot window is used to import data from a single source or multiple sources into tables that can be used to create pivot tables which can use data from multiple sources. PowerPivot is also used to create and manage relationships, create DAX calculations and more.

You will see the PowerPivot application listed as an Add-In on the Excel Options dialog box, as illustrated in Figure 3-1, after it has been installed. Open Excel ⇒ File tab ⇒ Options ⇒ Add-Ins, displays the screen shown in the figure.

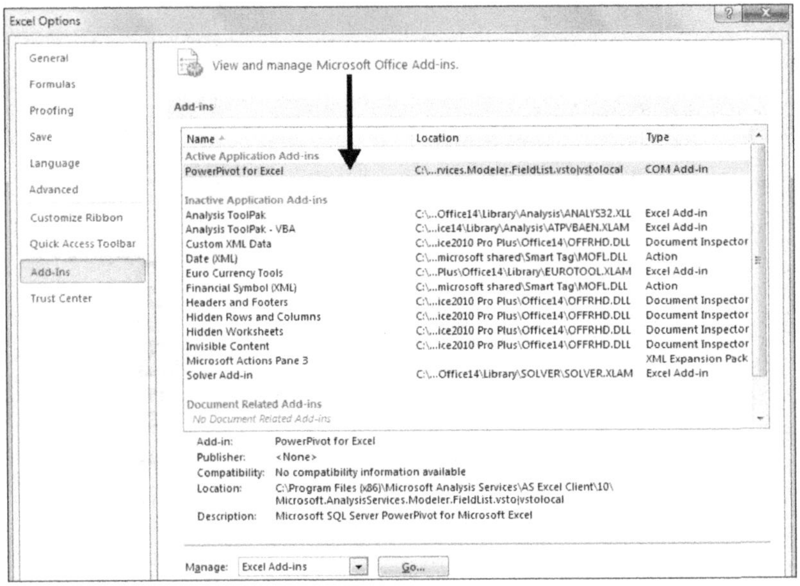

Figure 3-1 Excel Add-Ins options illustrated

PowerPivot Tab On The Excel Ribbon

Figure 3-2 shows the PowerPivot tab on the Excel ribbon. The buttons are explained in Table 3-1.

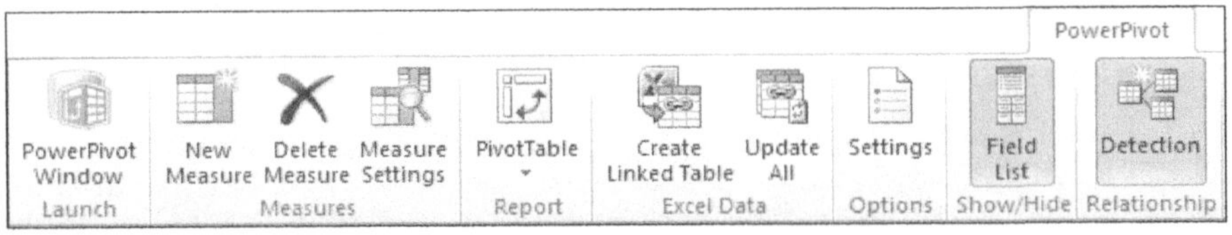

Figure 3-2 PowerPivot tab on the Excel ribbon

Button	Description
PowerPivot Window	Opens the PowerPivot window.
New Measure	Is used to create a new calculated field using a DAX formula. PowerPivot refers to calculated fields as **MEASURES**. They are more powerful than the calculated fields that can be created in Excel.
Delete Measure	Deletes the selected measure in the PowerPivot Field List.
Measure Settings	Opens the dialog box shown in Figure 3-3. The options on this dialog box are used to change the name or formula of the selected measure.
PivotTable	The options shown in Figure 3-4 are used to select the layout of pivot tables or pivot charts that you want to create from PowerPivot data. The options are explained later in Table 3-4.
Create Linked Table	Is used to create a PowerPivot table that is linked to data in an Excel table, instead of copying and pasting the data into the PowerPivot table.
Update All	Is used to update the data in all of the PowerPivot tables that are linked to Excel tables.
Settings	Opens the dialog box shown in Figure 3-5. The options on this dialog box are used to collect information about your PowerPivot environment.
Field List	Is used to display or hide the PowerPivot Field List shown in Figure 3-6. The options are used to help design a pivot table that is based on data in a PowerPivot table. It is similar to the PivotTable Field List shown in Figure 3-7, which is used in Excel to create pivot tables based on data in Excel.
Detection	Is used to enable or disable relationships from automatically being created between tables.

Table 3-1 PowerPivot tab buttons explained

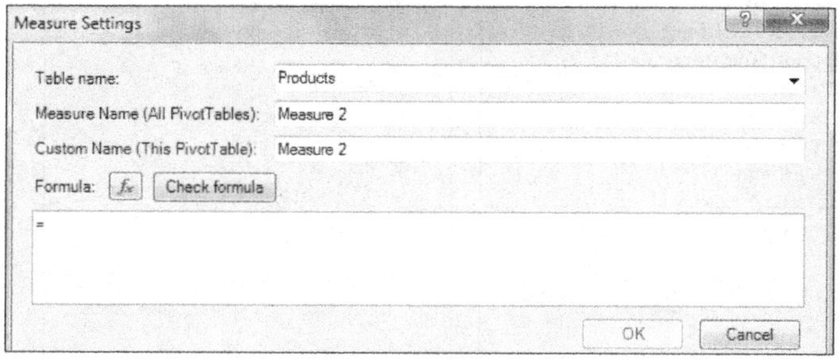

Figure 3-3 Measure Settings dialog box

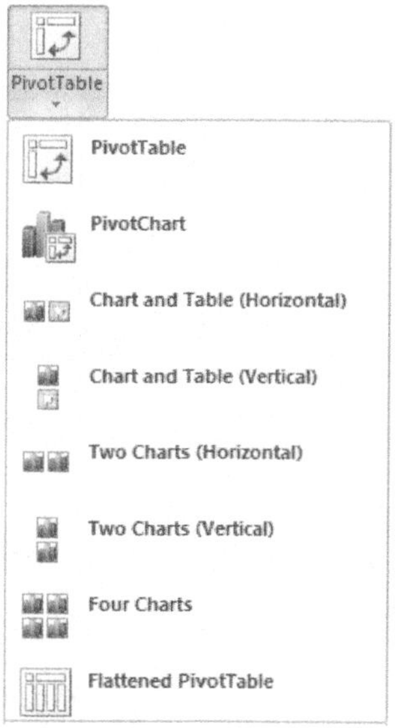

Figure 3-4 PivotTable button options

The options on the **SUPPORT & DIAGNOSTICS** tab are used to enable tracing, which is used for troubleshooting PowerPivot issues.

The options on the **CUSTOMER EXPERIENCE** tab are used to provide automatic feedback to Microsoft about problems that you experience with PowerPivot.

The options on the **LANGUAGE** tab are used to select a different language for the text that is displayed in PowerPivot.

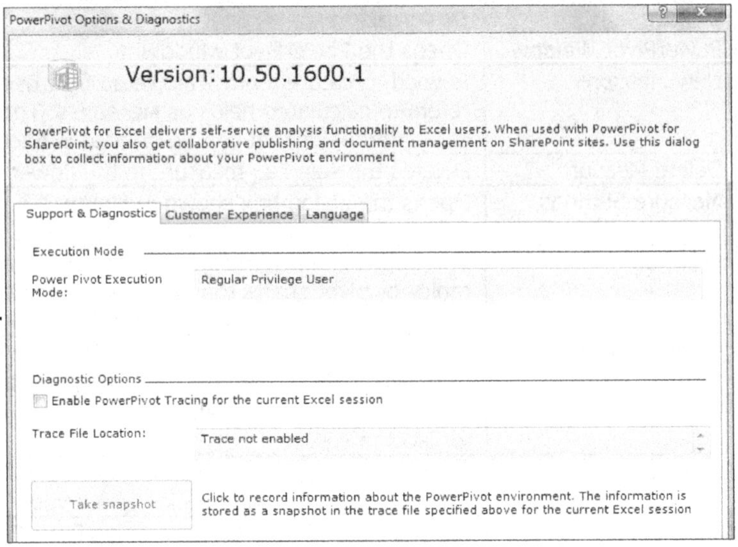

Figure 3-5 PowerPivot Options & Diagnostics dialog box

The PowerPivot Field List is only displayed when a pivot table that is using data from a PowerPivot table is selected.

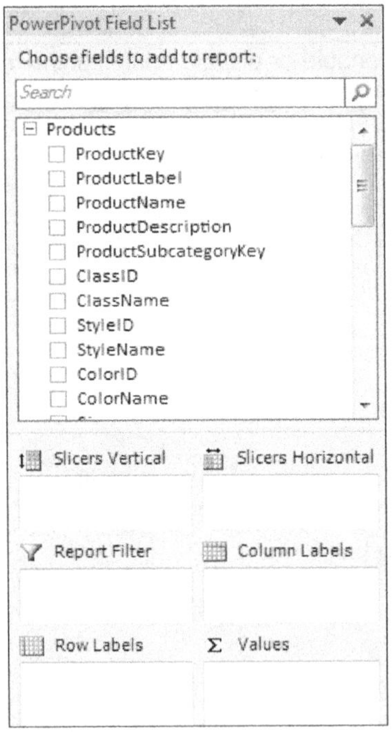

Figure 3-6 PowerPivot Field List

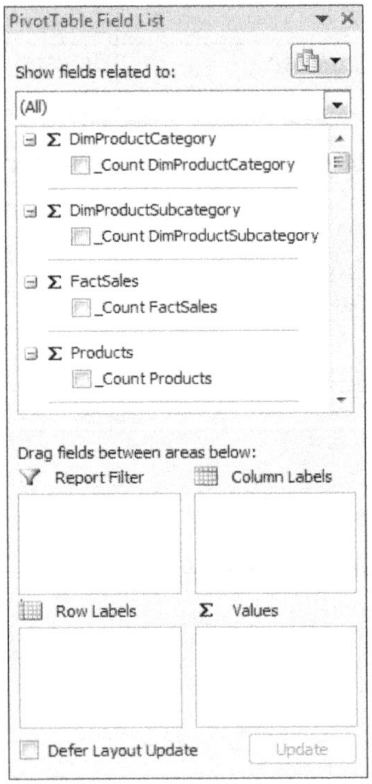

Figure 3-7 PivotTable Field List

PowerPivot For Excel Window

When you click the PowerPivot Window button shown earlier in Figure 3-2, you will see the window shown in Figure 3-8. As you learned in Chapter 2, this is where you import data and customize the data in PowerPivot tables. Table 3-2 explains the illustrated parts of the PowerPivot window.

This window displays the data on tabs. Each tab has data from a different table, query or view in a database or a different data source. This is how the relational data model is built.

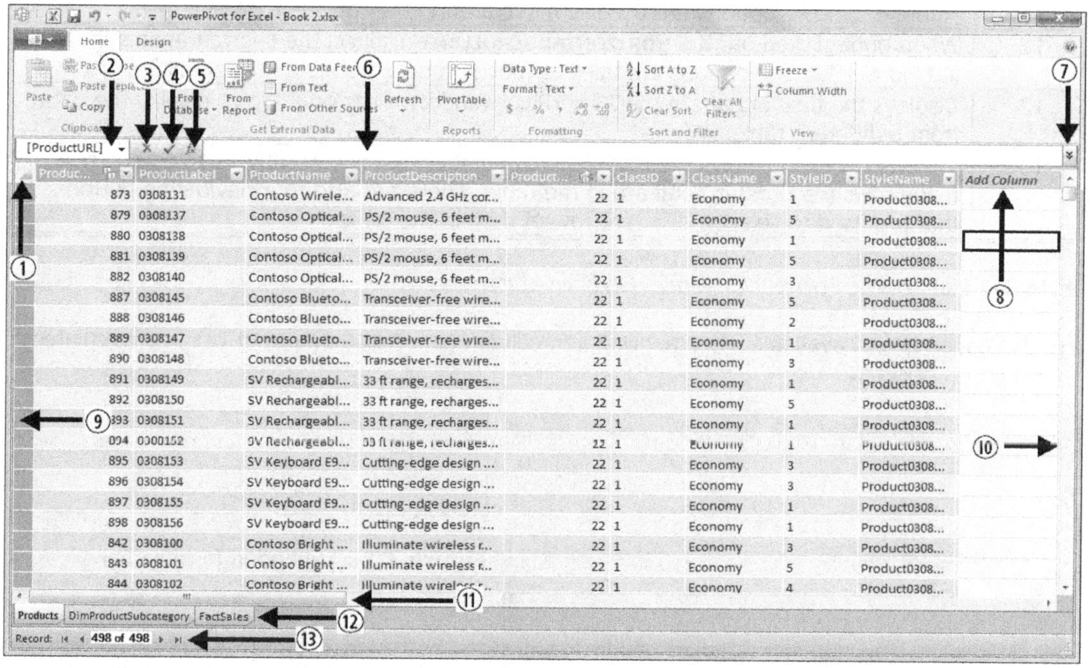

Figure 3-8 PowerPivot window

Option	Description
1	Clicking on this square selects the entire table.
2	Opens a drop-down list that displays a list of the columns that are in the table. Select the column that you want displayed. This option is useful if the table has more columns then can be displayed on the screen, without scrolling to the right.
3	Is used to delete the formula on the formula bar. (1)
4	Is used to apply the formula after you type it in. (1)
5	Displays the dialog box shown in Figure 3-9. The options on the dialog box are used to add a function to the calculated column. (1)
6	Is used to type in the formula to create the calculated column.
7	This button expands the formula bar, as shown in Figure 3-10. Doing this is helpful if the formula is long.

Table 3-2 Parts of the PowerPivot window explained

Option	Description
8	The column **ADD COLUMN** is a calculated column that is used to create a DAX formula. This column creates and adds a new column of data to the table. The data for the column comes from the formula that you create. You can create as many calculated columns in a table as needed.
9	Click in this box to select the corresponding row. This option is often used to select data that you want to copy.
10	When right-clicked on, the **VERTICAL SCROLLBAR** displays the shortcut menu shown in Figure 3-11. The options are used to move around the table vertically.
11	When right-clicked on, the **HORIZONTAL SCROLLBAR** displays the shortcut menu shown in Figure 3-12. The options are used to move around the table horizontally.
12	Displays the tabs of data in the PowerPivot window. Click on a tab to display the data from a different table.
13	The **STATUS BAR** displays the row (record) number that is currently selected and how many rows (records) in total are in the table. There are also four navigation buttons that are used to select a different row of data in the table.

Table 3-2 Parts of the PowerPivot window explained (Continued)

(1) This option is only available when a calculated column (the Add Column) or cell in a calculated column is selected.

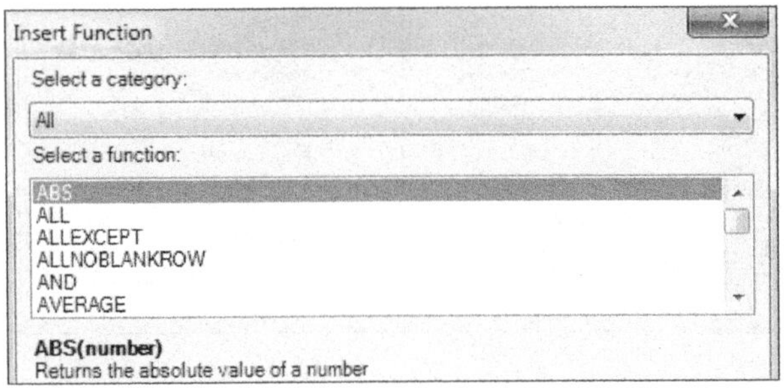

Figure 3-9 Insert Function dialog box

Figure 3-10 Expanded formula bar

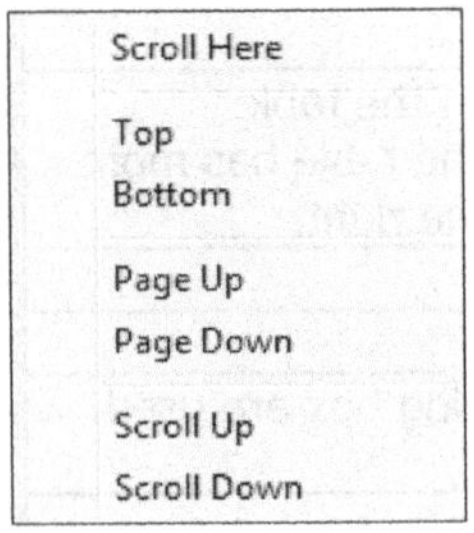

Figure 3-11 Vertical scrollbar shortcut menu

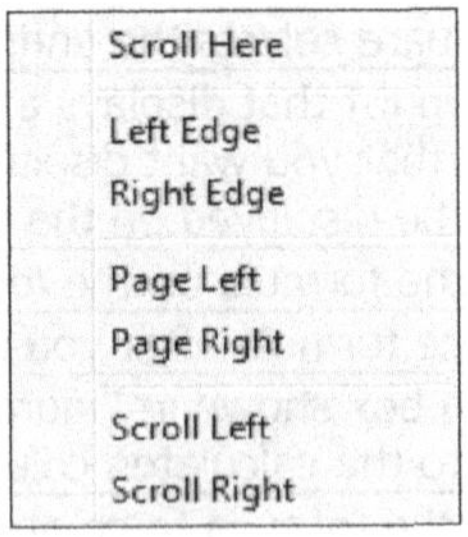

Figure 3-12 Horizontal scrollbar shortcut menu

PowerPivot Quick Access Toolbar

As shown earlier in Figure 3-8, the PowerPivot window has a Quick Access toolbar.

The customization options are shown in Figure 3-13. This toolbar does not have all of the customization options that its namesake in Excel has.

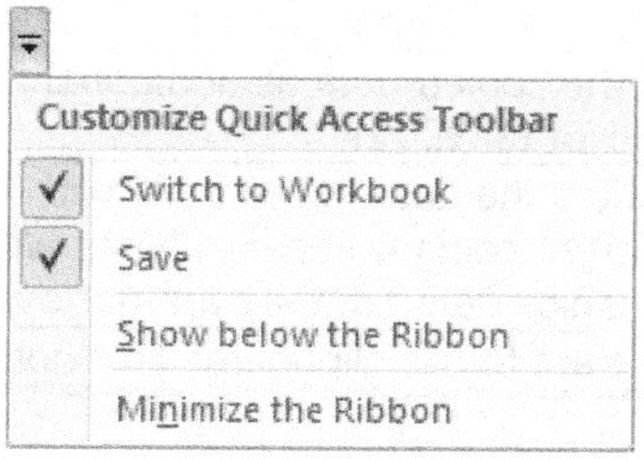

Figure 3-13 PowerPivot Quick Access Toolbar options

PowerPivot Window Ribbon

The button to the left of the Home tab displays the options shown in Figure 3-14. I could not find a name for this button. The options are links to a feature in Excel. When one of the options is selected, the PowerPivot window is minimized and the Excel window and option that you selected is displayed. The options are explained below.

SAVE Saves the changes in workbook.

SAVE AS Opens the Save As dialog box, which is used to save the workbook with a different file name or save the workbook with the same name in a different folder.

PUBLISH Opens the Save As dialog box, which is also used to publish (upload) the workbook to your Windows Sky Drive account or to a SharePoint server.

CLOSE Closes the PowerPivot window, then displays the Excel window.

Figure 3-14 Button options

PowerPivot Window Home Tab

The options on the tab shown in Figure 3-15 are used to import data into PowerPivot, add formatting to the imported data and sort and filter the data if needed. The options in each group are explained below.

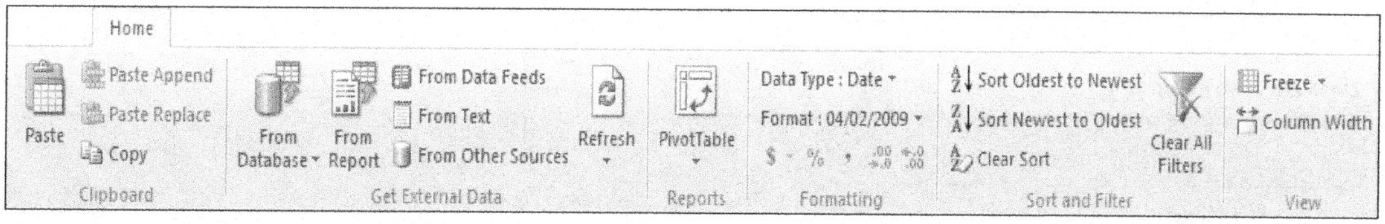

Figure 3-15 Home tab options

Clipboard Group

The options in this group are used to paste data from the Windows clipboard into a PowerPivot table or copy data from a PowerPivot table to the clipboard. The table-like data that you paste into a PowerPivot table can come from another software package like Microsoft Word. The options are explained in Table 3-3.

Option	Description
Paste	Pastes the copied data into a new PowerPivot table.
Paste Append	Pastes the copied data as additional rows to the bottom of an existing PowerPivot table. (2)
Paste Replace	Overwrites the data in the table with the data that you copied to the clipboard. The current column header names will not be changed. If the table already has relationships defined, they are not over written when the data is replaced. (2)
Copy	Copies data to the clipboard. This option is the same as using **CTRL+C**.

Table 3-3 Clipboard group options explained

(2) This option is only available when a PowerPivot table was initially created by using the Paste command. The data that you want to paste has to have the same number of columns as the PowerPivot table has that you want to paste the data to.

Get External Data Group

The options in this group are used to import data into a PowerPivot table. In order to import the data, you have to create a connection to the data source. The data connection options in this group are covered in Chapter 4.

REFRESH The options on this button are used to get updated data from an external data source for the PowerPivot tables in the workbook.

If you want to refresh the data for the PowerPivot table that is currently displayed, select the Refresh option shown in Figure 3-16.

If you want to refresh the data in all of the PowerPivot tables in the workbook that can be refreshed, select the Refresh All option.

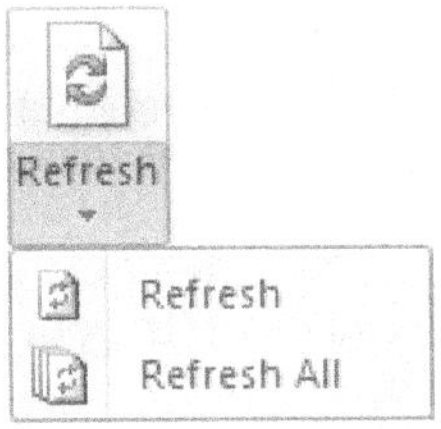

Figure 3-16 Refresh options

When either of the refresh options are selected, the dialog box shown in Figure 3-17 is displayed. It shows the progress of the data refresh. If there are any problems with the data refresh, you will see a link in the Message column.

If you click the **STOP REFRESH** button on the Data Refresh dialog box, data that was updated or imported is removed from the PowerPivot table and the original data in the table is restored.

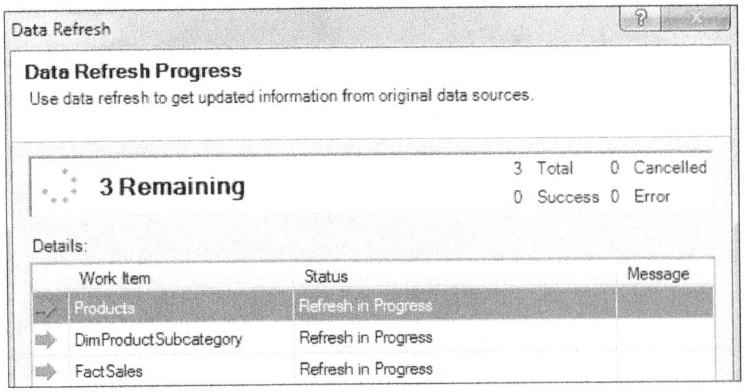

Figure 3-17 Data Refresh dialog box

Reports Group

The **PIVOTTABLE** button is used to create a pivot table or pivot chart that is based on data in a PowerPivot table, by selecting an option shown in Figure 3-18.

The options are explained in Table 3-4.

Pivot tables and pivot charts can be placed on an existing or new worksheet in the workbook.

All of the exercises in this book use the Existing Worksheet option.

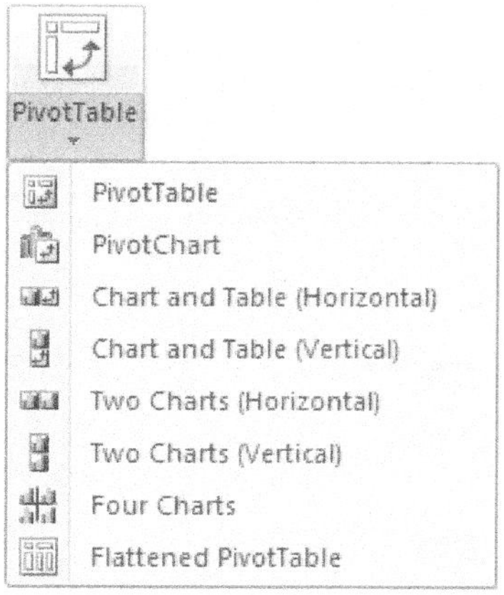

Figure 3-18 PivotTable button options

PivotTable And PivotChart Options
Even though the Insert Tab in Excel has options to create a pivot table and pivot chart, you cannot use those options if the data that you want to use for the pivot table or pivot chart is in a PowerPivot workbook. You have to select one of the pivot table or pivot chart options shown above in Figure 3-18 or shown earlier in Figure 3-4.

Layout Option	Description
PivotTable	Is used to create one pivot table.
PivotChart	Is used to create one pivot chart.
Chart and Table (Horizontal)	Is used to create a pivot chart and pivot table side by side. (3)
Chart and Table (Vertical)	Is used to create a pivot chart and pivot table with the pivot table positioned below the chart. (3)
Two Charts (Horizontal)	Is used to create two pivot charts, side by side. (4)
Two Charts (Vertical)	Is used to create two pivot charts, one positioned below the other. (4)
Four Charts	Is used to create four pivot charts that are independent of each other. The slicers apply to all charts.
Flattened PivotTable	Is used to create a pivot table. Data values are not arranged as row and column headers. Instead, new columns are added to a pivot table and a Total row is added after each group. Figure 3-19 shows a regular pivot table. Figure 3-20 shows the same pivot table with the Flattened PivotTable layout applied. This option is often used when the pivot table needs to be printed.

Table 3-4 PivotTable button options explained

(3) The data in the table and chart are independent of each other. The slicers apply to both.
(4) The data in the charts are independent of each other. The slicers apply to both charts.

	A	B	C	D	E
1	StoreType	Online			
2					
3	**Sum of SalesAmount**	**Column Labels**			
4	**Row Labels**	**2007**	**2008**	**2009**	**Grand Total**
5	**⊟Contoso Asia Online Store**	**156883859.6**	**188427344.5**	**212850715.8**	**558161919.9**
6	Audio	1392089.651	3845074.381	6291990.679	11529154.71
7	Cameras and camcorders	53105292.45	58530245.16	58853219.11	170488756.7
8	Cell phones	17463766.24	18727338.05	25224586.92	61415691.21
9	Computers	61730570.51	69293994.96	77309017.96	208333583.4
10	Music, Movies and Audio Books	3678032.351	3803581.908	3302814.112	10784428.37
11	TV and Video	19514108.38	34227110.08	41869086.99	95610305.45
12	**⊟Contoso Europe Online Store**	**167679516.4**	**170444136.2**	**175239722.4**	**513363375.1**
13	Audio	1671060.3	3349933.152	5007450.127	10028443.58
14	Cameras and camcorders	57331963.15	53269536.98	46157400.89	156758901
15	Cell phones	18198798.43	16433105.71	19823942.39	54455846.53

Figure 3-19 Pivot table

G	H	I	J	K
StoreType	Online			
Sum of SalesAmount		CalendarYear		
StoreName	ProductCategoryName	2007	2008	2009
Contoso Asia Online Store	Audio	1392089.651	3845074.381	6291990.679
Contoso Asia Online Store	Cameras and camcorders	53105292.45	58530245.16	58853219.11
Contoso Asia Online Store	Cell phones	17463766.24	18727338.05	25224586.92
Contoso Asia Online Store	Computers	61730570.51	69293994.96	77309017.96
Contoso Asia Online Store	Music, Movies and Audio Books	3678032.351	3803581.908	3302814.112
Contoso Asia Online Store	TV and Video	19514108.38	34227110.08	41869086.99
Contoso Asia Online Store Total		156883859.6	188427344.5	212850715.8
Contoso Europe Online Store	Audio	1671060.3	3349933.152	5007450.127
Contoso Europe Online Store	Cameras and camcorders	57331963.15	53269536.98	46157400.89
Contoso Europe Online Store	Cell phones	18198798.43	16433105.71	19823942.39
Contoso Europe Online Store	Computers	64859018.44	64252887.1	68548449.65

Figure 3-20 Pivot table with the Flattened PivotTable layout applied

Formatting Group

The options in this group are used to change the data type and to format the data in PowerPivot tables. Select the column of data that you want to apply the formatting to or change the data type of, before selecting an option in this group. The options are explained in Table 3-5.

Formatting Options

Keep the following in mind when using the options in the Formatting group.

① The options are only for formatting the data in the PowerPivot table. The formatting applied to the data in the PowerPivot table is not carried over to a pivot table that is created from the data.

② The data in the PowerPivot table cannot be printed.

Option	Description
Data Type	Displays the data type of the selected column. The options available to change the data type to, depend on the data type of the selected column. For example, Figure 3-21 shows the data type options that text data can be changed to. Figure 3-22 shows the data type options that dates can be changed to.
Format	Is used to select a format for the data in a column, as shown in Figure 3-23.
Apply Currency Format	This option is only enabled for columns that have numeric data. Select one of the options shown in Figure 3-24 to display the data in currency format.
Apply Percentage Format	Displays the numbers in percent format.
Thousands Separator	Displays the numbers with a comma.
Decrease Decimal	Moves the decimal point in the number one digit to the right. (5)
Increase Decimal	Moves the decimal point in the number one digit to the left. (5)

Table 3-5 Formatting group options explained

(5) This option does not change the actual data, it only changes how the data is displayed.

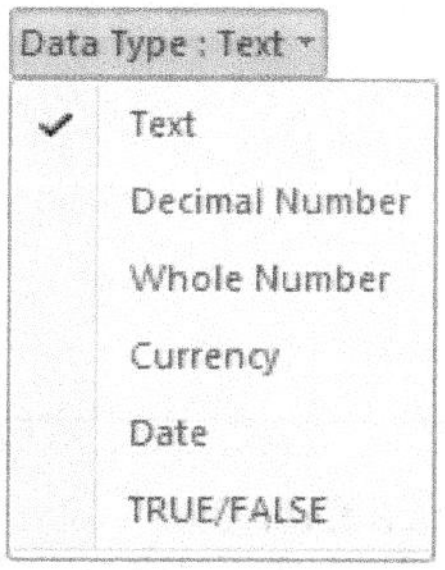

Figure 3-21 Text data type options

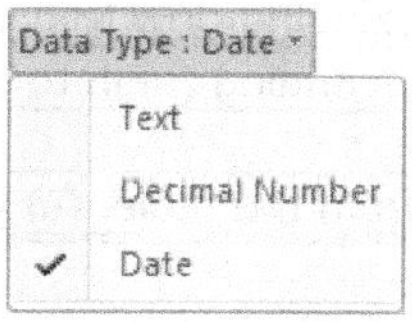

Figure 3-22 Date data type options

The **FORMAT** options that are available depend on the data type of the selected column.

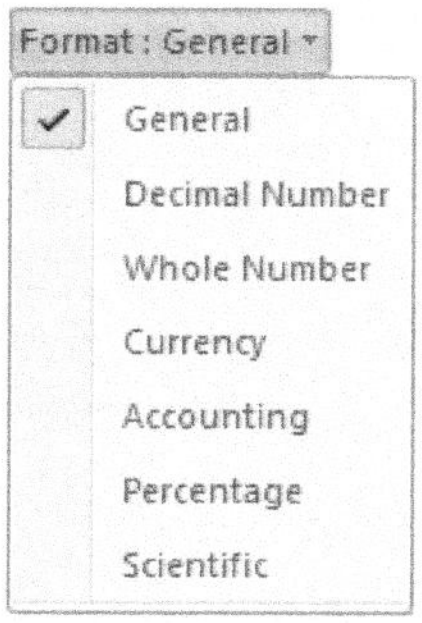

Figure 3-23 Whole Number format options

Figure 3-24 Currency format options

Sort And Filter Group

To use the options in this group, a column of data has to be selected first. The options are explained in Table 3-6.

> The names of the two sort options at the top of the Sort and Filter group change slightly, based on the data type of the selected column. Regardless of the name, the sort order is the same. In Figure 3-15 shown earlier, the column selected for the screenshot has dates. Figure 3-25 shows the sort option names when text data is selected.

Figure 3-25 Text data sort options

Option	Description
Sort A to Z	Sorts the data in ascending (low to high) order.
Sort Z to A	Sorts the data in descending (high to low) order.
Clear Sort	Removes the sort.
Clear All Filters	Removes all filters from the table. (6)

Table 3-6 Sort And Filter group options explained

(6)

> **How To Remove Some Filters And Leave Others**
> If you only want to remove some filters, right-click on the column that has a filter that you want to remove, then select Filter ⇒ Clear Filter From "Column Name", as shown in Figure 3-26.

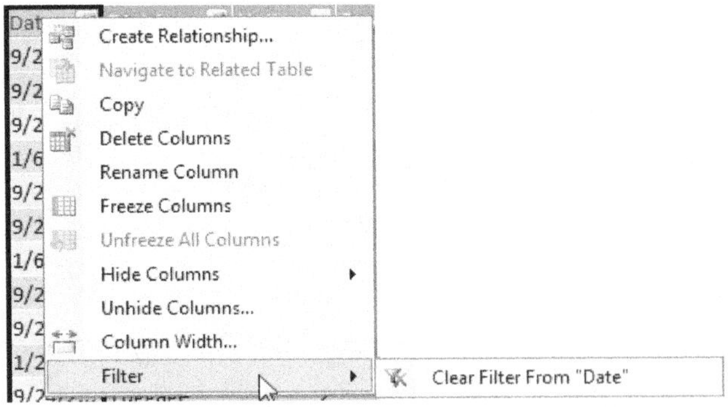

Figure 3-26 Clear Filter option

View Group

The options in this group are used to change how the columns are displayed. The options are explained in Table 3-7.

Option	Description
Freeze	Select the Freeze option shown in Figure 3-27 to move the selected columns to the left. The columns that this option is applied to will always be visible when you scroll to the right. The option is similar to the Freeze Panes option on the View tab in Excel. The difference is that the columns that this option is applied to, are moved to the left most columns in the table. This means that you could move the 29th and 30th columns to the far left of the PowerPivot table.
Column Width	Is used to change the width of the selected columns by typing the new width in the dialog box shown in Figure 3-28. (7)

Table 3-7 View group options explained

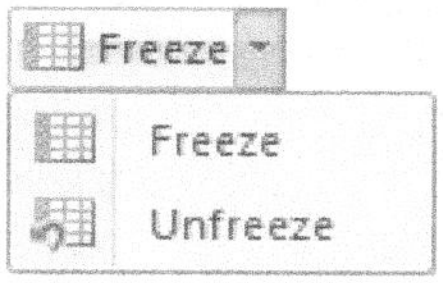

Figure 3-27 Freeze column options

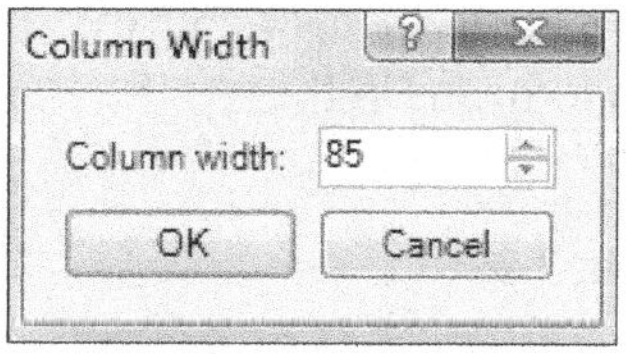

Figure 3-28 Column Width dialog box

(7) Unlike Excel, PowerPivot does not display pound signs (####) in a cell when a column is not wide enough to display the data. Instead, an ellipsis is added to the end of the cell, as shown in Figure 3-29. This lets you know that all of the data in the cell is not being displayed.

Figure 3-29 Narrow column

PowerPivot Window Design Tab

The options on the tab shown in Figure 3-30 are used to add columns to the PowerPivot table, change table properties, modify existing data source connections and create relationships between tables. The options in each group are explained below.

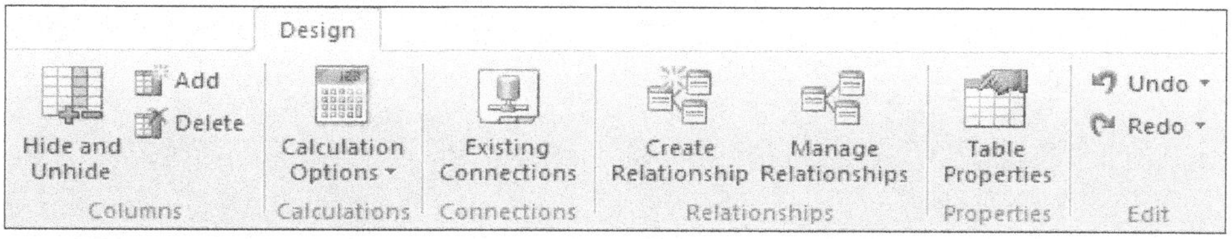

Figure 3-30 Design tab options

Columns Group

The options in this group are used to hide, add and delete columns. The options are explained in Table 3-8.

Option	Description
Hide and Unhide	Is used to hide or display columns of data in a PowerPivot table and in a pivot table in Excel, by adding or removing check marks on the Hide and Unhide Columns dialog box.
Add	Is used to add a column after the last column. This option is used to create a DAX calculated column.
Delete	Is used to permanently delete columns from the table. Ctrl+Click does not allow multiple columns to be selected.

Table 3-8 Columns group options explained

Calculations Group

CALCULATION OPTIONS The options shown in Figure 3-31 are used to select how and when formulas in the PowerPivot window are calculated.

The options are explained in Table 3-9.

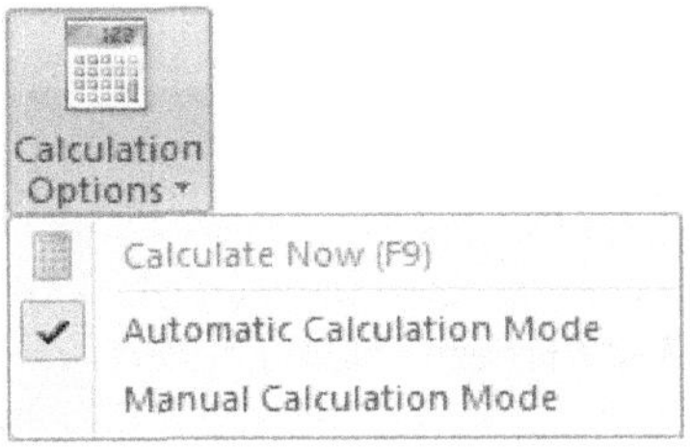

Figure 3-31 Calculation Options

Option	Description
Calculate Now	All of the formulas in the workbook are recalculated now.
Automatic Calculation Mode	When a formula is changed or any change in the workbook is made, the formulas are recalculated.
Manual Calculation Mode	Disables automatic calculation. If this option is currently selected, select the Calculate Now option to recalculate the formulas.

Table 3-9 Calculation options explained

Connections Group

EXISTING CONNECTIONS Is used to display the data sources that are already connected to the workbook. If you need to import more data from a data source listed on this dialog box you can, by selecting the data source from the list, as shown in Figure 3-32.

The options on this dialog box are also used to refresh data and edit the connection properties.

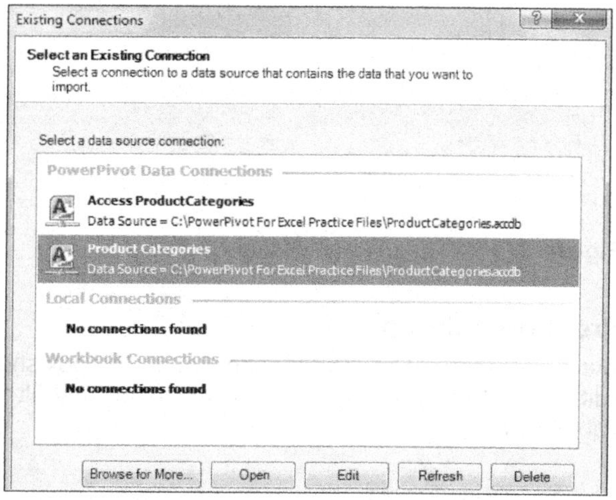

Figure 3-32 Existing Connections dialog box

Relationships Group

The options in this group are used to link tables based on related data in a column in each table. The relationship is what allows PowerPivot to display and use data from different tables in the same pivot table or pivot chart. The options are explained in Table 3-10.

Option	Description
Create Relationship	Is used to create a relationship between two tables in the PowerPivot window on the dialog box shown in Figure 3-33.
Manage Relationships	Opens the dialog box shown in Figure 3-34. The options are used to create, edit, view and delete relationships in the PowerPivot workbook.

Table 3-10 Relationships group options explained

This dialog box replaces using **VLOOKUP** in Excel.

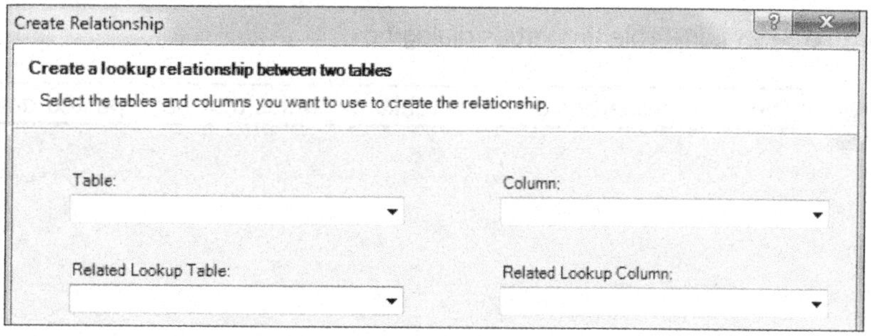

Figure 3-33 Create Relationship dialog box

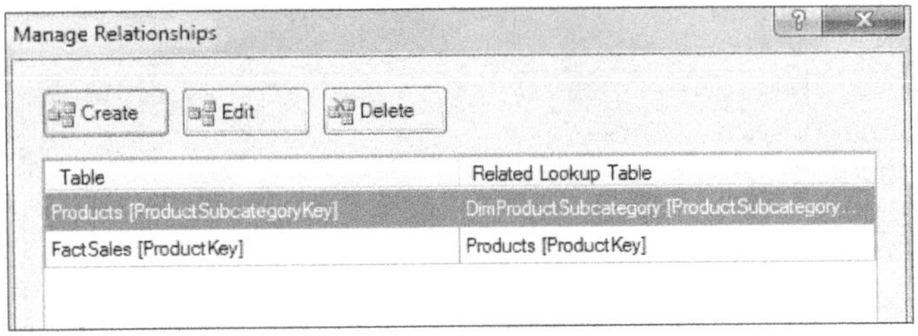

Figure 3-34 Manage Relationships dialog box

Properties Group

TABLE PROPERTIES This button opens the dialog box shown in Figure 3-35. The options are used to edit table information and select how columns and filters are mapped. The options are explained in Table 3-11.

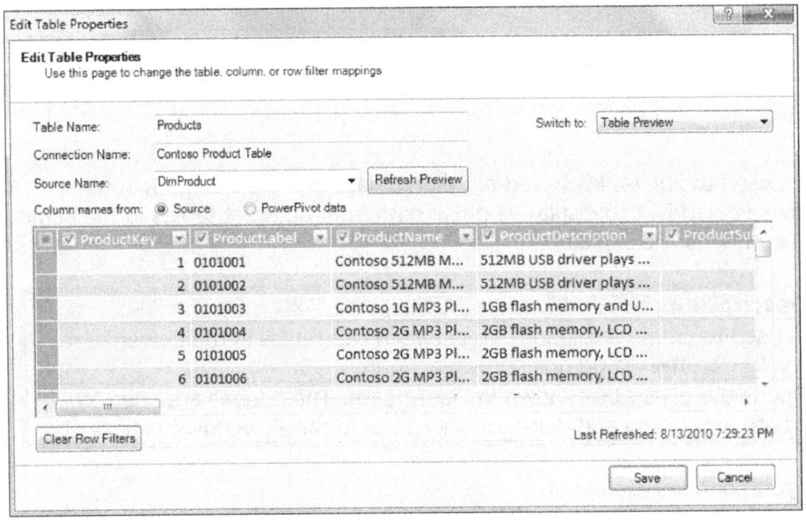

Figure 3-35 Edit Table Properties dialog box

The table properties of linked tables or tables that have pasted data cannot be edited.

Option	Description
Table Name	Displays the name of the table in the PowerPivot window before the Table Properties button was clicked.
Connection Name	Displays the name of the connection for the table in the Table Name field.
Source Name	Displays the current table by default. If the data source of the connection has more than one table, the drop-down list is enabled on this field. This allows you to select a different table that you want to replace the current table with. If you select a table that has a different structure then the current table, you will see a message similar to the one illustrated at the bottom of Figure 3-36, which lets you know that the columns are different. You can select to add all of the fields from the new table by clicking in the box in the upper left corner of the grid or individually select fields. Once you have made the changes, click the Save button.
Refresh Preview button	Is used to display the data in the selected source table.
Column Names From	Is used to select where the column names that are displayed come from.
Switch To drop-down list	The **TABLE PREVIEW** option displays a few rows of data. The **QUERY EDITOR** option displays the options shown in Figure 3-37. This screen displays the SQL statement used to select the data for the table. If you edit the query, click the Save button. The Validate and Design buttons are explained in the next chapter. [See Chapter 4, Import By Query]

Table 3-11 Edit Table Properties dialog box options explained

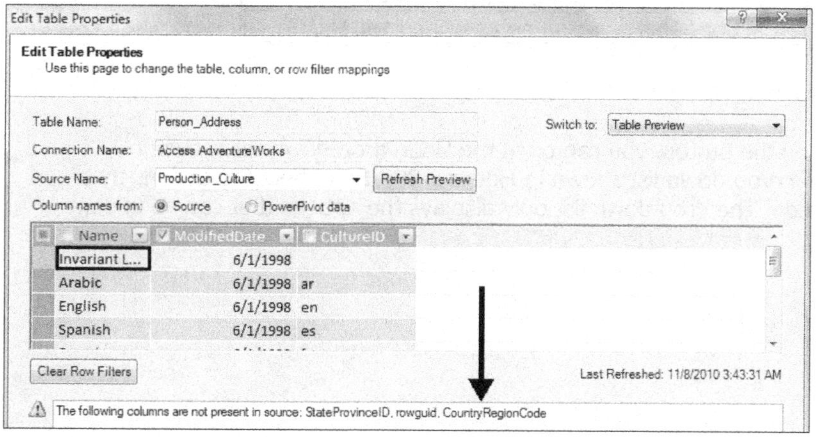

Figure 3-36 Different table structure warning message

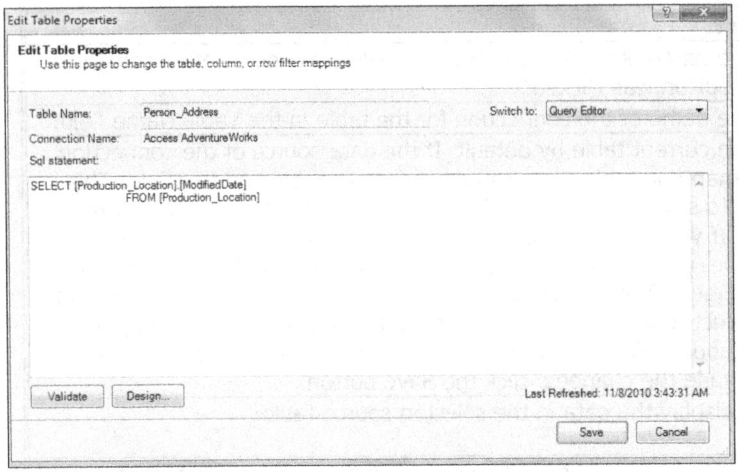

Figure 3-37 Edit Table Properties Query Editor screen

Edit Group

The options in this group are used to add or remove features that have been applied to the PowerPivot tables. The options are explained in Table 3-12.

Option	Description
Undo	Undoes the last action. This is the same as using **CTRL+Z**. (8)
Redo	Reapplies the last action. This is the same as using **CTRL+Y**. (8)

Table 3-12 Edit group options explained

(8) In addition to clicking on the button, you can open the Undo drop-down list shown in Figure 3-38 or the Redo drop-down list shown in Figure 3-39, then select the options that you want to undo or redo. The drop-down list only displays the options that can be undone or reapplied.

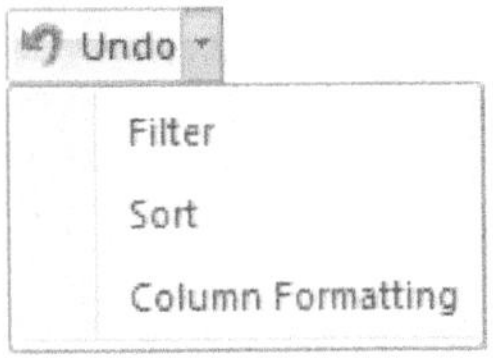

Figure 3-38 Undo drop-down list options

Figure 3-39 Redo drop-down list options

PowerPivot Window Linked Table Contextual Tab

Unlike the other tabs on the PowerPivot ribbon, the Linked Table contextual tab is part of the Table Tools. This tab is only available after an Excel table is linked to a PowerPivot table.

The options on the tab shown in Figure 3-40 are used to refresh the PowerPivot data that is linked to an Excel table and select how the data should be refreshed. The options are explained in Table 3-13.

Figure 3-40 PowerPivot Linked Table contextual tab

Option	Description
Update All	Updates all PowerPivot tables that are linked to tables in Excel.
Update Selected	Updates the selected PowerPivot table that is linked to a table in Excel.
Excel Table	Displays the name of the Excel table that the selected PowerPivot table is linked to. The Excel table names in the list come from the Table Name field on the Table Tools Design tab. This may be different then the name of the tab that the data is on. The drop-down list on this button only displays the Excel tables that are linked to a table in the PowerPivot window. If the Excel table name has changed, you have to type in the new name here to maintain the link.
Go to Excel Table	Is used to display the Excel table that is linked to the PowerPivot table that is currently displayed.
Update Mode	Is used to select how the linked PowerPivot table data is updated.

Table 3-13 Linked Table contextual tab options explained

Refreshing Data vs Recalculating Formulas
Refreshing data is different then recalculating formulas. Refreshing data replaces the existing data in the PowerPivot table with an updated copy of the data from the data source. Recalculating formulas does not update data that was imported or pasted into the PowerPivot table. It reruns the DAX formulas that you created against the data that is currently in the PowerPivot table. To have the most current information in pivot tables, refresh the data then recalculate the formulas.

PowerPivot Window Shortcut Menus

Like Excel, the grid in the PowerPivot window has two shortcut menus; one for cells and one for columns. The options on these shortcut menus are explained below.

PowerPivot Window Cell Shortcut Menu

The shortcut menu shown in Figure 3-41 is displayed when you right-click on a cell in a PowerPivot table. The options are explained in Table 3-14.

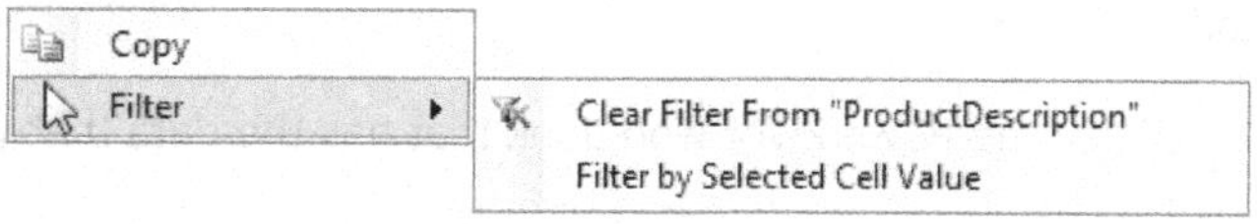

Figure 3-41 PowerPivot window cell shortcut menu

Option	Description
Copy	Is used to copy the data in the selected cells and paste them into a new PowerPivot table.
Filter	The options on the submenu shown on the right of Figure 3-41 above are used to only display rows of data in the table that have the value in the cell that you select. The first option **CLEAR FILTER FROM**, removes the filter. These filter options are a subset of the filter options for the column. [See Chapter 5, Using The Preview And Filter Options] Figure 3-42 shows the data without a filter applied. Figure 3-43 shows the same data with a filter applied.

Table 3-14 PowerPivot window cell shortcut menu options explained

ProductKey	ProductLabel	ProductName	ProductDescription
887	0308145	Contoso Blueto...	Transceiver-free wire...
888	0308146	Contoso Blueto...	Transceiver-free wire...
889	0308147	Contoso Blueto...	Transceiver-free wire...
890	0308148	Contoso Blueto...	Transceiver-free wire...
891	0308149	SV Rechargeabl...	33 ft range, recharges...
892	0308150	SV Rechargeabl...	33 ft range, recharges...
893	0308151	SV Rechargeabl...	33 ft range, recharges...
894	0308152	SV Rechargeabl...	33 ft range, recharges...
895	0308153	SV Keyboard E9...	Cutting-edge design ...
896	0308154	SV Keyboard E9...	Cutting-edge design ...

Figure 3-42 Data without a filter applied

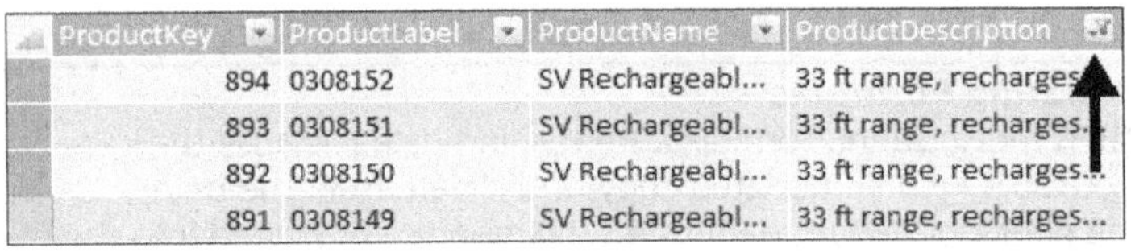

ProductKey	ProductLabel	ProductName	ProductDescription
894	0308152	SV Rechargeabl...	33 ft range, recharges...
893	0308151	SV Rechargeabl...	33 ft range, recharges...
892	0308150	SV Rechargeabl...	33 ft range, recharges...
891	0308149	SV Rechargeabl...	33 ft range, recharges...

Figure 3-43 Data with a filter applied

Notice the icon in the upper right corner of the Product Description column illustrated above in Figure 3-43. That is the filter icon, which indicates that the data in the table is filtered on this column.

Create A PowerPivot Table From Data In The PowerPivot Window

As you read above in Table 3-14, the Copy option on the cell shortcut menu is used to create a new table from data in an existing PowerPivot table. The steps below show you how to create a new table.

1. Open the PowerPivot workbook that has the data that you want to use to create a new table.

2. Open the PowerPivot window and click on the tab that has the data that you want to copy to a new table.

3. Select the cells that you want to copy to a new PowerPivot table.

4. Home tab ⇒ Clipboard group ⇒ Copy button.

   Home tab ⇒ Clipboard group ⇒ Paste button.

   You will see the dialog box shown in Figure 3-44.

   The dialog box displays the name of the table that you copied the cells from and the data that you selected to paste into the new table.

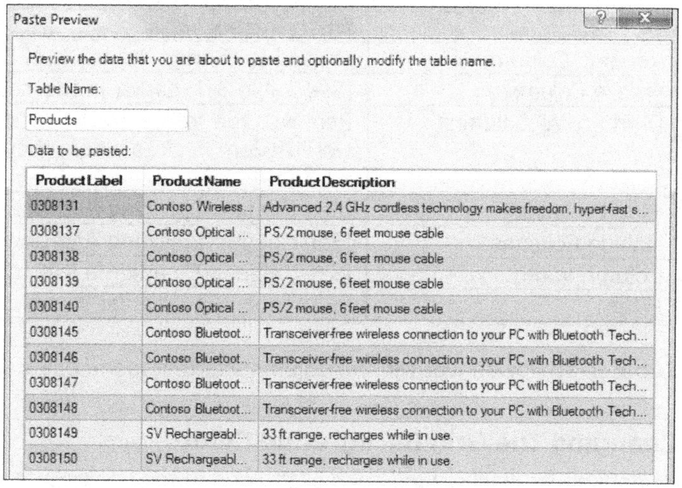

Figure 3-44 Paste Preview dialog box

5. More than likely, you want this data on a new tab. In the Table Name field type in a new name for the table, then click OK. A new table and tab will be created in the PowerPivot window. Save the changes to the workbook.

PowerPivot Window Column Shortcut Menu

Some of the options on the shortcut menu shown in Figure 3-45 are shortcuts to options on the PowerPivot window tabs.

Right-click on a column heading to display this shortcut menu.

The options are explained in Table 3-15.

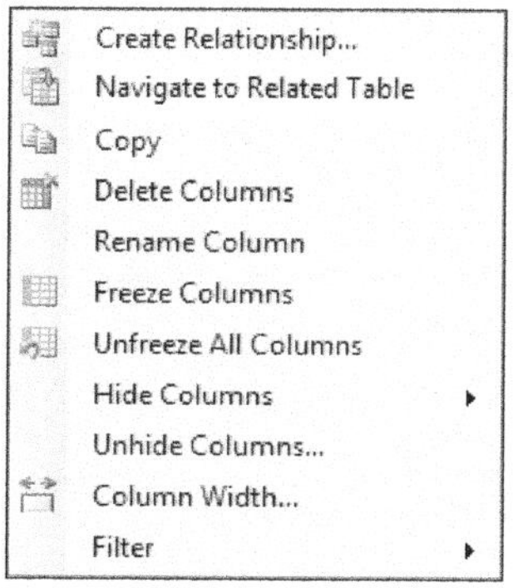

Figure 3-45 Column shortcut menu

Option	Description
Create Relationship	Is used to join two PowerPivot tables to be able to use the data from both tables in the same pivot table or pivot chart.
Navigate to Related Table	This option is only available for a column that has been used to create a relationship. When this option is selected, the table that the column is linked to is displayed. The lookup column in the related tabled is selected.
Copy	[See Table 3-14, earlier in this chapter]
Delete Columns	Deletes the selected columns from the table.

Table 3-15 PowerPivot window column shortcut menu options explained

Option	Description
Rename Column	Is used to change the name of the selected column.
Freeze Columns	[See Table 3-7, earlier in this chapter]
Unfreeze All Columns	Removes the freeze option but does not move the columns that were frozen, back to where they were before the freeze option was applied.
Hide Columns	[See Chapter 8, Hiding And Unhiding Columns]
Unhide Columns	[See Chapter 8, Hiding And Unhiding Columns]
Column Width	[See Table 3-7, earlier in this chapter]
Filter	[See Table 3-14, earlier in this chapter]

Table 3-15 PowerPivot window column shortcut menu options explained (Continued)

Changing The Grid Background Color

By default, the background color of the grid in the PowerPivot window is green. If you do not like the green, you can change it by following the steps below.

1. Display the Excel window of the PowerPivot workbook that you want to change the background color of.

2. Page Layout tab ⇒ Themes group ⇒ Themes. You should see the options shown in Figure 3-46.

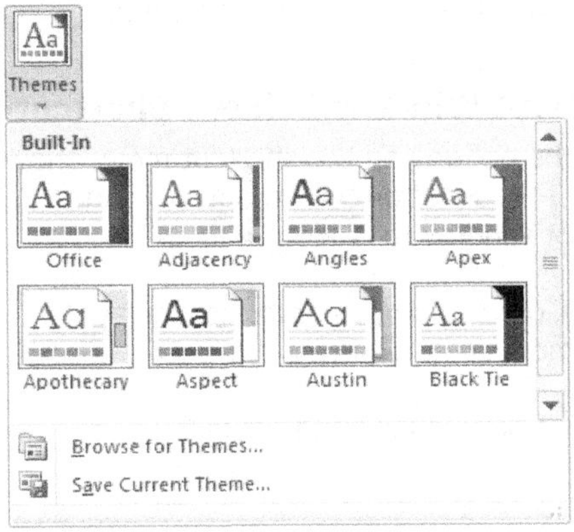

Figure 3-46 Themes options

3. Select a different theme from the list or click on the Browse For Themes link at the bottom of the list, then select a theme that is on your hard drive or in another location.

4. Save the changes, then close the PowerPivot window and reopen it to see the new theme color.

Customize The Quick Access Toolbar In Excel

Throughout this book you will create a lot of workbooks, open a lot of existing workbooks and save existing workbooks with a new file name. You may find it easier and faster to have options for these tasks on the Quick Access toolbar. The steps below show you how to add them to the toolbar. Customizing the Quick Access toolbar in Excel is not required to complete the exercises in this book.

1. Open Excel.

2. Click on the Customize Quick Access Toolbar button illustrated in Figure 3-47.

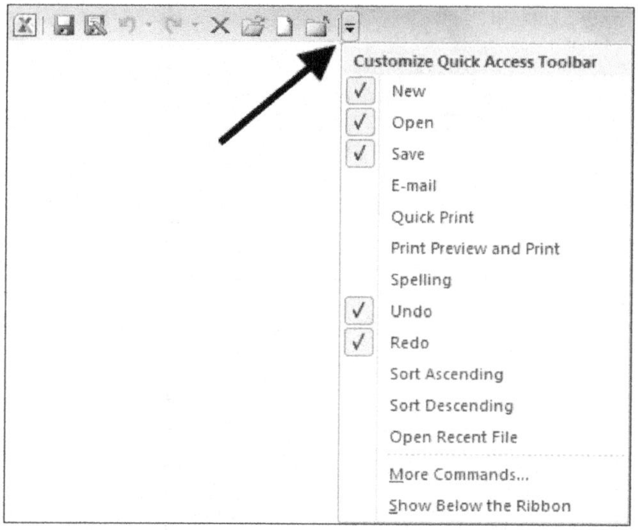

Figure 3-47 Quick Access Toolbar

3. Select any of the options shown above in Figure 3-47 that are currently not selected on your computer.

4. Select the **MORE COMMANDS** option on the menu shown above in Figure 3-47. The Excel Options dialog box will open.

5. In the left column, click on the **SAVE AS** option, then click the Add button.

6. Rearrange the items in the column on the right so that they are in the order from left to right that you want them to appear in, on the Quick Access toolbar. To move an option, click on it, then click the Move Up or Move Down button to place the item where you want it. Figure 3-48 shows how I have the options arranged on the toolbar, but you can put the options in the order that works best for you.

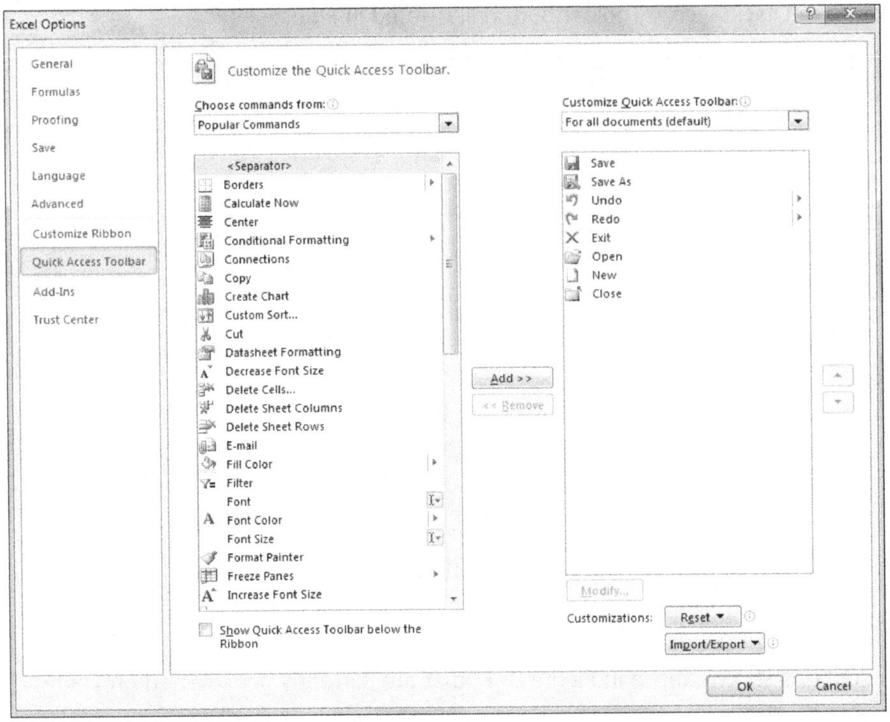

Figure 3-48 Excel Options dialog box Quick Access Toolbar options

7. When you are finished, click OK to close the dialog box.

THE TABLE IMPORT WIZARD

In this chapter you will probably learn more than you want to about the Table Import Wizard. You will also learn about the types of databases that can be used to import data into PowerPivot.

CHAPTER 4

Overview

The Table Import Wizard will take you step-by-step through the process of setting up a connection to a data source and selecting the data to import into PowerPivot. As you read in Chapter 1, data can be imported from a variety of sources. Data is imported as tables into PowerPivot. Each table is automatically placed on its own tab in the PowerPivot window, just like tabs in an Excel worksheet.

Unlike some wizards in other software packages that I have used and written about, I am happy to say that the Table Import Wizard is very straight forward. What I like is that each screen on the wizard has a sentence or two that explains in non technical terms what task needs to be completed.

PowerPivot Supported Data Sources

As you will see, PowerPivot supports a variety of data source types. Table 4-1 lists the supported data sources and other information that you may find helpful.

Data Source	File Type	Versions (If Applicable)
SQL Server database		SQL Azure, SQL Server 2005, 2008, 2008 R2
Analysis Services Cube		Analysis Services, SQL Server 2005, 2008, 2008 R2
Access	.mdb, .accdb	2003, 2007, 2010
Oracle		
Teradata		V2R6, V112
Sybase		V15 and higher
Informix		V11 and higher
IBM DB2		8.1
SQL Parallel Data Warehouse		2008 R2
OLE DB/ODBC		
Data Feeds		Atom 1.0 format, Microsoft Reporting Services
SharePoint Report		Reports that have an Atom icon in the header
PowerPivot Workbook	.xlsx, .xlsm, .xlsb, .xltx, .xltm	
Excel	.xlsx, .xlsm, .xlsb, .xltx, .xltm	Excel 97-2003, 2007, 2010
Text	.txt, .csv, .tab	

Table 4-1 PowerPivot supported data sources

Importing Data

Importing data is the most important part of the process of being able to use PowerPivot. Without data, PowerPivot can't be used. A benefit that PowerPivot has over traditional BI tools is that the data comes straight into PowerPivot, instead of having to be stored in a data warehouse for staging and then imported into the BI tool. Because of its flexibility, PowerPivot can import data from a rather impressive list of data sources.

Importing Data That You Will Not Use To Create Pivot Tables Or Pivot Charts
You have the option of importing as much data as you want. Keep in mind that the import can fail if your computer does not have enough RAM to support the amount of data in the import. One way to reduce the chance of the import failing, is to not import columns or rows of data that you will not use to create the pivot table or pivot chart. PowerPivot provides filter and query options on the Table Import Wizard that can be used to reduce the number of records and number of columns that are imported.

Table Import Wizard Overview

Because an important aspect of PowerPivot is importing data and the Table Import Wizard is the tool used to import data, I felt that it deserved its own chapter. In Chapter 1, the term relational database was briefly discussed.

In step 1 below, you will learn about the options in the Get External Data group, shown in Figure 4-1, on the Home tab of the PowerPivot window ribbon.

Figure 4-1 Get External Data group options

Step 1: Select The Data Source

In this step you select the database, text file, spreadsheet, data feed or other data source that has the data that you want to import. The data source options are explained below.

FROM DATABASE Displays the options shown in Figure 4-2. The options are used to import data from different Microsoft databases. The options are explained in Table 4-2.

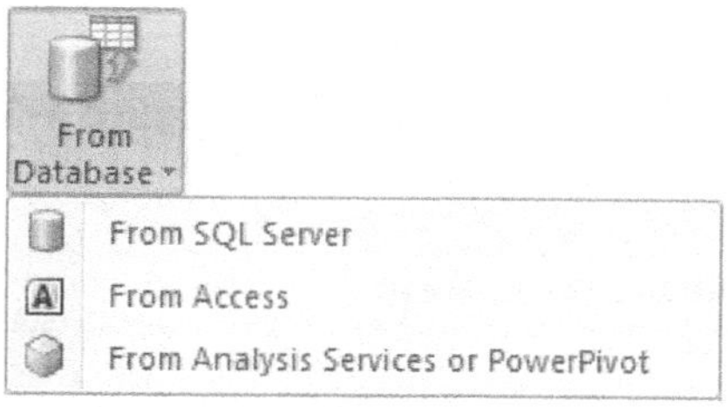

Figure 4-2 From Database options

Option	This Option Is Used To Connect To A . . .
From SQL Server	SQL Server database. The options shown in Figure 4-3 are used to connect to this type of database.
From Access	Access database. This database software comes with some editions of Microsoft Office or it can be purchased as a stand alone product. Unlike the other options on the From Database drop-down list, Access databases can reside on your computers hard drive or on a server. Figure 4-4 shows the connection options.

Table 4-2 From Database options explained

Option	This Option Is Used To Connect To A . . .
From Analysis Services or PowerPivot	SQL Server Analysis Services, which is similar to connecting to an SQL Server database. The difference is that you will use an **MDX** query for the Analysis Services instead of an SQL query. This option is also used to connect to and import data from a PowerPivot workbook that has been published to a SharePoint server. As shown in Figure 4-5, the options are similar to the SQL Server database connection options.

Table 4-2 From Database options explained (Continued)

When you open the Server Name drop-down list, PowerPivot will automatically search for servers that the computer is connected to.

If the search takes a while, your computer may not be connected to any servers.

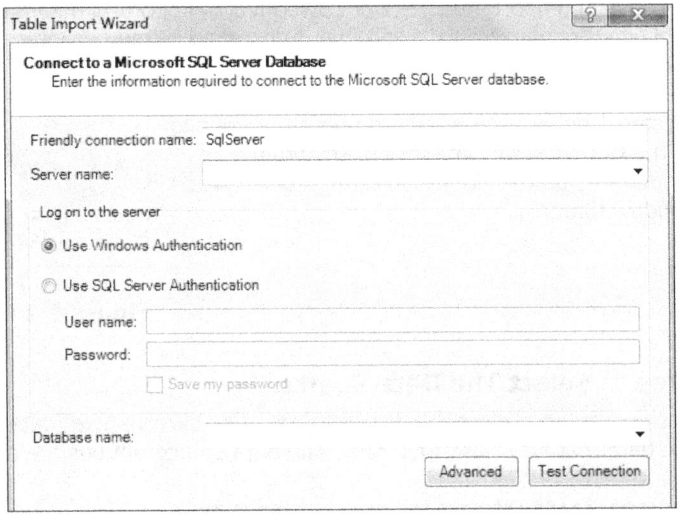

Figure 4-3 Microsoft SQL Server database connection options

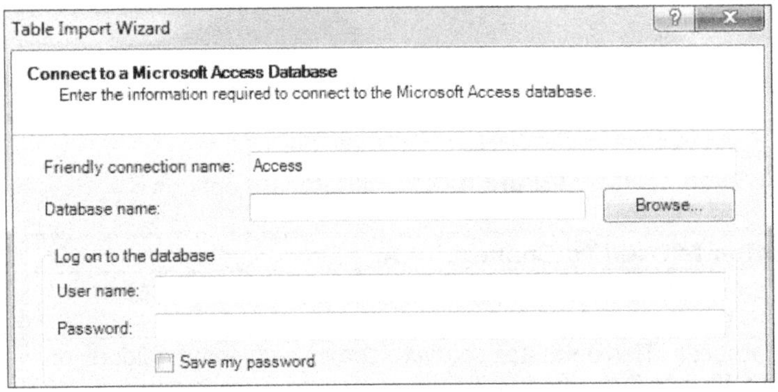

Figure 4-4 Microsoft Access database connection options

> Microsoft Access databases that have already been published to a SharePoint server cannot be imported into PowerPivot.

Unlike the Server Name field in an SQL Server connection, the Server or File Name field on the SQL Server Analysis Services screen shown in Figure 4-5, does not have a drop-down list that you can select a server from.

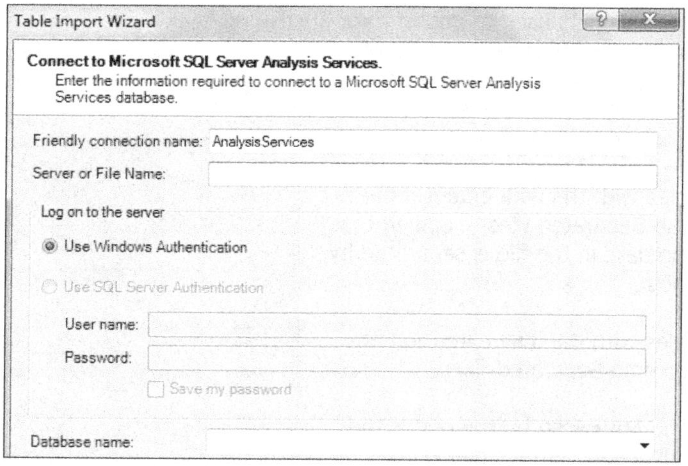

Figure 4-5 SQL Server Analysis Services/PowerPivot connection options

> **Importing Analysis Services OLAP Cubes**
> Select the From Analysis Services or PowerPivot option when you want to import data from an Analysis Services OLAP cube. Because OLAP cube files do not contain tables, an MDX query must be used to import the data. PowerPivot has an MDX editor that you can use to create queries for OLAP data. [See Chapter 13, Figure 13-19]

FROM REPORT Is used to import data from a Microsoft SQL Server 2008 R2 Reporting Services report, by using the options on the dialog box shown in Figure 4-6.

The data from these reports can be imported as a data feed.

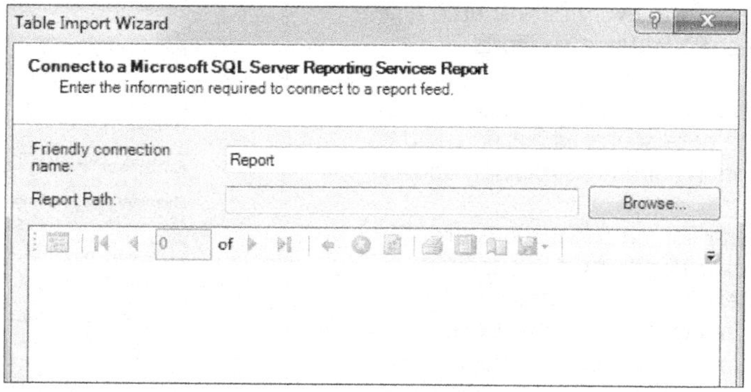

Figure 4-6 Microsoft SQL Server Reporting Services Report connection options

FROM DATA FEEDS Is used to import data from an Atom data feed, from an online data source (corporate or public), by using the options shown in Figure 4-7.

RSS DATA FEEDS are not supported.

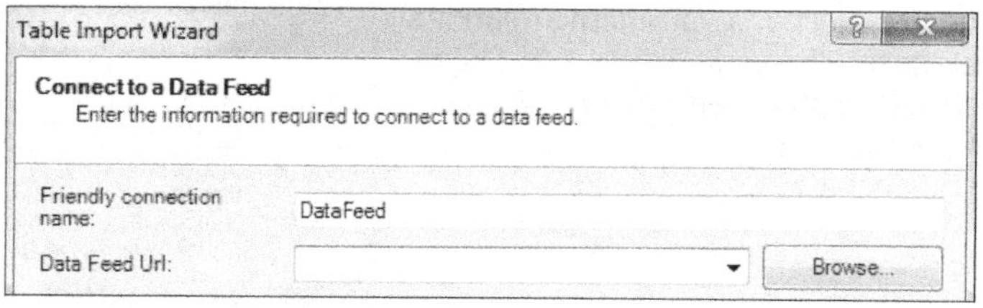

Figure 4-7 Data Feed connection options

FROM TEXT Is used to import data from a text file that is in one of these formats: .txt, .tab or .csv, by using the options shown in Figure 4-8.

Files with the **.TAB** extension are Tab Separated files, meaning that the data in the file is separated by tabs.

Files with the **.CSV** extension are Comma Separated files.

The **ADVANCED** button opens the Advanced Settings dialog box, which is covered in Chapter 6.

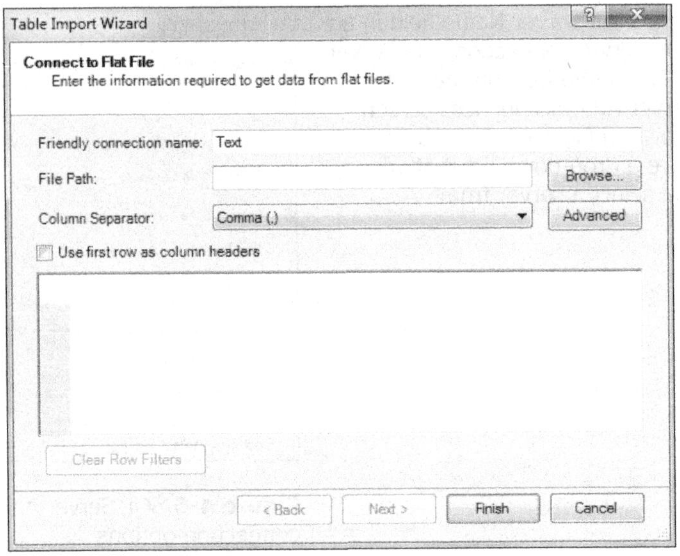

Figure 4-8 Flat File (text) connection options

FROM OTHER SOURCES displays the options shown in Figure 4-9.

This screen can be used to import data from every data source type that PowerPivot supports.

Usually this option is selected when the data source is not one of the options already explained above.

Data source connections are PowerPivot workbook specific, meaning that if workbook 1 is connected to database 1 and workbook 2 needs to import data from database 1, a connection to database 1 will have to be created in workbook 2.

The next section explains the relational databases shown in Figure 4-9. These database options also use the Table Import Wizard.

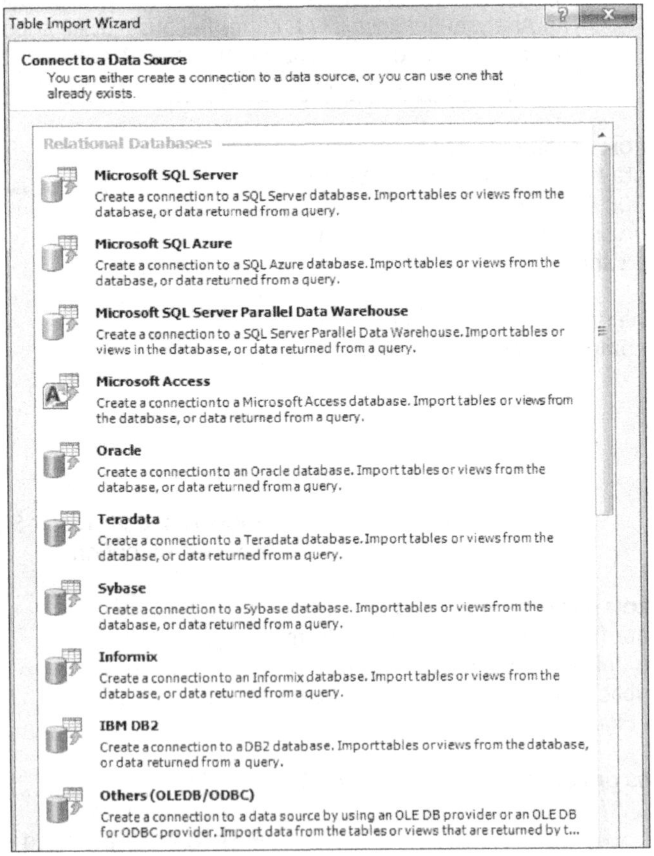

Figure 4-9 Connect To A Data Source screen options

Relational Databases

Earlier in this chapter you learned about the database connections that have their own option in the Get External Data group section on the Home tab. This section discusses the relational database options shown above in Figure 4-9 that were not already discussed.

Microsoft SQL Azure is a cloud computing database service that is based on the Microsoft SQL Server platform. Data feeds can be set up in cloud-based databases. For more information see www.microsoft.com/windowsazure.

Microsoft SQL Server Parallel Data Warehouse is a scalable data warehouse solution that is capable of storing hundreds of terabytes of data.

Oracle, Teradata, Sybase, Informix and **IBM DB2** are all enterprise level relational database management systems owned by different companies. Drivers for these databases do not come with PowerPivot. If you need to connect to one of these types of databases, you have to get and install the drivers. Many of these databases use the connection options shown in Figure 4-10.

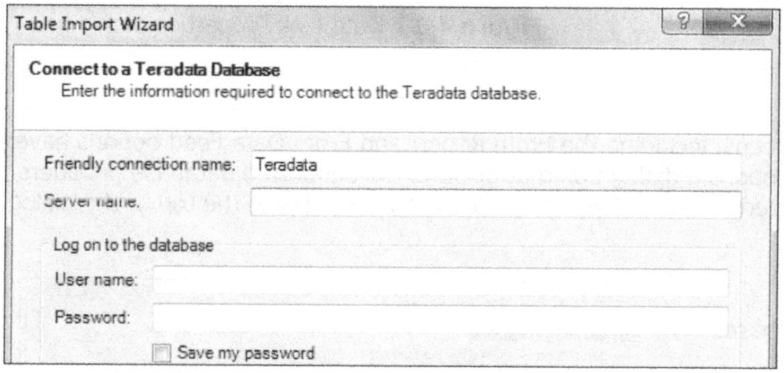

Figure 4-10 Enterprise database connection options

Others (OLEDB/ODBC) Select this option if the database that you want to connect to is not in the list of databases discussed above, as long as it is OLE DB or ODBC compliant.

Examples of this type of database are FoxPro and dBASE. When the Others option is selected and the Next button is clicked, the screen shown in Figure 4-11 is displayed.

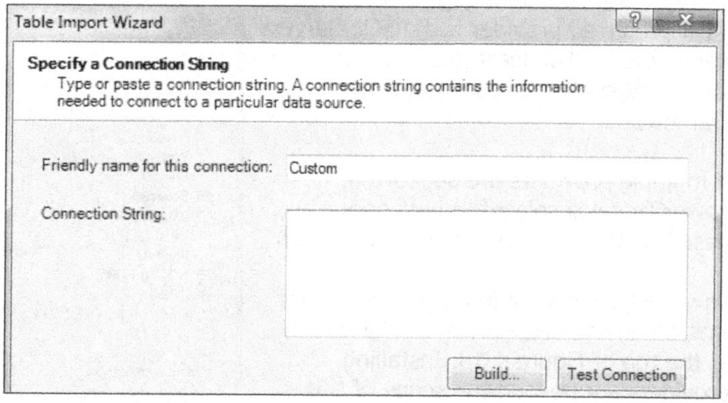

Figure 4-11 OLEDB/ODBC connection options

The options on this screen are used to add the information needed to connect to the database that you want to import data from. If you have no idea how to create a connection string, quickly click the **BUILD** button shown above in Figure 4-11, to display the dialog box shown in Figure 4-12. If you want to see a connection string, see Chapter 6, Figure 6-21.

The options on this dialog box are used to create the connection by selecting the appropriate provider. If you have never created a connection string, you will probably find using this dialog box easier then creating the connection string on your own.

More than likely, you will select the **ODBC DRIVERS** option on this dialog box, if you do not see the database type that you want to connect to in the list and then click the Next button to select the data source.

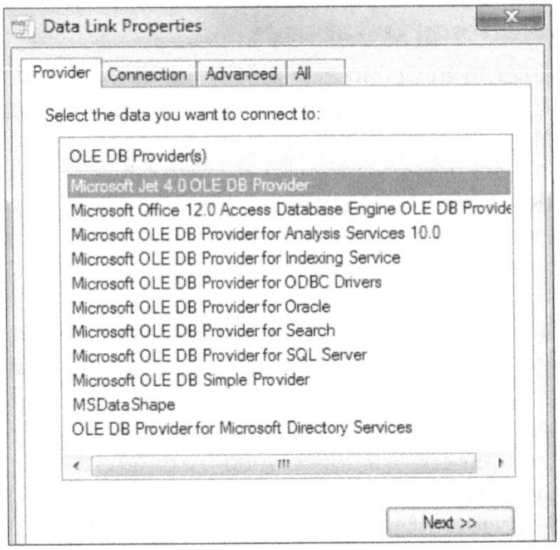

Figure 4-12 Data Link Properties dialog box

Database Providers

All of the database connection screens, including the From Report and From Data Feed options have an **ADVANCED** button. This button opens a dialog box that displays the supported database providers for the data source that you selected. The providers are in the drop-down list at the top of the dialog box.

Figure 4-13 shows the advanced properties for an SQL Server database.

The order that the providers are listed in the drop-down list is the preferred order of use. For example, in Figure 4-13, the most preferred provider is the SQL Server Native Client. The least preferred provider for this type of database is the .Net Framework.

If multiple providers are supported, PowerPivot will select the best one, based on the providers that are installed.

PowerPivot does not install the providers that are in the drop-down list illustrated at the top of Figure 4-13. Installing providers are beyond the scope of this book.

As shown, the SQL Server database has multiple providers that PowerPivot supports. Other databases may not.

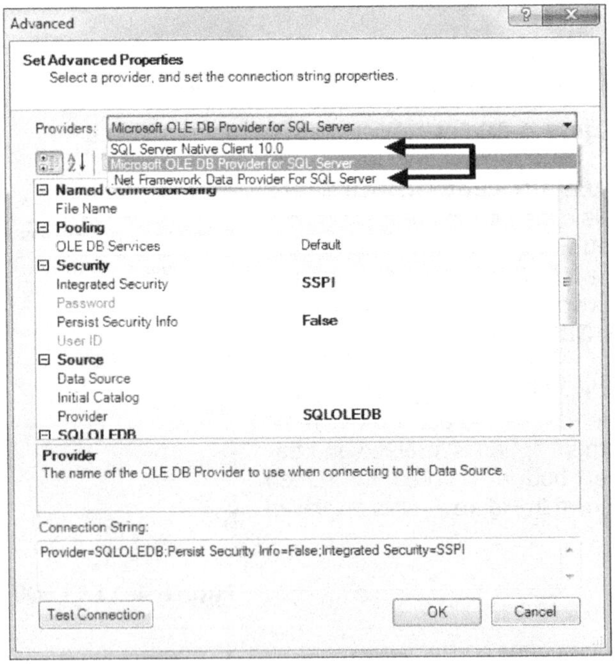

Figure 4-13 Advanced properties for an SQL Server database

Figure 4-14 shows the advanced properties for a Microsoft Access database.

Some of the providers may already be installed on your computer because of other software that is installed that uses the same type of database.

For example, the provider for Access will already be installed if Access is installed on your computer.

If multiple providers are in the drop-down list, but all of them are not installed, PowerPivot automatically selects one that is installed.

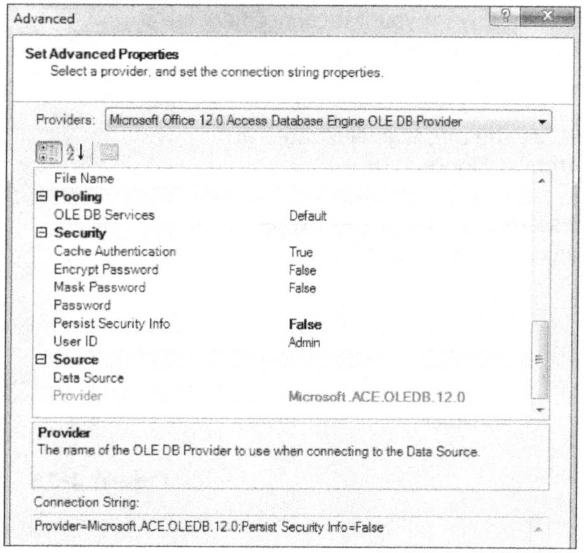

Figure 4-14 Advanced properties for a Microsoft Access database

What may not be obvious is that the majority of the advanced property options can be changed.

When you click in the column on the right of some options, you can type in the setting that you want.

For other options, when you click in the column on the right, you will see a drop-down list of options that you can select from, as illustrated in Figure 4-15.

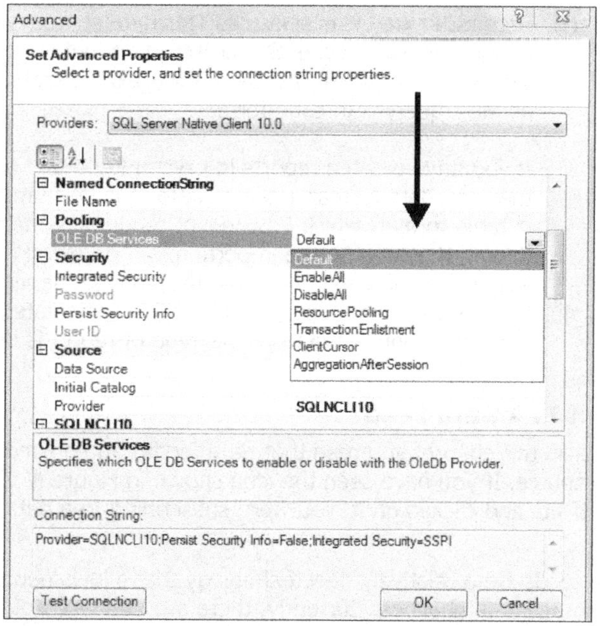

Figure 4-15 Property options illustrated

PowerPivot will warn you if it cannot find the drivers needed for the database type that you want to use.

You will see the message illustrated at the bottom of Figure 4-16.

The message will let you know what driver needs to be installed.

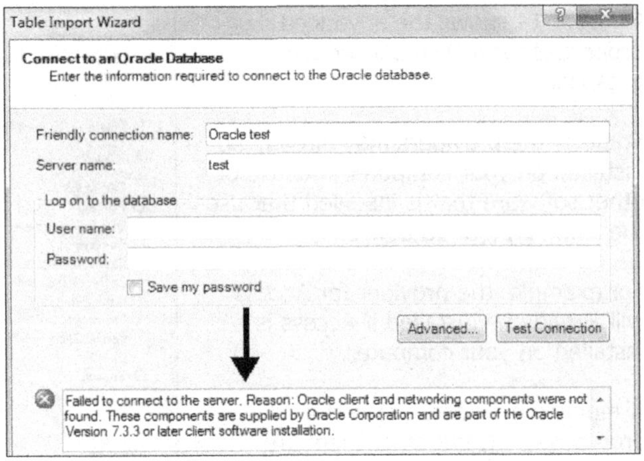

Figure 4-16 Provider not installed message illustrated

Other Data Sources

In addition to the data sources already discussed in this chapter there are two more data source options, as explained below.

① **MICROSOFT ANALYSIS SERVICES** This data source option is used to connect to a Microsoft Analysis Services cube. Select this option when the data that you want to import will be retrieved from a **MULTI DIMENSIONAL EXPRESSIONS (MDX)** query. The data retrieved from an MDX query is in cube format.

If you have created reports in Crystal Reports™ using an OLAP cube, you are familiar with the cube data format. Usually, data in cube format is summary type data. Cube data is not in table format, which PowerPivot requires. Fortunately, you do not have to manipulate the data in the cube before importing it into PowerPivot. During the import process, PowerPivot will import the cube data from the Analysis Services query into table format.

② **REPORT** This data source option is used to create a connection to a Microsoft Reporting Services report. Data from this type of report is imported into PowerPivot from a data feed.

What Is A Data Feed?

Earlier in this chapter you read that data feeds can be used as a data source. If you have seen the icon shown in Figure 4-17 on a web site and clicked on it, you were subscribing to a data feed.

Figure 4-17 Data Feed icon

Data feeds are a relatively new technology that allows people to receive updates to the data when the source data changes. Currently, there are two types of data feeds that PowerPivot supports as explained below.

① **REPORTING SERVICES REPORTS** like Microsoft Reporting Services, which was discussed earlier in this chapter. This option is near the bottom of the Connect to Data Source screen on the Table Import Wizard.

② **GENERIC DATA FEEDS** This is the type of data feed that you may have already subscribed to or are already familiar with. Select the From Data Feeds option on the PowerPivot Home tab to use this option.

Using .Atomsvc Documents

In addition to being able to select a Microsoft Reporting Services file or typing in the data feed URL, you can use an .atomsvc document. This is the Microsoft Data Feed Provider for PowerPivot. This is an XML file that defines one or more data feeds. This type of document contains pointers to at least one data feed or service that provides data feeds. You can open the .atomsvc file or use a URL address to access the .atomsvc document.

There are two **DATA FEED FORMATS**: Atom and RSS. PowerPivot for Excel only supports Atom data feeds.

There are two **DATA FEED ACCESS TYPES**: Those that require a logon account to access the data feed or a public data feed, which does not require a logon account.

Step 2: Select How To Import The Data

This step is only for a database connection, which includes data feeds. This step is not used for text or spreadsheet files. As the name of the screen suggests, the options on this screen are used to select how the data will be imported.

Figure 4-18 shows the table and query import options for a database. They are explained below.

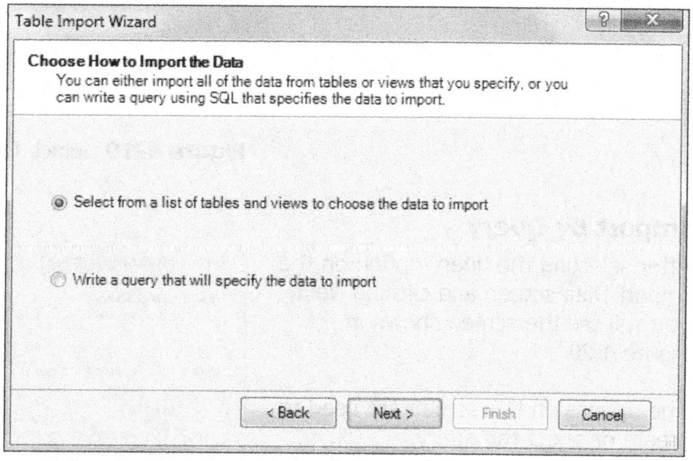

Figure 4-18 Database import options

① **Select The Tables And Views** This process is explained below in the Import Tables section.
② **Use A Query To Select The Data** This process is explained below in the Import By Query section.

Step 3: Select And Filter The Data That Will Be Imported

This step requires you to select the data that will be imported. If there are records or columns of data that you do not need to import from the data source, you should remove them before the data is imported into PowerPivot. If you are not going to import all of the fields in the external data source, make sure that the fields that you are not going to import are not key fields, if you know that a relationship needs to be created for the table using the field.

Import Tables

After selecting the Tables and Views option on the Import Data screen and clicking Next, you will see the screen shown in Figure 4-19.

The options on this screen are used to select the tables or views to import and create filters if needed.

To select a table or view, click in the box to the far left of the table, as illustrated.

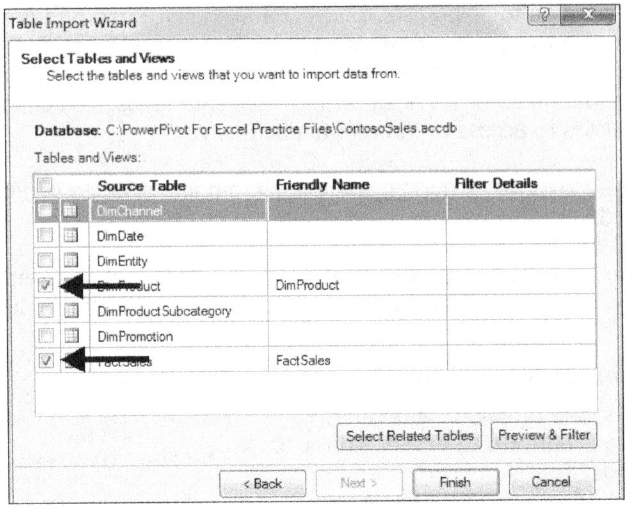

Figure 4-19 Select Tables and Views screen

Import By Query

After selecting the query option on the Import Data screen and clicking Next, you will see the screen shown in Figure 4-20.

The options on this screen are used to create or select the query.

If you type or copy and paste the SQL code on this screen, click the **VALIDATE** button. At the bottom of the screen you will see a message indicating that the SQL statement is valid or invalid.

Depending on the type of database that you are using, you will see a different query editor when you click the **DESIGN** button.

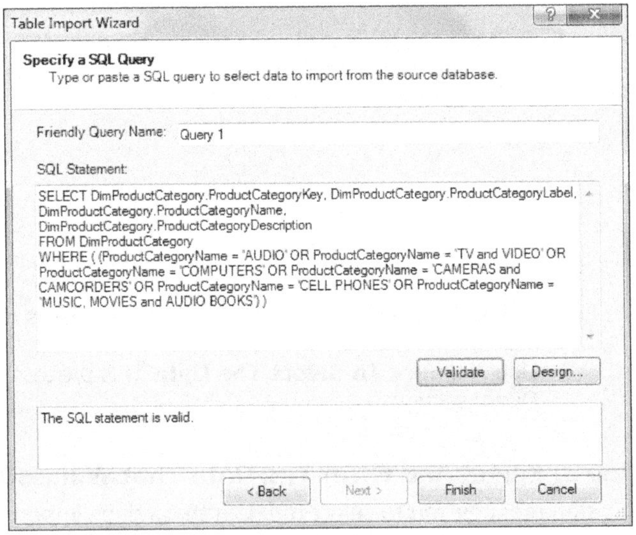

Figure 4-20 Specify a SQL Query screen

Figure 4-21 shows the query editor for a non SQL Server database. This editor has more functionality for creating a query then the SQL query screen shown above in Figure 4-20 has.

The **EDIT AS TEXT** button (in Figure 4-21) is used to switch between the text-based query designer (Figure 4-21) and the graphical query designer (Figure 4-22). If the data source supports graphical query designers, this button will be enabled.

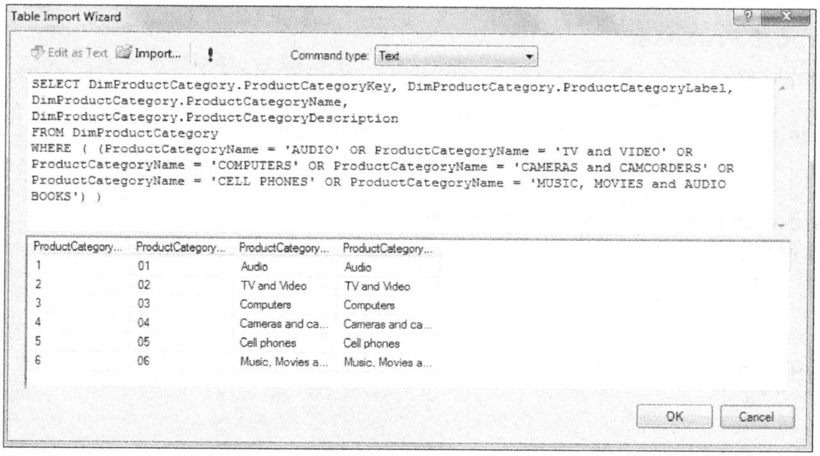

Figure 4-21 Non SQL Server query editor (text based)

Figure 4-22 shows the query editor for an SQL Server database. This query editor window will be familiar if you have used the Microsoft SQL Server 2008 R2 Report Builder 3 application. Notice that you can create relationships on the SQL Server query editor.

The **AUTO DETECT** button if clicked, will specify whether relationships are automatically detected from foreign keys in the database tables that are selected.

The **EDIT AS TEXT** button (in Figure 4-22) displays the query editor shown above in Figure 4-21.

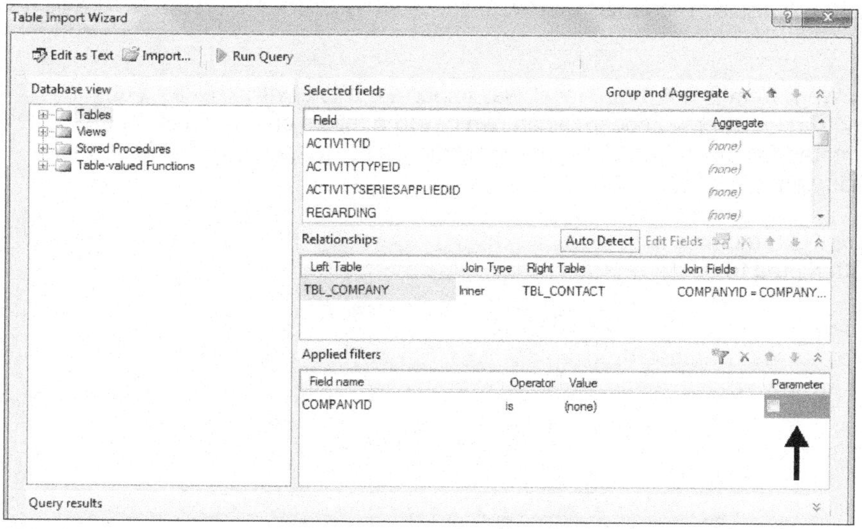

Figure 4-22 SQL Server query editor (graphical based)

> **Applied Filters Parameter Option**
> The Parameter check box in the Applied Filters section of the SQL Server query editor illustrated above in Figure 4-22 does not work.

Step 4: Finish The Import Process

The Finish button is not enabled on the Import Data screen.
(See Figure 4-18, shown earlier)

The Finish button is only enabled on the Select Tables and Views screen (See Figure 4-19 shown earlier) or the Specify A SQL Query screen (See Figure 4-20 shown earlier).

Clicking the Finish button on either of the screens just mentioned starts the data import process shown in Figure 4-23.

I stopped the import shown in the figure because I know that the Fact Sales table has a few million records.

This screen displays the status of each table that is being imported. If there are any problems during the import, you will see a **DETAILS** link in the Message column.

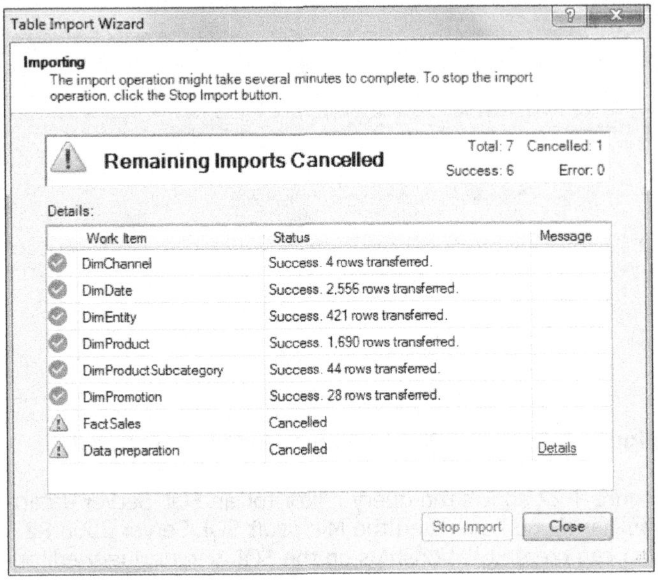

Figure 4-23 Importing screen

Clicking the **CLOSE** button will display the tables that were successfully imported, on tabs in the PowerPivot workspace.

The **DATA PREPARATION** Work Item is not a table that was imported. It is always the last entry in the list on the Importing screen. It only appears when two or more tables are imported that a relationship could be created for. It contains a list of the relationships that were created and their status for the tables that were imported.

As you can see in Figure 4-24, the first relationship that was attempted to be created failed.

The second relationship that was attempted, was successful.

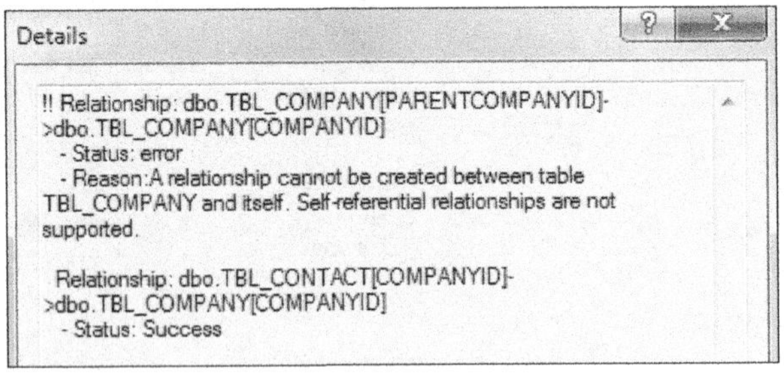

Figure 4-24 Details dialog box

IMPORTING DATA FROM A DATABASE INTO POWERPIVOT

CHAPTER 5

In this chapter you will learn how to import data from databases. You will also learn about the following:

- ☑ PowerPivot supported data types
- ☑ Views
- ☑ Stored procedures
- ☑ Using a query to import and filter data
- ☑ Filtering data during the import process

Overview

Chapter 3 briefly covered the options for importing data into PowerPivot tables. Chapter 4 covered the Table Import Wizard in detail. This chapter and the next one will show you how to import data from a variety of data sources into PowerPivot.

As the title of this chapter indicates, you will learn how to import data into PowerPivot tables from a database. The Table Import Wizard is used to accomplish this task. The next chapter covers importing data from other data sources.

The tables that are imported into PowerPivot should contain data that you will use to create a pivot table. If you have used VLOOKUP to get data from one worksheet into another, these worksheets are the related data that you should bring into PowerPivot to create a pivot table or pivot chart. Another way to put it is that you can join two or more worksheets of data without using VLOOKUP in PowerPivot.

PowerPivot Supported Data Types

PowerPivot supports the data types listed in the first column in Table 5-1. The first column in the table is how PowerPivot classifies data. The second column in the table is how DAX classifies data.

PowerPivot does not support all of the data types that some databases use. This means that some columns of data may not be displayed on the Preview Selected Table screen in the Table Import Wizard, which means that they may not be imported into PowerPivot.

While some databases support more than one variation of a data type listed in the first column, PowerPivot does not. If the original data type for the field is similar to one in the table, it will be mapped to a data type in the first column of Table 5-1.

PowerPivot Data Type	DAX Data Type	Description
Text	String	Usually contains regular text. Dates and numbers are displayed as text in this data type.
Decimal Number	64-bit real number	Positive and negative numbers with or without a decimal point. Zero is also a decimal number.
Whole Number	64-bit integer	Positive and negative numbers without a decimal point.
Date	Date/Time	DAX only supports dates and times after March 1, 1900.
Currency	Currency	Currency values are imported into the format of the currency format that the computer is set to use.
True/False	Boolean	A true or false value.
(Not available)	Blank	In DAX, this data type replaces SQL null values.

Table 5-1 PowerPivot supported data types explained

Importing Comment And Note Fields
At some point you will come across a table or file that has a comment or note field. As these fields will not be used to create a pivot table, you should not import the data because this type of field will take up unnecessary space in the PowerPivot workbook. This field type also prohibits the **VERTIPAQ** compression engine from doing the job that it was intended to do.

> **Excel Data Types**
> Keep in mind that Excel does not have data types. Instead, numeric data is formatted to match the data types in the first column of Table 5-1 above.

Selecting The Import Table Order

Because PowerPivot allows data from multiple data sources to be imported into the same PowerPivot workbook, the order that data is imported can be important if you need to create relationships between the tables of data that you import. The data source that will be used as the main table in PowerPivot should be imported first. Usually, this table will have the largest number of records. After that, the order that the remaining tables are imported in, is not as important unless one of the other tables will be used to create a relationship with a table other then the main table.

For example, if the following tables were going to be imported into the same PowerPivot workbook from multiple data sources, the order that they are listed in is the order that they should be imported in.

① Order Header
② Order Detail
③ Sales Reps
④ Product Details

Tables 2, 3 and 4 above are like lookup tables for the Order Header table because the Order Header table has fields (columns) that can be used to look up information in some of the other tables. For example, the Order Header table has a field for the sales rep for the order. This field is often known as an ID field. The Sales Reps table also has an ID field for each sales rep. This is how the sales reps name can be looked up in the Sales Reps table. The reasons that the order that tables of data are imported in is important, are explained below.

① The **AUTO DETECT** relationship functionality in PowerPivot expects the primary table to be the first table imported.
② The **POWERPIVOT FIELD LIST** dialog box displays the tables in the order that they were imported into PowerPivot.

Importing Data From A Database

Importing data from a database will probably be one of the most popular ways to add data to a PowerPivot table. The most popular way to import data from a database is to import directly from tables or views in the database. In addition to tables, databases can use queries and some databases have views or stored procedures, which are other ways to import data from a database into PowerPivot. Queries, views and stored procedures retrieve a subset of the data that is in the tables in the database, instead of retrieving all of the records in the selected tables.

For example, there could be a query that only retrieves orders from specific states. Unlike tables, queries, views and stored procedures do not store data. They contain code that specifies which records in the table should be retrieved or in the case of PowerPivot, records that should be imported. If you find that you are using the same criteria over and over to retrieve records or you are always applying the same filters to the same data, each time you import the data into PowerPivot, you can create a query that has all of the options that you need. Using a query, view or stored procedure will save you time when importing data from a database because you do not have to manually select the criteria on the Table Import Wizard dialog box. Views and stored procedures are discussed in more detail in the next two sections.

Views

Views or Business Views as they are also called, are a set of components, (Data Connections, Dynamic Data Connections, Data Foundations and Business Elements) that report designers and end users can use to access the data that is needed to create the report. Business Views are usually created by a Database Administrator, report designer or someone that has administrator rights to the database. Views allow one to gather data from a variety of tables and databases and combine the data into a "view". This makes it easier for end users to access the data.

A view is a **RECORDSET** (the result) of a query. Views usually display a subset of the data in a data source. Views are stored in the database and are like tables, but they do not have the physical characteristics of a table. For example, records cannot be added to or deleted from a view. Fields cannot be added to a view unless the view is modified to include more fields or the length of a field cannot be changed in a view like it can in a table.

Views are useful if you use the sorting, grouping and data selection (filter) options in PowerPivot. Views are created when the same recordset, calculation or query needs to be used in several reports or in the case of PowerPivot, several pivot tables. If you know that you will create several reports in Excel that use the same sorting, grouping or data selection options, you could create and save a view in the database, if you have the appropriate administrator rights to do so. Doing this means that you would not have to select the same options over and over again each time that you import data from the same table into PowerPivot. Instead of selecting all of the tables, fields and options in PowerPivot, select the view in the database that already has all of this information when importing data into a PowerPivot table.

Views are one way to optimize reports that use tables that have a lot of data. For example, a customer table may store all customers world wide. If there is a need to create several pivot tables that are specific to a certain country for marketing or sales analysis purposes, create a view (a query) that retrieves all of the customer records for the country. When the pivot tables are created for that country, select the "country view" if you will, as the data source, instead of the customer table. The import will run faster because it does not have to read the entire customer table to find the records for the specific country.

Stored Procedures

Stored procedures, like Views, do not contain data. They contain queries that are more complex then views, but less complex then commands.

The majority of the time, stored procedures are created by a DBA or programmer. Figure 5-1 shows the views and stored procedures in a database.

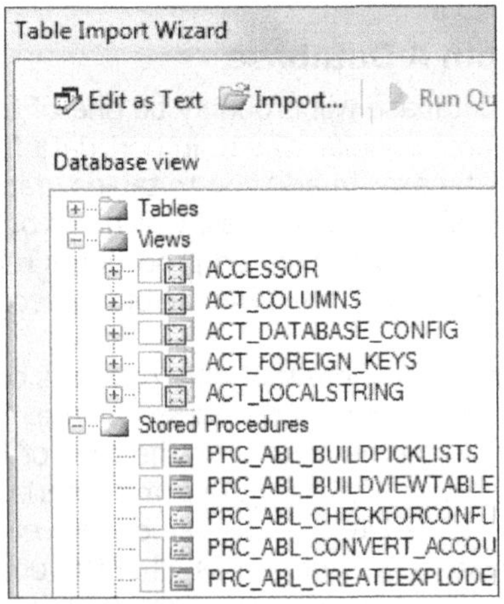

Figure 5-1 Views and stored procedures in a database

Testing A Data Source Connection
If the data source that you are using is on a server, including a web server, you can test to see whether or not your computer has successfully connected to the data source by clicking the **TEST CONNECTION** button on the Table Import Wizard dialog box. (See Figure 5-3 below) If the connection is successful, you will see the message shown in Figure 5-2.

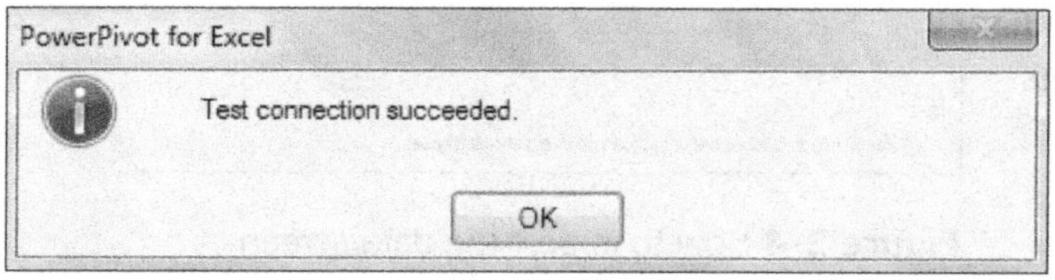

Figure 5-2 Successful connection message

Importing Exercises
Unless stated otherwise, before starting an importing exercise, open a new Excel workbook. On the PowerPivot tab in Excel, click the PowerPivot Window button to open the PowerPivot for Excel window.

Exercise 5.1: Importing Data From A Microsoft Access Database

The steps below show you how to import data from an Access database into PowerPivot tables.

1. Home tab ⇒ Get External Data group ⇒ From Database ⇒ From Access.
2. In the Friendly connection name field type `Contoso Product Table.`
3. Click the Browse button. In your folder, click on the ContosoSales.accdb database, then click the Open button.
4. You should have the options shown in Figure 5-3.

   If the database required a logon and password, you would enter the information on this dialog box.

   Click Next.

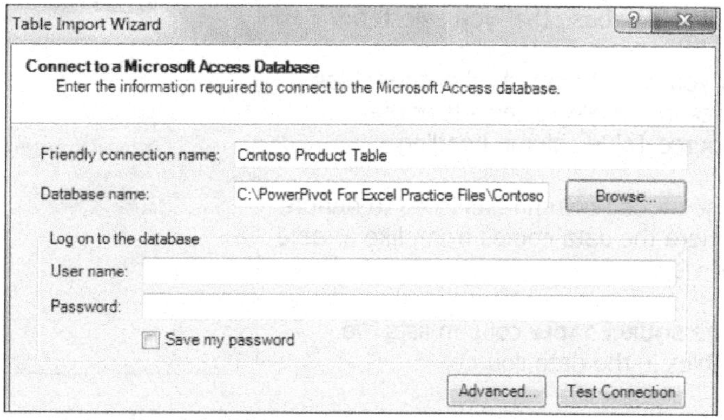

Figure 5-3 Connect to a Microsoft Access database screen

The options shown in Figure 5-4 are used to select how the data should be imported.

If you want all of the records or want to select specific tables or records in a table or view, select the first option. This option does allow you to create a filter.

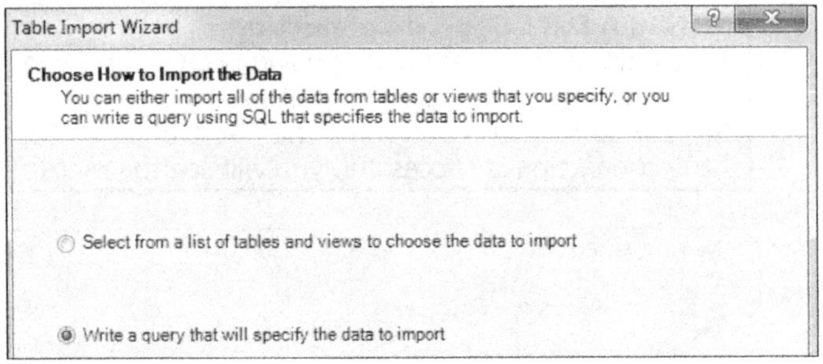

Figure 5-4 How to import the data screen

Select the second option if you only want to import records that meet specific criteria. This option requires you to write an SQL query or to select an existing SQL query.

Creating Queries For Access Databases
I have mentioned creating SQL queries on your own a few times and that you may have the need to get a DBA to create the queries for you. If you have used Access to create a database, you know that it allows you to create queries. You can create the SQL query in Access, then select the query option shown above in Figure 5-4 to select the query that you create.

5. Select the first option shown above in Figure 5-4, then click Next.

The options shown in Figure 5-5 are used to select the tables and views that have the data that you want to import into PowerPivot.

Above the grid you will see the name of the database that you selected.

If you want to select all of the tables, click in the box to the left of the Source Table column heading.

The second column has icons to denote where the data comes from, like a table or view.

The **SOURCE TABLE** column lists the tables in the data source.

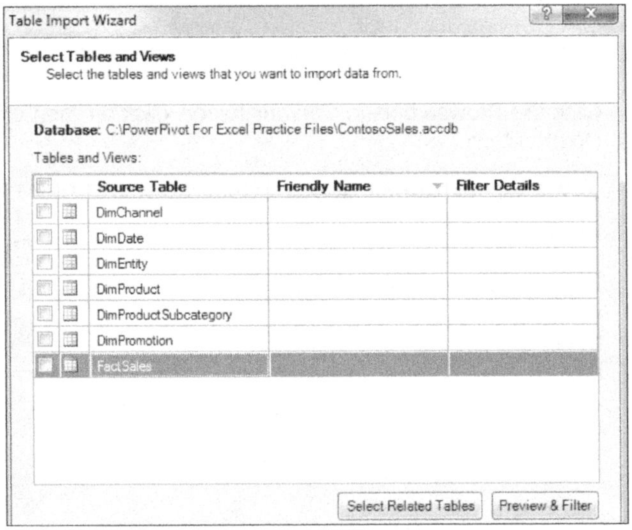

Figure 5-5 Select Tables and Views screen

The **FRIENDLY NAME** column displays the name of the table by default. If you want to use a different name for the table, type it in the cell. If you click on this column heading, you can change the sort order of the Tables and Views to be displayed in ascending or descending order by the friendly name instead of sorting on the Source Table name.

The **FILTER DETAILS** column displays a link that you can click on to see the filter criteria (that is created on the Preview Selected Table screen on the Table Import Wizard, shown later in Figure 5-8) for the table.

The **SELECT RELATED TABLES** button will retrieve and display the related tables for the source tables that are checked.

The **PREVIEW & FILTER** button is used to create filters and view data from the selected table.

6. Select the DimProduct source table. You will see that the Friendly Name field was automatically filled in with the default friendly name of the table.

7. Double-click in the Friendly Name column across from the DimProduct table, then type `Products` in the cell.

Preview The Related Tables

Now that you have selected a table, you can check to see if the table has any related tables. Related tables are often referred to as child tables in a database. In Excel, these related tables would be used as lookup tables.

1. Click the Select Related Tables button.

   Notice in Figure 5-6 that the DimProduct Subcategory and Fact Sales source tables are now checked.

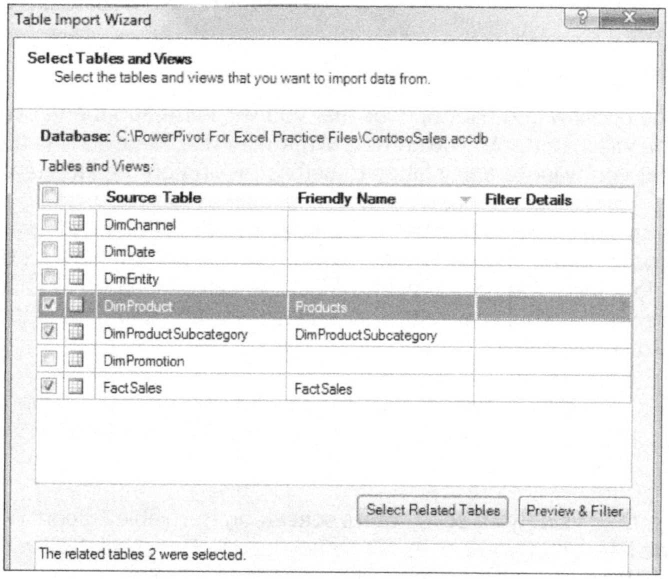

Figure 5-6 Related tables selected

At the bottom of the dialog box you will see a message indicating how many related tables PowerPivot found.

If you clicked the Select Related Tables button again, three more tables would be selected, as shown in Figure 5-7.

That is because the tables shown above in Figure 5-6 are now used as the tables to find the related tables for.

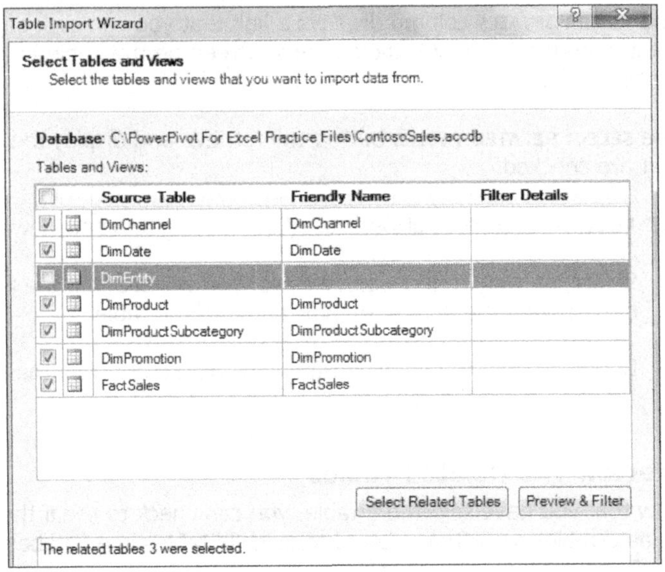

Figure 5-7 Additional related tables found

Using The Preview And Filter Options

The preview and filter options that you will learn about and use, can be applied to each table that you will import into PowerPivot. What may not be obvious is that you have to click on the table name that you want to apply filters to before clicking on the **PREVIEW & FILTER** button.

In this part of the exercise you will remove the Manufacturer and Brand Name columns from the Products table. Products that have a Unit Price greater than $100 will not be imported. The steps below show you how to filter the data to meet these specifications. The preview and filter options are very useful because they are used to review and reduce the amount of data that will be imported into PowerPivot.

1. With the Products table selected, click the Preview & Filter button. The options shown in Figure 5-8 display the columns of data from the table or view that was selected on the previous screen.

On the **PREVIEW SELECTED TABLE SCREEN** on the Table Import Wizard, you will see the table name that the filters that you create will be applied to. The check box in the column header is used to select whether or not the column will be imported. Clear the check mark if you do not want the column of data to be imported.

The filter option (the down arrow button on the column headings) on the Preview Selected Table screen works the same as it does in an Excel spreadsheet. Records that do not meet the filter requirements will not be imported. If you apply filters then change your mind, click the **CLEAR ROW FILTERS** button.

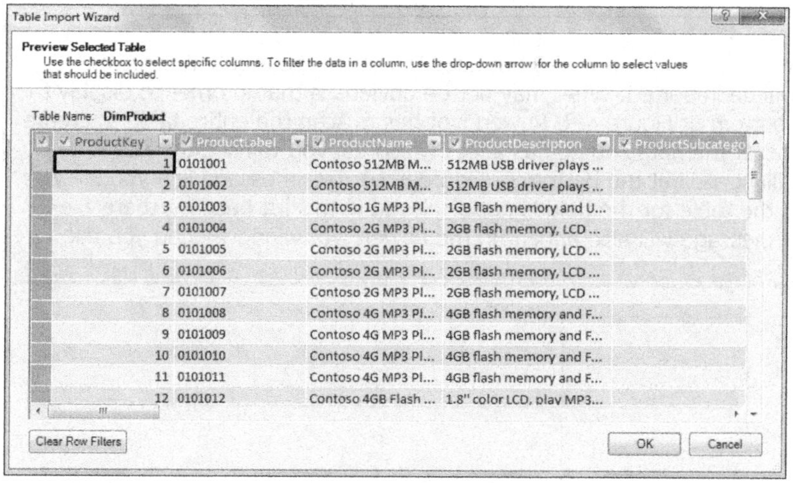

Figure 5-8 Preview Selected Table screen

2. Scroll to the right, then clear the check mark for the Manufacturer and Brand Name columns.

3. Scroll to the right until you see the Unit Price column.

   Click the down arrow button for the Unit Price column, which will display the options shown in Figure 5-9.

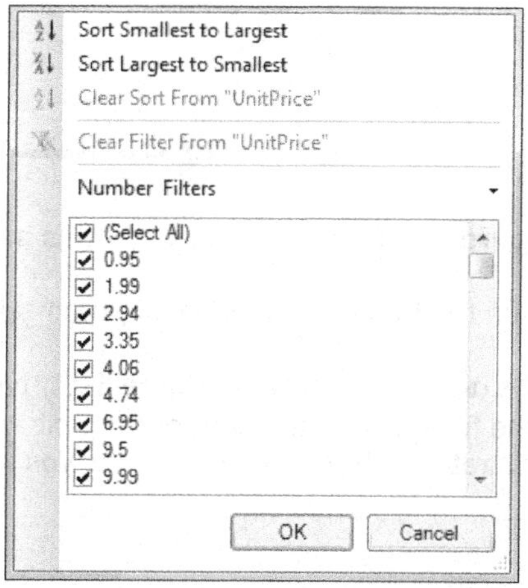

Figure 5-9 Filter options

> **Saving Filter Options**
> The filter options that you select are automatically saved with the PowerPivot database. This means that when you refresh the data in the table, the filters will be saved during the refresh process.

> **Using The Filter Options**
> The filter options shown above in Figure 5-9 are used to reduce the number of records (rows of data) that will be imported. What may not be obvious is that in order to display the list of options at the bottom of Figure 5-9, PowerPivot has to scan the entire table to create the list of filter options. If the data source has a lot of records, you will see the **NOT ALL ITEMS SHOWING** link, illustrated at the bottom of Figure 5-10. This message lets you know that all of the data in the table for the field is not displayed in this list because there are too many items. This message will also appear in the PowerPivot window when you use the filter option.

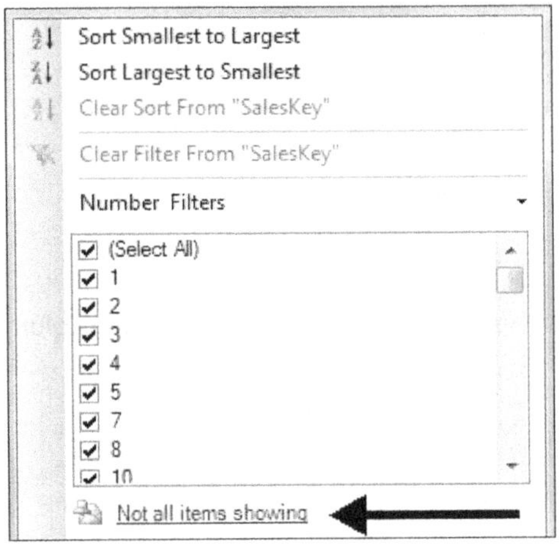

Figure 5-10 Filter with a lot of items message

4. Click on the Number Filters option, then select the **LESS THAN OR EQUAL TO** option.

5. On the dialog box shown in Figure 5-11, type `100.00` in the top field, then click OK. You will see the filter icon to the right of the Unit Price column heading, instead of the down arrow, as illustrated in Figure 5-12. This lets you know that a filter has been applied to the column.

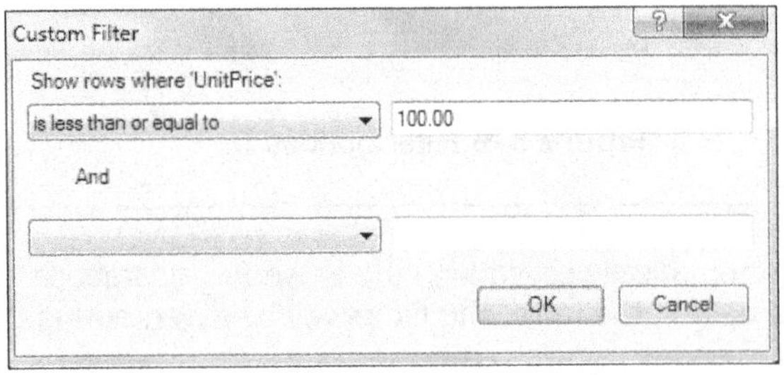

Figure 5-11 Custom Filter dialog box

Figure 5-12 Filter icon next to the column heading illustrated

6. Click OK to close the dialog box. On the Select Tables and Views screen, you should see the **APPLIED FILTERS** link in the Filter Details column for the Products table, as shown in Figure 5-13. If you click on this link, you will see the dialog box shown in Figure 5-14.

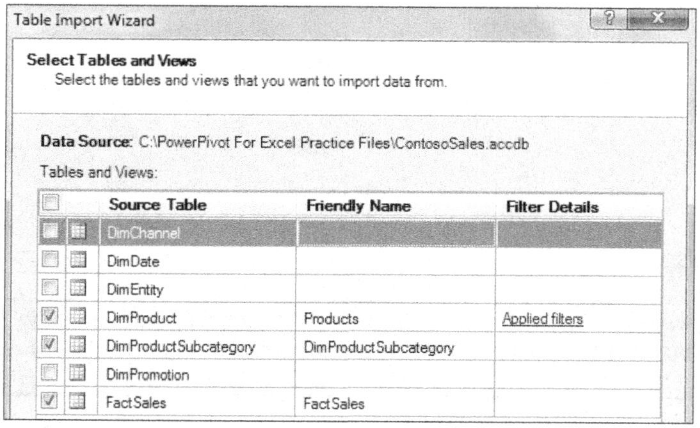

Figure 5-13 Filter applied to a table

This dialog box displays the criteria for the filter that you just created for the table.

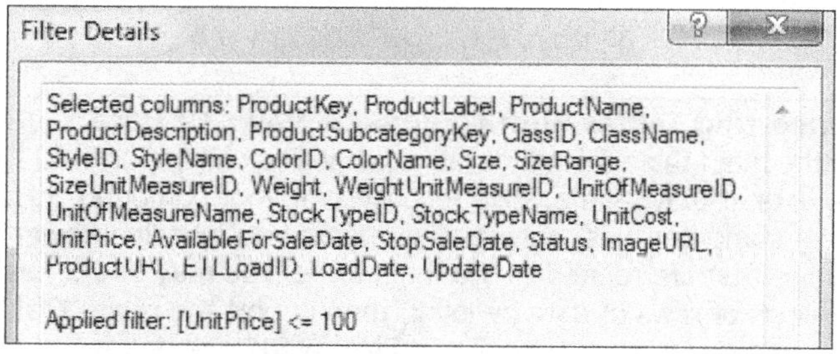

Figure 5-14 Filter Details dialog box

Finish The Import

1. Click the Finish button.
   The records will be imported.

   When the import is finished, you will see the results shown in Figure 5-15.

   The **STATUS** column displays how many rows of data (records) were imported from each table.

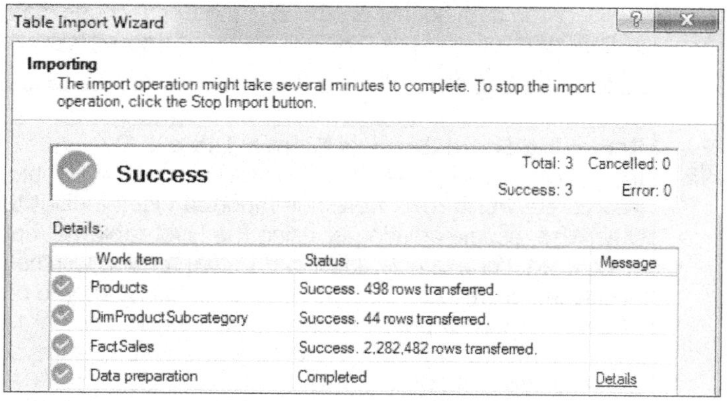

Figure 5-15 Importing screen

2. Click on the **DETAILS** link in the Message column on the Importing screen. The information shown in Figure 5-16 displays the relationships that were automatically created and whether or not they were successful.

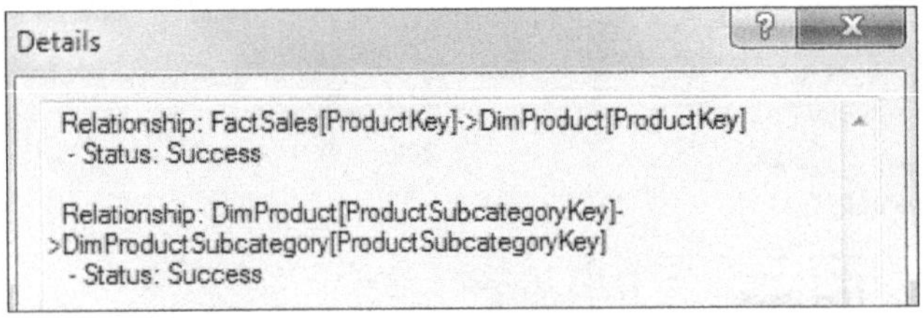

Figure 5-16 Data preparations details

During the import process, PowerPivot will try to recreate the relationships that are already set up between the tables in the database. The dialog box shown above in Figure 5-16 will also display relationships that PowerPivot could not recreate.

3. Click OK, then click the Close button. You should see three tabs of data in the PowerPivot window.

4. Save the workbook as `E5.1 Import from an Access database`.

Importing Tables With Millions Of Rows Of Data
If the main table from a database that you will import into PowerPivot has millions of rows of data, it may take a while, especially if your computer does not have a lot of RAM or if your computer was running slow before you installed PowerPivot. If you also need to import tables that are related to the main table, you may find it easier to import the table with millions of rows of data by itself, then import the related tables. To import tables from an existing connection in the PowerPivot workbook, follow the steps below. You do not have to create a new connection.

1. Open the workbook that you want to import more data into.
2. PowerPivot Window ⇒ Design tab ⇒ Connections group ⇒ Existing Connections button.
3. Select the data source on the Existing Connections dialog box.
4. Click the Open button. You will see the Choose How To Import The Data screen on the Table Import Wizard dialog box.

Removing Some Records From a Table
If you are not going to import all records (rows) in a table, a good practice would be to incorporate which rows were not imported when a pivot table is created based on the table. Otherwise, people creating or using the pivot table will not know that all of the data is not being used. For example, later in this chapter you will learn how to filter the data in a table to only import records that meet the criteria. When you or someone else uses the workbook to view or create a pivot table, will you really remember that you created this import criteria a week or month from now? Probably not. And for sure, someone else that uses the workbook will not know.

Overall, I personally prefer to use filters on the pivot table then to filter data during the import process in this scenario. I do think that if the requirements for the pivot table are date driven, like only needing to see records from the year 2002 to the present, records prior to 2002 should be filtered out during the import process.

Exercise 5.2: Import Data From A Database Using A Query

In the previous exercise you imported data from a database using tables. You created a filter that reduced the number of rows that would be imported from a table. You also removed columns of data which reduced the amount of data that was imported.

In this exercise you will use a query to select the tables and records in an Access database that will be imported into PowerPivot. If you cannot write SQL code, hopefully you have access to someone that can, if you have the need to use queries. The benefit that queries provide is that they can be used over and over and you do not have to import all of the records from the data source and then delete rows or columns from the PowerPivot table that you do not need.

1. Home tab ⇒ Get External Data group ⇒ From Database ⇒ From Access.
2. In the Friendly connection name field type `Product Database`.
3. Click the Browse button.

   In your folder, click on the ProductCategories.accdb database, then click the Open button.

   You should have the options shown in Figure 5-17.

   Click Next.

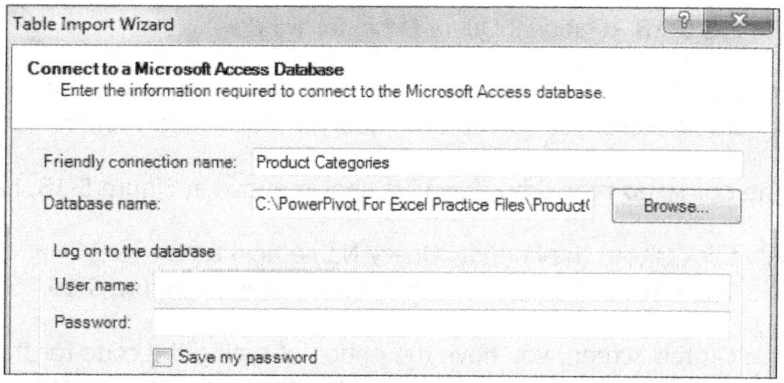

Figure 5-17 Database connection options

4. Select the second option, which will allow you to select a query or create a query, then click Next.
5. Click the **DESIGN** button, then click the Import button.
6. In your folder, click on the SQL Query file, then click the Open button. You should see the contents of the query file that you selected, at the top of the window. This is the SQL query code.

If you wanted to view the data that the query will retrieve to import into PowerPivot, click the **RUN** button (the red exclamation mark button). At the bottom of the window you will see some of the records that will be imported into a PowerPivot table, as shown in Figure 5-18.

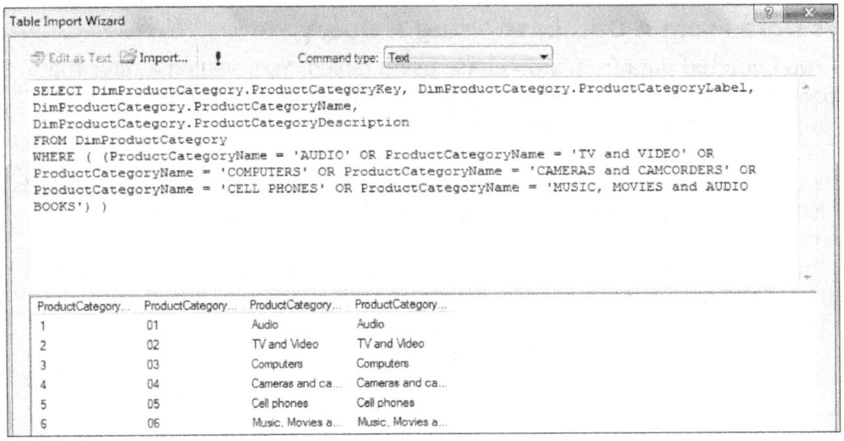

Figure 5-18 Relational Query Designer window

If the query does not run, does not retrieve any records or retrieves records that you do not think should be there, you can edit the query in this window and re-run it.

The **COMMAND TYPE** drop-down list shown above in Figure 5-18, has a stored procedures option.

7. Click OK. In the Friendly Query Name field type `Find Products Query`.
   The screen should have the options shown in Figure 5-19.

   On this screen, you have the option of typing the code for the query or selecting the file that has the code. If you typed or edited the query on this screen, click the **VALIDATE** button to make sure that the query does not have any syntax errors.

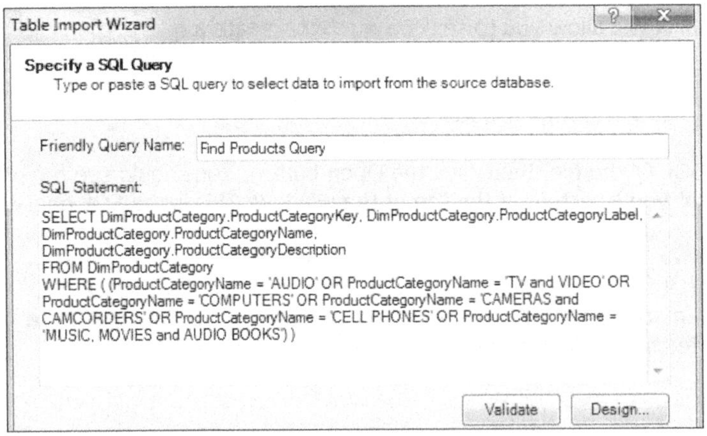

Figure 5-19 Specify a SQL Query screen

> The name that you enter in the Friendly Query Name field will be used as the table name on the tab in the PowerPivot window.

8. Click the Finish button. The records will be imported. When the import is finished, click the Close button so that the records will be added to a table in PowerPivot.

9. Notice that the name on the tab is the query name that you entered. Save the workbook as `E5.2 Use a query to import data.`

Exercise 5.3: Filter Records Before They Are Imported Into PowerPivot

In the previous exercise the query that was used to import records from the database contained the filter criteria. In Exercise 5.1 you created a filter for one of the tables that was imported. In this exercise you will import data from a table and create filters during the import process to reduce the number of records that are imported into a PowerPivot table.

1. Home tab ⇒ Get External Data group ⇒ From Database ⇒ From Access.

2. In the Friendly connection name field type `Filter Records.`

3. Click the Browse button. In your folder, click on the Import DB.accdb database, then click the Open button. Click Next.

4. Select the first option on the Import Data screen, then click Next.

5. Check the Customers and Orders tables.

Create The Customers Table Filter

In this part of the exercise you will create a filter to only import records of customers in CA, NV and WI.

1. Select the Customers table, then click the Preview & Filter button.

2. Scroll to the right and open the filter list for the State/Province column.

3. Change the options so that only CA, NV and WI are selected, as shown in Figure 5-20.

   Click OK twice to close both dialog boxes.

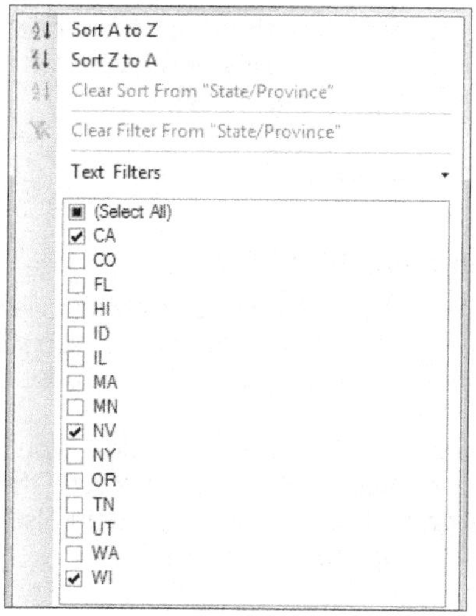

Figure 5-20 State/Province filter options

Create The Orders Table Filter

In this part of the exercise the goal was to create a filter to only import orders for one month. The problem is that there is a bug that does not allow filtering on a date field on the Preview Selected table screen on the Table Import Wizard dialog box. If you followed the steps below, you will see the error message shown in Figure 5-21. For now, read the information in this section, then go to the next section, "Finish The Import" and complete the exercise.

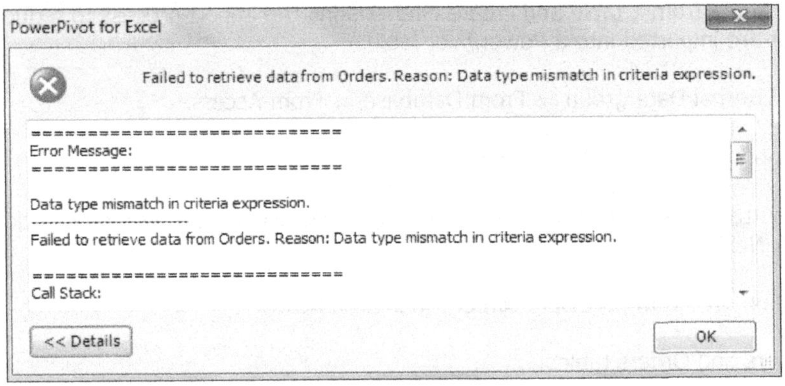

Figure 5-21 Data type mismatch error message

1. Select the Orders table, then click the Preview & Filter button.

2. Open the filter list for the Order Date field. Only select the four dates in June 2006, then click OK twice.

Finish The Import

1. Click the Finish button, then click the Close button. If you preview the data in the Customers table, you will see that all seven records in the table are in one of the three states that you created the filter for during the import.

2. Save the workbook as `E5.3 Import Filtered Records`.

Previewing Data In A View

At the beginning of this chapter, I discussed views as being a source of data in a database that you can import. At the bottom of Figure 5-22, you will see the Top Customers source table. Notice that the icon is different. When you hold the mouse pointer over the icon, it displays the word View.

When you preview the records in the view, you will see as shown in Figure 5-23, that the data looks like data from a single table. That is because the query that retrieves the data for the view can retrieve data from different tables. You can also create filters for a view to limit the number of records that are imported into PowerPivot.

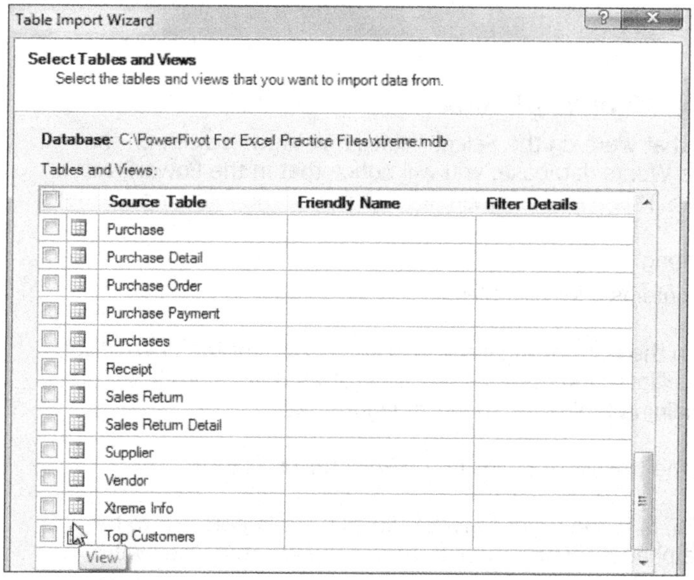

Figure 5-22 View icon on the Select Tables and Views screen

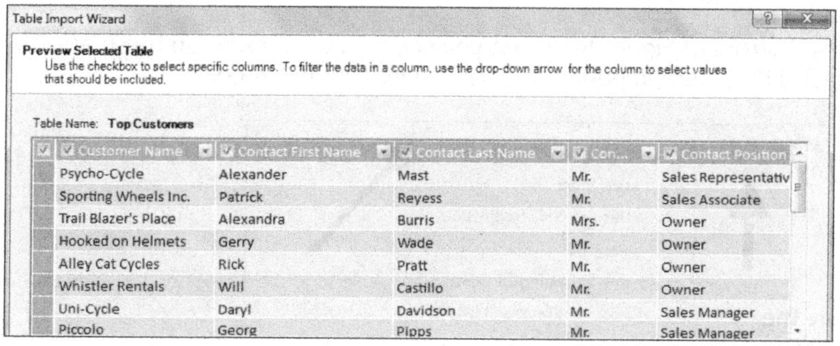

Figure 5-23 Records from a view

Exercise 5.4: Northwind Database Import

In this exercise you will import data from a database. The difference is that you will import the tables without the level of step-by-step instructions that the previous exercises provided.

1. Import the following tables and views from the Northwind database: Customers, Employees, Order Details, Orders, Products and Suppliers tables, then select the Order Subtotals view.

2. Save the workbook as `E5.4 Northwind database`.

Exercise 5.5: Adventure Works Database Import

In this exercise you will import all of the tables in the database.

1. Import all of the tables in the Adventure Works database into a PowerPivot workbook.

2. Save the workbook as `E5.5 Adventure Works database.`

View All Of The Data In A PowerPivot Workbook

If you looked at the number of tables that were on the Select Tables and Views screen on the Table Import Wizard for the Adventure Works database, you will notice that in the PowerPivot window you do not see all of the tables. This happens when at least one of the following is true:

① The table or tab names are long.
② The PowerPivot workbook contains a lot of tables.

When either of these options is true, to the right of the last tab at the bottom of the PowerPivot window, you will see a button with an ellipsis and down arrow, as illustrated in Figure 5-24. Click on this button to display the remaining tables, as shown in Figure 5-25.

Keep the following in mind when viewing the list of tables in the PowerPivot window.

① The list shown in Figure 5-25, is in the order that the tables were imported into the workbook. They are not in alphabetical order unless that is the way that they were imported into PowerPivot.
② The only tables on the list shown in Figure 5-25 are the ones that are not visible across the bottom of the PowerPivot window. The smaller the PowerPivot window is, the more tables will be displayed in the list.
③ Notice at the top and bottom of Figure 5-25 that you see arrows. Clicking on these arrows will display more tables that were imported into the PowerPivot workbook.

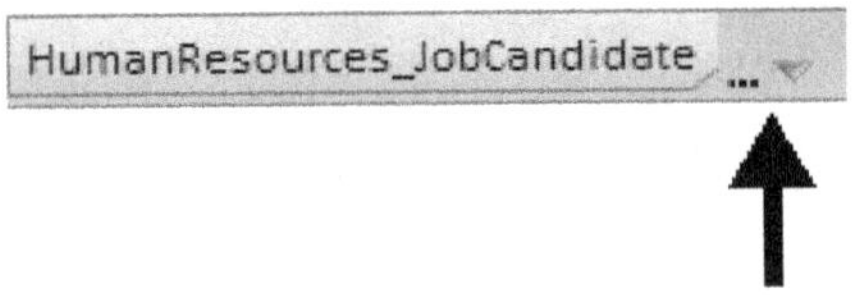

Figure 5-24 Button to display the tables that are not currently shown across the bottom of the PowerPivot window

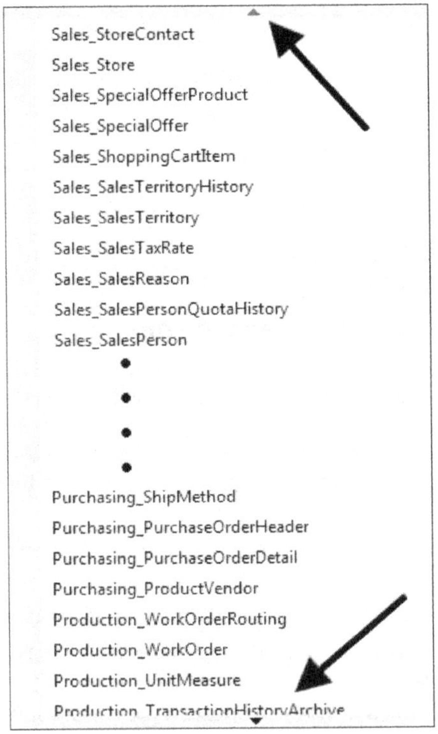

Figure 5-25 Additional tables in the workbook

IMPORTING OTHER TYPES OF DATA INTO POWERPIVOT

In this chapter you will learn how to import data from the following types of data sources:

- ☑ A text file
- ☑ Excel workbook
- ☑ A .csv file
- ☑ A data feed

You will also learn how to import data from multiple sources into one PowerPivot workbook.

Overview

In the previous chapter you learned how to import data into PowerPivot from databases. It is quite possible that most, if not all of the data that you need to import is in a database. This chapter covers other data sources that can be used to import data.

One of the most important tasks to take care of is making sure that the data that will be imported is in a layout that PowerPivot supports. This is more of an issue for data that will be imported from Excel or a text file, then data in a database.

For example, the data shown in Figure 6-1 is not in a layout that PowerPivot supports. There are blank rows. If this spreadsheet was imported into PowerPivot, you would not get the expected results because PowerPivot does not rearrange data during the import process. Figure 6-2 shows the same data in a layout that PowerPivot supports. The first row has the headings and the data starts in row 2. There are no empty rows.

	A	B	C	D
1	StoreId	Store Manager	StoreName	City
2	State: WA			
3				
4	1	35	Contoso Seattle No.1 Store	Seattle
5	2	35	Contoso Seattle No.2 Store	Seattle
6	3	36	Contoso Kennewick Store	Kennewick
7	4	37	Contoso Bellevue Store	Bellevue
8				
9	State: TX			
10	66	88	Contoso Houston No.1 Store	Houston
11	67	88	Contoso Houston No.2 Store	Midland
12	68	88	Contoso Houston No.3 Store	Russellville

Figure 6-1 Incorrect layout in Excel

	A	B	C	D	E
1	StoreId	Store Manager	StoreName	City	State
2	1	35	Contoso Seattle No.1 Store	Seattle	WA
3	2	35	Contoso Seattle No.2 Store	Seattle	WA
4	3	36	Contoso Kennewick Store	Kennewick	WA
5	4	37	Contoso Bellevue Store	Bellevue	WA
6	66	88	Contoso Houston No.1 Store	Houston	TX
7	67	88	Contoso Houston No.2 Store	Midland	TX
8	68	88	Contoso Houston No.3 Store	Russellville	TX

Figure 6-2 Correct layout in Excel to be imported into PowerPivot

Importing Tips For Text Files And Excel Worksheets

The tips discussed below will make it easier for you to import data into PowerPivot from Excel and text files.

① There should not be any blank rows or columns in the range of data that will be imported. There can be blank cells.
② There should only be one row of column headings.
③ The data should start on the first row below the column headings.

Importing Data vs Linking Tables vs Pasting Data

In this chapter you will learn how to import data from different data sources into PowerPivot tables. In Chapter 7, you will learn how to link an Excel table to a PowerPivot table and how to paste data to a create a table in PowerPivot.

While having all of these options available to get data into a PowerPivot table is good, keep the following in mind if the PowerPivot workbook will be published on a SharePoint server. Only PowerPivot workbooks with imported data can be updated in SharePoint. PowerPivot workbooks stored on a SharePoint server that have data from linked tables or pasted data cannot be updated on the SharePoint server.

To update PowerPivot workbooks with linked or pasted data, they have to be updated in PowerPivot for Excel and then published back to the SharePoint server. Therefore, if the workbook will be published on a SharePoint server, it is probably a good idea to only use the linked table and pasted data options for data that does not need to be updated on a regular basis or for data that does not need to be updated at all.

Text Files

Text (.txt) files do not have any formatting like bold, italic or font size. To be used in Excel, this file type has to have rows of data, as shown in Figure 6-3. Each row of data has fields (columns). The fields are usually separated by commas.

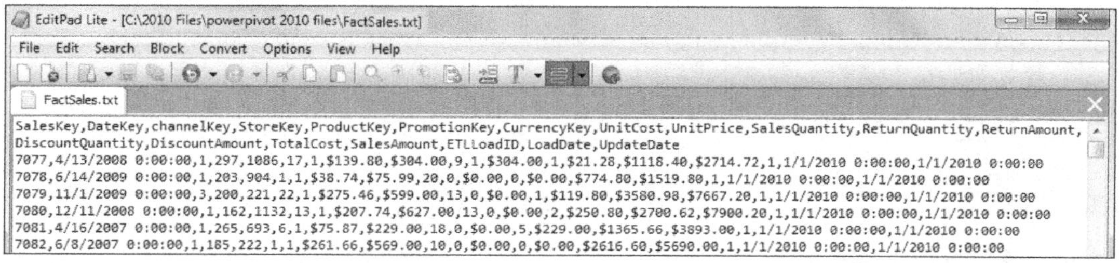

Figure 6-3 Text file

Exercise 6.1: Import Data From A Text File

In this exercise you will learn how to import data into a PowerPivot table from a text file.

1. Home tab ⇒ Get External Data group ⇒ From Text.
2. In the Friendly connection name field type `Import Fact Sales`.
3. Check the **USE FIRST ROW AS COLUMN HEADERS** option.

> If you want the column headers to be imported, but forget to select the option before selecting the file to import, you can select the option after the preview records from the data source are displayed at the bottom of the screen shown in Figure 6-4.

4. Click the **BROWSE** button, then navigate to your folder. Double-click on the Fact Sales.txt file. The data will now be imported. When the process is finished, your dialog box should look like the one shown in Figure 6-4.

> The Table Import Wizard dialog box does not display all of the data that will be imported. 50 rows of data are displayed as a preview, on the screen shown in Figure 6-4.

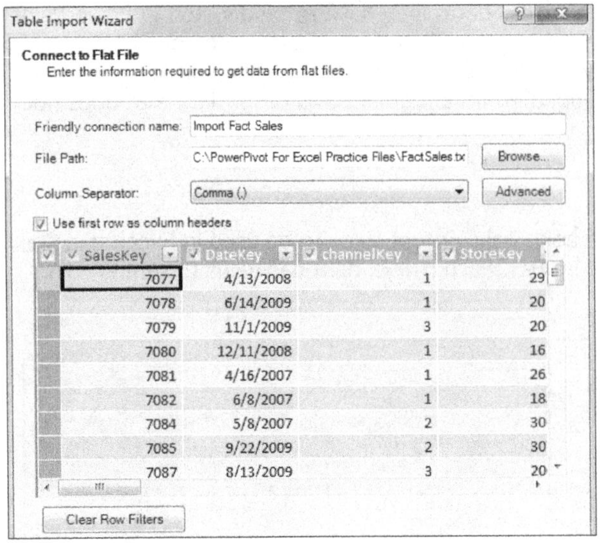

Figure 6-4 Imported data

The options in the **COLUMN SEPARATOR** drop-down list on the screen shown above in Figure 6-4 are used to select what character is used in the file to separate the fields in the file that will be imported.

The character is in parenthesis, as shown in Figure 6-5. If you are not sure which character is used, view the file before starting the import process.

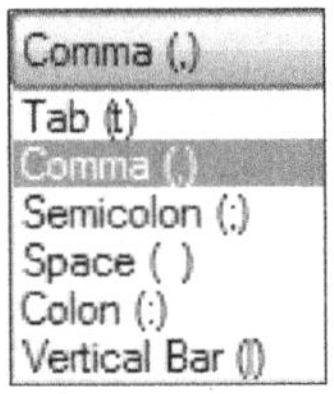

Figure 6-5 Column separator options

The **ADVANCED** button on the screen shown earlier in Figure 6-4, opens the dialog box shown in Figure 6-6.

The options on this dialog box are used to select a different encoding option.

ENCODING is a way to format data.

LOCALE is used to select a language that will be used for ordering (sorting) the records and for the date and time formats.

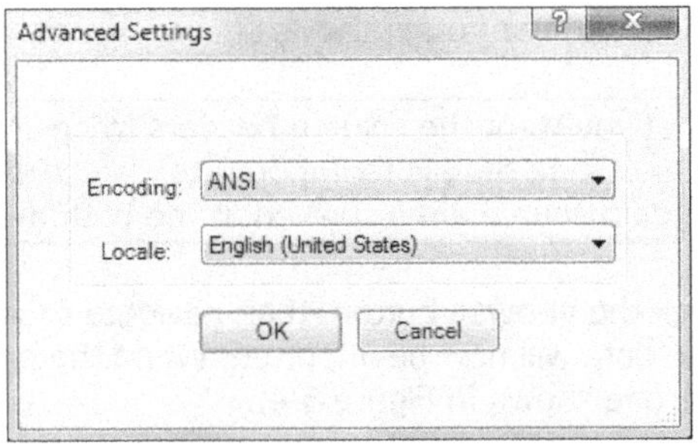

Figure 6-6 Advanced Settings dialog box

5. Click the Finish button. The data will now be imported, as shown in Figure 6-7. When the import is finished, you will see the imported table in the **WORK ITEM** column on the dialog box, as well as, how many rows of data were imported. Figure 6-7 shows that over 2.2 million rows of data were imported from the text file.

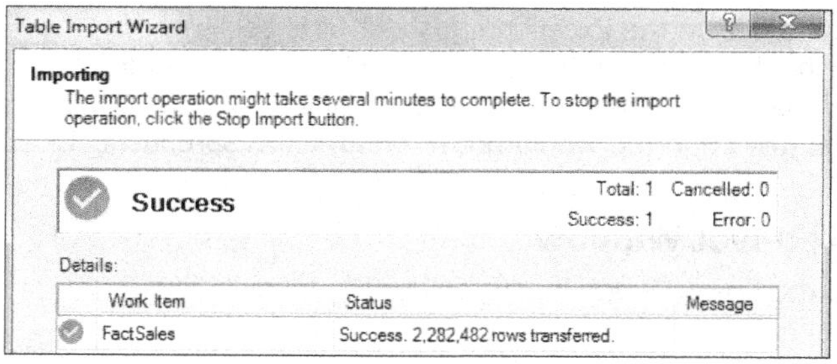

Figure 6-7 Import progress wizard screen

> **Large Data Files**
> As you saw above in Figure 6-7, PowerPivot is capable of handling data files that have millions of records (rows of data). In the interest of saving processing time on your computer, the remaining import exercises will not import this many records. I just wanted you to see that it really can be done and from a text file no less <smile>.

6. Click the Close button. You will now see the data on a tab in the PowerPivot window, as shown in Figure 6-8.

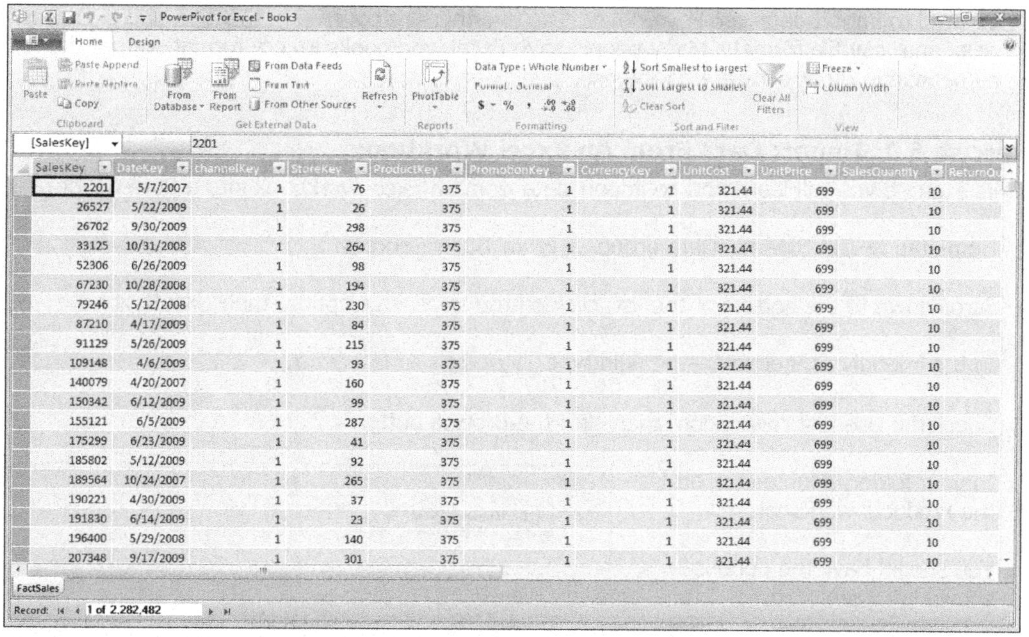

Figure 6-8 PowerPivot table with imported data

Save The PowerPivot Workbook

1. Click the Save button on the Quick Access toolbar.

2. If necessary, navigate to the folder that you want to save the workbook in, then type in the name for the workbook. For this exercise navigate to your folder if necessary, then type `E6.1 Import Fact Sales text file` as the file name.

If you are wondering why the imported data is not on the Excel spreadsheet, it is because PowerPivot data is not stored in Excel worksheets. It has to be stored in the PowerPivot window because that is how the data is saved to the database attached to the workbook. Never mind the fact that the 2 millions rows of data that you just imported would not fit on an Excel spreadsheet.

How To Rename A Tab In The PowerPivot Window

If you want to change the name of a tab in the PowerPivot window, follow the steps below.

1. Right-click on the tab that you want to rename and select Rename on the shortcut menu shown in Figure 6-9.

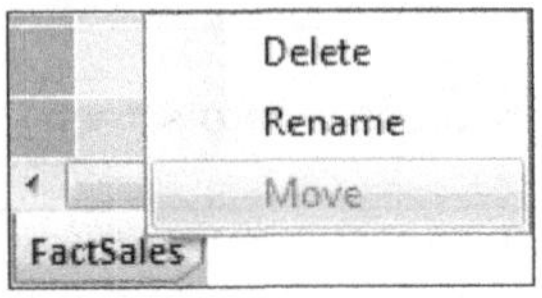

Figure 6-9 Tab shortcut menu

2. Type in the new name for the tab, then press Enter.

Importing Data From Excel Workbooks

In the previous exercise you imported data from a text file. There are several Excel file types that can be used to import data into PowerPivot. The two that are covered in the next two exercises are the **.XLSX** and **.CSV** file formats. Many people save Excel workbooks in .csv format so that the file can be opened in other software packages.

Exercise 6.2: Import Data From An Excel Workbook

In this exercise you will learn how to import data from an Excel workbook into a PowerPivot table.

1. Home tab ⇒ Get External Data group ⇒ From Other Sources.

2. Scroll down to the bottom of the list, click on the **EXCEL FILE** option, then click Next.

3. In the Friendly connection name field type `Import Products`.

4. Check the Use first row option, then click the Browse button.

5. In your folder, double-click on the Products workbook.

   You should have the options shown in Figure 6-10.

   Click Next.

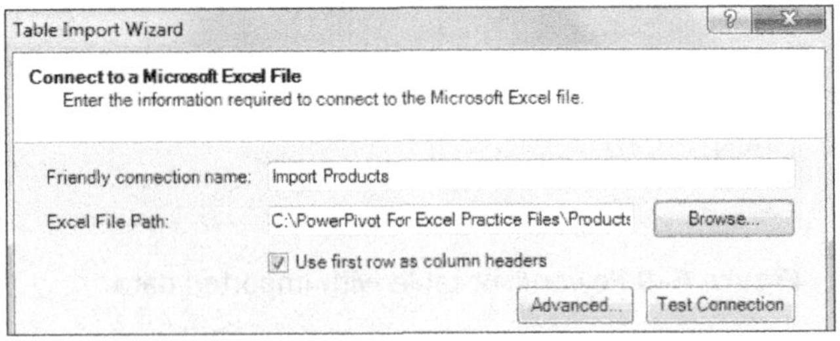

Figure 6-10 Excel workbook connection options

6. Check the DimProduct table shown in Figure 6-11, then click Finish.

   When the import is finished, you will see that 1,690 records were imported.

   Click the Close button.

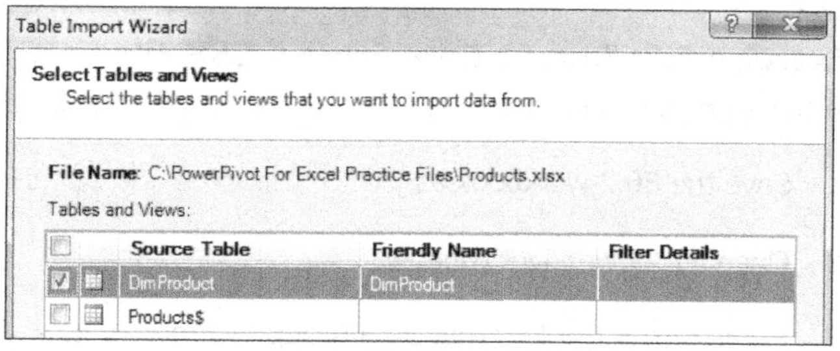

Figure 6-11 Select Tables and Views screen

7. Save the workbook as `E6.2 Import product data from Excel.`

> **Handling Non Adjacent Data On A Worksheet**
> In the exercise that you just completed, the data on the worksheet that you used had the data in adjacent rows and columns and did not contain any charts or other objects. If the worksheet that you need to import data from looks like the one shown in Figure 6-12, the PowerPivot table will look like the one shown in Figure 6-13. This is probably not what you were expecting to see. PowerPivot does not automatically rearrange data before or after it is imported.

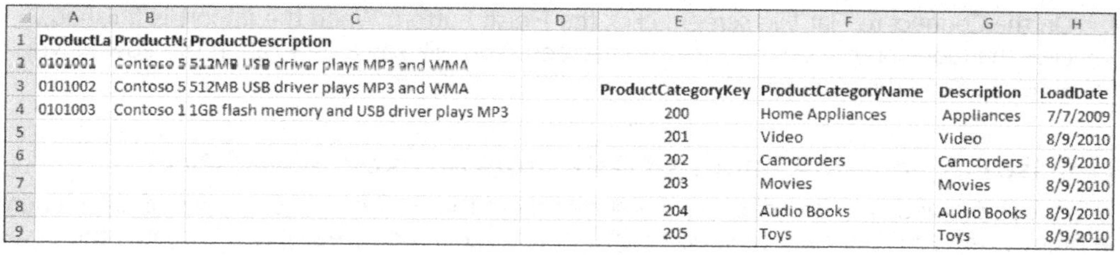

	A	B	C	D	E	F	G	H
1	ProductLa	ProductN:	ProductDescription					
2	0101001	Contoso 5	512MB USB driver plays MP3 and WMA					
3	0101002	Contoso 5	512MB USB driver plays MP3 and WMA		ProductCategoryKey	ProductCategoryName	Description	LoadDate
4	0101003	Contoso 1	1GB flash memory and USB driver plays MP3		200	Home Appliances	Appliances	7/7/2009
5					201	Video	Video	8/9/2010
6					202	Camcorders	Camcorders	8/9/2010
7					203	Movies	Movies	8/9/2010
8					204	Audio Books	Audio Books	8/9/2010
9					205	Toys	Toys	8/9/2010

Figure 6-12 Worksheet with non adjacent data

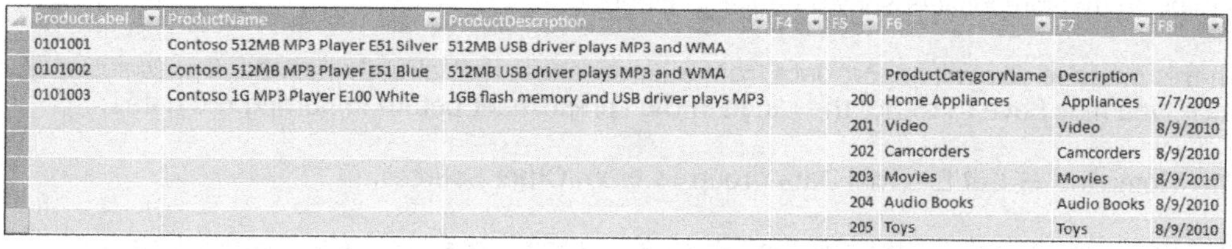

ProductLabel	ProductName	ProductDescription	F4	F5	F6	F7	F8
0101001	Contoso 512MB MP3 Player E51 Silver	512MB USB driver plays MP3 and WMA					
0101002	Contoso 512MB MP3 Player E51 Blue	512MB USB driver plays MP3 and WMA			ProductCategoryName	Description	
0101003	Contoso 1G MP3 Player E100 White	1GB flash memory and USB driver plays MP3		200	Home Appliances	Appliances	7/7/2009
				201	Video	Video	8/9/2010
				202	Camcorders	Camcorders	8/9/2010
				203	Movies	Movies	8/9/2010
				204	Audio Books	Audio Books	8/9/2010
				205	Toys	Toys	8/9/2010

Figure 6-13 Result of the non adjacent data imported into a PowerPivot table

CSV Files

Like the text files that you learned about earlier in this chapter, .csv files are also text files because they do not contain any formatting, even though they are saved in a workbook. This file type is most often created as an export file from a database or a spreadsheet. Having the ability to import data into PowerPivot from .csv files opens up a lot of possibilities, especially if you do not have direct access to data that is stored in an enterprise system. You can get the IT department to export the data from an enterprise system and save it in a .csv file for you.

Exercise 6.3: Import Data From A CSV File

In this exercise you will import data from a .csv file into an existing PowerPivot workbook.

1. Save the E6.2 workbook as `E6.3 Import data from a csv file`.
2. Open the PowerPivot window.
3. Home tab ⇒ Get External Data group ⇒ From Text.
4. In the Friendly connection name field type `CSV file`.
5. Check the Use first row option, then click the Browse button.
6. Navigate to your folder, then open the File Type drop-down list on the Open dialog box and select the **COMMA SEPARATED FILES (*.CSV)** option shown in Figure 6-14.

   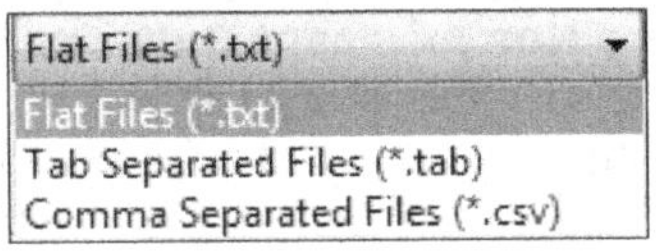

   Figure 6-14 File Type drop-down list options

   Click on the Products.csv file, then click the Open button.

7. On the Connect to Flat File screen, click the Finish button. When the import is finished, click the Close button on the Importing screen. You will see a new tab in the PowerPivot window. Save the changes.

Exercise 6.4: Import A Range Of Data From An Excel Spreadsheet

In Exercise 6.2 you imported data from a spreadsheet that had over 1,500 rows of data. There may be times when you only need to import part of the data in the spreadsheet. If that is the case, you can create one or more ranges in the spreadsheet and select the range on the Tables and Views screen on the Table Import Wizard. This would be helpful when the data on the spreadsheet looks similar to the spreadsheet shown earlier in Figure 6-12.

In this exercise you will import data from a spreadsheet that already has the ranges set up. On your own, you may have to create the range in the spreadsheet before importing the data.

1. Home tab ⇒ Get External Data group ⇒ From Other Sources.
2. Scroll down to the bottom of the list, click on the **EXCEL FILE** option, then click Next.
3. In the Friendly connection name field type `Import by Range Name`.
4. In your folder, click on the Products With Range Names workbook, then click the Open button. Click Next.

5. On the Select Tables and Views screen, you will see the options shown in Figure 6-15.

   Check the Range 2 table.

   Remember that each table or view that is selected on this screen is imported to a separate tab in the PowerPivot window.

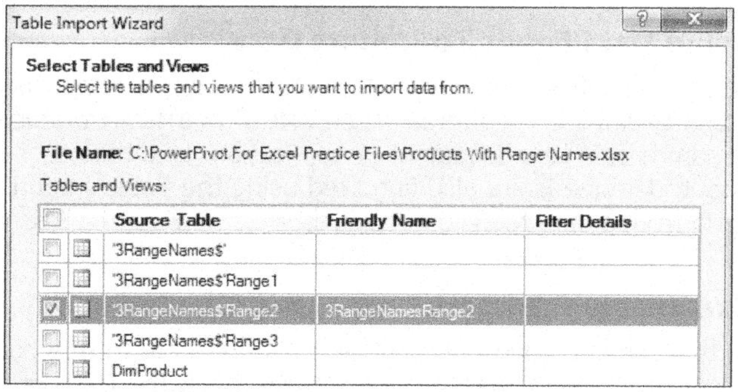

Figure 6-15 Range selected to be imported

6. Click Finish. When the import is finished, you will see the window shown in Figure 6-16.

   Notice that less records were imported in this exercise then there were in Exercise 6.2. That is because the range only contained 501 rows of data.

   Click the Close button.

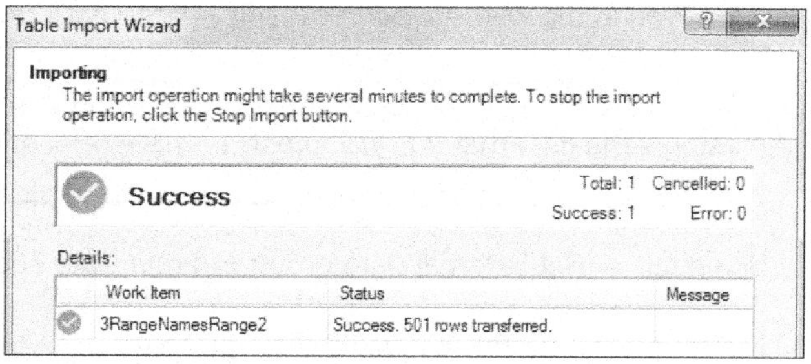

Figure 6-16 Import results

Even though the Products table in Exercise 6.2 came from a different workbook then the Products table in this exercise, the data in both spreadsheets is the same.

Notice that there are no column headings for the data in the PowerPivot workbook. That is because the range of data that was selected, does not have column headings because the range is not at the top of the spreadsheet. If you know that you will import data from a spreadsheet that has a range, add column headings to it if needed.

7. Save the workbook as `E6.4 Import by Range Name.`

Viewing The Range

If you opened the Products With Range Names workbook in Excel, then opened the Name Manager dialog box (Formulas tab ⇒ Defined Names group ⇒ Name Manager) shown in Figure 6-17, you could see the cells for each range.

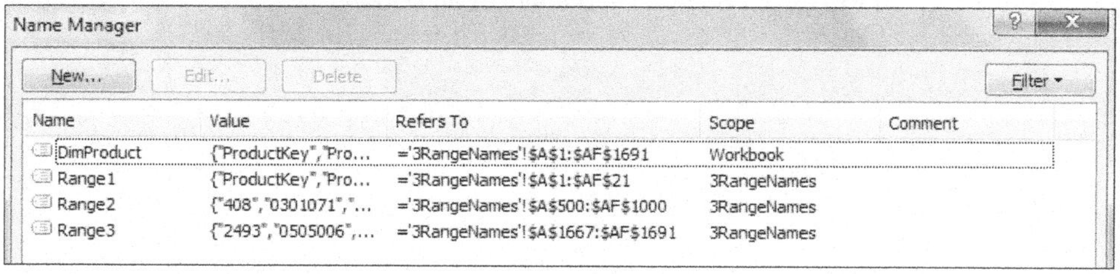

Figure 6-17 Range information for the spreadsheet

Using Data Feeds To Import Data

Select this option when the data that you need to import is on a web site, corporate intranet or is in a SharePoint list. A data feed is an **XML DATA STREAM** that is created from an online source. This data stream is sent to a document or application. Like the other import options that you have learned about, data feeds are also imported using the Table Import Wizard. Data imported into a PowerPivot table from a data feed can be refreshed.

Exercise 6.5: Import Data From A Data Feed

In this exercise you will learn how to import data from a public data feed on a government web site. There are two options that you can use to get the Data Feed URL, as discussed below.

① Select an **.ATOMSVC** document.

② Type in the web site address (URL) of the data feed.

> As you will see by the web site address used in this exercise, a **CLOUD-BASED** database stores the data that you will import in this exercise. Cloud-based databases were briefly covered in Chapter 4.

1. Home tab ⇒ Get External Data group ⇒ From Data Feeds.
2. In the Friendly connection name field type `Public Data Feed`.
3. Type `http://ogdi.cloudapp.net/vi/dc/banklocations/` in the **DATA FEED URL** field.
4. Click the Test Connection button to make sure that your computer is connected to the database. If the test fails, make sure that you typed the URL in correctly, in step 3 above and that the computer is connected to the Internet.

   You should have the options shown in Figure 6-18.

   Click Next.

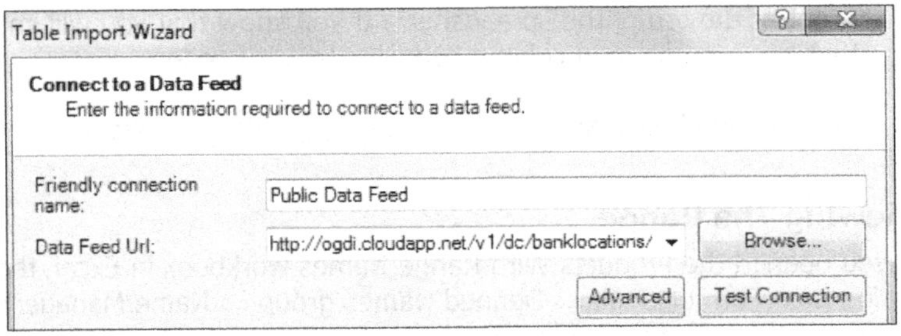

Figure 6-18 Data Feed connection options

The options shown in Figure 6-19 display the tables and views that the data feed has.

Like other types of data that can be imported, you can give the Source Table in a data feed a different name and filter the data, before it is imported into a PowerPivot table.

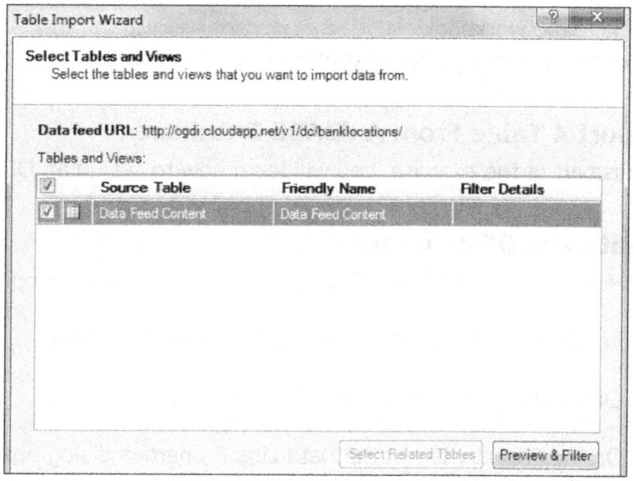

Figure 6-19 Data Feed Table and Views screen

5. Click the Finish button. When the import is finished, click the Close button on the Importing screen. You will see the data from the data feed in the PowerPivot window.

6. Save the workbook as `E6.5 Import data from an Atom data feed`.

Importing Data From Multiple Sources Into One PowerPivot Workbook

In Chapter 4 you read about the data sources that PowerPivot supports. Many of the database options that PowerPivot supports requires having access to a server. To demonstrate using multiple data sources in the same PowerPivot workbook, the next two exercises will use data sources that do not require a connection to a server.

Exercise 6.6: Import Tables From Multiple Sources

In this exercise you will import a list of orders from a Comma Separated Values (.csv) file and a table of order detail records from a dBASE database. The data in tables from multiple sources does not have to be related. This is helpful if you need to create several pivot tables in the same workbook that have unrelated data.

Import Data From A CSV File

1. Home tab ⇒ Get External Data group ⇒ From Text.

2. In the Friendly connection name field type `Import Orders CSV`.

3. Check the Use first row option, then click the Browse button.

4. Select the Import Orders.csv file.

5. Clear the check mark for the following fields, so that they will not be imported: Shipper ID, Ship Name, Ship Address, Ship City, Ship State, Ship Zip and Ship Country.

6. Click the Finish button, then click the Close button after the data is imported.

7. Save the workbook as `E6.6 Import from a dBASE database`. Leave the workbook open to complete the next part of the exercise.

Import A Table From A dBASE Database

In this part of the exercise, you will learn how to set up an ODBC connection for a database.

Create The ODBC Connection

1. Home tab ⇒ Get External Data group ⇒ From Other Sources.
2. Select the **OTHERS** Data Source option, then click Next.
3. Click the **BUILD** button on the Connection String screen.
4. On the Provider tab of the Data Link Properties dialog box, select the OLE DB Provider for ODBC Drivers option.
5. On the Connection tab open the **USE DATA SOURCE NAME** drop-down list and select dBASE Files, as illustrated in Figure 6-20.

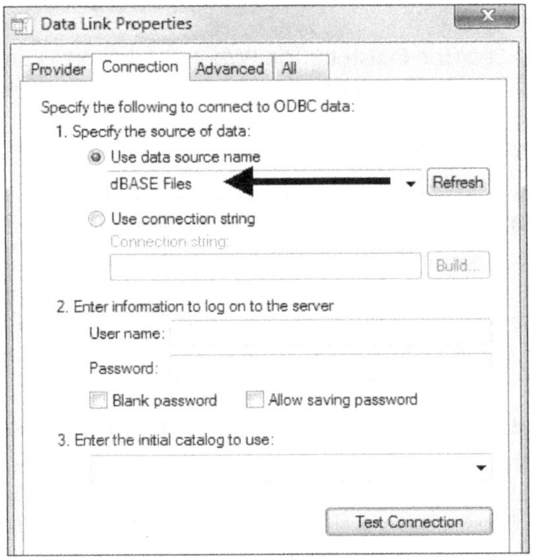

Figure 6-20 Connection tab options

6. Type `C:\PowerPivot For Excel Practice Files` in the Enter the initial catalog to use field.
7. Click the Test Connection button. This test confirms that there is at least one dBASE database in the folder that you selected. Click OK to confirm the connection, then click OK to close the Data Link Properties dialog box.

Import The Data

1. In the Friendly connection name field type `dBASE connection.`

   You should have the connection string shown in Figure 6-21.

   Click Next.

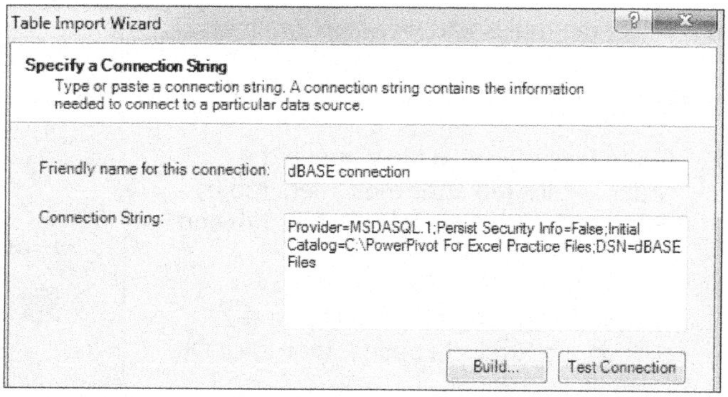

Figure 6-21 Connection string options

2. Select the tables and views option, then click Next.
3. Check the Order De table if it is not already checked.
4. Change the Friendly Name to `Order Details`, then click the Finish button. You should see the Order Details table from the dBASE database in the PowerPivot window. Save the changes to the workbook.

Exercise 6.7: Import Data From A Text File And A Database

In this exercise you will import data from a text file and three tables from an Access database.

Import A Text File

1. Home tab ⇒ Get External Data group ⇒ From Text.
2. In the Friendly connection name field type `Customers.`
3. Check the Use first row option, then click the Browse button.
4. Select the Import Text File.txt file.
5. Remove the following columns: E-mail Address, Home Phone, Mobile Phone, Web Page, Notes and Attachments. Click Finish.
6. Rename the tab in the PowerPivot window to `Customers.`
7. Save the workbook as `E6.7 Import from a text file and a database.`

Import Multiple Tables

In this part of the exercise you will import three tables from a database.

1. Home tab ⇒ Get External Data group ⇒ From Database ⇒ From Access.
2. In the Friendly connection name field type `Import 3 tables.`

3. Select the Import DB database, then click Next.

4. Select the tables and views option, then click Next.

5. Select the Orders, Order Details and Products tables, then click Finish.

6. In the PowerPivot window, move the Order Details tab after the Orders tab by right-clicking on the Order Details tab and selecting Move.

   On the dialog box shown in Figure 6-22, click on the Products option, then click OK.

   Save the changes to the workbook.

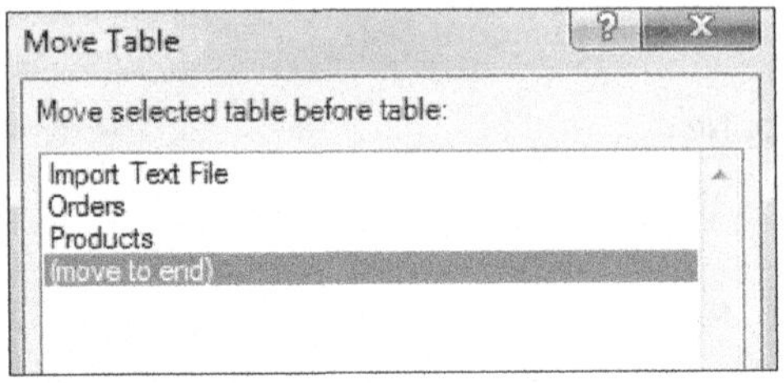

Figure 6-22 Move Table dialog box

> **Rearranging The Tab Order In The PowerPivot Window**
> You just learned how to use the Move Table dialog box to rearrange the order of the tabs. Like the tabs in an Excel workbook, you can use drop and drag to rearrange the order of the tabs in the PowerPivot window.

Exercise 6.8: Import Tables In Order

In Chapter 4 you read that the order that tables are imported are important if you plan to create relationships. It is also important for the PowerPivot Field List dialog box.

In Exercise 6.7, the Order Details table was imported before the Orders table. This means that there is a possibility that the auto detection feature created a link that will produce unexpected results. In this exercise you will import four tables.

Import The Customers And Orders Tables

1. Home tab ⇒ Get External Data group ⇒ From Database ⇒ From Access.

2. In the Friendly connection name field type `Customers-Orders`.

3. Select the Import DB database, then click Next.

4. Select the tables and views option, then click Next.

5. Select the Customers and Orders tables, then click Finish.

Import The Order Details And Products Tables

1. Home tab ⇒ Get External Data group ⇒ From Database ⇒ From Access.

2. In the Friendly connection name field type `Order Details-Products`.

3. Select the Import DB database, then click Next.

4. Select the tables and views option, then click Next.

5. Select the Order Details and Products tables, then click Finish.

6. Save the workbook as `E6.8 Import tables in order.`

Exercise 6.9: Import From Databases And Excel Workbooks

In this exercise you will import data from two Access databases and two Excel workbooks. This workbook will be used later in the book to create a pivot table.

1. Open a new workbook, then open the PowerPivot window.

2. Import all of the tables in the Contoso Sales database.

3. Import the DimProductCategory table in the Product Categories database.

4. Import the DimGeography worksheet in the Geography workbook.

5. Import the Stores worksheet in the Stores workbook.

6. Save the workbook as `E6.9 Contoso database.`

Getting Data Out Of A PowerPivot Table

All of the exercises in this chapter have shown you how to get data into a PowerPivot table. There may be times when you need to get data out of a PowerPivot table. An example that comes to mind is when you need to make changes to the data or you need all or part of the data for another project and cannot find the data source. The steps below show you how to get data out of a PowerPivot table and into a spreadsheet.

1. Open the workbook that has the PowerPivot table data that you want to paste into a spreadsheet.

2. Open the PowerPivot window.

3. Select the entire table by clicking on the square to the left of the first column heading if you want to paste the entire table into the spreadsheet or select the cells that you want to paste into the spreadsheet.

4. On the Home tab click the Copy button.

5. Click on the spreadsheet either in the current workbook or open a different workbook, depending on where you want to paste the data.

6. Press Ctrl+V, then save the changes to the workbook that you pasted the data into.

LINKING TABLES, PASTING AND APPENDING DATA

In this chapter you will learn how to do the following:

- ☑ Link an Excel table to a PowerPivot table
- ☑ Copy and paste data
- ☑ Append data
- ☑ Handle bad data

CHAPTER 7

Linking Data In Excel To A PowerPivot Table

In Chapter 6 you learned how to import Excel data into a PowerPivot table. You also learned that you cannot make changes to the data in a PowerPivot table and that if you needed to change the data you would have to make the changes in the data source and then refresh the data or import the data again.

Importing is not the only way to get data into a PowerPivot table. There are other options: Linking to tables in Excel, pasting data and appending data. They are explained below.

① A **LINKED TABLE** is a table that is created in an Excel spreadsheet. It is linked to a PowerPivot table in the same workbook. After the initial link to the data in an Excel workbook is set up, the data in the PowerPivot table will be updated with the new or modified data in the table in Excel. In environments where spreadsheets are on a server and updated by a few people on a regular basis, linking to the spreadsheet will save you a lot of work.

The first three exercises in this chapter will show you how to link a PowerPivot table to data in a spreadsheet. The good thing about linking to data is that new records (rows of data) that have been added to the original table on the spreadsheet are automatically added to the PowerPivot table.

② **COPY AND PASTE** the data into a PowerPivot table. This option is the same process as copying and pasting data between any other types of documents. Keep in mind that once data is pasted into a PowerPivot table, there is no connection back to the data source. This means that if the data source now has 2,500 more records, you have to copy and paste the new records into the PowerPivot table. For a small amount of data, that may be acceptable, but what about data sources that have tens of thousands of new records added on a regular basis? Do you really want to keep copying and pasting that many records on a regular basis?

In order to copy and paste the new records in the data source into the PowerPivot table, you would have to know specifically which records are new. How will you handle data that has been deleted from the source, but is still in your PowerPivot table? As you can see, the data in a PowerPivot table can quickly become outdated. The best solution is to link to the data source. The benefit that linking has is that the data in the PowerPivot table can be automatically updated.

③ **APPENDING DATA** into a PowerPivot table is similar to copying and pasting. The differences are that the data that you want to append to a PowerPivot table has to have the same data type in each column that the data in the PowerPivot table has. Another difference is that the data that you want to append must have the same number of columns that the PowerPivot table has.

Creating Tables

If the data that you want to link to is not in a table, you can follow the steps in Exercise 7.1, in the "Prepare The Data To Be Linked" section, before the **CREATE LINKED TABLE BUTTON** is clicked. This is not a requirement because if you click the Create Linked Table button and the data in the spreadsheet is not in table format, you will be prompted to create the table before you can create the link.

One benefit of creating the table first is that you can change the table name, which is the name that will be used for the PowerPivot table. This will keep you from having to rename the table in PowerPivot.

Linked And Pasted Tables
If you plan to publish a PowerPivot workbook to a SharePoint server, keep in mind that linked and pasted tables cannot be updated from SharePoint. To update the data you have to update the data in PowerPivot for Excel, then republish it to the SharePoint server.

Linked Table Advantage
The advantage of creating and maintaining data in a worksheet in Excel instead of importing it, is that as you add to or edit the data in the worksheet, the data in the corresponding table in the PowerPivot window is updated automatically.

Linked Table Issue
I noticed that relationships [Covered in Chapter 9] are not picked up by auto detection like they are when data is imported. I don't know if this is the way that it is suppose to be or if it is a bug.

Exercise 7.1: Link Data In An Excel Table To A PowerPivot Table

In this exercise you will learn how to link data in an Excel workbook to a PowerPivot table.

Prepare The Data To Be Linked

In this part of the exercise you will convert the data in the spreadsheet to a table. In your own workbooks, if the data in the spreadsheet is already in a table you can skip step 3.

1. Close all open workbooks and PowerPivot windows.
2. Save the Store Data workbook as `E7.1 My Store Data`.
3. Click in a cell that has data, then press Ctrl+T.

   You will see the dialog box shown in Figure 7-1. You should see the range A1:S307 in the field.

   Check the My table has headers option, if it is not already checked, then click OK.

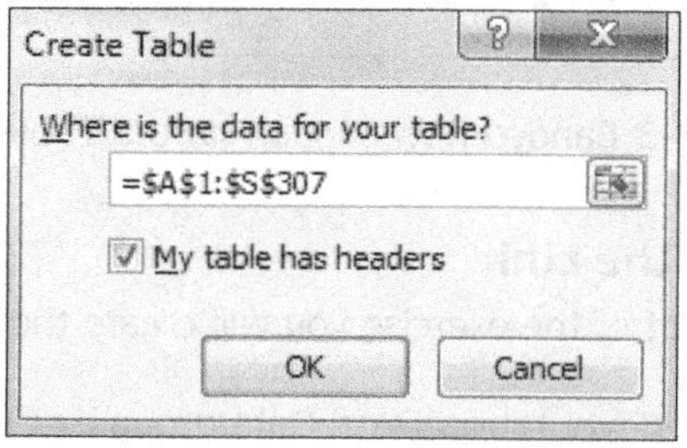

Figure 7-1 Create Table dialog box

Name The Table

By default, Excel creates generic table names like Table 1, Table 2, Table 3, etc., so it is a good idea to change the table name to something meaningful.

1. On the Table Tools Design tab in Excel, type `Stores` in the Table Name field, as illustrated in Figure 7-2, then click on any cell in the table.

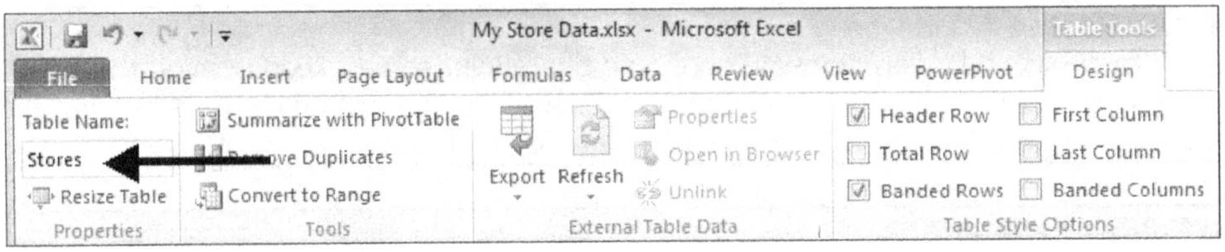

Figure 7-2 Table Name field illustrated

Converting Data To Table Format

Once data in a spreadsheet is converted to a table, you will see some differences, as explained below.

① Bands of color are automatically added to the rows in the table. You can remove the band formatting by clearing the check mark for the **BANDED ROWS** option, illustrated in Figure 7-3.

② Auto Filter drop-down lists are added to the first row of the table as shown in Figure 7-4. The first row is usually the header row. You can turn this feature off.

③ If you scroll down the spreadsheet, the column letters will be replaced with the data in the first row, which should be the column headings, as shown in Figure 7-4. This only happens when the Freeze Column option is not enabled.

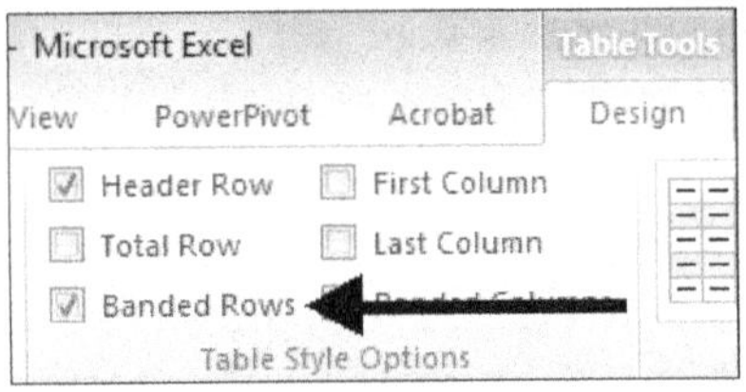

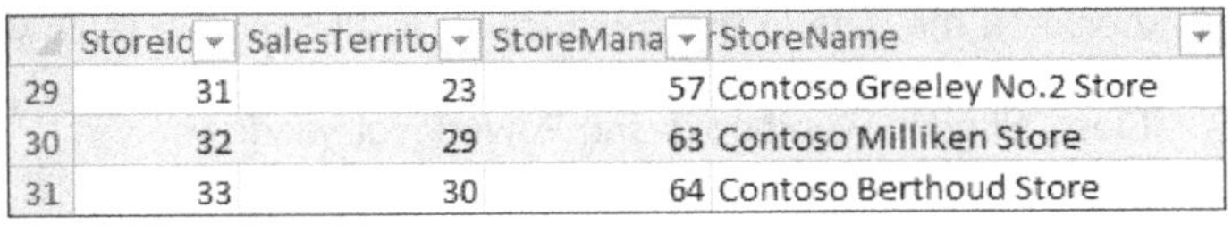

	StoreId	SalesTerrito	StoreMana	StoreName
29	31	23	57	Contoso Greeley No.2 Store
30	32	29	63	Contoso Milliken Store
31	33	30	64	Contoso Berthoud Store

Figure 7-4 Column letters replaced with column headings

Figure 7-3 Banded Rows option on the Table Tools Design tab illustrated

Create The Link

In this part of the exercise you will create the link between the Excel table and the PowerPivot table.

1. PowerPivot tab ⇒ Excel Data group ⇒ Create Linked Table button. You will see the data in the PowerPivot window.

If you look at the tab in the lower left corner of the PowerPivot window, you will see a link icon in front of the tab name, as illustrated in Figure 7-5. This is how you can visually see which tables in the PowerPivot window have linked data.

Notice that the tab name is the name of the table on the Excel worksheet.

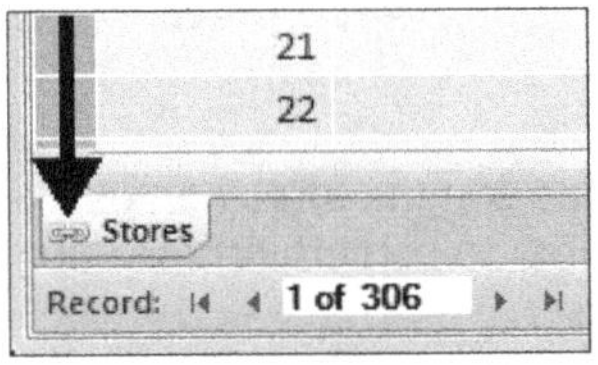

Figure 7-5 PowerPivot table tab with link icon

Modify The Excel Data

In this part of the exercise you will modify data in the Excel table and observe how the changes are automatically updated in the PowerPivot table.

1. On the Stores worksheet in the E7.1 workbook, type the date `12/31/2009` in the Close Date column (Column K) for the first two rows of data.

2. Without saving the changes, view the data in the PowerPivot table.

   The first two rows in the PowerPivot table should look like the ones shown in Figure 7-6.

   Save the changes.

Status	OpenDate	CloseDate
On	4/12/2004	12/31/2009
On	2/14/2004	12/31/2009
On	2/12/2004	
On	3/1/2004	

Figure 7-6 Data updated in the PowerPivot table

Add Data To A Table In Excel

In Figure 7-5 shown earlier, you saw that there are 306 rows of data in the PowerPivot table. In this part of the exercise you will paste rows of data from a different workbook to the end of the Excel table in the E7.1 workbook. If done correctly, the data that you paste to the end of the table in Excel will also be added to the PowerPivot table.

1. Open the New Stores workbook.
2. Select the range A2:S21, then press Ctrl+C.
3. Switch to the E7.1 workbook, then scroll to the end of the table.
4. Right-click in the first empty row below the table and select Paste.
5. View the PowerPivot table. It should now have 326 rows of data. Save the changes.
6. Close the New Stores workbook.

> **Inserting And Deleting Rows Of Data**
> An Excel table that is linked to a PowerPivot table is no different then a table that is not linked, in terms of inserting and deleting rows of data. If you insert a row of data in the Excel table, it is added to the PowerPivot table. The same applies to deleting rows of data in the Excel table, they are automatically removed from the PowerPivot table.

Exercise 7.2: Linking To Non Table Data

In the previous exercise you created a link to data that was already in an Excel table. It is not a requirement that the data that you want to link to, already be in an Excel table. During the process of creating the link to data on a worksheet, you are automatically prompted to create a table if the data is not already in a table. In this exercise, you will create links for data that is on three worksheets in an Excel workbook.

1. Save the Import Spreadsheet workbook as `E7.2 Link non table data`.
2. On the Customers tab, click in a cell that has data.

3. PowerPivot tab ⇒ Excel Data group ⇒ Create Linked Table button.

Selecting A Different Table Range In Excel
By default, PowerPivot will select the entire range of adjacent cells on the worksheet. If you do not want to import all of the data in the range that Excel selects, click the button at the end of the range on the Create Table dialog box shown in Figure 7-7, then select the range of cells that you want to import. Compare the range shown in the figure to the one shown on your screen.

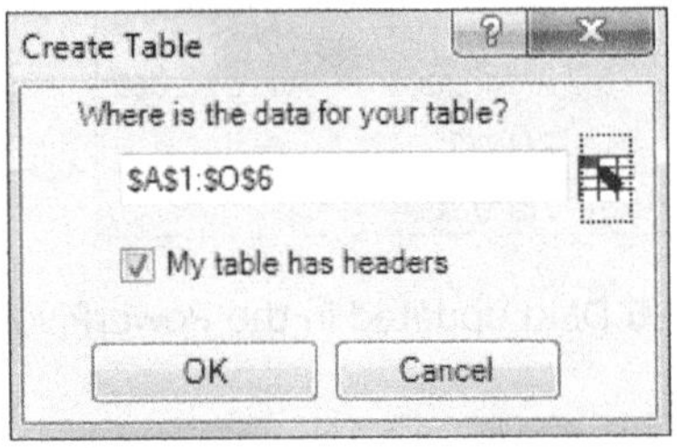

Figure 7-7 Different range selected

4. You will see the Create Table dialog box shown above. You should see the range A1:Q30. Click OK.

5. In the PowerPivot window, rename the tab to `Customers`, then save the changes.

6. Repeat steps 2 to 5 above to create links for the data on the Orders worksheet (use the range A1:T49) and the Order_Details worksheet (use the range A1:J59). Rename the tables in the PowerPivot window accordingly.

7. Save the changes to the workbook.

Using Multiple Data Sets On The Same Worksheet

In the previous exercise you learned how to link to data that originally was not in an Excel table. In the workplace, it is not uncommon to see a worksheet that looks like the one shown in Figure 7-8.

The data on the worksheet could have been placed on separate tabs in the workbook. It is just a matter of preference. As you read earlier, Excel data must be in table format to be linked to a PowerPivot table. You also read that data in non adjacent cells cannot be created as one table. The good news is that each of the three data sets shown in Figure 7-8 can be saved as a table and then linked to tables in PowerPivot.

	A	B	C	D	E
1	Customers				
2					
3	Customer ID	Last Name	First Name	City	State
4	1	Bedecs	Anna	Seattle	WA
5	2	Gratacos Solsona	Antonio	Boston	MA
6	3	Axen	Thomas	Los Angelas	CA
7	4	Lee	Christina	New York	NY
8	5	O'Donnell	Martin	Minneapolis	MN
9	6	Pérez-Olaeta	Francisco	Milwaukee	WI
10	7	Xie	Ming-Yang	Boise	ID
11	8	Andersen	Elizabeth	Portland	OR
12	9	Mortensen	Sven	Salt Lake City	UT
13	10	Wacker	Roland	Chicago	IL
14	11	Krschne	Peter	Miami	FL
15	12	Edwards	John	Las Vegas	NV
16	13	Ludick	Andre	Memphis	TN
17	14	Grilo	Carlos	Denver	CO
18	15	Kupkova	Helena	Honolulu	HI
19	16	Goldschmidt	Daniel	San Francisco	CA
20	17	Bagel	Jean Philippe	Seattle	WA
21	18	Autier Miconi	Catherine	Boston	MA
22	19	Eggerer	Alexander	Los Angelas	CA
23					
24					

	G	H	I	J	K
1	Order Header				
2					
3	Order ID	Customer	Order Date	Shipped Date	Payment Type
4	30	1	1/15/2006	1/22/2006	Check
5	31	4	1/20/2006	1/22/2006	Credit Card
6	32	12	1/22/2006	1/22/2006	Credit Card
7	33	8	1/30/2006	1/31/2006	Credit Card
8	34	4	2/6/2006	2/7/2006	Check
9	35	12	2/10/2006	2/12/2006	Check
10	36	3	2/23/2006	2/25/2006	Cash
11	37	17	3/6/2006	3/9/2006	Credit Card
12	38	5	3/10/2006	3/11/2006	Check
13	39	8	3/22/2006	3/24/2006	Check
14	40	10	3/24/2006	3/24/2006	Credit Card
15	42	9	3/24/2006	4/7/2006	Check
16	43	11	3/24/2006	4/7/2006	Credit Card
17	45	18	4/7/2006	4/7/2006	Credit Card
18	46	9	4/5/2006	4/5/2006	Check
19	47	13	4/8/2006	4/8/2006	Credit Card
20	48	8	4/5/2006	4/5/2006	Check
21					
22					
23					
24					

	M	N	O	P	Q
1	Order Details				
2					
3	ID	Order ID	Product ID	Quantity	Unit Price
4	27	30	34	100	14.00
5	28	47	80	30	3.50
6	29	31	7	10	30.00
7	30	31	51	10	53.00
8	31	48	80	10	3.50
9	32	32	1	15	18.00
10	33	44	43	20	46.00
11	34	33	19	30	9.20
12	35	34	19	20	9.20
13	36	35	48	10	12.75
14	37	36	41	200	9.65
15	38	37	8	17	40.00
16	39	38	43	300	46.00
17	40	39	48	100	12.75
18	41	40	81	200	2.99
19	42	41	43	300	46.00
20	43	45	6	10	25.00
21	44	46	4	10	22.00
22	45	42	19	10	9.20
23	46	43	80	20	3.50
24	47	43	81	50	2.99

Figure 7-8 Multiple data sets on a worksheet

Exercise 7.3: Create Three PowerPivot Tables From One Worksheet

In this exercise you will convert the three data sets shown above in Figure 7-8 into three tables and link them to individual tables in PowerPivot.

1. Save the Multiple Data Sets workbook as `E7.3 Multiple data sets.`
2. Click in a cell in the Customer data section.
3. PowerPivot tab ⇒ Excel Data group ⇒ Create Linked Table button.
4. You should see the range A3:E22. Click OK to close the Create Table dialog box.
5. In the PowerPivot window, rename the table to `Customers`, then save the changes.
6. Repeat steps 2 through 5 above for the Order Header (range G3:K20) and Order Details (range M3:Q24) sections of the worksheet to create linked tables.
7. Save the changes to the workbook.

Linked Table Errors

Linking Excel table data to a PowerPivot table provides the ability to keep the data in the PowerPivot table updated easily. If you use a lot of spreadsheets, over time you may not remember which tables are linked to PowerPivot tables.

If you make certain changes to the linked table in Excel, they will cause errors in the PowerPivot table. If any of the changes listed below are made to a linked table in Excel, an error will occur.

① The linked table in Excel is deleted.
② The name of the table in Excel is changed.
③ The data type for a column in the Excel table is changed.

Exercise 7.4: Create And Fix Linked Table Errors

Normally, you would not create an error on purpose, but it is necessary to create errors in this exercise to demonstrate how to fix an error.

Create The Errors

In this part of the exercise, you will create errors in an Excel table to learn how to fix errors in the next part of this exercise.

1. Save the E7.1 workbook as `E7.4 Linked table errors`.
2. Right-click on the Close Date column (Column K) and select Format Cells.
3. On the Number tab, select the Currency category option, then click OK.
4. On the Table Tools Design tab, change the Table name to `yesterday`.
5. Save the changes, then open the PowerPivot window.

Generate And Fix The Errors

In the previous part of the exercise you made changes to the linked table data in Excel. By default, PowerPivot does not automatically let you know that there are any problems with the data. The way that you find out that there is a problem with the data in PowerPivot is to refresh the data in the PowerPivot window.

1. Table Tools Linked Table tab ⇒ Update All button.
2. You will see the dialog box shown in Figure 7-9.

   This is how you know that something has changed in the linked table in Excel.

   Click the Options button.

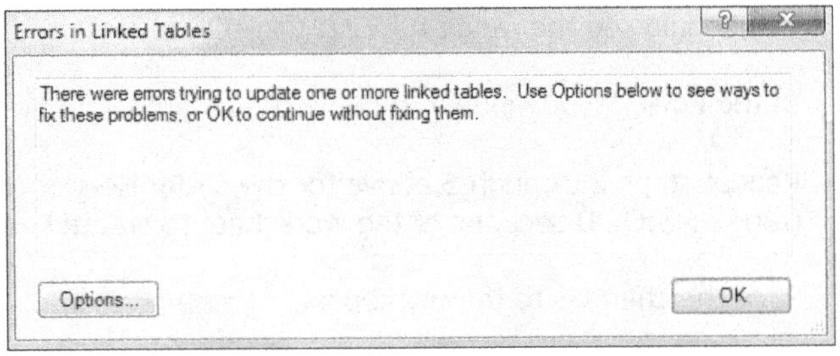

Figure 7-9 Errors In Linked Tables dialog box

Using The Select Action Dialog Box

This dialog box is used to select what to do when the link between the PowerPivot table and the Excel table has changed.

The options shown in Figure 7-10 are used to let you know that the table name has changed and what the options are to fix the error.

Table 7-1 explains the options on the dialog box.

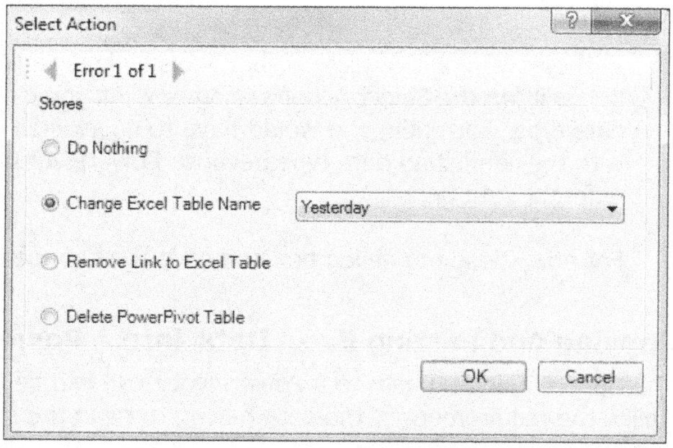

Figure 7-10 Select Action dialog box

Option	Description
Do Nothing	Selecting this option leaves the error unchanged. The error dialog box shown earlier in Figure 7-9 will continue to appear every time that data in the PowerPivot table is refreshed.
Change Excel Table Name	This option is used to type in a new table name for the table in Excel or to select a new table from the drop-down list. The drop-down list contains the names of Excel tables in the workbook.
Remove Link To Excel Table	Selecting this option removes the link between the Excel and PowerPivot tables. Selecting this option means that the data in the PowerPivot table will no longer be updated.
Delete PowerPivot Table	Selecting this option deletes the link and PowerPivot table.

Table 7-1 Select Action dialog box options explained

1. In this exercise you want to continue to use the table. Select the **CHANGE EXCEL TABLE NAME** option, then click OK. If the Excel workbook had more than one table, you would see the other table names in the drop-down list.

2. You may see the message shown in Figure 7-11. It lets you know that a table could not be updated. Click OK.

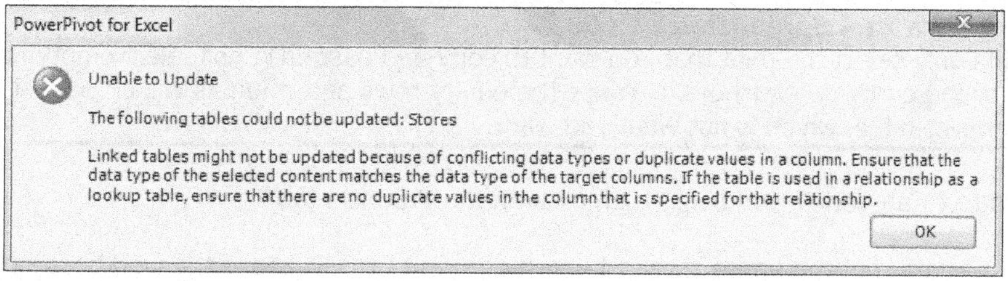

Figure 7-11 Unable to update table message

3. In Excel, Table Tools Design Tab ⇒ Type `Stores` in the Table Name field, then save the changes.

4. In the PowerPivot window, Table Tools Linked Table tab ⇒ Update All button ⇒ Options button. You will see the Select Action dialog box. As you can see there is nothing about the conflicting data type. Currently, you would have to check each column in the Excel table to find the column with the conflicting data type because PowerPivot does not let you know which column has a different data type.

5. For now, close the dialog box and save the changes to the workbook.

Copying And Pasting Excel Data Into A PowerPivot Table

The option of adding data to a PowerPivot table can be used for a small or large amount of data. Unlike the requirement of the data having to be in the same workbook for linking data in a table in Excel to a PowerPivot table, copying and pasting data does not have this requirement. This means that the data that you want to paste into a PowerPivot table can be in a different workbook or other data source, like a web page. This is usually the reason why copying and pasting is used instead of linking data. You can select all of the data on the spreadsheet to copy and paste or just the portion of the data on the spreadsheet that you need.

Limitation Of Copying And Pasting Data
If the source data that is pasted into a PowerPivot table is updated and the changes are needed in the PowerPivot table, all of the data has to be pasted into the PowerPivot table again because pasted data cannot be updated in a PowerPivot table. This process is also known as **REPLACING DATA**. Individual rows of pasted data cannot be replaced. Therefore, pasting data is best suited for data that does not change or data that does not change often.

Having Several Workbooks Open At The Same Time
As you will see, it is very easy to have several workbooks and PowerPivot windows open at the same time while going through this book. It can get confusing, especially when you are copying and pasting between workbooks. It may be easier to close all workbooks and PowerPivot windows at the end of each exercise. Doing this is optional.

Exercise 7.5: Copying And Pasting Data

In this exercise you will copy data in an Excel spreadsheet in one workbook and paste it into a PowerPivot table in a new workbook.

Selecting Data In A Spreadsheet To Copy
You should only select the data that you want to copy and paste. Do not select empty rows, columns or the entire spreadsheet, because the empty rows and columns will be pasted into the PowerPivot table, which is not what you want.

1. Open the Product Categories workbook, then click on the Products tab.

2. Select all of the data, not the entire spreadsheet, then press Ctrl+C. Leave the workbook open for the next exercise.

3. Open a new workbook, then open the PowerPivot window.

4. Home tab ⇒ Clipboard group ⇒ Paste button. You will see the Paste Preview dialog box with the data that you copied from the other workbook.

5. In the Table Name field, type `Products.`

   If the Use first row as column headers option is not selected, select it now.

   Your dialog box should look like the one shown in Figure 7-12.

   Click OK.

   The PowerPivot table will be created.

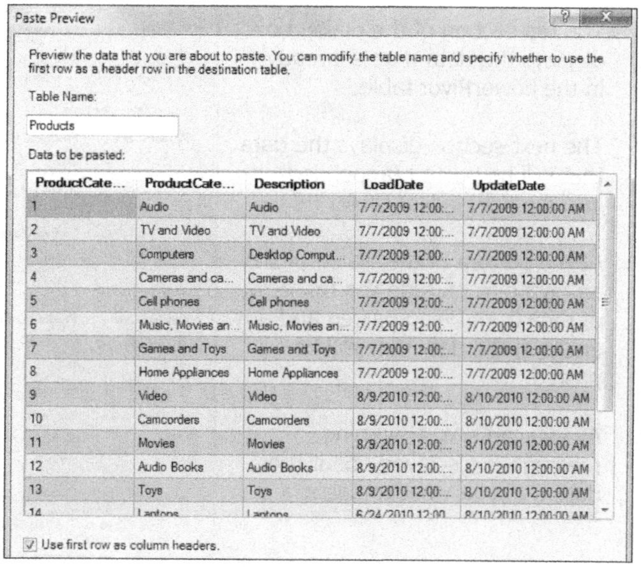

Figure 7-12 Paste Preview dialog box

6. Save the workbook as `E7.5 Copy and paste.`

Appending Data

There may be times after you have copied and pasted the initial data into a PowerPivot table or imported data into a PowerPivot table, that you need to add more data to the PowerPivot table. The new data can either come from the original spreadsheet or a different spreadsheet. The data that you want to append can also come from a different file type, like a .csv file. As long as the structure of the new data is the same structure as the data that you will append it to, appending the new data will work.

When appending data, it is not a requirement to copy the column headings.

Exercise 7.6: Append Data To A PowerPivot Table

In this exercise you will append data to the PowerPivot table that you created in the previous exercise.

1. Save the E7.5 workbook as `E7.6 Append Data.`

2. Open the Product Categories workbook, then click on the Append_Products tab.

3. Select the range A1:E8, then press Ctrl+C. Leave the workbook open for the next exercise.

4. Display the PowerPivot window in the E7.6 workbook.

5. Home tab ⇒ Clipboard group ⇒ Paste Append. You will see the dialog box shown in Figure 7-13.

   The top section of the dialog box displays the data that is already in the PowerPivot table.

   The next section displays the data that will be pasted (appended) into the PowerPivot table.

   At the bottom of the dialog box is an option to exclude the first row of data from being pasted and any errors in the data that will be pasted.

   As you can see, a warning message is displayed about the data that you want to paste.

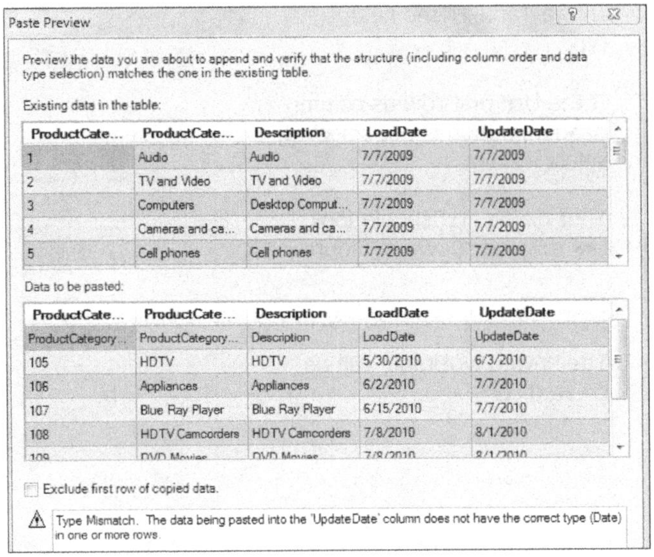

Figure 7-13 Paste Preview warning message

The **TYPE MISMATCH** message is letting you know that at least one cell in the Update Date column of the data that will be pasted, has data that is a different type then the same column in the PowerPivot table. In this case, the mismatch data is the column heading, because PowerPivot recognizes the Update Date column as a date field.

6. Check the **EXCLUDE FIRST ROW OF COPIED DATA** option. Notice that the Type Mismatch warning at the bottom of the dialog box is gone.

7. Click OK. The PowerPivot Products table now has 27 records, instead of 20. Save the changes.

Exercise 7.7: Appending Bad Data

As much as we strive to keep data correct and up to date, there will be data that does not meet the minimum requirements. In spreadsheets that do not have a lot of data, it is easier to fix bad data. Spreadsheets that have 100,000 rows for example, makes it a little more difficult to maintain the data. In the previous exercise, you saw an example of what PowerPivot considered bad data.

As you have read, when data is appended to an existing PowerPivot table, PowerPivot compares the data type of each column of the data that you want to append to the existing column in the same location in the PowerPivot table. In this exercise you will purposely try to append bad data to a PowerPivot table.

1. Save the E7.6 workbook as `E7.7 Appending Bad Data`.

2. Open the Product Categories workbook, then click on the Append_Bad_Data tab.

3. Select the range A1:E8, then press Ctrl+C. Leave the workbook open for the next exercise.

4. Display the PowerPivot table in the E7.7 workbook, then click the Paste Append button. You will see the dialog box shown in Figure 7-14.

   The warning message is letting you know that the first column in the PowerPivot table has been designated as a whole number data type format and that at least one row in the data that you want to append to the column has a different data type.

   In this exercise, selecting the Exclude first row option will not fix the problem.

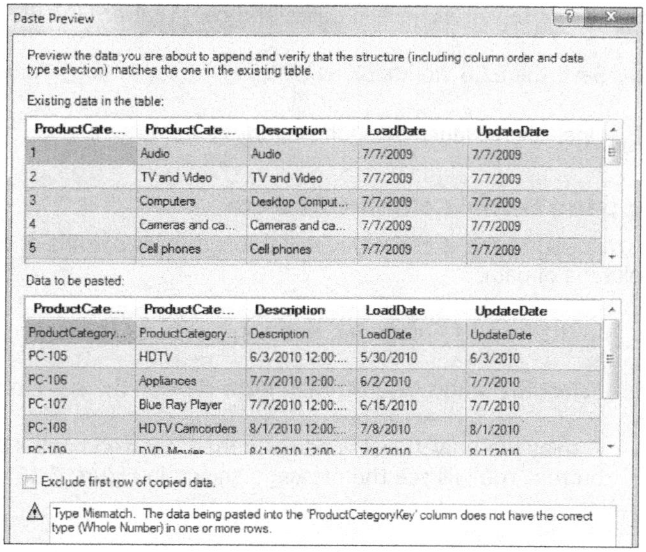

Figure 7-14 Paste Preview dialog box

5. Click the OK button. PowerPivot will attempt to paste the data.

   You will see the message shown in Figure 7-15 when you click the Details button.

   This message provides information on why the data could not be appended. While PowerPivot allows you to format data, it does not allow you to change the actual data.

   The only way to change the data is to change it in the source file, then append it again. It would be nice if the message would display all of the data errors at one time.

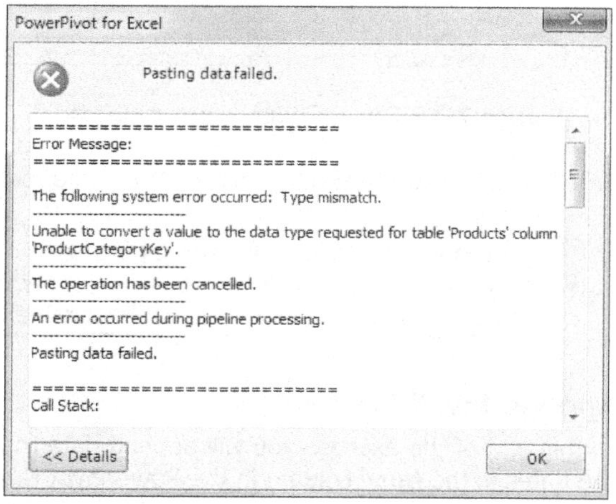

Figure 7-15 Paste data failed message

6. Click OK to close the message window, then close the PowerPivot window.

Different Types Of Bad Data

In the previous two exercises, you learned about appending bad data. These exercises showed you that the Type Mismatch validation feature is also used to check more than the actual data. The exercises that you will complete now, cover some of the more popular types of data errors that you may come across when appending or importing data.

Exercise 7.8: Appending More Bad Data

In this exercise you will attempt to append the following types of bad data: Fewer columns then the PowerPivot table has, invalid dates and cells that are missing data.

1. Save the E7.6 workbook as `E7.8 Append more bad data.`

2. Open the Product Categories workbook.

Append Fewer Columns Of Data

In this part of the exercise you will append four columns of data to a PowerPivot table that has five columns of data.

1. In the Product Categories workbook, click on the Fewer_Columns tab.

2. Select the range A2:D14, then right-click on the selected cells and select Copy.

3. Display the PowerPivot window in the E7.8 workbook. On the Home tab, click the Paste Append button. You will see the message shown in Figure 7-16.

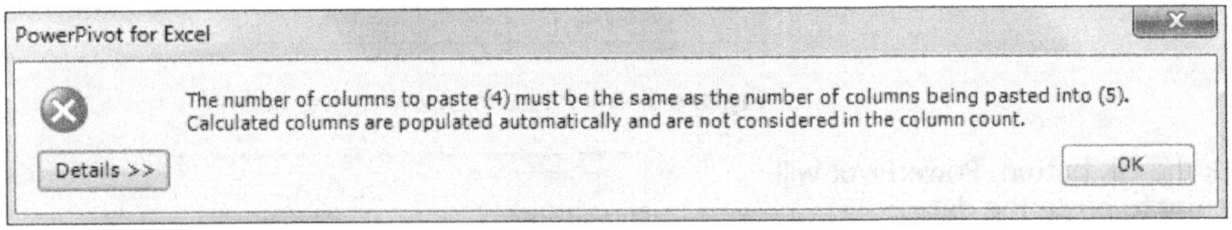

Figure 7-16 Fewer Columns error message

4. Click OK. You will see that the data is not appended to the PowerPivot table.

> **Appending More Columns Of Data**
> You will see the same message shown above in Figure 7-16 if you try to append more columns of data then the PowerPivot table has.

Append Invalid Dates

In this part of the exercise you will append data that has dates that are in a different format then the dates in the same column in the PowerPivot table.

1. In the Product Categories workbook, click on the Invalid_Dates tab.

   As illustrated in Figure 7-17, three of the dates are not valid.

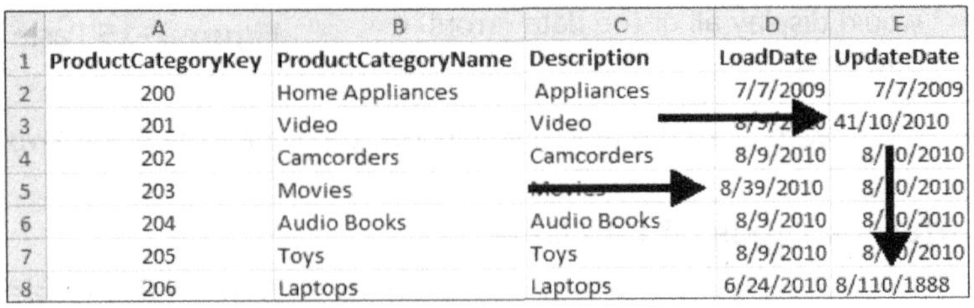

	A	B	C	D	E
1	ProductCategoryKey	ProductCategoryName	Description	LoadDate	UpdateDate
2	200	Home Appliances	Appliances	7/7/2009	7/7/2009
3	201	Video	Video	[illegible]	41/10/2010
4	202	Camcorders	Camcorders	8/9/2010	8/[illegible]0/2010
5	203	Movies	[illegible]	8/39/2010	8/[illegible]0/2010
6	204	Audio Books	Audio Books	8/9/2010	8/[illegible]0/2010
7	205	Toys	Toys	8/9/2010	8/[illegible]/2010
8	206	Laptops	Laptops	6/24/2010	8/110/1888

Figure 7-17 Invalid dates illustrated

2. Select the range A2:E8, then right-click on the selected cells and select Copy.

3. Display the PowerPivot window in the E7.8 workbook.

   On the Home tab, click the Paste Append button.

   You will see that data in the Update Date column does not have the correct data type, as shown in Figure 7-18.

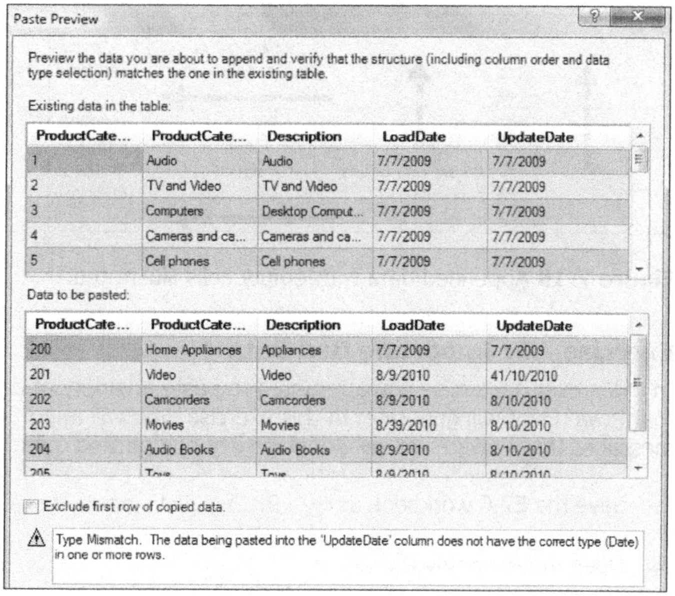

Figure 7-18 Type mismatch message for dates

4. Click OK. You will see the Paste data failed message letting you know that the data that you want to append cannot be appended. Click OK.

> **Pasting Invalid Dates**
> The steps above walked you through attempting to append data that has invalid dates. As you saw, the data could not be appended. You can paste data with invalid dates, but the data type for the column will automatically be changed to text instead of date.

Append Empty Cells

If you have created a pivot table in Excel, you know that an empty cell in a numeric column can change the function or formula that is used to calculate the values. In this part of the exercise you will append a range of data that has empty cells.

1. In the Product Categories workbook, click on the Missing_Data tab.
2. Select the range A2:E11, then right-click on the selected cells and select Copy.
3. Display the PowerPivot window in the E7.8 workbook. On the Home tab, click the Paste Append button.
4. You will see the Paste Preview dialog box. Notice that no errors are reported. Click OK.
5. If you scroll to the bottom of the Products table in the PowerPivot window, you will see the appended data with the empty cells, as shown in Figure 7-19. You will also see that the data type of the Product Category Key column is still a whole number. Save the changes.

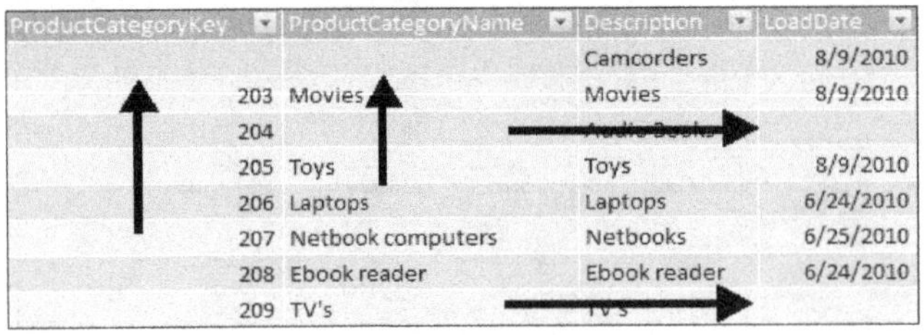

Figure 7-19 Appended data with empty cells illustrated

Exercise 7.9: Importing Bad Data

In the previous exercise you attempted to paste a variety of data to see the types of error messages that PowerPivot will generate. In this exercise, you will import data to see the types of error messages that PowerPivot will generate when importing data.

1. Save the E7.6 workbook as `E7.9 Import bad data`.
2. Open the PowerPivot window.

Import Data With Different Date Formats

In this part of the exercise you will import a date column that has two date formats in it.

1. Home tab ⇒ Get External Data group ⇒ From Other Sources ⇒ Excel File, then click Next.
2. In the Friendly connection name field type `Date Format`.
3. Select the Use first row option, then click the Browse button.
4. Select the Product Categories workbook. Click Open, then click Next.
5. Select the Date Format table, then click Finish. When the import is finished, click the Close button, then save the changes.

Notice in the Load Date column in the PowerPivot table shown in Figure 7-20, that the first three dates in August have the same format as the other dates in the column.

That is because Excel converted them. If you look at the data on the Date_Format tab on the Products Categories workbook shown in Figure 7-21, you will see that the three dates are in a different date format.

ProductCategoryKey	ProductCategoryName	Description	LoadDate	UpdateDate
200	Home Appliances	Appliances	7/7/2009	7/7/2009
201	Video	Video	8/9/2010	8/10/2010
202	Camcorders	Camcorders	8/9/2010	8/10/2010
203	Movies	Movies	8/9/2010	8/10/2010
204	Audio Books	Audio Books	8/9/2010	8/10/2010
205	Toys	Toys	8/9/2010	8/10/2010
206	Laptops	Laptops	6/24/2010	8/10/2010
207	Netbook computers	Netbooks	6/25/2010	8/10/2010
208	Ebook reader	Ebook reader	6/24/2010	8/10/2010
209	TV's	TV's	6/26/2010	8/10/2010
210	Air conditioners	AC	6/26/2010	8/10/2010
211	Music	Music	6/26/2010	8/10/2010
212	Dishwashers	Dishwashers	6/26/2010	8/10/2010

Figure 7-20 Date_Format tab in PowerPivot

	A	B	C	D	E
1	ProductCategoryKey	ProductCategoryName	Description	LoadDate	UpdateDate
2	200	Home Appliances	Appliances	July 7, 2009	7/7/2009
3	201	Video	Video	August 9, 2010	8/10/2010
4	202	Camcorders	Camcorders	August 9, 2010	8/10/2010
5	203	Movies	Movies	August 9, 2010	8/10/2010
6	204	Audio Books	Audio Books	8/9/10	8/10/2010
7	205	Toys	Toys	8/9/10	8/10/2010
8	206	Laptops	Laptops	6/24/10	8/10/2010
9	207	Netbook computers	Netbooks	6/25/10	8/10/2010
10	208	Ebook reader	Ebook reader	6/24/10	8/10/2010
11	209	TV's	TV's	6/26/10	8/10/2010
12	210	Air conditioners	AC	6/26/10	8/10/2010
13	211	Music	Music	6/26/10	8/10/2010
14	212	Dishwashers	Dishwashers	6/26/10	8/10/2010

Figure 7-21 Date_Format tab in Excel

Import Data With Invalid Dates

In this part of the exercise you will import data that has invalid dates.

1. Home tab ⇒ Get External Data group ⇒ From Other Sources ⇒ Excel File, then click Next.
2. In the Friendly connection name field type `Invalid Dates`.
3. Select the Use first row option, then click the Browse button.
4. Select the Product Categories workbook. Click Open, then click Next.
5. Select the Invalid_Dates table, then click Finish. When the import is finished, click the Close button.

Notice in Figure 7-22 that three cells in the date columns are empty. In this example, that is because Excel could not convert the data in the cells illustrated earlier in Figure 7-17.

ProductCategoryKey	ProductCategoryName	Description	LoadDate	UpdateDate
200	Home Appliances	Appliances	7/7/2009	7/7/2009
201	Video	Video	8/9/2010	
202	Camcorders	Camcorders	8/9/2010	8/10/2010
203	Movies	Movies		8/10/2010
204	Audio Books	Audio Books	8/9/2010	8/10/2010
205	Toys	Toys	8/9/2010	8/10/2010
206	Laptops	Laptops	6/24/2010	

Figure 7-22 Empty cells in the PowerPivot table

6. Save the changes.

How To Change The External Data Source Used By A Connection

In Chapter 3 you read about the **EXISTING CONNECTIONS** option on the PowerPivot Design tab. You may have the need to change the current data source for a PowerPivot table. Examples of when you would need to change the connection information is if the location of the data source has changed or if the data source now has a new name. Another reason that you may have the need to change the connection information is that there are tables in the data source now that were not there when you originally created the connection that you need to use to create a pivot table or modify an existing one.

You must select the same type of data source as the one that you are going to change. This means that if the current data source is a text file, you cannot select a database file now. The steps below show you how to change the connection for an external data source.

1. Open the PowerPivot window in the workbook that you need to change the connection information of.

2. Design tab ⇒ Existing Connections button. As shown in Figure 7-23, you will see the connections for the workbook.

   In this scenario, the location of the Product Categories database has changed.

   Click on the connection that you want to change, then click the Edit button. You will see the Edit Connection dialog box.

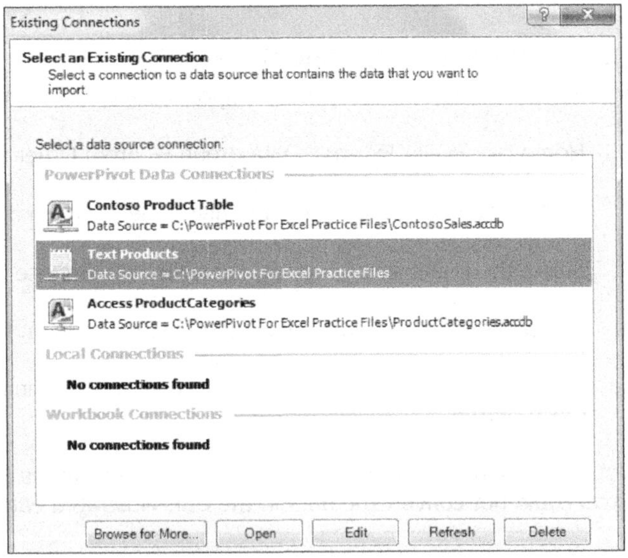

Figure 7-23 Existing Connections dialog box

3. Click the Browse button, then navigate to the location of the new file (in this case the file is a database) that you want to connect to.

   Click on the file in the new location, then click the Open button.

   You should see the new location and file name in the field before the Browse button, as shown in Figure 7-24.

   Notice the message at the bottom of the dialog box. This message lets you know that PowerPivot recognizes that the data source has changed and that the data needs to be refreshed.

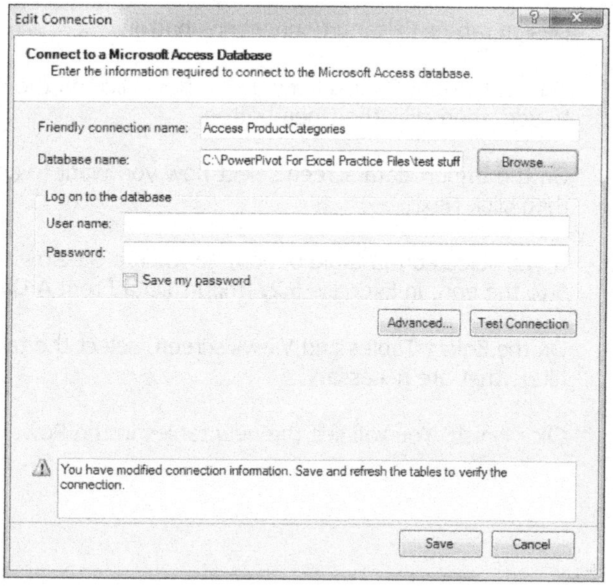

Figure 7-24 Edit Connection dialog box

4. Click the Save button.

   You should see the new location of the data source that you changed.

   Compare the Data Source path illustrated in Figure 7-25 for the Product Categories database to the one shown earlier in Figure 7-23.

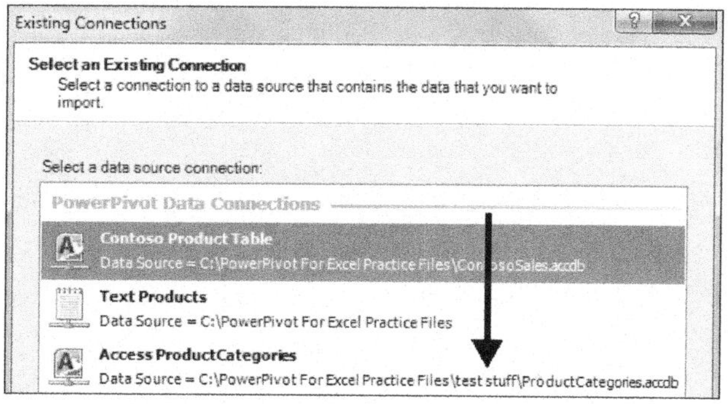

Figure 7-25 Modified connection illustrated

5. Select the connection, then click the Refresh button. Click the Close button on the Data Refresh dialog box.

6. Click the Close button on the Existing Connections dialog box, then save the changes to the workbook.

How To Import Data From A New Table In An Existing Data Source

Over time, the structure of a database (or Excel workbook for that matter) may change and new tables will be added. If that is the case and you want to import data from a new table in a database that already has a connection to the PowerPivot workbook, follow the steps below to add the new table. These steps also work for adding data from an Excel workbook. The difference is that you skip steps 4 and 5 for Excel workbooks.

1. Open the PowerPivot window in the workbook (that has an existing connection) that you want to add a table to.

2. Design tab ⇒ Existing Connections button.

3. On the Existing Connections dialog box, click on the database that has the tables that you want to add, then click the Open button.

4. On the Import data screen select how you want to add the data, either by tables or by query, then click Next.

5. If you selected the table option, go to step 6 below. If you selected the query option, follow step 5 to the end, in Exercise 5.2, Import Data From A Database Using A Query.

6. On the Select Tables and Views screen, select the tables that you want to add, then create any filters that are necessary.

7. Click Finish. You will see the new tables in the PowerPivot window. Save the changes.

FILTERING AND SORTING DATA

In addition to learning how to sort and filter the data in tables in the PowerPivot window, you will also learn about the following:

- ☑ How to change data types
- ☑ Formatting data
- ☑ Filtering differences between PowerPivot and Excel
- ☑ Freeze columns
- ☑ Rearrange columns
- ☑ Change column widths
- ☑ Hide and unhide columns

CHAPTER 8

Overview

Now that you have learned how to import data from a variety of data sources, linked to data in Excel worksheets, pasted and appended data, it is time to learn how to format, filter and sort the data in preparation of analyzing the data in the PowerPivot window. These features do not interfere with creating relationships or using the data to create pivot tables.

In Chapter 5 you learned how to filter records while using the Table Import Wizard to select which records in a table would be imported into PowerPivot. Filtering records in the PowerPivot window basically works the same way. Filtering records in the PowerPivot window is useful when you need to analyze the data in the table in PowerPivot in preparation to create pivot tables. Often, the columns used to filter data are good choices for slicers for a pivot table.

Changing Data Types

Once the data is imported into PowerPivot you may need to change the data type for some columns of data in a table in the PowerPivot window. Chapter 3 explained the formatting options on the Home tab in the PowerPivot window. They are used to change the data type. During the data import process, the data being imported is mapped to one of the data types listed below.

① Text
② Decimal Number
③ Whole Number
④ Currency
⑤ Date
⑥ True/False

> If the data being imported does not match or cannot be converted to one of the data types listed above, the column of data will not be imported.

If you select a data type that is not compatible with the data in the column, you will see a warning message similar to the one shown in Figure 8-1.

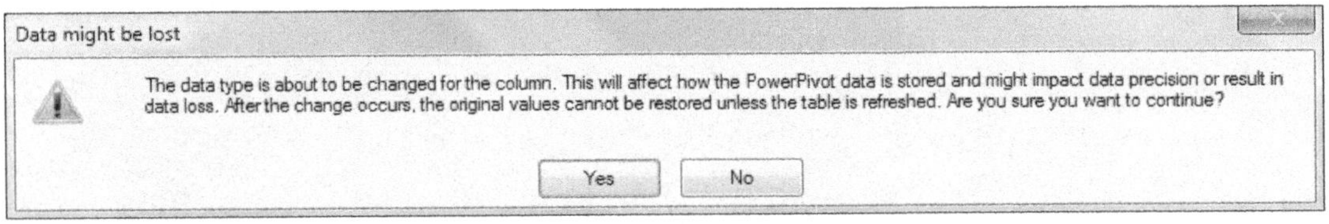

Figure 8-1 Data might be lost message

Not all of the data types are available for each column of data. The options shown in the Data Type drop-down list in the Formatting group are the options that are most compatible with the data in the selected column. Keep in mind that just because a data type is in the drop-down list does not mean that the data in the column, can or should be converted to one of the data types in the list.

For example, Figure 8-2 shows the Whole Number data type options for the Shipper ID field shown on the left of the figure. If you selected the True/False option, you would see the warning message shown above in Figure 8-1.

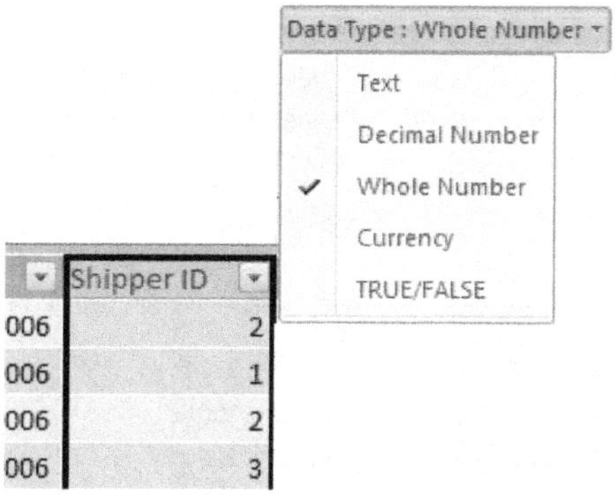

Figure 8-2 Whole Number data type options

Figure 8-3 shows the Text data type options and the data in the Ship Name column. If you selected the Currency data type, you would see the warning message shown in Figure 8-4. This message lets you know why the column of data could not be converted to the data type that you selected.

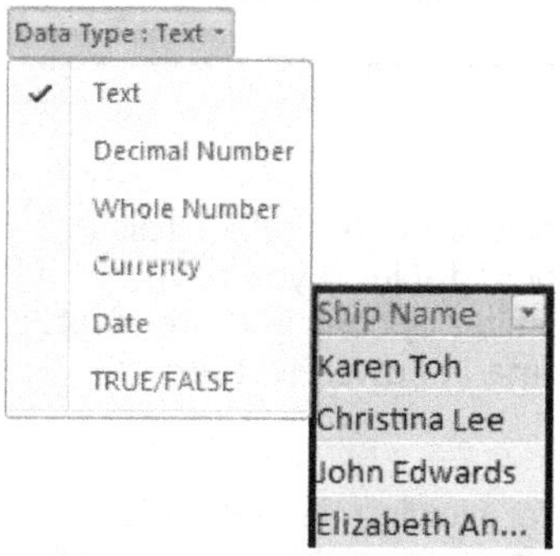

Figure 8-3 Text data type options

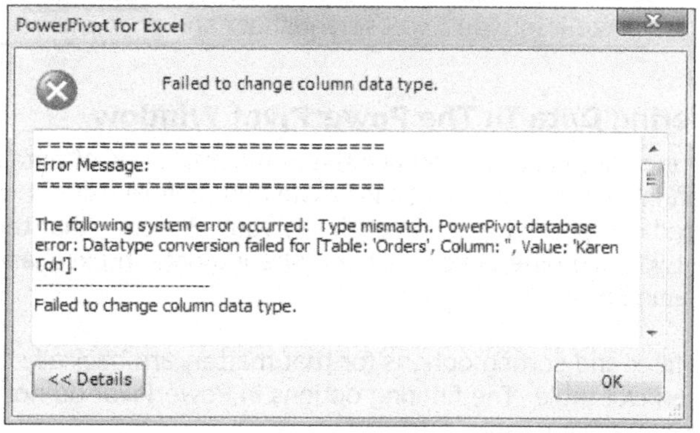

Figure 8-4 Failed change of data type message

Formatting Data

If the reason that you want to change the data type is because you want to see data in a slightly different format, it may be a better choice to change how the data is formatted. The difference between changing the data type of a column and changing the formatting of a column is that the data in the column is not physically changed if it is formatted. Formatting a column just changes the way that the data is displayed.

Figure 8-5 shows columns of data that have the Whole Number data type with each of the available formatting options. The column heading name is the formatting option that is applied to the data in the column.

Figure 8-6 shows columns of data that have the Date data type with some of the available formatting options. The column heading name is the formatting option that is applied to the data in the column.

General	Decimal Number	Whole Number	Currency	Accounting	Percentage	Scientific
17	17.00	17	$17.00	17.00	1,700.00 %	1.70E+001
25	25.00	25	$25.00	25.00	2,500.00 %	2.50E+001
26	26.00	26	$26.00	26.00	2,600.00 %	2.60E+001

Figure 8-5 Whole Number formatting options

M D YYYY	MM DD YYYY	Weekday Month DD YY	M D	M D YY Time	Month YYYY
4/12/2004	04/12/2004	Monday, April 12, 2004	4/12	4/12/04 12:00 AM	April, 2004
2/14/2004	02/14/2004	Saturday, February 14, 2004	2/14	2/14/04 12:00 AM	February, 2004
2/12/2004	02/12/2004	Thursday, February 12, 20...	2/12	2/12/04 12:00 AM	February, 2004
3/1/2004	03/01/2004	Monday, March 01, 2004	3/1	3/1/04 12:00 AM	March, 2004

Figure 8-6 Dates with different formatting options

No Printing From The PowerPivot Window
You cannot print from the PowerPivot window. If the PowerPivot table does not have more than one million rows (Excels row limit), you can copy the data in the PowerPivot table and paste it into an Excel spreadsheet and print the data from Excel.

Filtering Data In The PowerPivot Window

Filtering data is used to reduce the number of rows of data that are displayed in the table. This is helpful when you want to analyze the data before using it to create a pivot table. If you have filtered data in an Excel spreadsheet, you will notice that there are less filter options in PowerPivot. The two main differences between filtering data in Excel and filtering data in PowerPivot are explained below.

The filter and sorting options for that matter, are basically only useful for viewing the data in a PowerPivot table. The filtering options in PowerPivot do not have any effect when the data is used to create a pivot table.

① Excel has more **OPERATORS** then PowerPivot, but I suspect that this will change in the future. Figure 8-7 shows the filter operators for a Number field in Excel. Figure 8-8 shows the filter operators for a Whole Number field in PowerPivot. Figure 8-9 shows the filter operators for a Date field in Excel. Figure 8-10 shows the filter operators for a Date field in PowerPivot. Notice that PowerPivot only supports the equals and not equal operators for dates, while Excel supports a variety of operators for dates.

② **CUSTOM FILTER** Select this option when the filter options on the shortcut menu shown in Figure 8-8 are not sufficient enough to create the filter that you need in PowerPivot. Selecting this option in Excel opens the dialog box shown in Figure 8-11. Selecting this option in PowerPivot opens the dialog box shown in Figure 8-12. The first thing that I noticed was that the Custom Filter dialog box in PowerPivot does not support the **OR** operator. This leaves less ways that PowerPivot data can be filtered.

Using The (Select All) Filter Option In PowerPivot
This option is checked by default, as illustrated in Figure 8-8. It causes all of the options below it to also be checked by default. If you clear this option all of the options below it are also cleared. This is helpful when you only want to use a few of the options to filter the data because you can select them one by one.

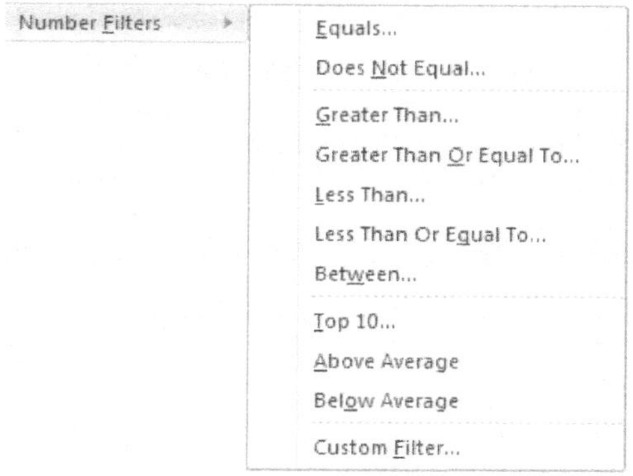

Figure 8-7 Excel Number operators

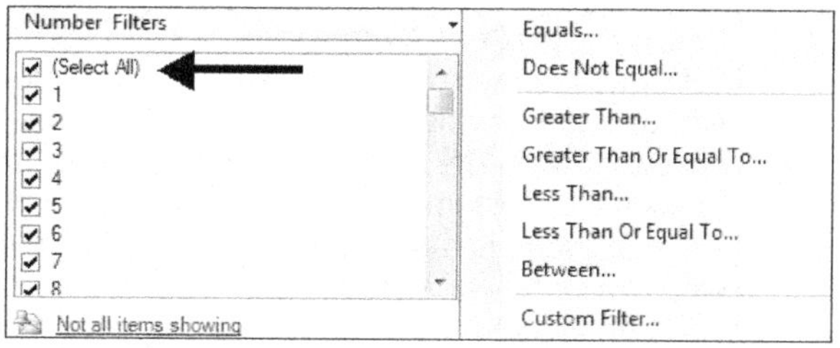

Figure 8-8 PowerPivot Whole Number operators

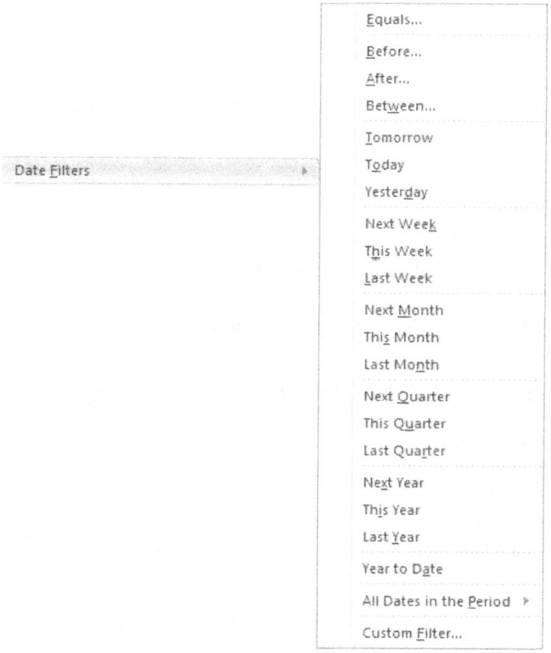

Figure 8-9 Excel date operators

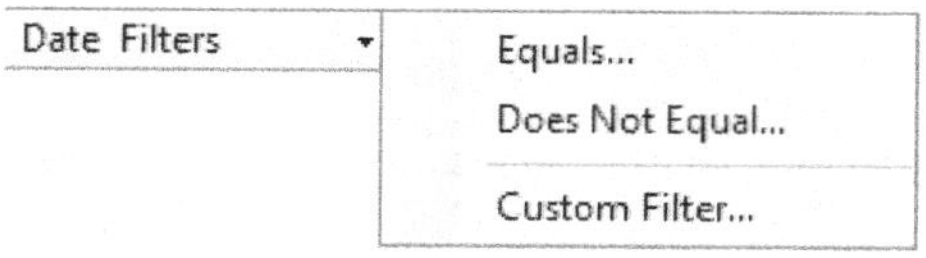

Figure 8-10 PowerPivot date operators

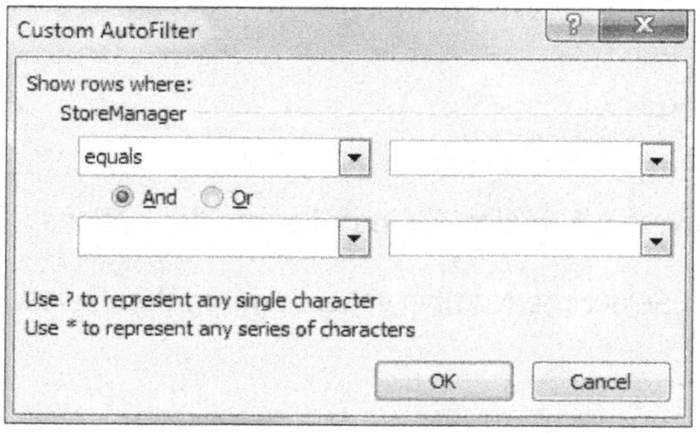

Figure 8-11 Excel Custom Auto Filter dialog box

Figure 8-12 PowerPivot Custom Filter dialog box

> **Using PowerPivot Operators**
> Select an operator when the filter options below the operator type starting with (Select All), as shown earlier on the left side of Figure 8-8, will not handle your needs. All of the operators open the Custom Filter dialog box. The difference between selecting an operator to open the Custom Filter dialog box instead of selecting the Custom Filter option on the shortcut menu is that the operator is selected by default on the Custom Filter dialog box when it is opened, as shown in Figure 8-13. Compare this dialog box to the one shown above in Figure 8-12.

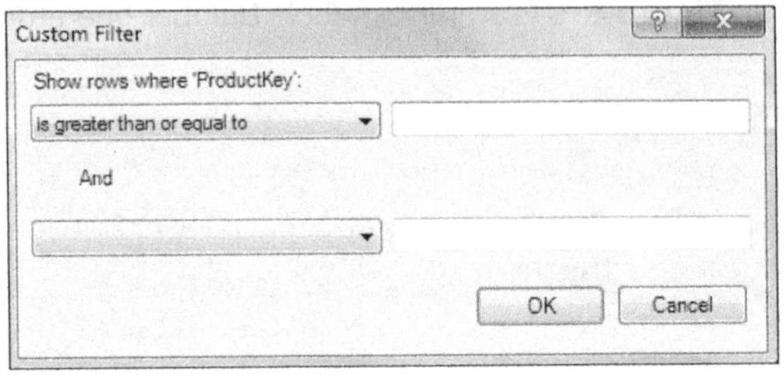

Figure 8-13 Custom Filter dialog box opened by selecting an operator first

Exercise 8.1: Using Filters In PowerPivot

In this exercise you will learn how to filter data in a PowerPivot table by filtering the Stores table to only show stores in the United States that have less than 30 employees that are still open.

1. Save the E7.1 workbook as `E8.1 Filter Data`, then open the PowerPivot window.
2. Select the filter list for the Region Country Name column, then clear the (Select All) option.
3. Scroll down the list and select United States, as shown in Figure 8-14, then click OK.

   Notice that the table now displays 220 rows of data instead of 326 rows.

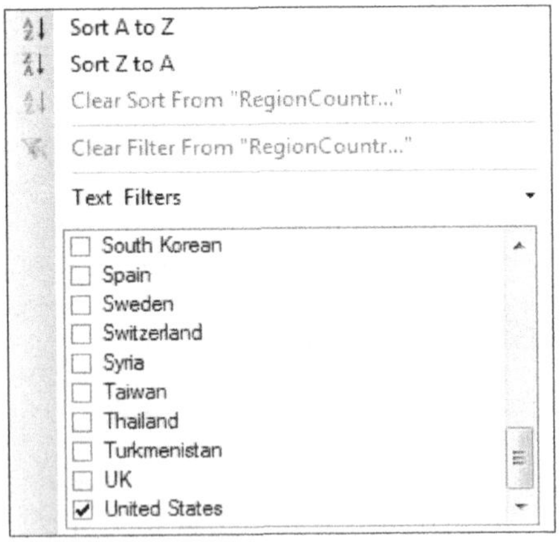

Figure 8-14 Region Country Name filter options

4. Open the filter list for the Employee Count column. Select the Number Filters option, then select the Less Than operator.

5. Type `30` in the field, as shown in Figure 8-15, then click OK.

   Notice that the table now displays 161 records.

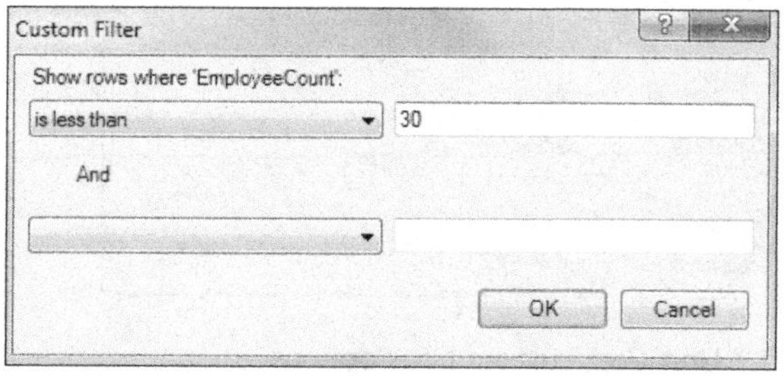

Figure 8-15 Employee Count column custom filter options

6. Open the filter list for the Close Date column, then clear the (Select All) option.

7. Check the (Blanks) option illustrated in Figure 8-16.

   In this exercise this means that the store is still open.

   Click OK, then save the changes.

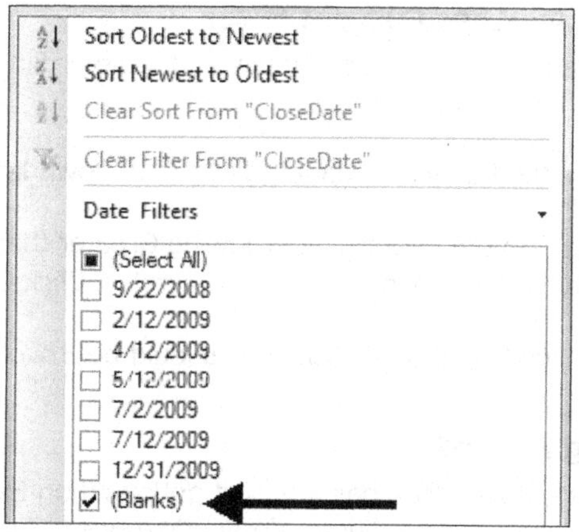

Figure 8-16 (Blanks) option illustrated

Based on the filters that you created, there are 149 stores in the United States that are open and have less than 30 employees.

Exercise 8.2: Creating Custom Filters

In this exercise you will create a custom filter to only display records with a Unit Cost between $1 and $100 and a Discount Quantity between 3 and 4.

1. Save the E6.1 workbook as `E8.2 Custom Filters`.

2. Open the PowerPivot window.

3. Open the Unit Cost filter drop-down list, then select the **BETWEEN** operator.

4. Type `1.00` in the field across from the Greater than or equal to operator. Type `100.00` in the field across from the Less than or equal to operator. You should have the options shown in Figure 8-17.

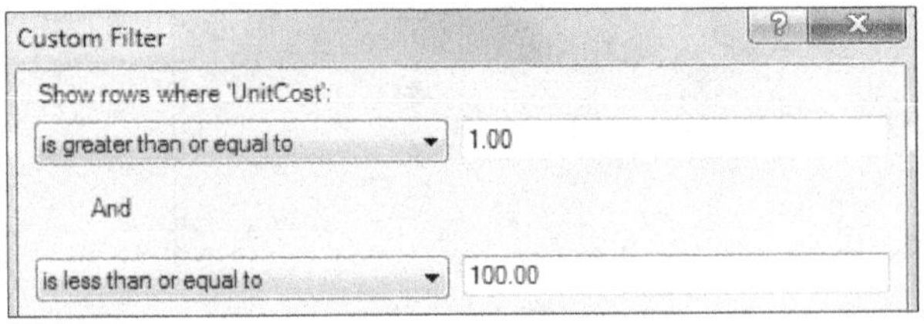

Figure 8-17 Unit Cost custom filter options

5. Click OK. Notice that the number of records has been reduced to 1.2 million from over 2 million. Save the changes.

Create Another Custom Filter

In this part of the exercise you will add another filter to only display records with a Discount Quantity between 3 and 4.

1. Open the Discount Quantity filter drop-down list, then select the Between operator.
2. Type 3 in the field across from the Greater than or equal to operator. Type 4 in the field across from the Less than or equal to operator. Click OK.
3. The number of rows displayed should be 316,772. Save the changes.

Sorting Records

Like filters, PowerPivot has less sort options than Excel. The sort options that are available are to sort a column in ascending or descending order. Currently, only one column in the PowerPivot table can be sorted on at a time. If you sort on Column A, then sort on Column C, the sort from Column A is removed, then the table is sorted on Column C. Sorting the data in a PowerPivot table does not have any effect when the data is used to create a pivot table.

Exercise 8.3: Using The Freeze Option

As you read in Chapter 3 Table 3-7, the Freeze option will move the selected columns to the far left of the table. These columns will always be visible without having to scroll. If you have used the Freeze Panes option in Excel, you will notice that the Freeze option in PowerPivot only supports freezing columns. Freezing rows is not supported.

Usually, tables in a database have many, if not all of the ID fields as the first fields in a table, as shown in Figure 8-18. That is a database standard. For end users, these fields are not the ones that will be used for analysis. In the table shown in Figure 8-18, it may be more helpful to move the Product Name, Standard Cost and List Price columns to the beginning of the table.

> **Freezing Columns**
> Once a column is frozen, you cannot move it to the right without removing the Freeze option.

Supplier IDs	ID	Product Code	Product Name	Description	Standard Cost	List Price	Reorder Level
10	3	NWTCO-3	Northwind Traders Syrup		$7.5	$10	25
10	4	NWTCO-4	Northwind Traders Cajun Seasoning		$16.5	$22	10
10	5	NWTO-5	Northwind Traders Olive Oil		$16.0125	$21.35	10
2;6	6	NWTJP-6	Northwind Traders Boysenberry Spread		$18.75	$25	25

Figure 8-18 ID columns at the beginning of the table

The steps below show you how to use the Freeze option to rearrange the column order.

1. Save the E6.7 workbook as `E8.3 Freeze option`.

2. Click on the Products tab in the PowerPivot window, then click on the Product Name column.

3. Home tab ⇒ View group ⇒ Freeze button ⇒ Freeze. The Product Name column should now be the first column in the table.

4. Select the Standard Cost and List Price columns.

5. Home tab ⇒ View group ⇒ Freeze button ⇒ Freeze. The Standard Cost and List Price columns should be the second and third columns in the table. The beginning of the table should look like the one shown in Figure 8-19.

Product Name	Standard Cost	List Price	Supplier IDs	ID
Northwind Traders Syrup	$7.5	$10	10	3
Northwind Traders Cajun Seasoning	$16.5	$22	10	4
Northwind Traders Olive Oil	$16.0125	$21.35	10	5
Northwind Traders Boysenberry Spread	$18.75	$25	2;6	6

Figure 8-19 Freeze option applied to three columns

Notice the black vertical line after the List Price column. This line is used to visually indicate which columns have the freeze option applied. Compare this table to the one shown earlier in Figure 8-18.

6. Scroll to the right until you see the Target Level column. You will still see the Product Name, Standard Cost and List Price columns on the left. Save the changes.

Rearranging The Column Order

This option is used to move the selected columns to another part of the table. If you have the need to change the order of the columns, follow the steps below.

1. Open the PowerPivot workbook that has the columns that you want to rearrange, then open the PowerPivot window.

2. Click on the column heading of a column that you want to move.

3. Drag the column heading to the right or left until it is in the location that you want, then release the mouse button.

4. Save the changes.

Hiding And Unhiding Columns

Having the ability to hide columns in a PowerPivot table that you currently do not need for analysis can be helpful. If you are not sure that a column of data should be deleted, hide it instead. The steps below show you how to hide and unhide columns, as well as view the hidden columns.

How To Hide Columns

1. Open the PowerPivot workbook that has columns that you want to hide, then open the PowerPivot window.

2. Click on the tab that has a column that you want to hide.

3. Right-click on the column that you want to hide ⇒ Hide Columns.

   You will see the options shown in Figure 8-20. The options are explained in Table 8-1.

   Select the option that corresponds to where you want to hide the selected column. The column will be hidden in the locations that you select.

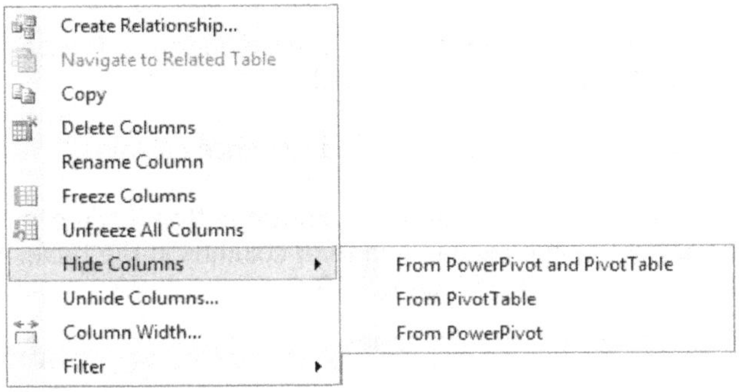

Figure 8-20 Hide Columns options

Option	Hides The Selected Column In The . . .
From PowerPivot and PivotTable	PowerPivot window and the PowerPivot Field List.
From PivotTable	PowerPivot Field List.
From PowerPivot	PowerPivot window.

Table 8-1 Hide Columns options explained

Hiding More Than One Column At The Same Time
There are two ways to hide columns on a tab in the PowerPivot window, as explained below.

① Design tab ⇒ Columns group ⇒ Hide and Unhide button. You will see the dialog box shown in Figure 8-21.
② To hide more than one adjacent column at a time, click on the left most column that you want to hide. Hold the left mouse button down, then drag the mouse to the right until all of the columns that you want to hide have a thick black border around them, as shown in Figure 8-22, then go to step 3 above in the "How To Hide Columns" section.

This dialog box provides the same functionality as removing check marks from columns in the PowerPivot window.

The benefit that this dialog box provides is the ability to hide a column in the pivot table.

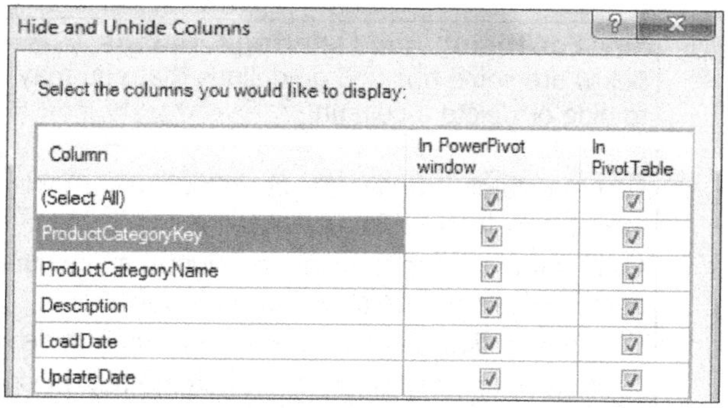

Figure 8-21 Hide and Unhide Columns dialog box

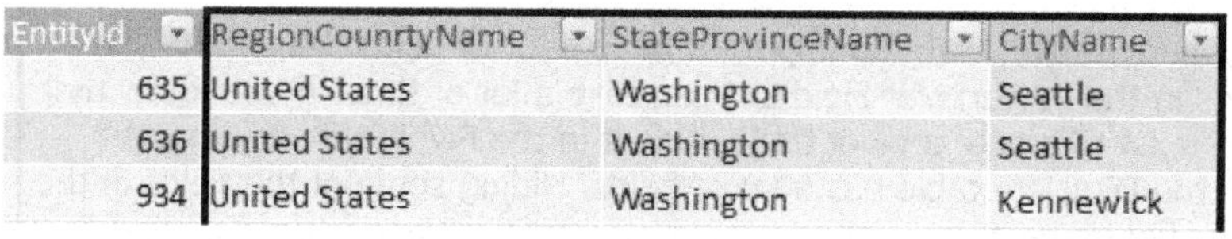

Figure 8-22 Multiple adjacent columns selected

How To Unhide A Column

There are two ways to open the Hide and Unhide Columns dialog box, as discussed below.

Option 1: Use The Option On The PowerPivot Ribbon

1. Open the PowerPivot workbook that has a column that you want to unhide, then open the PowerPivot window.

2. Design tab ⇒ Columns group ⇒ Hide and Unhide button. You will see the dialog box shown earlier in Figure 8-21.

3. Add a check mark to the column that you want to display (unhide), then click OK and save the changes to the workbook.

Option 2: Use The Column Shortcut Menu

1. Right-click on a column heading and select **UNHIDE COLUMNS**, as shown earlier in Figure 8-20.

2. Save the changes to the workbook.

Tips For Hiding And Deleting Columns
Below are some tips and guidelines that you may find helpful in deciding whether or not to hide or delete a column.

① If a column is deleted from a PowerPivot table, the data in the column is no longer available to be used in a pivot table.
② If you are going to delete a column, make sure that it is not a column that is needed to create a relationship with another table.
③ When in doubt about deleting a column, hide it instead.
④ Hide columns of data used to create relationships in the PivotTable section shown earlier in Figure 8-21. The reason to consider doing this is because these fields are rarely used to create a pivot table because the end user probably will not understand the values in the field.
⑤ As you have seen, many tables that you imported have a lot of fields. Having to sift through all of the fields in the PowerPivot Field List can take a lot of time. If you know that some fields will not be used to create a pivot table, hide it in the PivotTable column. As shown in Figure 8-23, the DimDate table has a lot of fields. Hiding some of the fields in the PowerPivot Field List would be helpful.

Figure 8-23 Fields in one table displayed in the PowerPivot Field List

CREATING RELATIONSHIPS

In this chapter you will learn about the following:

- ☑ Relational databases
- ☑ Primary key fields
- ☑ Types of relationships
- ☑ Relationship requirements
- ☑ Auto detection of relationships
- ☑ Manual creation of relationships
- ☑ Managing relationships

CHAPTER 9

Overview

Chapter 1 provided an overview of what relationships are. The ability to create relationships to join tables in PowerPivot and use the data to create pivot tables may be the number one reason that many people will use PowerPivot. This is because it is easier to create the relationship (a link between tables) then it is to use VLOOKUP. Relationships also allow for more robust analysis of the data then VLOOKUP provides. As if that is not enough reason to use PowerPivot, don't forget its ability to import millions of records (rows of data).

A relationship is a connection between two tables. Relationships are created between a column that the two tables have in common. Relationships between tables allow for a higher level of analysis because columns of data from different PowerPivot tables can be used to create one pivot table. Data in one table can be filtered by data in another table, which provides even more flexibility and control over the data that is displayed in a pivot table.

What Is A Data Model?

The previous section discussed relationships between tables of data in a PowerPivot workbook. Chapter 2 demonstrated from beginning to end how to get data from an external data source, import it into PowerPivot and then create a pivot table. Relationships between tables makes this possible without having to use the VLOOKUP function in Excel.

Relationships are based on tables in what is known as a data model. A data model is a list of tables with lines between them that point to the field in the table that they have in common. These lines represent the relationships between the tables. In Chapter 2 Figure 2-19, you saw a data model for the SalesOrderHeader, SalesTerritory and ShipMethod tables. In this data model, there are two relationships, as listed below.

① The TerritoryID field is used to create the relationship between the SalesOrderHeader and SalesTerritory tables.
② The ShipMethodID field is used to create the relationship between the SalesOrderHeader and the ShipMethod tables.

Data modeling is an important concept to understand because even though PowerPivot has an auto detection option, at best, it only works on database tables that are imported into PowerPivot at the same time. You will see examples of this later in this chapter.

Types Of Data Models

There are two types of data models, as explained below.

① The **PHYSICAL DATA MODEL** is how the data is stored in a tables in a database. This model is often referred to as the "back end" model because it is usually not displayed to end users. This is the model that IT people work with the most. This structure is the most efficient way to store the data because other then the key field, the data is not duplicated in several tables. Instead, relationships are created between the tables so that all of the data in a database can be accessed. This is known as **DATA NORMALIZATION**.
② The **LOGICAL DATA MODEL** is what end uses see and are most familiar with. This model is often referred to as the "front end" model because it only displays the fields that end users need to get their job done.

For example, to enter new orders, an end user would use an application that has a series of data entry screens (also known as the interface) to enter new orders. This interface would show the customer name and address fields, but not the CustomerID field. If Excel was used to enter orders and a customer placed multiple orders, the spreadsheet would have the same customer name and address in several rows. This is known as **DATA DENORMALIZATION.**

Data Normalization vs Data Denormalization

In the previous section you read about the two types of data models, physical and logical. Normalization is the process of removing redundancy in the tables in a database. In the logical data model example discussed above, the redundant fields would be the customer name and address fields. When normalized, these fields would be put into a new table and the order fields would be put into two other tables. Interestingly enough, this data redundancy is what the logical data model requires. This is known as denormalization.

While normalization requires more tables to be created in a database to store the information, the file size of the database is smaller then if all of the data for each order was stored in one table.

How PowerPivot Handles Data
PowerPivot uses what is known as a **COLUMNAR DATABASE.** This type of database reduces the need to figure out a normalization strategy. If a value occurs more than once in a column, it is only saved once in the database. The other occurrences of the value in the column are replaced with a reference to the first occurrence. For example, in a customers table a zip code will often appear more than once in the zip code column. The first occurrence of the zip code is saved. The remaining occurrences of the same zip code are replaced with a pointer to the first location in the column that has the zip code.

Relational Databases

The reason that PowerPivot tables can have relationships created between them is because there is at least one column of data in each table that has related data, like there are in databases, thus the term "Relational Databases". Yes, this is a complicated topic and there are a lot of books on the concepts associated with relational databases and how to create them, so I won't bore you with all of the details, but please hear me out and don't skip this section. Creating relationships in PowerPivot and creating relationships in a database have a lot in common.

While databases are not the primary focus of this chapter, it is important that you understand a little more than the fundamentals that were covered in Chapter 1. Now you will learn how all of the components fit together. The reason that you need to understand databases is because they will probably be the foundation of the pivot tables that you will create and modify using data in PowerPivot tables. If you have never created a database, or have very little experience creating them, the next few sections in this chapter will be your crash course in databases and relationships. Figures 9-1 and 9-2 illustrate the layout of two tables.

Orders			
Order ID	**Order Date**	**Order Amount**	**Cust ID**
1000	1/2/2005	$263.99	48
1001	1/2/2005	$322.45	57
1002	1/3/2005	$196.00	3
1003	1/4/2005	$124.99	48

Figure 9-1 Orders table layout

Orders Detail		
Order ID	Product ID	Quantity
1000	43	4
1000	76	2
1001	76	3
1001	10	2
1003	10	1
1004	25	3

Table Name
Field Names
Records

Figure 9-2 Orders Detail table layout

Primary Key Fields

Primary Key fields and ID fields are terms that are used interchangeably. I prefer to use the term ID field because primary key fields in databases usually have "ID" as part of the field name.

> ID is short for identification. It is jargon that the computer programming community uses to reference a field that can be used to link the data in one table to the data in another table. In PowerPivot, linking two tables is known as a relationship.

The majority of the tables in the sample databases that you use in the this book have at least one ID field. Hopefully, you will find that this is also true out in the real world. The reason ID fields are used is because by design they provide a way for each record in the table to have a unique way to be identified.

I have taught several database classes and almost without fail, this topic causes a lot of confusion. For some reason, people want to create links on string (text) fields. Please don't do that for tables in databases. It can cause you problems. However, creating relationships in PowerPivot tables on text fields is acceptable, in particular from data that does not come from a database.

If you needed to create a pivot table that showed all of the orders and what items were on each order, you would need a way to link the Orders and Orders Detail tables. Think of creating relationships as having the ability to combine two or more tables "virtually" and being able to display the result of this "virtual linking" in a pivot table.

This linking is different then linking to tables in Excel that you learned about in Chapter 7. The linking covered in Chapter 7 provides the ability to keep the data in a PowerPivot table up to date with the data in the spreadsheet that it is linked to. The relationship linking covered in this chapter refers to the process of joining two tables based on data in a column that the tables have in common.

In Figures 9-1 and 9-2 above, the common ID field is the Order ID field. If you look at the data in the Orders Detail table, you will see that some records have the same Order ID number. That's okay. This means that some customers placed orders with more than one item. Each record in the Orders Detail table represents one item that a customer ordered. If you were to "virtually" join the data in the tables shown in Figures 9-1 and 9-2 above, the virtual table would look like the one shown in Figure 9-3.

This "virtual" join is what happens when tables are **LINKED** (have a relationship). If all of this data was stored in one table instead of two, at the very minimum, the Order Date and Order Amount fields would be repeated for every record that is in the Orders Detail table. Repetition of data is why this information is stored in two tables in a database instead of one. It is considered poor database table design to have the same information (other than fields that are used to join tables) stored in more than one table.

Orders				Orders Detail		
Order ID	Order Date	Order Amount	Cust ID	Order ID	Product ID	Quantity
1000	1/2/2005	$263.99	48	1000	43	4
1000	1/2/2005	$263.99	48	1000	76	2
1001	1/2/2005	$322.45	57	1001	76	3
1001	1/2/2005	$322.45	57	1001	10	2
1002	1/3/2005	$196.00	3			
1003	1/4/2005	$124.99	48	1003	10	1
				1004	25	3

Figure 9-3 Virtually joined tables

Usually if you see a record in the Orders Detail table, like Order ID 1004 shown above in Figure 9-3, or any child table that is in a **PARENT-CHILD RELATIONSHIP**, there is a problem with the data in at least one of the tables because all of the records in the child table should have at least one matching record in the parent table. Parent tables are used to get data from a child table.

Types Of Database Relationships

To create an orders report would require at least two tables in a database. These tables are linked by a common field, the Order ID field. This field is what connects (joins) data from both tables and allows you to use data from both tables seamlessly.

An ID field in the Orders table is how you find the matching record (known as a **ONE-TO-ONE RELATIONSHIP**) or records (known as a **ONE-TO-MANY RELATIONSHIP**, which is the most popular type of relationship) in another table. These are the two most common types of relationships. The **MANY-TO-MANY RELATIONSHIP** is a third type of relationship. It is not used as much as the other two relationship types.

PowerPivot Relationships

Relationships between two PowerPivot tables sort of works in the reverse of what you may be use to. They work in a **MANY-TO-ONE RELATIONSHIP** because the table on the left is the "many" table and the table on the right is the "one" table. The good thing though is that you can create relationships with PowerPivot tables in the traditional "one" table being on the left and the "many" table being on the right. Fortunately, if you create a relationship between tables that PowerPivot wants in the opposite direction, you will see the message shown in Figure 9-4.

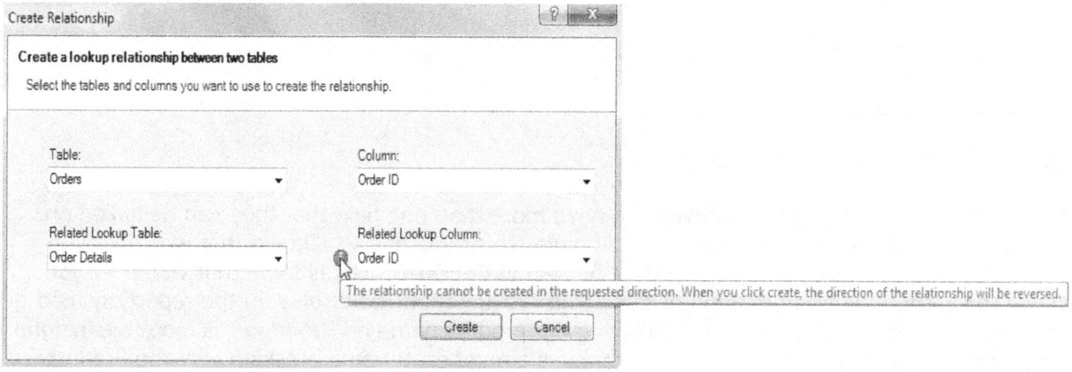

Figure 9-4 Relationship warning message

How Relationships Work

More than likely, many of the pivot tables that you create will require data from more than one table in a database. Pivot tables that display the equivalent of a Product List report will probably only use one table, so there is no linking involved. For reports that require two or more tables, the tables need to be linked by creating a relationship between them.

When you need to view or modify existing relationships, you can do so by opening the Manage Relationships dialog box. Even though some of the time the relationships that you need are automatically created in PowerPivot for you, it is important to understand what is going on behind the scenes, as they say.

The best way to understand the basic concept of creating relationships between tables is to look at the records or a portion of the records in the tables that need to have a relationship created. When you create a pivot table that is based on data that you are not familiar with, you should take the time to look at the data in the tables.

Figures 9-5 and 9-6 show the records in the Employee and Employee Addresses tables in a database.

The field that these tables have in common is the Employee ID field.

This would be the primary field used to create a relationship between these two tables.

Employee : Table

Employee ID	Supervisor ID	Last Name	First Name	Position	Birth Date	Hire Date
1	5	Davolio	Nancy	Sales Representati\	12/8/1972	3/29/1991
2		Fuller	Andrew	Vice President, Sale	2/19/1969	7/12/1991
3	5	Leverling	Janet	Sales Representati\	8/30/1971	2/27/1991
4	5	Peacock	Margaret	Sales Representati\	9/19/1973	3/30/1992
5	2	Buchanan	Steven	Sales Manager	3/4/1975	9/13/1992
6	5	Suyama	Michael	Sales Representati\	7/2/1963	9/13/1992
7	5	King	Robert	Sales Representati\	5/29/1972	11/29/1992
8	5	Callahan	Laura	Inside Sales Coordi	1/9/1974	1/30/1993
9	5	Dodsworth	Anne	Sales Representati\	1/27/1976	10/12/1993
10	2	Hellstern	Albert	Business Manager	3/13/1968	3/1/1993
11	10	Smith	Tim	Mail Clerk	6/6/1973	1/15/1993
12	10	Patterson	Caroline	Receptionist	9/11/1979	5/15/1993
13	2	Brid	Justin	Marketing Director	10/8/1977	1/1/1994
14	13	Martin	Xavier	Marketing Associate	1/30/1975	1/15/1994
15	13	Pereira	Laurent	Advertising Speciali:	12/9/1970	2/1/1994

Record: 1 of 15

Figure 9-5 Employee table data

Employee Addresses : Table

Employee ID	Address1	Address2	City	Region	Country	Postal Code
1	507 - 20th Ave. E.		Port Moody	BC	Canada	V3D 4F6
2	908 W. Capital Way	Suite 100	Coquitlam	BC	Canada	V3H4J7
3	722 Moss Bay Blvd.		Vancouver	BC	Canada	V6M 8S9
4	4110 Old Redmond Rd		Richmond	BC	Canada	V5S 6H7
5	14 Garrett Hill		London		UK	SW1 8JR
6	Coventry House		London		UK	EC2 7JR
7	Edgeham Hollow	Apt #243	London		UK	RG1 9SP
8	4726 - 11th Ave. N.E.		New Westmins	BC	Canada	V7J 5G5
9	7 Houndstooth Rd.		Nottingham		UK	WG2 7LT
10	13920 S.E. 40th Street		Burnaby	BC	Canada	V2C 8H3
11	30301 - 166th Ave. N.E.	Apt #3D	North Vancouve	BC	Canada	V3K 2G9
12	16 Maple Lane		West Vancouve	BC	Canada	V3L 5S3
13	2 impasse du Soleil		Haguenau	Bas-Rhin	France	67500
14	9 place de la Liberté		Schiltigheim	Bas-Rhin	France	67300
15	7 rue Nationale		Strasbourg	Bas-Rhin	France	67000

Record: 15 of 15

Figure 9-6 Employee Addresses table data

Depending on the table structure, tables can have more than one field that they can be linked on. An example of this would be the Orders Detail table. This table has an ID field that would let you link it to the Orders table. There is a Product ID field in the Orders Detail table that would let you retrieve the Product Name from another table (the Product table) to display on the report, instead of displaying the Product ID number. Displaying the product name on the report is more meaningful then displaying the Product ID field, which contains a number. If you are asking why the Product Name is not stored in the Orders Detail table, there are two reasons, as explained below.

① The ID field takes up less space then the Product Name field, thereby keeping the size of the Orders Detail table and any other table that stored the Product Name field instead of the Product ID field smaller.

② If a Product Name has to be changed for any reason, it only has to be changed in the Product table. Every report that the Product Name field is used on would automatically be updated with the revised product name. If the product name was stored in the Orders Detail table, every record in the Orders Detail table that had that product name would have to be changed, as well as, any other table that stored the product name. That would be a lot of extra work.

Keys And Columns

Earlier in this chapter you read about relational databases and primary key fields. Key fields or columns are the same as the other fields in a database table or column in a PowerPivot table. The difference is that they do not contain data that is usually displayed. Their purpose is to allow data in two or more tables to be joined and displayed together.

PowerPivot uses slightly different terminology then databases do for key fields, as explained below.

① **PRIMARY KEY** (PK) is a unique value that is used to select a specific row of data in the table. (1)

② **FOREIGN KEY** (FK) is a unique value that is used to select a specific row or rows of data in another table. Foreign keys are used to link to the primary key field in another table. Usually, foreign keys are in main tables and are used to get data from a lookup table.

③ **ALTERNATE KEY** is a secondary unique value that is used to select a specific row of data in the table. (1)

④ **COMPOSITE KEY** is a unique value that is created by combining the values in two or more fields. PowerPivot does not support this type of key, but you can create a calculated field to combine the data in two or more columns in PowerPivot.

(1) Either of these keys can be used to select a row in the table. For example, a Products table can have a Product ID field and a Manufacturers Code ID field. Both of these fields are in the table and each product has both fields, which have unique values. These ID fields can be used to look up data in other tables.

Relationship Requirements

While having the ability to create relationships between tables sounds like it will provide a lot more flexibility, it can be time consuming to set up the relationships that you need. In addition to the requirements PowerPivot has for creating relationships that are explained below, the size of the PowerPivot workbook can grow a lot because you may have to import the same table of data more than once to be able to create all of the relationships that are needed to create a complex pivot table.

① **MANY-TO-MANY RELATIONSHIP** PowerPivot does not support this type of relationship, but DAX functions can be used to imitate this type of relationship.

② **ONLY ONE RELATIONSHIP PER TABLE** Tables can contain more than one column of data that a relationship can be created for, but PowerPivot can only handle one relationship between the same two instances of tables. An instance in this scenario is one copy of a table. If you need to create more than one relationship for the same table, you have to import the table into PowerPivot again and give the second table a different name.

③ **COMPATIBLE DATA TYPES** The column in each table that will be used to create a relationship must have the same or compatible data type. For example, the primary key column in the main table can have a whole number data type and the lookup column in the second table can have a text data type. In this example, the lookup column could not be a date, currency or True/False data type.

④ **COMPOSITE KEYS** PowerPivot does not support this type of key being used to create a relationship. Instead, you have to combine the values in the columns before creating the relationship. There are two options for combining values: 1) Import the columns and create a calculated column using DAX or 2) Combine the values in the data source and import the new column.

⑤ **SELF JOINS** In many types of databases, this is known as a **RECURSIVE JOIN**. This type of join uses one column in the table to reference data in another column in the same table. PowerPivot does not support this type of relationship.

⑥ **ONLY ONE RELATIONSHIP PER COLUMN** A primary key column cannot be used to create multiple relationships. If you need to use the same column in a table to create a relationship with another table, you would have to import another instance of the table into PowerPivot and use the copy to create the second relationship.

⑦ **UNIQUE COLUMN OF DATA FOR EACH TABLE** A table used to create a relationship must have one column that has a unique value that can be used to identify each row of data. (2)

⑧ **UNIQUE LOOKUP COLUMN** The values in the look up column must be unique. (2)

(2) This means that no two rows of data can have the same value in this column. At most, there can only be one empty cell in this column. This is because empty cells are the same as a blank cell, which is a data type. [See Chapter 5, PowerPivot Supported Data Types]

Relationship Creation Options

There are two ways that relationships can be created in PowerPivot: Using the Auto detection option and creating relationships manually. They are explained below.

Using Auto Detection

As the name implies, this type of relationship is automatically created. The Table Import Wizard will automatically try to import relationships between tables that are stored in the database. If you want auto detection to create the majority of relationships, make sure that the column names are the same or very similar in the tables that will be imported into PowerPivot. This also applies to data being imported from different data sources. The process that auto detection uses, is as follows.

① Data types for the columns that will possibly be used to create a relationship must have a whole number or text data type.

② If the column names are the same or similar and have an acceptable data type. Examples of similar names are Customer ID, Cust ID and Customer_ID.

> **Turning Off Auto Detection**
> Before you import tables of data, click the **DETECTION** button on the PowerPivot tab on the Excel ribbon, if you want to create all of the relationships yourself. This will stop relationships from being created during the import process.

When creating a pivot table from PowerPivot data, you may see the message illustrated in Figure 9-7. This message lets you know that you may need to create a relationship. If you click the **CREATE** button, PowerPivot will look at the tables in the PowerPivot window to see if any additional relationships can be created. During this process you will see the dialog box shown in Figure 9-8.

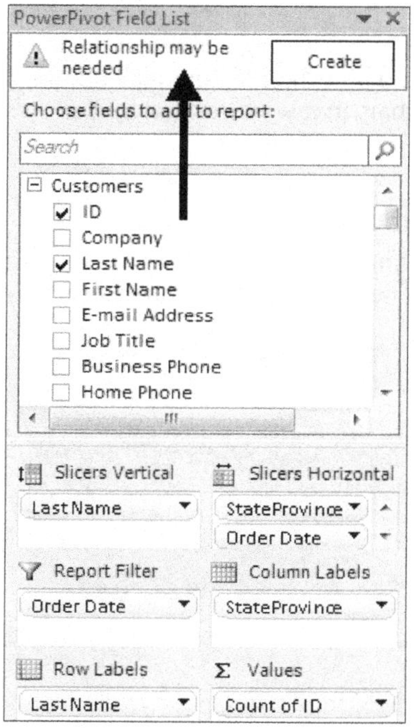

Figure 9-7 Prompt to create more relationships illustrated

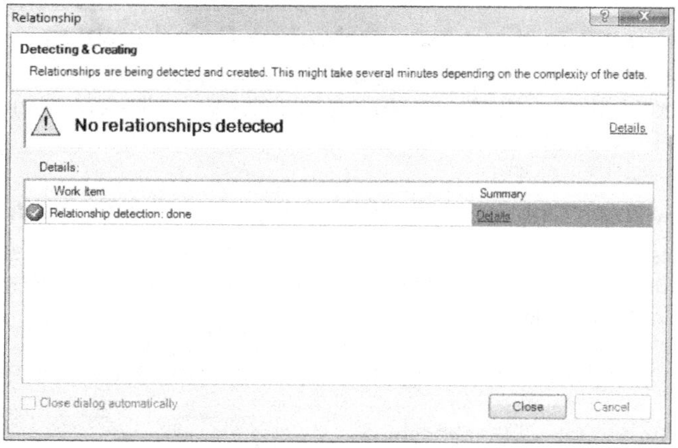

Figure 9-8 Relationship dialog box for Detecting & Creating relationships

In Exercise 2.2 you saw the relationship warning message shown above in Figure 9-7 when you added a field from a table that was imported into the PowerPivot workbook after the pivot table in the workbook had already been created. This can happen for a few reasons including column names in the PowerPivot tables have been renamed.

Relying On Auto Detection
While it may seem like a good idea to let auto detection find and create the relationships that you need, it is very possible that the process that auto detection uses may not detect a relationship that you need. If you find that to be the case, you will have to create the relationship manually.

Creating Relationships Manually

This option is used to create relationships that were not automatically created. This will also be helpful if the data has **NAMED SETS** because auto detect does not recognize named sets and their fields. Named Sets are covered in Chapter 13.

INFERRED RELATIONSHIPS This is a type of auto detection relationship that occurs when two relationships are manually created between three tables. For example, if Relationship #1 and 2 below were created manually, relationship #3 is inferred and will automatically be created.

Relationship #1 Orders table and Products table
Relationship #2 Products table and Product Types table
Relationship #3 Orders table and Product Types table

Exercise 9.1: View Auto Detection Relationships

What may not be clear is that some relationships created by the auto detection feature may not be correct. Why, I am not sure. In this exercise you will view relationships that were created by the Auto Detection feature.

View Auto Detection Relationships In The E6.7 Workbook

In Exercise 6.7 you imported a customer table from a text file and an order, order detail and product table from an Access database. The steps below show you how to view the relationships that were automatically created.

1. Open the E6.7 workbook, then open the PowerPivot window.
2. Design tab ⇒ Relationships group ⇒ Manage Relationships button.

   You should see the relationships shown in Figure 9-9.

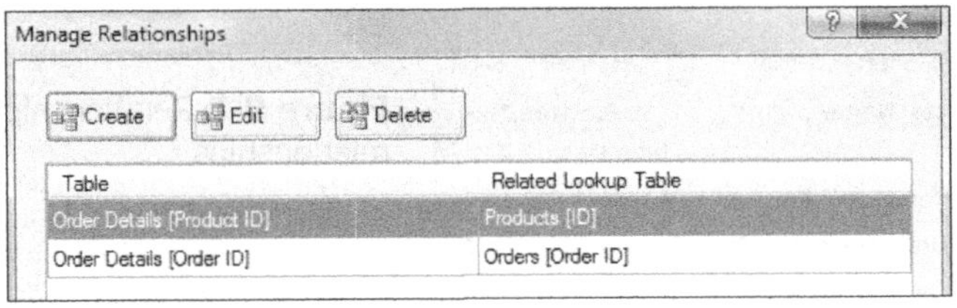

Figure 9-9 Exercise 6.7 relationships

Notice that the table in the Table column is the "many" table, meaning that there could be more than one row of data in the table that has the same matching record in the table in the Related Lookup Table column. If you are a programmer or have created databases, this is the complete opposite of how linking (relationships) work in databases.

View The Auto Detection Relationships In The E6.8 Workbook

In Exercise 6.8 you imported a customer, order, order detail and product table from an Access database. The steps below show you how to view the relationships that were automatically created.

1. Open the E6.8 workbook, then open the PowerPivot window.
2. Design tab ⇒ Relationships group ⇒ Manage Relationships button.

   You should see the relationships shown in Figure 9-10.

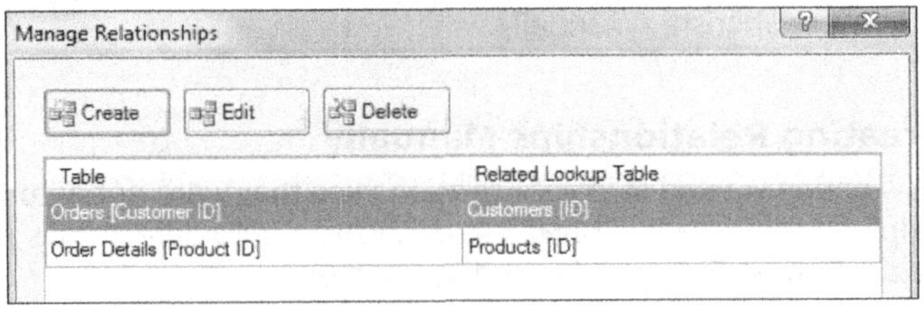

Figure 9-10 Exercise 6.8 relationships

In Exercise 6.7 and Exercise 6.8 the same data was imported into PowerPivot tables. Notice that the relationships that were created are different (See Figures 9-9 and 9-10 above). The difference is that in Exercise 6.7 no relationship was created between the Orders and Customers tables. The Customer table was imported from a text file and the other tables were imported from a database. Text files do not have or save relationship information like databases do.

Relationships Are Not Automatically Created When Importing From The Same Database Twice

In Exercise 6.8, no relationship was created between the Orders and Order Details tables, even though both tables were imported from the same database. They were imported at different times. This lets you know that PowerPivot does not check tables already in the workbook during the import process to see if there are any relationships that can be created between the tables already in the workbook and the tables that are being imported into the database, even if they are from the same database. Keep this in mind if you have to import from the same database more than once in the same workbook. When fields from tables that do not have a relationship are added to a pivot table, you will see a message stating that a relationship may need to be created.

Exercise 9.2: Create Your First Relationship

In this exercise you will create a relationship between data that was imported from a table and data that was imported from a view into PowerPivot tables.

The relationships shown in Figure 9-11 were created automatically when the data was imported.

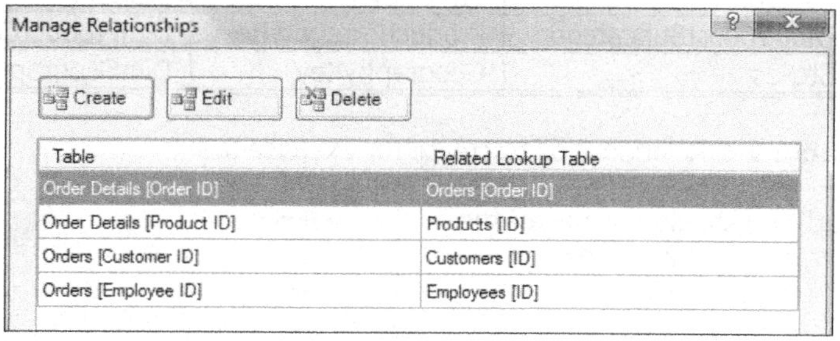

Figure 9-11 Auto detection created relationships

1. Save the E5.4 workbook as `E9.2 Create a relationship`.
2. In the PowerPivot window, Design tab ⇒ Relationships group ⇒ Create Relationship button.
3. Open the Table drop-down list and select the Order Subtotals table, then open the Column drop-down list and select the Order ID field.
4. Open the Related Lookup Table drop-down list and select the Orders table, then open the Related Lookup column drop-down list and select the Order ID field.
5. You should have the options shown in Figure 9-12. Click the Create button, then save the changes.

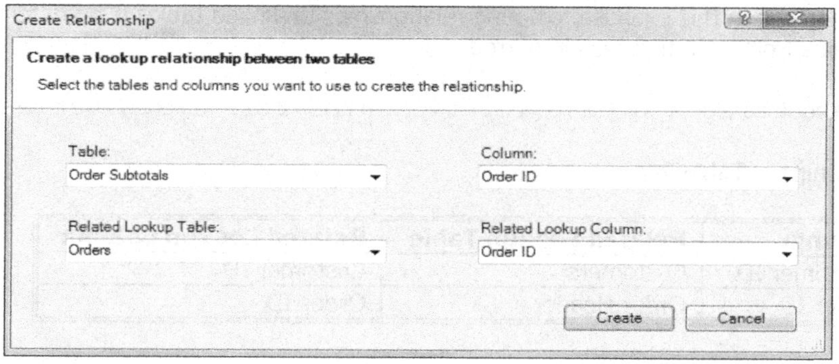

Figure 9-12 Create Relationship dialog box

Exercise 9.3: Create Relationships In A PowerPivot Workbook

In Exercise 6.9 you created a PowerPivot workbook that contains tables from two databases and two Excel workbooks. During the import process, five relationships were automatically created. Not all of the relationships were created automatically that will be needed to create a pivot table in Chapter 11. In this exercise, you will create the rest of the relationships.

1. Save the E6.9 workbook as `E9.3 Create three relationships.`

2. Create the relationships in Table 9-1.

Table	Column	Related Lookup Table	Related Lookup Column
FactSales	StoreKey	Stores	StoreKey
DimProductSubcategory	ProductCategoryKey	DimProductCategory	ProductCategoryKey
Stores	GeographyKey	DimGeography	GeographyKey

Table 9-1 Relationships to create for Exercise 9.3

3. You should have all of the relationships shown in Figure 9-13.

   Save the changes.

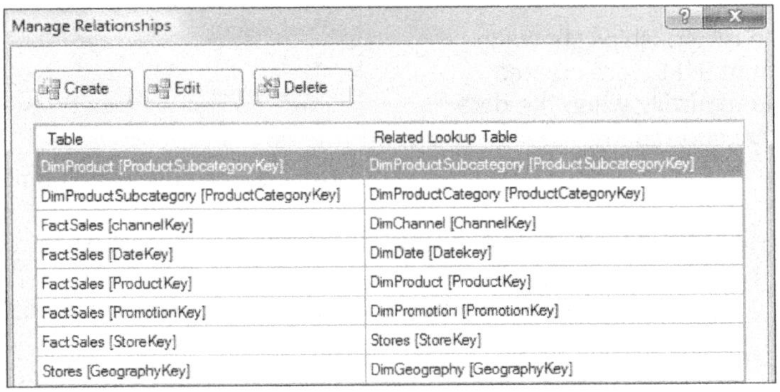

Figure 9-13 E9.3 workbook relationships

Exercise 9.4: Creating Relationships For Linked Tables

In Exercise 7.3 you created three linked tables from data on a single worksheet in a workbook. Even though the linked tables have a common field, no relationships were automatically created. I do not know if it is a bug that auto detection does not work for PowerPivot tables that are linked to Excel tables. As you will see in this exercise, creating relationships on linked tables is no different then creating relationships from data that was imported.

1. Save the E7.3 workbook as `E9.4 Create relationships for linked tables.`

2. Create the relationships in Table 9-2.

Table	Column	Related Lookup Table	Related Lookup Column
Order Header	Customer ID	Customers	Customer ID
Order Details	Order ID	Order Header	Order ID

Table 9-2 Relationships to create for Exercise 9.4

3. Save the changes.

4. Click on the Customers tab, then open the Create Relationship dialog box. You will see the message shown at the bottom of Figure 9-14. This message is letting you know that based on the tables currently in the PowerPivot workbook that there are no more relationships can be created with the Customer table.

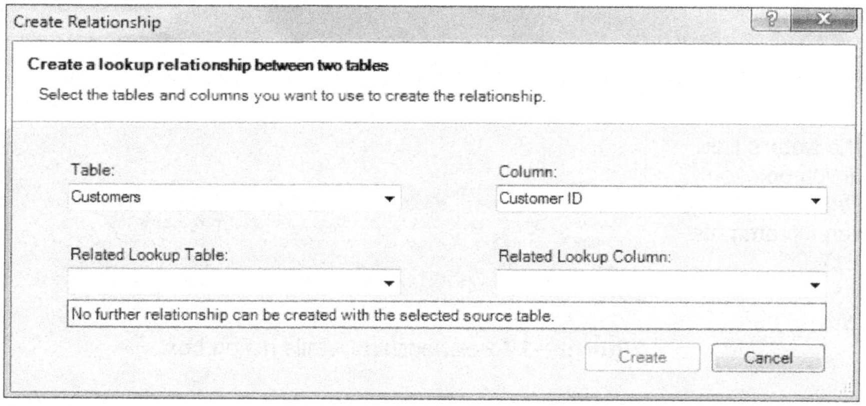

Figure 9-14 Relationship message

Seeing The Power Of Relationships

There is nothing stopping you from creating a pivot table that uses fields from PowerPivot tables that do not have relationships. PowerPivot will create a pivot table based on the fields that you select. The three tables that you created relationships for in Exercise 9.4 is a good example.

If you opened the E7.3 workbook (which has the same tables as the E9.4 workbook), you could create the pivot table shown in Figure 9-15, using data from all three tables, even though there are no relationships were for the tables.

At first glance, the pivot table may look okay, until you realize that the values in the Sum of Quantity column are all the same.

The other thing that you should notice is the message at the top of the PowerPivot Field List which states that a relationship may need to be created.

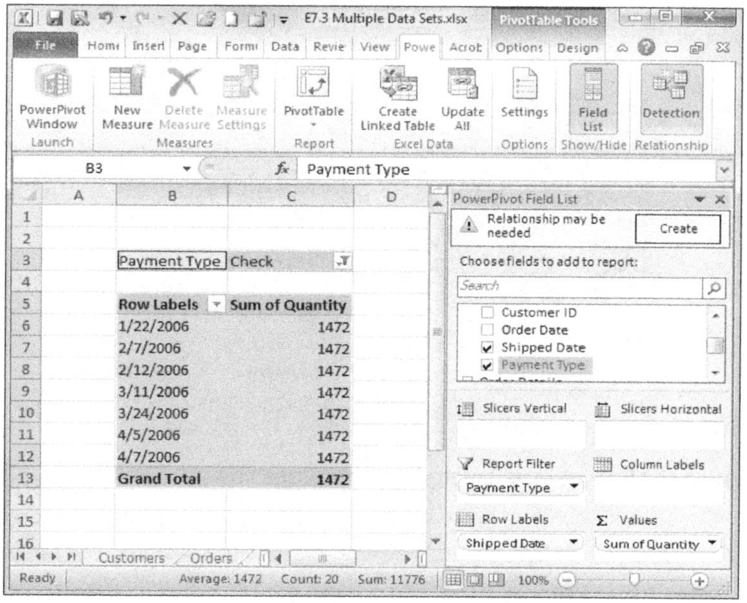

Figure 9-15 Pivot table created from tables without a relationship

If you clicked the **CREATE** button, shown above in Figure 9-15, you would see the dialog box shown in Figure 9-16.

Ironically, PowerPivot did not find any tables that it could create a relationship for.

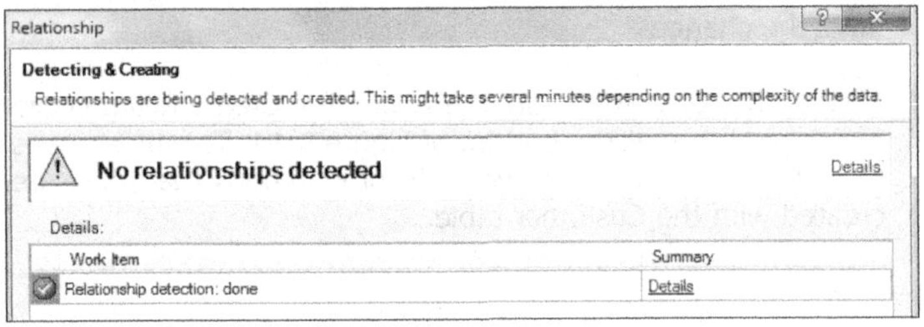

Figure 9-16 Relationship dialog box

If you clicked on the Details link at the top of the dialog box you would see the explanation of why no relationships were created, as shown in Figure 9-17.

Interesting, don't you think?

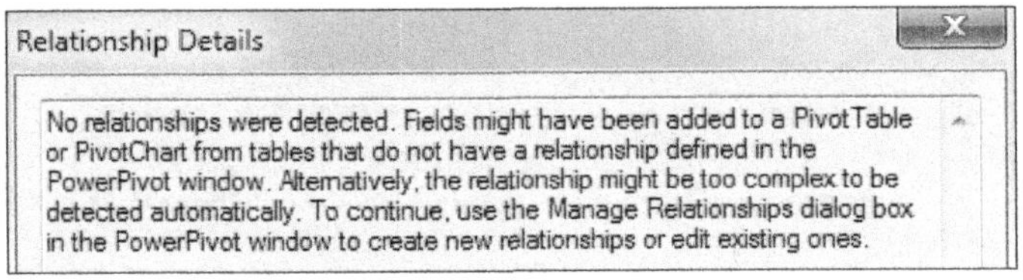

Figure 9-17 Relationship Details dialog box

If you created the same pivot table in the E9.4 workbook, the values in the Sum of Quantity column would be calculated correctly, as shown in Figure 9-18.

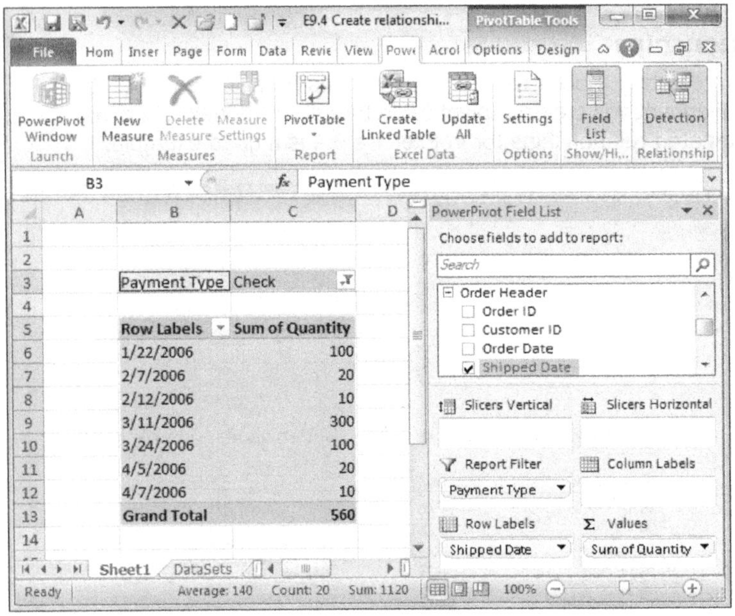

Figure 9-18 Pivot table created with relationships

CREATING DATA ANALYSIS EXPRESSIONS (DAX)

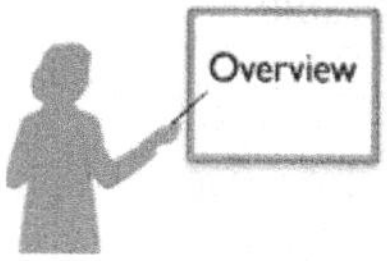

In this chapter you will learn about the following:

☑ DAX function types
☑ DAX operators
☑ DAX expressions (formulas)
☑ DAX function categories
☑ Filter functions
☑ Context evaluation

Overview

DAX is a new programming language that extends the functionality of formulas created in Excel. DAX allows for more complex analysis, calculations and grouping. If you are familiar with creating formulas in Excel, you should find the syntax of DAX formulas easy to learn. For example, like Excel formulas, DAX formulas start with an equal sign and is followed by an expression or function. Unlike Excel, DAX does not use cell references or ranges in formulas. DAX references column and table names. DAX also uses operators and values.

While some DAX expressions are similar to Excel formulas and functions, they are different because they are designed for groups of data, like columns, instead of single cells of data. This means that the DAX expression that you create in the Add Column in a PowerPivot table is automatically applied to every cell in the column. In Excel, each cell can have a different formula. If you want all of the cells in a column in Excel to have the same formula, you have to use the Fill option to add the formula to each cell in the column.

DAX has functions that Excel does not have. This includes functions that provide the ability to perform analysis on tables of data that are related and functions to perform dynamic analysis. Prior to PowerPivot, this type of analysis required learning a multi-dimensional programming language.

DAX Function Types

The reason that you create formulas is because the result of the formula needs to be placed on the pivot table that you are going to create. As you saw in Chapter 2, you can create pivot tables that do not require you to create formulas. DAX has over 130 functions that fall into one of the two types: Calculated columns, which are discussed below or measures, which are covered in Chapter 13.

Calculated Columns

These are the expressions that are similar to Excel formulas. A calculated column is added to an existing PowerPivot table and is based on data in tables. When you create this type of expression, it is automatically applied to every cell in the column. You cannot create a different formula for different rows in a PowerPivot table. After you imported data into a PowerPivot table you should have seen that the last column in the table has the heading **ADD COLUMN**. This column is automatically added to the table. This is where you create a calculated column. The column heading can be renamed. You can create as many calculated columns as needed.

Figure 10-1 shows the formula to concatenate (combine) the First Name and Last Name fields. This is a popular expression to create because the first and last names are often stored in separate fields in a table in a database, but need to be displayed on the pivot table as one column.

Figure 10-2 shows a calculated column that calculates the line item total for each product ordered.

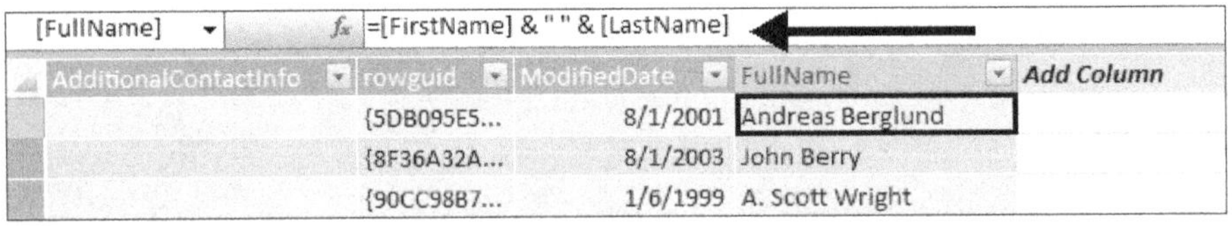

Figure 10-1 Calculated column formula that combines two fields illustrated

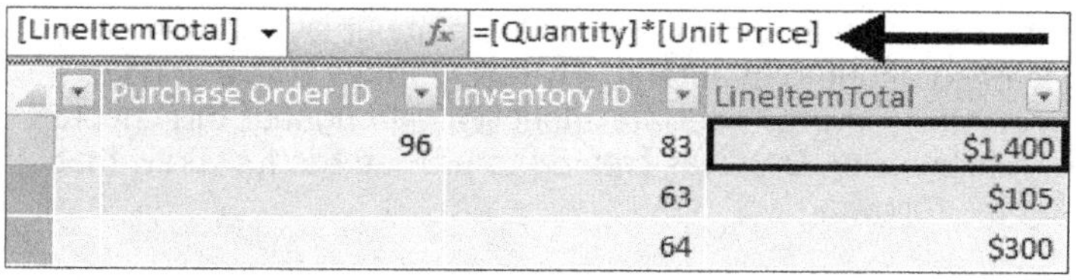

Figure 10-2 Calculated column for a line item total formula illustrated

Column Name Requirements

By default when you create a new calculated column, the name of the column defaults to **CALCULATEDCOLUMN1**. The column heading can be renamed, as long as the following conditions are met.

① The column name cannot have spaces at the beginning or end of the name. (1)

② The following characters cannot be used in the column name:
( ) [ ] { } < > = + ! $ % & ? * | / \ . , ; : ' (1)

③ Analysis Services reserved keywords are not used. (1)

④ Each column name must be unique in the workbook. This includes table names, measures or other calculated columns.

⑤ Any other column that uses the column that you are going to rename in its formula, has to be updated after the column is renamed.

(1)

This rule also applies to table names.

Excel Functions vs DAX Functions

DAX functions are based on Excel functions. This means that there are some features of the functions that are the same and some features of the functions that are different. Some of the differences and similarities are discussed below.

① DAX has lookup functions that are similar to the **ARRAY** lookup function in Excel. The difference is that the DAX functions require that the tables that will be used with the function have a relationship created between them.

② DAX functions only work with a column or table of data. Excel functions work with cells or a range of cells.

③ Some of the DAX functions use calculations that are based on a table of values for input or return a table of values. This means that DAX functions can reference columns and tables. Excel does not have any functions that return a table of values. The closest functionality that Excel has is that some of its functions can work with arrays.

④ DAX date and time functions return a **DATE TIME** data type. Excel date and time functions return a serial number that represents the data.

Why Is There A Need For DAX Formulas And Functions?

As you know, PowerPivot is an add-in for Excel. Add-ins in general add more functionality to the software that they were created for. In the case of PowerPivot for Excel, a lot of the formula functionality that it adds to Excel is beyond the capabilities that Excel formulas have.

This formula functionality includes context evaluation, which you will learn about later in this chapter and relationships, which you learned about in Chapter 9. Therefore, there was a need to create an environment that could support this (new to Excel) functionality. Throughout this chapter you will learn how to use some of this functionality. DAX was created to provide the functions that support these enhancements, including the following.

① Functions that can calculate a total for all years or all sales reps.
② Functions that can use tables as arguments to filter a another table.
③ Functions that can navigate table relationships.

DAX Syntax Overview

As you read at the beginning of this chapter, a DAX formula is very similar to an Excel formula. Understanding the terms explained below will help make learning DAX a little easier.

① **EXPRESSION** Is used to define a constant, reference to a column, a literal or Boolean test.
② **OPERATORS** Dictate what to do with the values in the expression, like add them together or compare one value to another. If necessary, PowerPivot will automatically convert string values to numbers and numbers to string values if an operator requires it. The operators that DAX supports are covered in the next section.
③ **FUNCTIONS** Are pre-built formulas that perform a variety of math and logic tests.
④ **VALUES** Are used in expressions and formulas. They can come from other formulas, a column in a table or the table itself.

DAX Operators

DAX supports the operators listed below. Some of the operators work the same as the operators in Excel.

① + Addition
② - Subtraction
③ * Multiplication
④ / Division
⑤ ^ Exponents
⑥ =, <>, >,>=,<,<= Comparison
⑦ & Concatenating text
⑧ && Creates an AND condition (2) (3)
⑨ ! NOT operator (2)
⑩ || Creates an OR condition (2) (3)

(2) This operator is used for evaluating Boolean expressions.
(3) DAX does not support the AND and OR operators in Excel. Instead use these operators.

DAX Expressions

DAX expressions are used in the PowerPivot window to create a wide range of calculations from summing a column of data to calculations that use data from more than one table. These formulas are saved in the PowerPivot table. In addition to these formulas, PowerPivot also has measures, which are formulas used to create pivot tables. Below are examples of DAX formulas. Throughout this chapter you will see more examples.

Example #1 =[Qty]*[Price]
This is a basic multiplication expression of two columns in the same table. (4)

Example #2 =Orders[Qty]*Orders[Price]
This expression provides the same result as the expression shown above in Example #1.
The difference is that this expression uses the **TABLE NAME[COLUMN NAME]** format. This format is known as **QUALIFYING A COLUMN**. This is the preferred way to create formulas because it avoids confusion over which table the column is in. Yes, it is a little more typing if you do not use the Auto Complete option discussed later in this chapter, but trust me, over time you won't notice the extra keystrokes and your life will be a little easier, especially when you need to know what table a column is in. (4)

Example #3 =(Orders[Order Total]<100) && Orders[Ship Time] = 2)
This expression checks to see if the value in the Order Total field is less than 100 and that the value in the Ship Time field equals 2. This expression by itself does not produce any output.
It would be the logical test part of an IF statement.

Example #4 =Billing[City] &", " & Billing[State] &" " & Billing[Zip Code]
This formula concatenates (combines) the values in three columns. This will put the City, State and Zip Code into the same new column in the PowerPivot table. (4)

(4) If this expression was placed in a calculated column, it would be calculated for each row in the PowerPivot table. This is known as **ROW CONTEXT** because all of the values used are in the same row in the table.

Example #5 =SUMX(REALATEDTABLE(Orders), Orders[Order Amount])
This formula is more advanced then the previous examples in this section. It uses data from two tables. This formula calculates the total of all orders for each customer. This formula would be placed in the Customer table. It adds (sums) all of the values in the Order Amount column in the Orders table for each customer and places that value in a calculated column in the Customers table.

The **SUMX** function calculates the sum of the Order Amount field for each customer order in the Orders table.

RELATEDTABLE is a DAX function that is used to find all of the rows in the second table, in the example above, the Orders table.

Auto Complete

Like Excel, the PowerPivot window supports the **AUTO COMPLETE** feature (also known as **INTELLISENSE**) for creating formulas in the formula bar. The feature is used to select qualified names of columns and tables. It will also display a list of functions. A benefit of using Auto Complete to create formulas instead of typing the formula, is that it will add some of the syntax for the function when you double-click on an item in the drop-down list.

Use Auto Complete For Field Names

If you want to use a field name in the current table, type a left bracket [in the formula bar.

Doing this will display a list of the field names in the drop-down list, as shown in Figure 10-3.

Double-click on the item in the drop-down list that you want to add to the formula that you are creating.

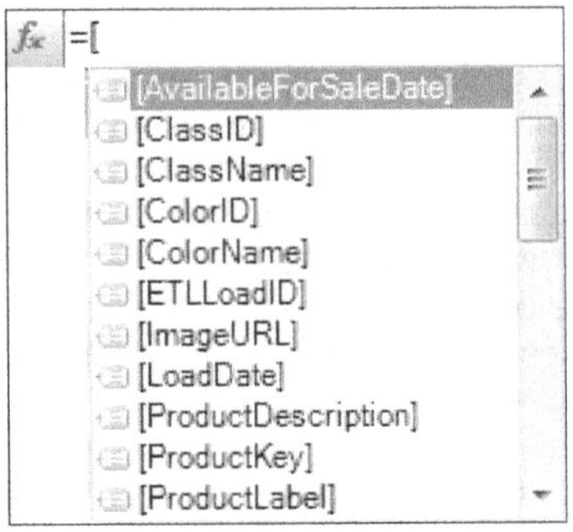

Figure 10-3 Auto Complete drop-down list

Use Auto Complete For Qualified Names And Functions

Because columns in different tables can have the same name, it is best to use what is known as **QUALIFIED NAMES**, which are the table name and the column name.

To display a list of qualified names, type the first letter of the table name or function, as shown at the top of Figure 10-4. The functions that start with the letter that you typed are displayed at the top of the drop-down list and the table names and field names are displayed after the functions.

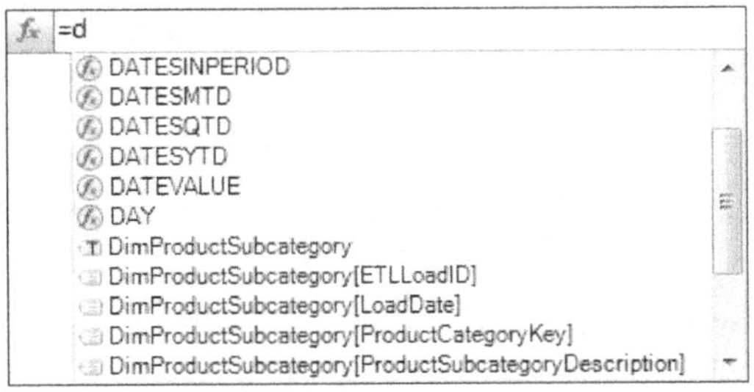

Figure 10-4 Functions and qualified names in the Auto Complete list

Table Names With Spaces In Formulas

Table names that have spaces will generate a syntax error if it is used in a formula. If you know that a table name that has spaces will be used in a formula, there are three options that I am aware of to resolve this, as listed below.

① Put the table name in single quotes like this, 'Transaction History'[StatusID].

② You can rename the table during the import process.

③ After the data is imported, you can rename the tab in the PowerPivot window.

The first option is the preferred option because you are not permanently altering the table. I will admit that I renamed a table used in this book. For this book, I renamed the Order Details table to be one word. I did it because I type all formulas manually. I am also not use to seeing table names with spaces (a throwback from my programming days <smile>).

You may want to rename the Order Details table. That way you can use the formulas in some of the exercises in this book exactly as they are displayed, without having to worry about adding additional syntax. If you do not want to rename the table, you have to put single quotes around the table name when using it in a formula.

Exercise 10.1: Use A DAX Operator In A Formula

In this exercise you will create a calculated column to calculate the line item total for each row in the Order Details table that you saw earlier in Figure 10-2.

1. Save the E5.4 workbook as `E10.1 Line item total formula.`
2. Display the Order Details table.
3. Click on a cell in the Add Column. Type `=[Quantity]*[Unit Price]`, as shown earlier at the top of Figure 10-2.
4. Press Enter. The calculated column will be created.
5. Right-click on the calculated column and select Rename Column.
6. Type `Line Item Total` as the column name, then press Enter. The calculated column should look like the one shown earlier in Figure 10-2. Save the changes.

DAX Function Categories

The eight categories of DAX functions are listed below in Table 10-1. Like the operators, DAX supports many of the Excel functions. There are some differences in how some of the functions work in DAX. Each of the categories is explained in the sections that follow.

DAX Function Category	Excel Functions Supported In DAX In The Same Category
Text	CONCATENATE, EXACT, FIND, FIXED, LEFT, LEN, LOWER, MID, REPLACE, REPT, RIGHT, SEARCH, SUBSTITUTE, TRIM, UPPER, VALUE
Date and Time	DATE, DATEVALUE, DAY, EDATE, EOMONTH, HOUR, MINUTE, MONTH, NOW, SECOND, TIME, TIMEVALUE, TODAY, WEEKDAY, WEEKNUM, YEAR, YEARFRAC
Logical	AND, TRUE, FALSE, IF, IFERROR, NOT, OR
Time Intelligence	There is no equivalent in Excel.
Information	ISBLANK, ISERROR, ISLOGICAL, ISNONTEXT, ISNUMBER, ISTEXT
Filter	There is no equivalent in Excel.
Statistical	AVERAGE, AVERAGEA, COUNT, COUNTA, COUNTBLANK, MAX, MAXA, MIN, MINA
Math and Trigonometric	ABS, CEILING, EXP, FACT, FLOOR, INT, LN, LOG, LOG10, MOD, MROUND, PI, POWER, QUOTIENT, RAND, RANDBETWEEN, ROUND, ROUNDDOWN, ROUNDUP, SIGN, SQRT, SUM, TRUNC

Table 10-1 DAX function categories

DAX also has functions that are used to create tables of data. However, the values in these tables cannot be used as the final value in a calculated column or measure. These tables of data can only be used as an argument in another function.

The **DAX FUNCTION REFERENCE** contains detailed information for the operators and functions used in DAX Analysis Expressions formulas. The link is http://technet.microsoft.com/en-us/ff452127.aspx.

> **Function Tips**
> Below are some tips that you may find helpful if this is your first time creating formulas. They refer to the syntax in the left column of the tables in this chapter that explain functions.
>
> ① Arguments enclosed in <> are required.
> ② Arguments enclosed in [ ] are optional.

Text Functions

The functions in this category are used with text data. Most of the functions are used to manipulate text (string) data. The majority of these functions are the same as the text functions in Excel. They can be used to search a field for specific characters, find the length of a field or concatenate fields. Some functions can be used to replace characters. Other functions convert the text to all uppercase as shown in Example #6, or all lowercase. The functions are explained in Table 10-2.

Function/Syntax	Description
BLANK()	Checks to see if the field is zero. If it is, a blank value is returned.
CONCATENATE(<text1>, <text2>)	Converts values to string fields if necessary, then combines the values in the text fields into one field. (5)
EXACT(<text1>, text2>)	Compares the values in the two fields and returns TRUE if the content in both fields is identical or returns FALSE if the content is not identical. (6)
FIND(<find_text>, <within_text> [,<start_num>])	Searches for the first place that the value is in the field. The <start_num> argument specifies where in the field to start the search. (6)
FIXED(<number>, <decimals> [,<no_commas>])	Rounds the value to the number of decimal places in the decimals argument, which has a default value of two. Use TRUE in the <no_commas> argument if you do not want decimal places. Use FALSE for this argument if you want decimals places in the value.
FORMAT(<value>,<format_string>)	Converts the value to text, based on the formatting in the <format_string> argument.
LEFT(<text>,<num_chars>)	Retrieves the specified number of characters from the beginning of the text string.
LEN(<text>)	Counts the number of characters in the field.
LOWER(<text>)	Converts all of the characters in the field to lower case letters.
MID(<text>,<start_num> [,<num_chars>])	Retrieves characters from the middle of the field, starting from the position in the <start_num> argument.
REPLACE(<old_text>,<start_num>, <num_chars> <new_text>)	Replaces part of the value in the <old_text> field, starting with the value in the <start_num> field with the content in the <new_text> for the number of characters specified in the <num_chars> field.

Table 10-2 Text functions explained

Function/Syntax	Description
REPT(<text>, <num_times>)	Repeats the content in the field, the number of times specified in the <num_times> argument.
RIGHT(<text>, <num_chars>)	Finds the last number of characters specified in the <num_chars> argument in the field.
SEARCH(<search_text>,<within_text> [,<start_num>])	Returns the number of the character where the specified character is found in the field. (6)
SUBSTITUTE(<text>, <old_text>, <new_text> [,<instance_num>])	Replaces the existing text with new text.
TRIM(<text>)	Removes all spaces in the field except the single space between words.
UPPER(<text>)	Converts all of the characters in the field to uppercase case letters.
VALUE(<text>)	Converts a text string that has a number to a number.

Table 10-2 Text functions explained (Continued)

(5)

CONCATENATE Function Limitation
In DAX, the CONCATENATE function only allows two arguments. Use the operator instead.

(6) This function is case sensitive.

Example #6 =UPPER(Customer[State])
This formula converts the value in the State field to all uppercase characters.

In Excel 2010, the Text function has been renamed to **FORMAT**. The FORMAT function can also be used with non text fields. An example of when this function would be useful is if you need to use part of a date field in a different format, as shown in Examples #7 and #8. These two examples convert the numeric values to a string (text) value.

Example #7 =FORMAT([Ship Date], "DDD")
This formula converts the day portion of the date to a three character day of the week, like Sun, Mon, Tue.

Example #8 =FORMAT([Ship Date], "MMM")
This formula converts the month portion of the date to a three character month, like Jun, Jul, Aug.

Exercise 10.2: Combine Two Columns Of Data

The formula in Example #4 shown earlier combines the data from three columns into a new column. A common use of this type of formula is to combine the first and last names into one column so that the name can be displayed together. That is the formula that you will create in this exercise.

1. Save the E10.1 workbook as `E10.2 Combine columns of data`.
2. Display the Customers table.
3. In the Add Column type `=[First Name} & " " & [Last Name]`, as shown in Figure 10-5. There is a space between the quotes. It will put a space between the first and last names when they are displayed.

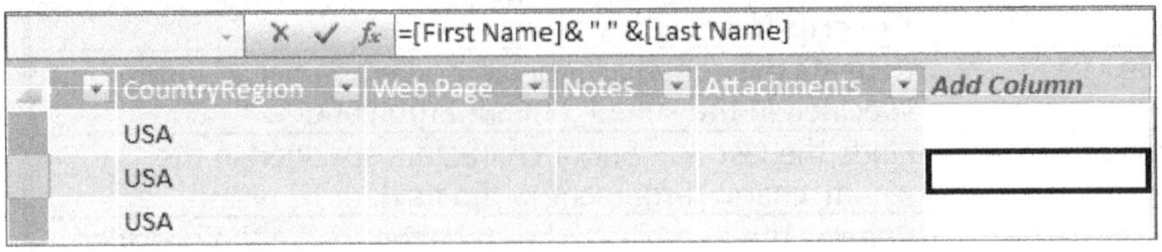

Figure 10-5 Concatenation formula

4. Press Enter. Rename the calculated column to `Customer Full Name.`

   The column should look like the one shown in Figure 10-6. Save the changes. This field can be used in a pivot table like any other column in the table, even though it contains the values from two other columns.

Customer Full Name
Anna Bedecs
Antonio Gratacos Solsona
Thomas Axen
Christina Lee

Figure 10-6 Calculated column

> **Sorting By Name**
> The exercise above taught you how to combine the first and last name for display purposes. You may have the need to sort the names in alphabetical order by last name, but display the names as shown above in Figure 10-6. If that is the case, create another calculated column, use the formula shown earlier in Figure 10-5, but put the last name field first, then the first name field. This is the column that you sort on and use the Customer Full Name column shown above in Figure 10-6 as the column that is displayed.

Exercise 10.3: Add Data From Another Table In The PowerPivot Workbook

As you saw in Exercise 10.2, two columns of data can be combined and that there are some formatting options available. Concatenating columns is not restricted to only using columns in the same table. You can concatenate columns of data from other tables in the PowerPivot workbook. Sometimes doing this makes the result of a sort in a table easier to understand.

For example, the sales reps name is not stored in the same table as the orders.

If you wanted to sort the Orders table by sales rep, you would have to sort on the Sales Person ID field, as shown in Figure 10-7.

Conta...	SalesPersonID	Territo...
41	268	4
154	268	4
364	275	5
8	275	5
364	275	5

Figure 10-7 Table sorted on an ID field

While sorting on the ID field works as intended, it is not as useful to the person viewing the data as it would be if the table was sorted on the sales reps name. In this exercise you will create a formula to add the sales reps name from a different table to the Orders table. This will let you view the data in the Orders table in a more meaningful way. In the workbook used in this exercise, the sales reps names are in the Employee table.

1. Save the E10.2 workbook as `E10.3 Add data from another table.`

2. Display the Orders table.

3. In the Add Column type `=Employees[First Name] & " " & Employees[Last Name]`, as shown in Figure 10-8.

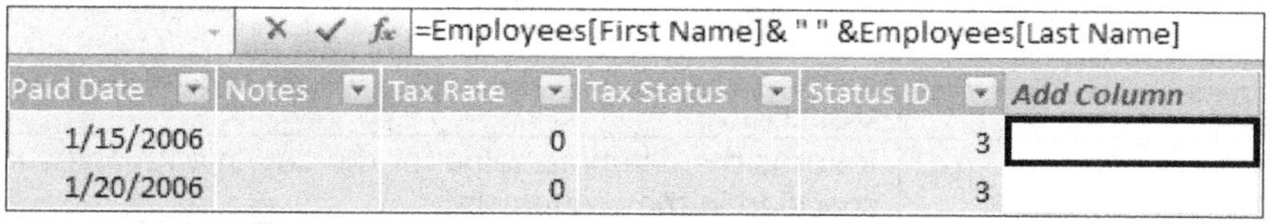

Figure 10-8 Formula to display data from another table

4. Press Enter. As you can see, there is an error in the formula. Clicking the **SHOW ERROR** button shown in Figure 10-9 will display the error message in Figure 10-10.

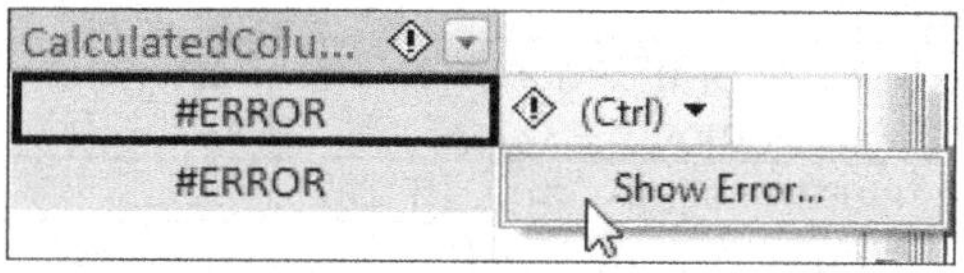

Figure 10-9 Show Error button

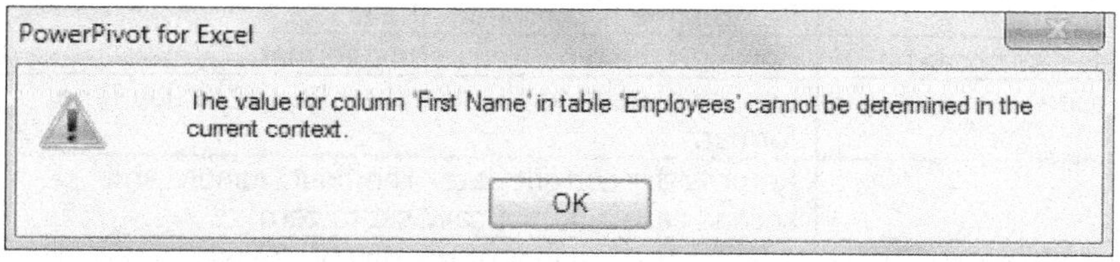

Figure 10-10 Context error message

At first you may think that there is no relationship between the Orders and Employees tables, but that is not the case. The message is telling you that PowerPivot cannot find a match for the current record in the Employees table. Later in this chapter you will learn about **ROW CONTEXT** and will fix this formula then.

5. Save the changes.

Date And Time Functions

The DAX date and time functions are similar to the Excel date and time functions. Some of the more popular date and time functions are MONTH, YEAR, NOW and TODAY. The functions are explained in Table 10-3.

Function/Syntax	Description
DATE(<year>, <month>, <day>)	Returns the datetime value for the day, month and year specified in the arguments.
DATEVALUE(<date_text>)	Converts the date to datetime format. This function uses the date/time settings on the computer that does the conversion.
DAY(<date>)	Returns the day number portion of the date.
EDATE(<start_date>, <months>)	Returns the date based on the months before or after the start date. (7)
EOMONTH(<start_date>, <months>)	Returns the last day of the month before or after the specified number of months. (7)
HOUR(<datetime>)	Returns the hour in military time. (0 to 23)
MINUTE(<datetime>)	Returns the minute from the field.
MONTH(<datetime>)	Returns the month from the field.
NOW()	Returns the current date and time.
SECOND(<datetime>)	Returns the second from the field.
TIME(<hour>,<minute>,<second>)	Converts the time to datetime format.
TIMEVALUE(<time_text>)	Converts the time that is in text format to datetime format.
TODAY()	Returns the current date. The hour, minute and seconds are automatically set to zero.
WEEKDAY(<date> [,<return_type>])	Returns the number of the day of the week. (1-7) The default is 1 for Sunday.
WEEKNUM(<date> [,<return_type>])	Returns the week number of the date. (1 to 52) The default value is 1 for the first week of the year.
YEAR(<date>)	Returns the 4 digit year from the date field.
YEARFRAC(<start_date>, <end_date> [,<basis>])	Calculates the fraction of the year based on the number of days between the two dates.

Table 10-3 Date and Time functions explained

(7) A positive <months> value retrieves a date after the <start date>. A negative <months> value retrieves a date before the <start date>.

Example #9 =YEAR([Ship Date])
If the Ship Date is 9/19/2010 in the formula above, the YEAR function will return 2010.

Exercise 10.4: Use The FORMAT, MONTH And YEAR Functions

If you have looked at any of the sample PowerPivot pivot tables or pivot charts that you downloaded, you probably saw one that had slicers, like the ones illustrated in Figure 10-11. The options in a slicer come from a column of data in a PowerPivot table.

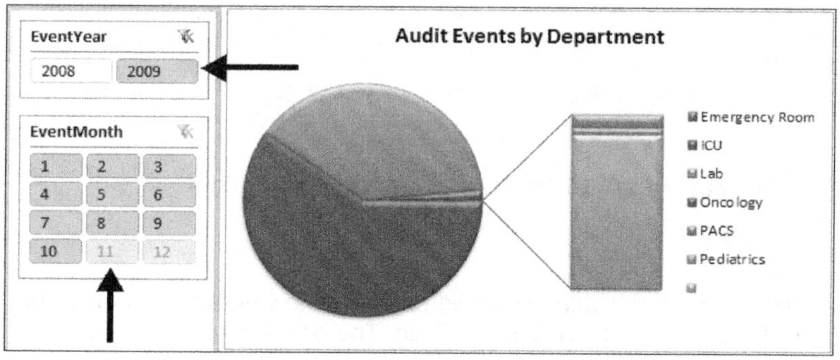

Figure 10-11 Slicers illustrated

If you have looked at data in the PowerPivot tables that you have used so far, you may have noticed that you did not see any columns that only have the year or month as the data. In order to create slicers like the ones shown above in Figure 10-11, portions of the date for each transaction needs to be in its own column.

In this exercise you will create three formulas, one for the order year, one for the order month number and one for the order month full name. This will let you create the slicers shown above in Figure 10-11.

1. Save the E5.5 workbook as `E10.4 Use the FORMAT, MONTH and YEAR functions.`

2. Display the Sales_SalesOrderHeader table.

Create The Order Month Number Formula

1. In the Add Column type `=month([OrderDate])`, as shown in Figure 10-12.

Figure 10-12 Month formula

2. Press Enter, then rename the calculated column to `Order Month.`

Create The Order Year Formula

1. In the Add Column type `=year([OrderDate]).`

2. Press Enter, then rename the calculated column to `Order Year.`

Create The Order Month Name Formula

In this part of the exercise you will use the FORMAT function to display the months full name. In Chapter 11 you will use this calculated column to display orders by the month name.

1. In the Add Column type `=FORMAT([OrderDate],"mmmm").`

2. Rename the calculated column to `Order Month Full Name.`

3. You should have the three new columns on the right side of Figure 10-13.

   Save the changes.

ModifiedDate	Order Month	Order Year	OrderMonthFullName
7/9/2001	7	2001	July
7/10/2001	7	2001	July
7/10/2001	7	2001	July

Figure 10-13 Month and year columns of data

Logical Functions

Most of the functions in this category check the value in a field to determine whether or not it meets the logical test condition. This test returns a value of True or False. The best known logical function is the **IF** function. The functions are explained in Table 10-4.

Function/Syntax	Description
AND(<logical1>,<logical2>)	Returns TRUE if both logicals evaluate to true. Returns FALSE if either logical evaluates to false.
FALSE()	Always returns the logical value FALSE.
IF(<logical_test>,<value_if_true>, <value_if_false>)	This function evaluates the logic test. If the test is true, the true portion of the expression is executed. If not, the false portion of the expression is executed.
IFERROR(<value>, <value_if_error>)	Returns the value specified if the expression returns an error, otherwise the value from the expression is returned.
NOT(<logical>)	Returns TRUE if the <logical> is FALSE. Returns FALSE if the result is TRUE.
OR(<logical1>,<logical2>)	Returns TRUE if either <logical> evaluates to true. Returns FALSE if both logicals evaluate to true.
TRUE()	Always returns the value TRUE. This function is used with a TRUE/FALSE data type field.

Table 10-4 Logical functions explained

AND and OR Functions Limitation
In DAX, these functions only allow two arguments. Use the AND and OR operators instead.

Example #10 =IF([Ship Date]>[Promise Date], "Shipped Late", "OK")
This formula will check to see if the Ship Date is greater than the Promise Date. The words "Shipped Late" will be placed in the cell in the calculated column if the formula evaluates as true. Otherwise, the word "OK" will be placed in the cell in the calculated column.

Exercise 10.5: Use The IF Function

In this exercise you will create a formula similar to the one shown above in Example #10.
The formula that you create will check to see if the shipped date is greater than the order date plus two days. If it is, add "Shipped Late" to the cell, otherwise, add "YES" to the cell.

The +2 adds two days to the order date. This part of the formula means that if the Order Date field contains 9/6/10 and the Shipped Date field contains 9/19/10, "Shipped Late" will be added to the cell for this row because Order Date +2 returns a date of 9/8/10, which is the expected date. Any date that is greater than 9/8/10 in this example is considered to be shipped late. You can use any number. +2 is just what I selected to demonstrate the concept with.

1. Save the E10.2 workbook as `E10.5 Use the IF function.`

2. Display the Orders table.

3. In the Add Column type `=IF([Shipped Date] > ([Order Date] +2), "Shipped Late", "Yes")`, then press Enter.

4. Rename the calculated column to `Order Shipped On Time`. The table should look like the one shown in Figure 10-14. Save the changes.

Figure 10-14 IF formula

Information Functions

The Information functions explained in Table 10-5 are often used as the first argument of the IF function because they return a true or false value. These functions are used to check to see if a field is blank, contains text or contains a number. The syntax for all of the functions is function name (<value>). The BLANK function refers to an empty cell.

Function	Returns TRUE If The Value Is . . .
ISBLANK	Blank.
ISERROR	Any error value.
ISLOGICAL	A logical Boolean value.
ISNONTEXT	Not text. A BLANK value is not considered text and returns TRUE.
ISNUMBER	A number. A BLANK value is not considered text and returns FALSE.
ISTEXT	Text. A BLANK value is not considered text and returns FALSE.

Table 10-5 Information functions explained

Exercise 10.6: Use The ISBLANK Function

As you read earlier, information functions are often used as the first argument of an IF statement. In this exercise you will create a formula that uses the ISBLANK function to check a column to see if any of the cells in the column are blank (empty). If a cell is empty, a message will be displayed.

1. Save the E10.5 workbook as `E10.6 Use the ISBLANK function.`

2. Display the Orders table.

3. In the Add Column type `=IF(ISBLANK([Payment Type]), "Payment Type Is Missing", "OK")`, then press Enter.

4. Rename the calculated column to `Check Payment Type`. The table should look like the one shown in Figure 10-15. Save the changes.

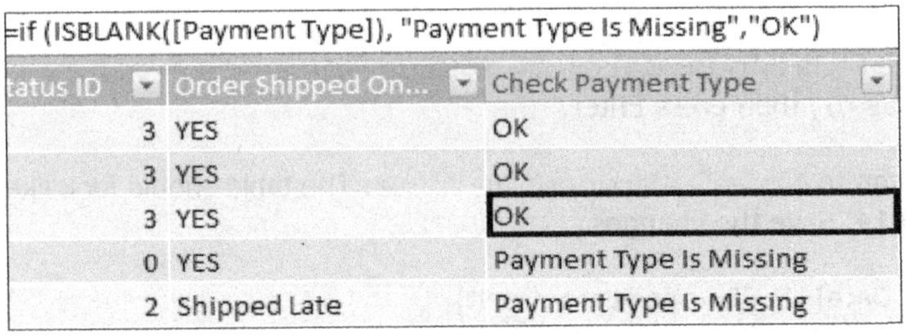

Figure 10-15 ISBLANK formula

Math And Trigonometric Functions

The functions in this category are the same as the ones in Excel. They are explained in Table 10-6.

Function/Syntax	Description
ABS(<number>)	Returns the absolute value of a number.
CEILING(<number>,<significance>)	Rounds the number to the nearest integer or nearest multiple of the <significance> value. (8)
EXP(<number>)	Returns e raised to the power of the number.
FACT(<number>)	Returns the factorial of the number.
FLOOR(<number>,<significance>)	Rounds the number down toward the nearest multiple of the <significance> value. (9)
INT(<number>)	Rounds the number down to the nearest integer. (10)
ISO.CEILING(<number> [,<significance>])	Rounds the number up to the nearest integer or nearest multiple of the <significance> value. (8)
LN(<number>)	Returns the natural logarithm of the number.
LOG(<number>, <base>)	Returns the logarithm to the specified base value. The default is base 10, but you can change the base number.
LOG10(<number>)	Returns the base 10 logarithm of the number.
MOD(<number>, <divisor>)	Returns the remainder of a division calculation.
MROUND(<number>, <multiple>)	Rounds the number to the <multiple> value. (9)
PI()	Returns the value of Pi, which is 3.14159265358979 to 15 digits.
POWER(<number>, <power>)	Returns the number raised to the <power> value.
QUOTIENT(<numerator>, <denominator>)	Returns the integer portion of the results of the <numerator> divided by the <denominator>. The remainder is discarded.
RAND()	Returns a random number greater than or equal to zero and less than 1.
RANDBETWEEN(<bottom>, <top>)	Returns a random number between the range specified.
ROUND(<number>, <num_digits>)	Rounds the number to a specific number of digits.
ROUNDDOWN(<number>, <num_digits>)	Rounds the number down toward zero.

Table 10-6 Math and Trigonometric functions explained

Function/Syntax	Description
ROUNDUP(<number>, <num_digits>)	Rounds the number up from zero.
SIGN(<number>)	Returns a 1 if the number is positive, a zero if the number is zero or a -1 if the number is negative.
SQRT(<number>)	Returns the square root of the number.
SUM(<column>)	Adds the values in a column instead of a range, like the function does in Excel.
TRUNC(<number> [, <num_digits>])	Removes the fractional part of the number. (10)

Table 10-6 Math and Trigonometric functions explained (Continued)

(8) These functions return the same value for positive numbers, but different values for negative numbers. CEILING rounds negative numbers down. ISO.CEILING rounds negative numbers up.
(9) This function does not work with negative numbers.
(10) These functions are similar because the both return integers.

Introduction To Aggregations

This section will provide a high level overview of aggregations and how they are used to create pivot tables and pivot charts. Understanding the power of aggregations will be very helpful when you create pivot tables. This is especially true if you have not created a lot of pivot tables prior to reading this book.

Chapter 9 covered relationships and how they are used to join tables to be able to create pivot tables that use data from more than one table. Hopefully, taking that knowledge and combining it with the knowledge that you will gain in this chapter about aggregations will make it easier to understand the data that is need to create a pivot table.

Aggregations Defined

Aggregations are used to group or summarize data. The way that data is displayed in a table makes it difficult to know totals, see trends in the data or answer "What-If" analysis type questions. For example, if you looked at the data in Figure 10-16, can you tell which sales rep had the most sales or what the top five selling products were? Probably not. When added to pivot tables, aggregations will allow the data shown in Figure 10-16 to be grouped or summarized to answer these questions and much more.

SalesOrderID	OrderDate	DueDate	ShipDate	CustomerID	SalesPersonID	SubTotal
71842	6/1/2004	6/13/2004	6/8/2004	460	285	$11.687
71841	6/1/2004	6/13/2004	6/8/2004	10	285	$102,044.1...
71840	6/1/2004	6/13/2004	6/8/2004	571	286	$1,117.094
71839	6/1/2004	6/13/2004	6/8/2004	611	279	$68,030.1615
71838	6/1/2004	6/13/2004	6/8/2004	319	286	$13,724.1893
71837	6/1/2004	6/13/2004	6/8/2004	579	275	$36,189.4664
71836	6/1/2004	6/13/2004	6/8/2004	254	280	$81,644.2102
71835	6/1/2004	6/13/2004	6/8/2004	621	280	$64,801.7394
71834	6/1/2004	6/13/2004	6/8/2004	633	289	$2,090.9556
71833	6/1/2004	6/13/2004	6/8/2004	182	283	$63,690.0778
71832	6/1/2004	6/13/2004	6/8/2004	88	282	$35,775.2113
71831	6/1/2004	6/13/2004	6/8/2004	322	282	$2,016.3408

Figure 10-16 Table of raw data

Tools To Create Aggregations

Believe it or not you have already used both of the aggregation creation tools if you have completed all of the exercises up to this point in the book. Just in case you skipped around in the book, the tools are explained below.

① The **POWERPIVOT WINDOW** is used to create formulas using aggregations. These formulas are created in calculated columns in tables.
② In the **POWERPIVOT FIELD LIST** measures (which are another type of aggregation) are used to create formulas, that are used in pivot tables. The aggregations are used to summarize data and count items in a group.

Understanding Groups

Grouping data is a way to put rows of data that have the same value in a column together so that a formula can be applied to get a sum, count, average or some other value for the group. Grouping data is similar to sorting data. The difference is that grouping allows a calculation to be used to get a value for the group. For example, if you needed to analyze sales by state, the group would be the State column. The formula for the group would be to add the order amount for each row that is in the group.

Another example would be if you wanted a count of orders by state. The formula for the group would be to count each order in the state. If the table that you are using does not have the column of data that you need to group on, you have the two options discussed below.

① Create a relationship to the table that does have the column of data that you need to create the group.
② Create a calculated column that will add the data that you need.

An example of this would be if you wanted a count of how many of each product was sold by state. An Order Details table usually has a Product ID field. While you could use the Product ID field in the table to get a count of how many of each product was sold and display it in the pivot table, as shown in Figure 10-17, as you can see, you do not know what the name of each product is.

Instead, if a relationship was created between the Product ID field in the Order Details table and the Product ID field in the Products table, the pivot table would look like the one shown in Figure 10-18, because you could use the Product Name field in the Products table. Which pivot table is easier to read?

	A	B	C	D	E	F	G	H	I	J	K	L	M	N
1	Count of Quantity	Column Labels												
2	Row Labels	CA	CO	FL	ID	IL	NV	NY	OR	TN	UT	WA	WI	Grand Total
3	1						1					1		2
4	3	1												1
5	4					2								2
6	5			1										1
7	6			1		1								2
8	7							1					1	2
9	8	1		1					1				1	4
10	17		1											1
11	19					1		1	2					4

Figure 10-17 Pivot table using the ID field as the group field

Count of Quantity	Column Labels												
Row Labels	CA	CO	FL	ID	IL	NV	NY	OR	TN	UT	WA	WI	Grand Total
Northwind Traders Almonds					1								1
Northwind Traders Beer		1				1						1	3
Northwind Traders Boysenberry Spread			1		1								2
Northwind Traders Cajun Seasoning					2								2
Northwind Traders Chai						1					1		2
Northwind Traders Chocolate		1						2				2	5
Northwind Traders Chocolate Biscuits Mix					1		1	2					4
Northwind Traders Clam Chowder	1		1						1	1			4
Northwind Traders Coffee				1		1			2		1		5

Figure 10-18 Pivot table using the Product Name field as the group field

Statistical Functions

The statistical functions have the same name in Excel and PowerPivot. The DAX version of these functions have been rewritten to work with columns and tables, which is what PowerPivot uses, instead of individual cells and a range of cells, which is what Excel uses. The statistical functions are explained in Table 10-7.

The DAX version of these functions cannot be used with Excel data unless they are modified. They can only be used with PowerPivot data. Not all of Excels statistical functions are supported in PowerPivot.

What The A And X Suffix Options Mean
As you will see, some DAX functions end with the letter A or X. The options are explained below.
The **A** suffix indicates a function that can be used with any data type.
The **X** suffix indicates a function that can be used to aggregate the result of the expression that is applied to each row of the table.

Function/Syntax	Description
AVERAGE(<column>)	Calculates the average of all the numbers in a column. (11)
AVERAGEA(<column>)	Calculates the average of all the values in a column. (12)
COUNT(<column>)	Counts the number of cells in the column that have numbers.
COUNTA(<column>)	Counts the number of cells in the column that are not empty. (12)
COUNTBLANK(<column>)	Counts the number of blank cells in a column.
COUNTROWS(<table>)	Counts the number of rows in a table or a table created from a function like FILTER.
MAX(<column>)	Finds the largest numeric value in the column. (11)
MAXA(<column>)	Finds the largest numeric value in the column. (12) (13)
MIN(<column>)	Finds the smallest numeric value in the column. (11)
MINA(<column>)	Finds the smallest numeric value in the column. (12) (13)
SUM(<column>)	Adds all of the numbers in a column. (11)

Table 10-7 Statistical functions explained

(11) This function only works with numeric values. Non numeric values and text are ignored.
(12) This function works with non numeric values, text and empty values.
(13) A zero is returned for text columns.

DAX Aggregate Statistical Functions

In the previous section you learned about the statistical functions that are similar to their Excel namesake. DAX has new aggregate functions that can reference rows in a table. The difference between these functions and the statistical functions is that aggregate functions use an expression as the second argument. These functions calculate the expression for each row in the table. The syntax for all of the aggregate functions is function name(<table>,<expression>). The functions are explained in Table 10-8.

Function	Description
AVERAGEX	Evaluates the expression for each row in the table, then calculates the average. (14)
COUNTAX	Counts the number of cells that are not blank. This means that cells with a formula will also be counted.
COUNTX	Counts the number of rows that evaluate to a number, contain a number or expression.
MAXX	Evaluates the expression to find the largest numeric value in a table, as shown in Example #11. (14)
MINX	Evaluates the expression to find the smallest numeric value in a table. (14)
SUMX	Returns the sum of the expression for each row in the table. (14)

Table 10-8 Aggregate functions explained

(14) The expression will return an error if the result is not numeric.

Example #11 =MAXX(OrderHeader, OrderHeader[Shipping Cost]+OrderHeader[InsuranceCost])
This formula finds the row in the OrderHeader table that has the largest total of shipping and insurance costs.

Example #12 =MAXX(FILTER(OrderDetails, [Product ID] = EARLIER ([Product ID])), OrderDetails [Quantity])
This formula goes through the entire OrderDetails table to find the largest single order for each product in the Products table.

Time And Intelligence Functions

The functions in this category are new. They are explained in Table 10-9. They will remind you of accounting functions because they allow you to compare today's sales to sales from a year ago, calculate the sales for the last 30 days, calculate sales for the last quarter and more. These functions use a range of dates to get the aggregate and related values. Functions in this category use a table of dates to calculate an aggregation or return a table of dates.

Function/Syntax	Description
CLOSINGBALANCEMONTH (<expression>, <dates> [,filter>])	Evaluates the expression at the end of the month specified. (15)
CLOSINGBALANCEQUARTER (<expression>, <dates> [,filter>])	Evaluates the expression at the end of the quarter specified. (15)

Table 10-9 Time and Intelligence functions explained

Function/Syntax	Description
CLOSINGBALANCEYEAR(<expression>, <dates> [,filter>]) [,<year_end_date>])	Evaluates the expression at the end of the year specified. (15)
DATEADD(<date_column>, <number_of_intervals>, <interval>)	Returns a table that has a column of dates based on the intervals specified. (15)
DATESBETWEEN(<column>, <start_date>, <end_date>)	Returns a table of dates that are between the start and end dates.
DATESINPERIOD(<date_column>, <start_date>, <number_of_intervals>, <intervals>)	Returns a table of dates that starts with the specified date through the number of intervals.
DATESMTD(<date_column>)	Returns a table with dates from the specified date column from the first day of the month to the current day of the month. (15)
DATESQTD(<date_column>)	Returns a table with dates from the specified date column from the first day of the quarter to the current day of the quarter. (15)
DATESYTD(<date_column> [,year_end_date])	Returns a table with dates from the specified date column from the first day of the year to the current day of the year of the quarter. (15)
ENDOFMONTH(<date_column>)	Returns the last date of the month in the date column specified. (15)
ENDOFQUARTER(<date_column>)	Returns the last date of the quarter in the date column specified. (15)
ENDOFYEAR(<date_column> [,year_end_date])	Returns the last date of the year in the date column specified. (15)
FIRSTDATE(<date_column>)	Returns the first date for the date column specified. (15)
FIRSTNONBLANK(<column>, <expression>)	Returns the first value in the column specified that is filtered by the current context where the expression is not blank.
LASTDATE(<date_column>)	Returns the last date in the current context for the date column specified.
LASTNONBLANK(<column>, <expression>)	Returns the last value in the column specified that is filtered by the current context where the expression is not blank.
NEXTDAY(<date_column>)	Returns a table with dates for the next day based on the first date specified in the date column. (15)
NEXTMONTH(<date_column>)	Returns a table with dates for the next month based on the first date specified in the date column. (15)
NEXTQUARTER(<date_column>)	Returns a table with dates in the next quarter based on the first date specified in the date column. (15)
NEXTYEAR(<date_column> [,year_end_date])	Returns a table with dates in the next year based on the first date specified in the date column. (15)
OPENINGBALANCEMONTH (<expression>, <dates> [,<filter>])	Evaluates the expression at the first date of the month. (15)
OPENINGBALANCEQUARTER (<expression>, <dates> [,<filter>])	Evaluates the expression at the first date of the quarter. (15)

Table 10-9 Time and Intelligence functions explained (Continued)

Function/Syntax	Description
OPENINGBALANCEYEAR(<expression>, <dates> [,<filter>] [,year_end_date])	Evaluates the expression at the first date of the year. (15)
PARALLELPERIOD(<date_column>, <number_of_intervals>, <intervals>)	Returns a table with a column of dates for a period parallel to the dates specified in the column. (15)
PREVIOUSDAY(<date_column>)	Returns a table of all dates for the day before the first date in the dates column. (15)
PREVIOUSMONTH(<date_column>)	Returns a table of all dates for the month before the first date in the dates column. (15)
PREVIOUSQUARTER(<date_column>)	Returns a table of all dates for the quarter before the first date in the dates column. (15)
PREVIOUSYEAR(<date_column> [,year_end_date])	Returns a table of all dates for the year before the first date in the dates column. (15)
SAMPLEPERIODLASTYEAR (<date_column>)	Returns a table of dates back one year in time from the date specified in the date column. (15)
STARTOFMONTH(<date_column>)	Returns the first date of the month from the specified date column. (15)
STARTOFQUARTER(<date_column>)	Returns the first date of the quarter from the specified date column. (15)
STARTOFYEAR(<date_column> [,year_end_date])	Returns the first date of the year from the specified date column. (15)
TOTALMTD(<expression>, <dates> [,<filter>])	Evaluates the expression for the month to date of the month specified. (15)
TOTALQTD(<expression>, <dates> [,<filter>])	Evaluates the expression for the dates in the quarter to the last date of the quarter specified. (15)
TOTALYTD(<expression>, <dates> [,<filter>] [,year_end_date])	Evaluates the expression for the year to date value of the year specified. (15)

Table 10-9 Time and Intelligence functions explained (Continued)

(15) This formula is evaluated in the **CURRENT CONTEXT**.

Filter Functions

The functions in this category are new and are used to apply filters to columns or tables of data. The Filter functions are used to create dynamic calculations and manipulate the data context. They work like the filter option does on a column in a PowerPivot table. These functions are not supported in Excel.

The Filter functions can be used with pivot tables, as well as in a calculated column and measure. Filters are used to select the rows of data that will be calculated. This is accomplished by using a table as input for the formula. A filter expression is created to query the data in the table to only retrieve the records that meet the condition of the filter. Filters are applied dynamically when the data is refreshed, updated or recalculated, depending on the current context of the data.

This section covers the following Filter functions in detail because they are more complex then other functions discussed in Table 10-10 and you may have the need to use them: FILTER, RELATED, RELATEDTABLE and CALCULATE.

Function/Syntax	**Description**
ALL(<table_or_column>)	Ignores any filters that may have been applied and returns all of the values in a column or all of the rows in a table. Use this function when you need to clear filters.
ALLEXCEPT(<table> [<column> [,<colummn2> [,...]]])	Is used to remove all of the context filters that have been applied, except the ones that you specify in the formula.
ALLNOBLANKROW (<table_or_column>)	Disregards context filters and returns all rows that are not blank or distinct values in a column except blank rows.
CALCULATE(<expression> [,<filter1> [,<filter2> [,...]]])	(16)
CALCULATETABLE(<expression> [,<filter1> [,<filter2> [,...]]])	Is used to evaluate a table expression in a context that has been modified by filters.
DISTINCT(<column>)	Returns a one column table that has unique values from the specified column. (17)
EARLIER(<column> [,number>])	(18)
EARLIEST(<table_or_column>)	(18)
FILTER(<table>, <filter>)	(16)
RELATED(<column>)	(16)
RELATEDTABLE(<table>)	(16)
VALUES(<column>)	The difference between this function and the DISTINCT function is that the VALUES function can also return an unknown value. (17)

Table 10-10 Filter functions explained

(16) This function is covered in detail later in this chapter.
(17) These functions return the same results. They return a one column table that has the unique values from a specific column. This function removes duplicate values.
(18) This function is explained at the end of the chapter.

FILTER Function

This function tells another function what data to use. Filters can be applied to formulas that use a table as an input value. Instead of using the table name in the formula, use the FILTER function. The result of a FILTER expression is a table that is passed to another function that performs a calculation. This table is not returned to the PowerPivot workbook. Instead, the table is embedded in another function.

Example #13 =SUMX(FILTER(SalesOrderHeader,[Order Date] > "09/19/2010"), [SubTotal])
This formula will retrieve all rows of data in the SalesOrderHeader table that have an order date that is greater than 9/19/2010, then sum the values of retrieved rows in the SubTotal column.

Using The RELATED Functions
For either of the RELATED functions discussed below to work, there must be a relationship between the table that uses the function and the table that has the column of data that the function references. This relationship can be direct, meaning both tables have the same field in common, like the Order Header and Order Details tables have. The relationship can also be from an **INFERRED RELATIONSHIP**. [See Chapter 9, Inferred Relationships]

Using The RELATED Functions (Continued)
For example, if you wanted to calculate the order total amount by region. The Customer table has the Region ID field. The Order Header table has the Customer ID field and Order Total Amount field. The Region table has the Region ID field and Region Name field. The formula would be placed in the Region table.

RELATED (Column) Function

This function is used for the "many" table in a many-to-one relationship, to retrieve the matching value in the "one" table. Use this function when the value being retrieved is from a column.

The RELATED function is more powerful then VLOOKUP in Excel for the following reasons:

① VLOOKUP only returns the first match, even though there may be more rows that meet the criteria requirement.
② As stated above in the tip box, this function requires a relationship between the tables. Having the relationship means that the lookup table does not have to be sorted in a specific way, nor do certain columns have to be in the left most columns in the lookup table like VLOOKUP requires.

Exercise 10.7: Use The RELATED Function

In this exercise you will use the RELATED function to add the Product Name field from the Products table to the Order Details table in the Northwind workbook.

1. Save the E10.6 workbook as `E10.7 Use the RELATED function.`

2. Display the Order Details table.

3. In the Add Column type `=RELATED(Products[Product Name])`, as shown in Figure 10-19, then press Enter.

`=RELATED(Products[Product Name])`

Figure 10-19 RELATED formula

4. You should see the product name for each row in the Order Details table. Rename the column to `Product Name`. Save the changes.

Exercise 10.8: Fix The Formula In Exercise 10.3

In Exercise 10.3 the goal was to create a formula in the Orders table to have the sales reps full name added to the Orders table. As you read earlier, the RELATED function is used to retrieve information from one table and add it to another table in the PowerPivot workbook. In this exercise you will fix the formula that you created in Exercise 10.3.

1. Save the E10.3 workbook as `E10.8 Add the RELATED function to a formula.`

2. Display the Orders table, then click in the calculated column with the error.

3. Change the formula so that it looks like the one shown at the top of Figure 10-20.

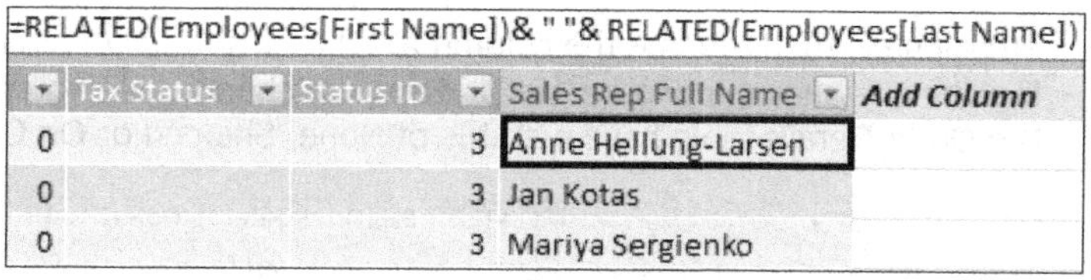

Figure 10-20 Revised formula for the E10.3 workbook

4. Rename the column to `Sales Rep Full Name`, then save the changes.

RELATEDTABLE (Table) Function

This function is similar to the RELATED function because it retrieves values from another table. The differences are explained below.

① The RELATEDTABLE function can be used in tables that have a one-to-many or many-to-one relationship.
② The RELATEDTABLE function cannot be used by itself to create a calculated column like the RELATED function can. This function provides an intermediate result that will be used as an argument for another function.
③ The RELATEDTABLE function returns a table that contains all of the rows from another table that are related to the current row in the table that the formula is in. This table is the intermediate result, discussed above.

Exercise 10.9: Use The SUMX And RELATEDTABLE Functions

In this exercise you will create a calculated column in three tables. The formula will use two functions. What you will see is that the same formula will produce a different total amount when used in different tables. Each table will use the same formula, as explained below to create a different total amount.

① In the Order Details Status table, the formula will be used to calculate the total amount of sales by status.
② In the Employees table, the formula will be used to calculate the total amount of sales by sales rep (employee).
③ In the Products table, the formula will be used to calculate the total amount of sales by product.

1. Save the E10.7 workbook as `E10.9 Use the SUMX and RELATEDTABLE functions`.

2. Import the Order Detail Status table, then display the table in the workbook.

3. Create a relationship between the Status ID field in the Order Details table and the Status ID field in the Order Details Status table.

Create The Formula In the Order Details Status Table

1. In the Add Column type `=SUMX(RELATEDTABLE(OrderDetails),OrderDetails[Line Item Total])`.

2. Press Enter, then rename the column to `Status Total Amount`. The table should look like the one shown in Figure 10-21. Save the changes. As you can see, none of the items in the Order Details table have a status of None, Shipped or On Order.

[Status Total Am(▾ | fx =sumx(RELATEDTABLE(OrderDetails), OrderDetails[Line Item Total])

Stat...	Status Name	Status Total Amount	Add Column
0	None	$0	
1	Allocated	$16,074.25	
2	Invoiced	$52,062.75	
3	Shipped		
4	On Order		
5	No Stock	$0	

Figure 10-21 SUMX and RELATEDTABLE formula in the Order Details Status table

Create The Formula In The Employees Table

The formula that you create in this part of the exercise will display the total amount of sales for each sales rep. All people in the Employees table will not have a value in this column. That is because all employees are not sales reps.

1. Copy the formula from the Order Details Status table that you created in the previous section of this exercise.
2. Display the Employees table.
3. Click in the Add Column. Paste the formula into the formula bar.
4. Rename the column to `Employee Sales Total.`
5. Move the column to the left, after the First Name field. The table should look like the one shown in Figure 10-22.

fx =sumx(RELATEDTABLE(OrderDetails), OrderDetails[Line Item Total])

Last Name	First Name	Employee Sales Total	E-mail Addre
Freehafer	Nancy	$22,255.25	nancy@north
Cencini	Andrew	$2,997.5	andrew@nor
Kotas	Jan	$5,787.5	jan@northwi
Sergienko	Mariya	$6,278	mariya@nort
Thorpe	Steven		steven@nort
Neipper	Michael	$6,378	michael@nor
Zare	Robert	$3,786.5	robert@nortl
Giussani	Laura	$680	laura@north
Hellung-Lars...	Anne	$19,974.25	anne@north

Figure 10-22 SUMX and RELATEDTABLE formula in the Employees table

Create The Formula In The Products Table

The formula that you create in this part of the exercise will display the total amount of sales for each product. If a product does not have a value in the Product Sales Total column, it means that the product has not been sold. This would be helpful in determining if the company should retire the product or try to create a better promotional campaign for the product so that it will sell.

1. Paste the formula in the Add Column on the Products table.

2. Rename the column to `Product Sales Total`.

3. Move the column to the left after the Product Name column. The table should look like the one shown in Figure 10-23. Save the changes.

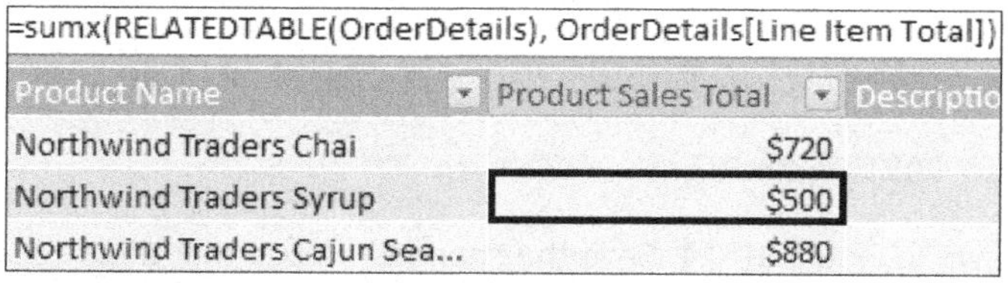

Figure 10-23 SUMX and RELATEDTABLE formula in the Products table

CALCULATE Function

I will admit that at first I found it difficult to conceptually visualize how this function works and what it is capable of. But being the fearless person that I am, I decided to cover it in detail in case other people have the same blank look that I did. This function evaluates the expression in the context of the current filter.

CALCULATE (Expression, SetFilter 1, SetFilter 2 . . .) is the syntax for this function. Using the SetFilter argument is optional.

The CALCULATE function is used to let a DAX expression be evaluated in a specific filter context. Based on the syntax for the function, this means that you can set a filter for the expression to be evaluated in.

For example, if you wanted to sum the Line Item Total column in the Order Details table for sales in the US, the expression would be Sum(Order Details[Line Item Total]). The filter would be Order Header [Country]="USA").

In Exercise 10.9 you used the SUMX and RELATEDTABLE functions to calculate the total amount of sales in three PowerPivot tables. The value was stored in the tables. That is appropriate because the goal was to allow all of the orders to be displayed in the pivot table.

The CALCULATE formula in Example #14 produces the same result as the RELATEDTABLE formula that you used in Exercise 10.9. Notice that this CALCULATE formula does not use the SetFilter argument.

Example #14 =CALCULATE(Sum(OrderDetails[Line Item Total]))

If another pivot table needs to display the same sales information for a specific country, you would use a SetFilter argument to select the country. The formula in Example #15 is what you would use.

Example #15 =CALCULATE(Sum(OrderDetails [Line Item Total]), Order Header [Country]="USA")

Exercise 10.10: Use The CALCULATE Function Without A SetFilter Argument

In this exercise you will add the formula shown earlier in Example #14 to one of the tables that you created the RELATEDTABLE formula in, in Exercise 10.9. Normally, you would not add two formulas to the same PowerPivot table that produced the same result. It is done in this exercise to demonstrate that there is a choice of functions that can product the same result.

1. Save the E10.9 workbook as `E10.10 Use the CALCULATE function without the SetFilter argument.`
2. On the Order Details Status tab, create the formula shown earlier in Example #14.
3. Rename the calculated column to `Calc_Formula.`
4. You should have the results shown in Figure 10-24. Save the changes. Notice that the CALCULATE formula produced the same result as the RELATEDTABLE shown earlier in Figure 10-21.

fx =CALCULATE(SUM(OrderDetails[Line Item Total]))

Status Name	Status Total Amount	Calc_Formula
None	$0	$0
Allocated	$16,074.25	$16,074.25
Invoiced	$52,062.75	$52,062.75
Shipped		
On Order		
No Stock	$0	$0

Figure 10-24 CALCULATE function without a SetFilter argument

Exercise 10.11: Use The CALCULATE Function With A SetFilter Argument

In this exercise you will use a formula similar to the one shown earlier in Example #15 as a calculated field. You will add the formula to the Customers table to create a total amount for all orders that the customer has placed that were shipped to an address in the USA.

1. Save the E10.10 workbook as `E10.11 Use the CALCULATE function with a SetFilter argument.`
2. On the Customers tab, create a calculated column with this formula.
   `=CALCULATE (Sum(OrderDetails[Line Item Total]), Orders[ShipCountryRegion]="USA"`
3. Rename the calculated column to `Calc_SetFilter.`

4. The formula and calculated column should look like the one shown in Figure 10-25.

   Save the changes.

=CALCULATE(Sum(OrderDetails[Line Item Total]),Orders[Ship CountryRegion]="USA")

Attach...	Customer Full Name	Calc_SetFilter	Add Column
	Anna Bedecs	$2,410.75	
	Antonio Gratacos Solsona		
	Thomas Axen	$2,550	
	Christina Lee	$4,949	
	Martin O'Donnell		
	Francisco Pérez-Olaeta	$8,007.5	

Figure 10-25 CALCULATE function with a SetFilter argument

The filter in the formula only allows orders that were shipped to an address in the USA to display a value. That would explain why there is no amount in some of the rows. If you look in the Order Details table, you will see that all of the orders have USA in the ShipCountryRegion column. Hmmm. Does that means that something is wrong with the formula? Possibly.

The Orders table has a Customer ID field. If you sort the data in the Orders table by the Customer ID field from smallest to largest, you will see that there are no orders for customers 2, 5 and 13. There are more customers without orders, but this is enough to test.

If you look in the Customers table, the calculated column that you created should be blank for Customer ID 2, 5 and 13, which it is. In the real world, this would be a problem because all customers should have at least one order.

This is why a few times in this book I have said that it is important to know the data that you are working with. I am sure that many people would have thought at least one of the following:

① The formula is wrong.
② A relationship was missing.
③ A relationship that was created was incorrect.

In reality, 2 and 3 above could not be a reason why there are empty cells in the calculated column, because the CALCULATE function requires that tables in the formula have a relationship. While it is good to check all possibilities of why the data looks the way that it does, just don't forget to check the data itself.

Understanding Context Evaluation

In previous chapters you learned how to filter PowerPivot tables by selecting criteria for columns in the table. Earlier in this chapter you learned about the FILTER function and how it is used to select the data that will be used by another function. Context is what makes dynamic analysis in pivot tables and pivot charts possible. Context refers to the ability to have formulas change to reflect the cell selection in a pivot table based on the users selection or current row and related data in a PowerPivot table.

Now that you have read about the variety of functions that DAX supports, it is time to understand how they are evaluated. This topic is especially important when you need to use some of the advanced DAX functions like CALCULATE or EARLIER.

The context that DAX expressions are evaluated in, happens in one of the three ways listed below. It is important to understand the context concept because the expressions that you create may not work as you expect and often the context evaluation is the reason why. An example of this was demonstrated earlier in Exercise 10.3. There are three types of context. Each context is explained in the sections that follow.

① **ROW CONTEXT** Evaluates the current row in a table.
② **FILTER CONTEXT** Evaluates the active rows in a calculation.
③ **QUERY CONTEXT** Evaluates the table to retrieve a subset of the data in the table.

Row Context

Calculated column formulas are evaluated for each row in a table. The row context is the values in each row and the values in columns that are related to the current row. For example, the formula shown in Figure 10-26 takes the value in the [Quantity] column and multiples it by the value in the [Unit Price] column in the current row. This may seem familiar because this is how formulas work in Excel.

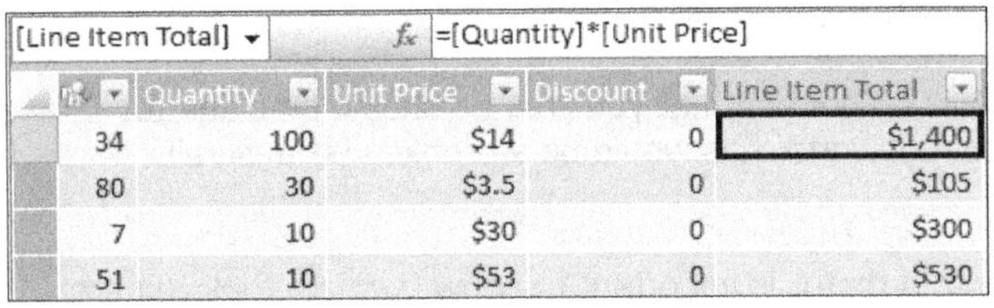

	Quantity	Unit Price	Discount	Line Item Total
34	100	$14	0	$1,400
80	30	$3.5	0	$105
7	10	$30	0	$300
51	10	$53	0	$530

Figure 10-26 Row Context example

If the Unit Price data was in the Products table instead of the Order Details table shown above in Figure 10-26, you would use the formula in Example #16 to access the Unit Price column.

Example #16 =[Quantity]+[RELATED] (Products [Unit Price])

Some functions get a value from the current row and use the value in a calculation for an entire table. An example of this type of function is EARLIER.

Row context will automatically use the relationships between tables to determine which rows in other tables are associated with the current row. An example of this was illustrated in the RELATED formula above in Example #16. Notice that no key was used in the formula to connect the current table (shown above in Figure 10-26) to the Products table.

If there is no row context, DAX cannot recognize the column name as a value. For example, if the same formula is created as a measure, an error is generated, as shown at the bottom of Figure 10-27. The error is generated because there is no row context (current row) for DAX to know what the value of [Quantity] is. DAX measures that you create cannot use the default five aggregate functions covered earlier in this chapter. Instead, measures that you create use SUMX.

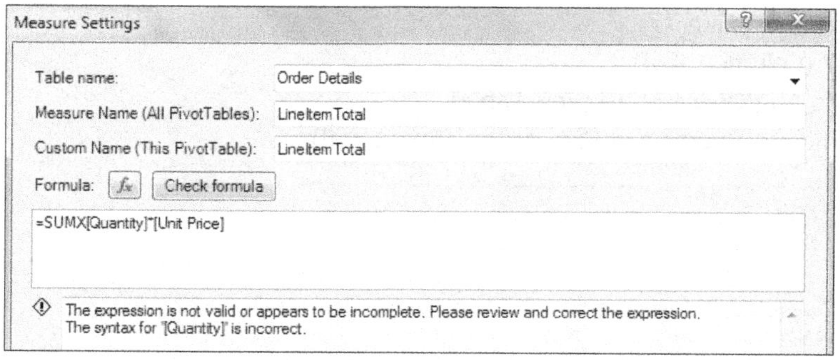

Figure 10-27 DAX measure row context error

Instead of row context that fills in values in a calculated column, row context can also be based on browsing through a table to apply the row context to each row of the table that is being browsed.

The **SUMX** function uses two arguments, a table to aggregate and an expression to be evaluated for each row in the table. For example, to fix the formula shown above in Figure 10-27 so that it will work, add **(TABLENAME,** after the SUMX function, as shown in Figure 10-28. This expression will be evaluated by using a row context for each row of the table.

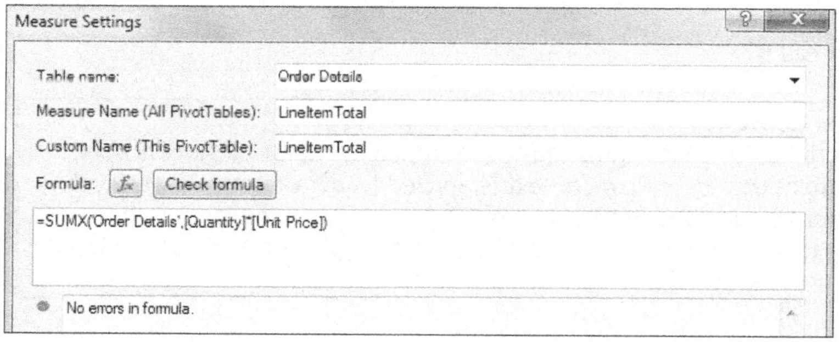

Figure 10-28 DAX measure formula fixed

Filter Context

This type of evaluation is a little more complicated than row context. Filter context is a set of allowed values for each column. The values are based on filters that are defined by the **FILTER** expression in a formula or filters that are applied to the row.

Measures are evaluated once for each cell in the Values drop zone on the PowerPivot Field List. Each cell has a distinct filter context which is based on the report filter, column labels, row labels and slicers that are used.

Filter context is added to a PowerPivot table or column when a formula has a filter argument. Filter context works on top of row and query contexts. This means that a filter expression controls the values used by the formula. It is important that end users that view and use pivot tables know about the filters that may be applied to the pivot table so that they understand how the data in the pivot table is filtered. For example, in Figure 10-29, the following filters were applied before the measure is evaluated for cell B7.

① Store Type = Online (Report Filter)

② Calendar Year = 2007 (Column Label)

③ Store Name = Contoso Asia Online Store (Row Label)

④ Product Category Name = Cameras and Camcorders (Row Label)

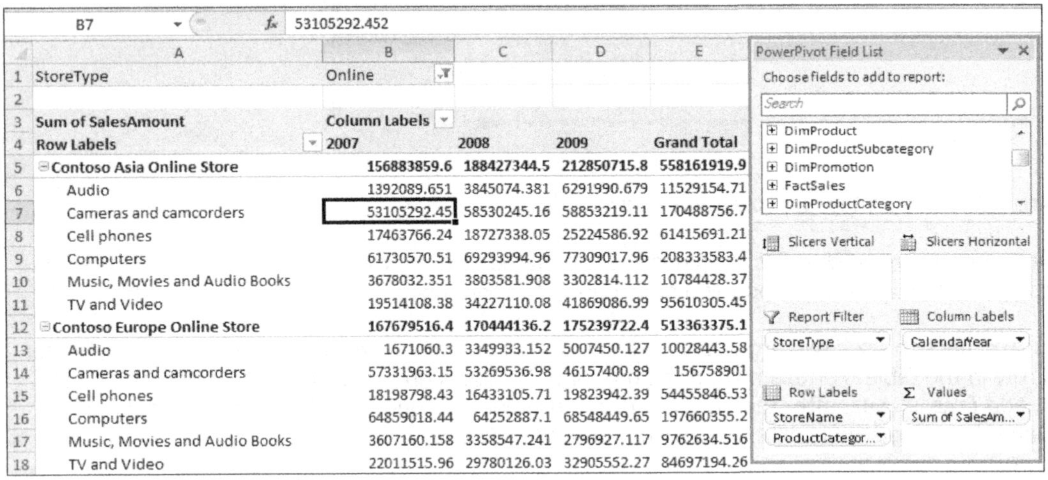
B7 53105292.452

	A	B	C	D	E
1	StoreType	Online			
2					
3	**Sum of SalesAmount**	**Column Labels**			
4	**Row Labels**	**2007**	**2008**	**2009**	**Grand Total**
5	**Contoso Asia Online Store**	**156883859.6**	**188427344.5**	**212850715.8**	**558161919.9**
6	Audio	1392089.651	3845074.381	6291990.679	11529154.71
7	Cameras and camcorders	53105292.45	58530245.16	58853219.11	170488756.7
8	Cell phones	17463766.24	18727338.05	25224586.92	61415691.21
9	Computers	61730570.51	69293994.96	77309017.96	208333583.4
10	Music, Movies and Audio Books	3678032.351	3803581.908	3302814.112	10784428.37
11	TV and Video	19514108.38	34227110.08	41869086.99	95610305.45
12	**Contoso Europe Online Store**	**167679516.4**	**170444136.2**	**175239722.4**	**513363375.1**
13	Audio	1671060.3	3349933.152	5007450.127	10028443.58
14	Cameras and camcorders	57331963.15	53269536.98	46157400.89	156758901
15	Cell phones	18198798.43	16433105.71	19823942.39	54455846.53
16	Computers	64859018.44	64252887.1	68548449.65	197660355.2
17	Music, Movies and Audio Books	3607160.158	3358547.241	2796927.117	9762634.516
18	TV and Video	22011515.96	29780126.03	32905552.27	84697194.26

Figure 10-29 Filter context for cell B7

> **Row Context vs Filter Context**
> If you are having some difficulty understanding the difference between these concepts, it may help to think of them this way. Row context is applied to data from a PowerPivot table, meaning no further calculations from calculated columns will take place once the data is added to a pivot table. Filter context is applied to data in a pivot table after filters in the pivot table have been applied.

Query Context

This type of evaluation refers to a subset of data that is created specifically for each cell in a pivot table depending on the row and column headers, report filters and slicers. When a value field or measure is added to a cell in a pivot table, the necessary calculations are run to populate each cell in the pivot table. This retrieved data set is the query context for each cell.

What you will notice is that the context will change depending on the drop zone that the formula is placed in for the pivot table or if the pivot table has filters or groups. The context can also change if the formula is used on a calculated column in a pivot table. Adding or removing slicers, row or column headings will also change the context.

How The Context Can Affect A Filter

In a PowerPivot table, the context is the values in the current row. When a DAX formula is added to a pivot table, the formula results can be affected by the context, which is the entire set or a subset of data. The subset of data in the pivot table is created by filters and slicers.

By design, pivot tables can create a context. This happens when a pivot table has groups. Only the data for the groups is displayed in the pivot table. This means that measures that are added to the pivot table are only calculated for the data in the pivot table, opposed to every row in the underlying PowerPivot table.

How Context And Functions Work

Below are some examples of functions and the context that is applied.

The **ALL** function can be used to clear filters that were applied by a query context. This function sets the context in a formula.

The **EARLIER** and **EARLIEST** functions are used to loop through tables by using calculations that reference a value from an inner loop. The functions are used to compare the value of the current row to all rows in the table. DAX does not support the **RANK** function. Use the EARLIER function instead.

The **FILTER** function is used to select the rows to include in the current context.

The **RELATED** function is used to expand the current row context to include values in a related column. This function is used for lookups.

CREATING PIVOT TABLES

In addition to learning how to create pivot tables, you will learn about the following in this chapter:

- ☑ Have a better understanding of the concept of Business Intelligence and how it relates to PowerPivot
- ☑ Pivot Table Tools contextual tabs options
- ☑ Pivot Table Options dialog box
- ☑ Field Settings dialog box
- ☑ Pivot table and pivot chart layout options
- ☑ PowerPivot Field List options
- ☑ Top N pivot tables

Overview

In this chapter you will learn how to create pivot tables using data from PowerPivot tables. You will also learn how to use the PowerPivot Field List and read about the differences between this field list and the PivotTable Field List that is part of Excel. While the focus of this chapter is on creating pivot tables, there will be some mention of pivot charts. The reason is to keep from presenting the same information in this chapter and in Chapter 12, which covers pivot charts.

The Pivot Table Tools contextual tabs options that are part of Excel are also covered because the options on these tabs can be used to enhance the pivot tables that are created from PowerPivot data.

Business intelligence is the first topic discussed in this chapter because it is a primary reason that people create pivot tables. These tools allow end users to perform some, if not all, of the analysis that is needed to make business decisions.

Business Intelligence is often called or referenced as BI for short. Even though the concept of business intelligence has been around for a while, there are still different schools of thought in the business community on what it is, what it isn't and how it should be implemented.

Generally speaking, business intelligence is the process of analyzing data, raw or otherwise and converting the analysis into knowledge (intelligence). Business intelligence, in the broad sense, is a collection of technology and applications that are used to gather, store, access and analyze data, often in an enterprise environment. This process is usually used to make business decisions or track business trends and changes. The typical business intelligence process includes querying, reporting, forecasting, data mining and statistical analysis.

Some of the goals of business intelligence analysis include being able to easily find new business opportunities, making decisions on existing processes, looking for ways to save money and having the ability to recognize where improvement is needed. While not the traditional type of report, the reports that are created from data imported into PowerPivot produce reports on a higher and more interactive level then what can be created in Excel.

Business intelligence, especially self-service (do it yourself) business intelligence, is gaining a lot of momentum because companies are looking to bring more decision making tools to their employees. This will allow end users at several levels in the company to obtain access to data that will help them make more accurate business decisions in a timely manner.

While giving end users more tools to get their jobs done more efficiently is a good strategy, they can also make mistakes that can do the opposite of what the tools were intended to do. I am not saying this to rain on your enthusiasm of learning PowerPivot. I just want you to be aware of the fact that if you do not have a very good understanding of the data that you work with in PowerPivot, the chances of making a mistake are high.

Getting Started With Pivot Tables And Pivot Charts

I have taught beginner and intermediate college level Excel classes and noticed that not a lot time is devoted to pivot tables and pivot charts, even though they are popular tools that are used in the workplace. Because I wrote this book primarily for people that do not have a lot of experience creating pivot tables and pivot charts, I feel that the more information that I can provide the better you will be to create pivot tables and pivot charts with ease.

The purpose of pivot tables is to analyze numeric data, primarily in a summarized format. By summarized format, I mean that there are usually not a lot of detail records in a pivot table. It is very common to see reports that have detail records and summary data in paper based reports. If this is the type of report that you are use to, think of it this way, the data in the PowerPivot window is the detail report and the pivot table is the summary report that is based on the detail report in the PowerPivot window. Pivot tables are also used to answer "What-If" scenario questions.

How Pivot Tables Are Created

Pivot tables are used to retrieve records from the data source that meet specific criteria. The pivot table takes the functionality of data in a pivot table in Excel one step further because it allows you to summarize the data that is in the rows in the pivot table. Pivot table reports are often used for comparison analysis. Examples of reports that can be created with pivot tables are:

① Sales by sales rep by year.
② Sales by region.
③ Summarizing the number of orders by year and by zip code, each sales rep has.
④ Sales of a specific product by sales rep, by month.
⑤ Summarizing how many customers by region purchased certain products by month or by year.

Pivot table reports often give new report designers difficulty. I suspect that this is because this type of report requires one to think in dimensions. If you have seen, used or created a **CROSS-TAB REPORT**, you will see that overall, the thought process of creating a pivot table is the same as creating a cross-tab report. Like spreadsheets, pivot tables have rows and columns. Each cell in a spreadsheet contains one piece of data. In a pivot table, the cell contains one piece of summary data (count, sum, average etc.) that is the equivalent of the sub totals for each group that is often used for data in a spreadsheet.

Behind the scenes, pivot tables take the detail records that you are use to seeing in a spreadsheet, as well as, the groups and summarizes the detail data and places the result in a cell. Hopefully, the following scenario will make the concept of pivot tables easier to understand.

Going From Spreadsheet Reports To Pivot Table Reports

This scenario will use the first pivot table example mentioned above; Sales by sales rep by year. The goal of this pivot table report from a spreadsheet report perspective is to show sales for a year by sales rep. The report shown in Figure 11-1 is a basic spreadsheet list report that sorts the sales, by sales rep and by year.

The report shown in Figure 11-1 contains all of the data one would need to determine sales by sales rep, by year, but because there aren't any totals for the groups (in this case, the groups are the sales reps), it would take a while to manually do the math, especially if there were hundreds of sales reps. Yes, I know what you are thinking, create a report that groups the data by sales rep, then by year and add totals. Figure 11-2 shows that report.

Can you tell how many saddles Robert King sold in total? Or can you tell me who had the lowest number of sales in 2004? Okay, I'll wait while you open the spreadsheet that has the data for the report shown in Figure 11-1 and get a calculator to add up the totals for the sales reps. [See the Chapter 11 Figure 11-1 workbook in the zip file] I can wait. I have patience <smile>.

Like the report shown in Figure 11-1, the report in Figure 11-2 has all of the raw data that you need to answer these questions.

Sales By Rep By Year

Last Name	First Name	Order Date	Order Amount	Customer Name
Davolio	Nancy	02/19/2003	$789.51	Belgium Bike Co.
Davolio	Nancy	02/19/2003	$58.00	Spokes for Folks
Davolio	Nancy	02/26/2003	$68.90	Mountain Madmen Bicycles
Davolio	Nancy	02/27/2003	$2,698.53	Pedals Inc.
Davolio	Nancy	02/27/2003	$1,079.70	Mountain Madmen Bicycles
Davolio	Nancy	02/27/2003	$1,529.70	Cycle City Rome
		.		
		.		
		.		
Suyama	Michael	02/14/2005	$5,893.20	Crazy Wheels
Suyama	Michael	02/19/2005	$6,005.40	Off the Mountain Biking
Suyama	Michael	02/19/2005	$7,685.25	To The Limit Biking Co.
Suyama	Michael	02/22/2005	$1,664.70	Bike-A-Holics Anonymous
Suyama	Michael	02/24/2005	$138.70	Tienda de Bicicletas El Pardo
Suyama	Michael	02/25/2005	$893.55	Whistler Rentals
Suyama	Michael	02/28/2005	$1,529.70	Belgium Bike Co.

Figure 11-1 Basic sorted report in Excel of sales by sales rep by year

Sales By Rep By Year

Last Name	First Name	Order Date	Order Amount	Customer Name
Nancy Davolio				
2003				
Davolio	Nancy	02/19/2003	$789.51	Belgium Bike Co.
Davolio	Nancy	02/19/2003	$58.00	Spokes for Folks
Davolio	Nancy	02/26/2003	$68.90	Mountain Madmen Bicycles
Davolio	Nancy	02/27/2003	$1,079.70	Mountain Madmen Bicycles
Davolio	Nancy	02/27/2003	$2,698.53	Pedals Inc.
Davolio	Nancy	02/27/2003	$1,529.70	Cycle City Rome
Davolio	Nancy	12/02/2003	$41.90	City Cyclists
Davolio	Nancy	12/03/2003	$10,259.10	Piccolo
Davolio	Nancy	12/03/2003	$14,872.30	Cyclopath
Davolio	Nancy	12/04/2003	$29.00	Spokes 'N Wheels Ltd.
Davolio	Nancy	12/07/2003	$890.61	Tienda de Bicicletas El Pardo
		.		
		.		
		.		
		.		
Davolio	Nancy	05/02/2005	$1,082.50	Warsaw Sports, Inc.
			$138,028.42	
			$660,756.95	
Janet Leverling				
2003				
Leverling	Janet	02/21/2003	$5,219.55	Tienda de Bicicletas El Pardo
Leverling	Janet	02/21/2003	$8,819.55	Bikes, Bikes, and More Bikes
Leverling	Janet	02/25/2003	$2,246.25	Folk och fä HB
Leverling	Janet	02/26/2003	$267.76	Hooked on Helmets
Leverling	Janet	02/26/2003	$61.35	Bike Shop from Mars

Figure 11-2 Data grouped by sales rep by year

The problem is that the data is spread out in the spreadsheet which makes it difficult for comparison analysis. As you will see after completing the exercises in this chapter, this same data in a pivot table report will be in an easy to read format. With a pivot table you can quickly answer questions like how many sales Robert King had for three products and which sales rep had the lowest number of sales in 2004.

How To Create The Report Shown Above In Figure 11-1 As A Pivot Table

Yes, I hear you grumbling and saying, "Great, I now see the advantages of creating a pivot table, but how do I get the data shown earlier in Figure 11-1 into pivot table format?" Okay, here goes:

① Usually, the field down the left side of a pivot table (that creates the rows) is the data element that there are more occurrences of. In this example, there are more sales reps then years. You can put the sales reps across the top of the pivot table and still get the same results, but you would probably find it a little awkward to read.

② The field that goes across the top (that creates the columns) represents the data element that there are less occurrences of. In this example, that would be the years.

③ The cells in the middle of the pivot table are the sum of order amounts that the sales rep had for the year. This is the equivalent to grouping and sorting data. This is how multiple rows of data in a spreadsheet are summarized in a pivot table. In this example, all of the order total amounts for one sales rep for one year are placed in one cell.

④ The totals at the bottom of the pivot table will tell you the total amount of sales for each year, for all sales reps and a grand total of sales for the entire pivot table in the lower right corner of the pivot table. These totals are automatically calculated in a pivot table. If you do not need these totals, you can remove them.

⑤ I have saved the best for last; the placement of the fields on the PowerPivot Field List. The fields for the rows and columns were answered above. That leaves the field for the cells in the middle of the pivot table. Recall the original report criteria: Sales by sales rep, by year. You have already determined that the sales rep field (the Employee Name field), is what will be used for the rows. You have also determined that the Order Year will be used for the columns. The only field left is the sales (the order amount). This is the field that goes in the Values drop zone section of the PowerPivot Field List. In this example, the cells represent a sum of order amounts.

The pivot table would look like the one shown in Figure 11-3.

Now you should be able to figure out which sales rep had the lowest sales amount each year.

	2003	2004	2005	Total
Davolio	$71,862.70	$450,865.83	$138,028.42	$660,756.95
Dodsworth	$29,049.94	$513,545.52	$140,253.75	$682,849.21
King	$21,093.75	$512,406.60	$215,255.59	$748,755.94
Leverling	$44,121.64	$447,235.19	$157,745.16	$649,101.99
Peacock	$38,458.39	$446,150.56	$147,190.82	$631,799.77
Suyama	$54,804.22	$496,881.48	$158,715.78	$710,401.48
Total	$259,390.64	$2,867,085.18	$957,189.52	$4,083,665.34

Figure 11-3 Sales per year, per sales rep pivot table

What Is The Difference Between A Pivot Table And A Pivot Table Report?

A **PIVOT TABLE**, like the one shown above in Figure 11-3 provides static summary information, meaning that there are no options for the person using the pivot table to provide What-If scenarios. Basically, all you can do with a pivot table like the one shown above in Figure 11-3 is look at the data that is presented in it.

A **PIVOT TABLE REPORT** is an interactive pivot table that includes filters and/or slicers that are used to cause the pivot table to display data based on the options that you select. This is how you provide What-If analysis functionality. For example, you could add filters or slicers for the Product Name and

Ship To State to the pivot table shown above in Figure 11-3. That would let you select the specific product sales for each sales rep, instead of all products.

PowerPivot Pivot Table And Pivot Chart Overview

Pivot tables and pivot charts are great business intelligence tools because they allow large amounts of data to be summarized and analyzed easily. As you read in Chapter 3 [See Table 3-4], there are eight layouts for pivot tables and pivot charts that you can select from. Many of these layout configurations are similar. If you understand how the three basic layouts work: One pivot table, one pivot chart and flattened pivot table, you should not have a problem using the other five layouts. These three layouts are discussed below.

Using One Pivot Table

Select this option when you need to create a pivot table without a pivot chart. Figure 11-4 shows the options when the PivotTable option is selected. Notice at the top of the window that the **PIVOTTABLE TOOLS** tabs from Excel are available. This means that you can use the options on the Options tab [See Figure 11-5] and the Design tab [See Figure 11-10], that you may already be familiar with, to enhance the PowerPivot pivot tables that you create.

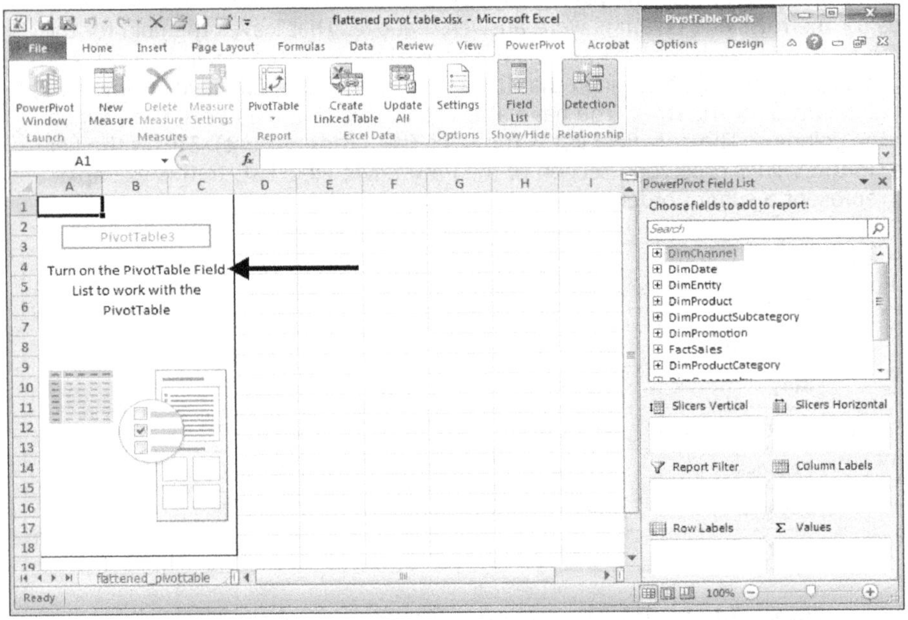

Figure 11-4 PowerPivot pivot table layout

> **Pivot Table Field List Warning**
> As illustrated above in Figure 11-4 on the left, is a warning that states that the PivotTable Field List is not enabled. Don't worry, you can ignore this warning because the correct field list is enabled. If you look on the right side of the figure you will see that the PowerPivot Field List is enabled. To create a pivot table or pivot chart using PowerPivot data you have to use the PowerPivot Field List. The PivotTable Field List cannot be used because it is not connected to the PowerPivot data.

Pivot Table Tools Contextual Tabs

The tabs shown in Figure 11-5 and Figure 11-10 are part of Excel, but are available when a pivot table is selected, even if the pivot table was created using data from a PowerPivot table. The options on these tabs are used to customize the appearance of pivot tables.

Options Tab

The dialog boxes that the Options and Field Settings buttons shown in Figure 11-5 open, may be useful when modifying a pivot table. These options are explained below.

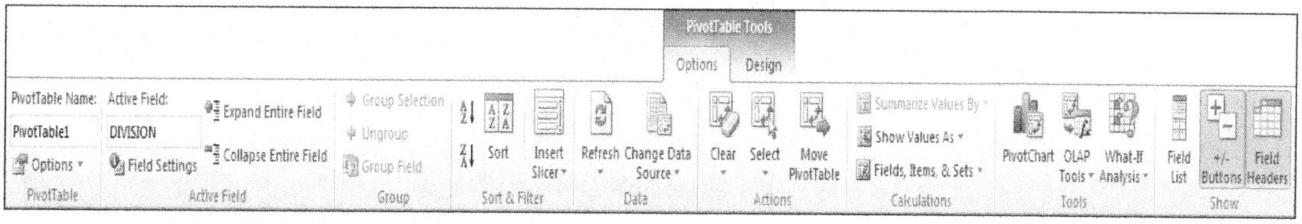

Figure 11-5 Options tab options

PivotTable Options Dialog Box

Clicking the **OPTIONS** button in the PivotTable group shown above in Figure 11-5, opens the dialog box shown in Figure 11-6.

The options on the first two tabs are used to change the layout, format, totals and filter options for the pivot table.

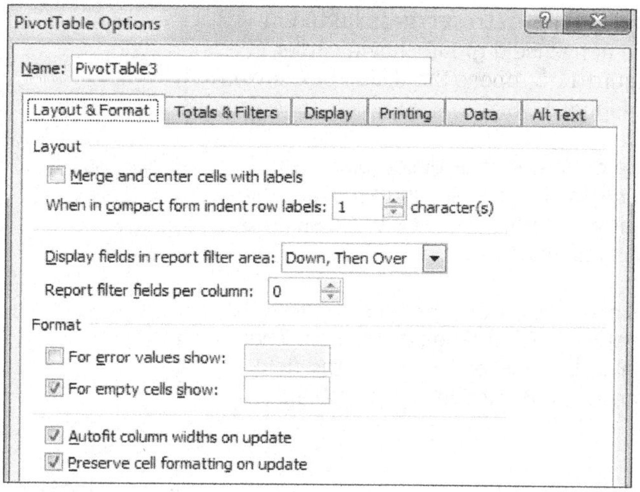

Figure 11-6 Layout & Format tab options

As shown in Figure 11-7, grand totals that are added by default to the pivot table, can be removed.

The way that filters change how the total amounts are calculated can also be changed.

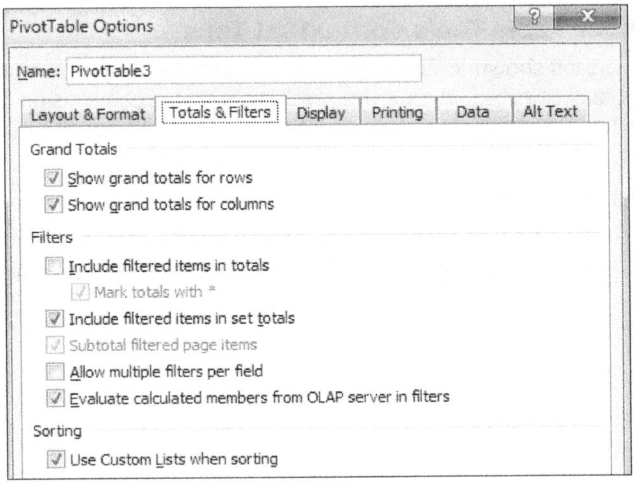

Figure 11-7 Totals & Filters tab options

Field Settings Dialog Box

Clicking the **FIELD SETTINGS** button in the Active Field group shown earlier in Figure 11-5, opens the dialog box shown in Figure 11-8.

The options on this dialog box are used to customize the field in the pivot table that was selected before this dialog box was opened.

As shown later in Figure 11-26, there is another Field Settings dialog box. That dialog box is used to change the field name that is used in a pivot table.

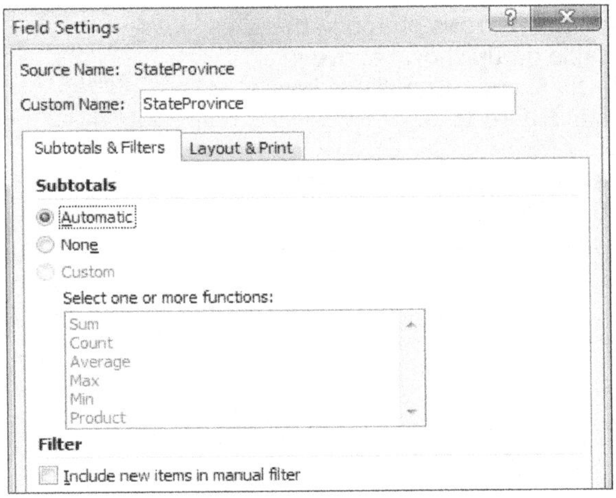

Figure 11-8 Subtotals & Filters tab options

If you know that the pivot table will be printed, you may have the need to change the default options shown in Figure 11-9.

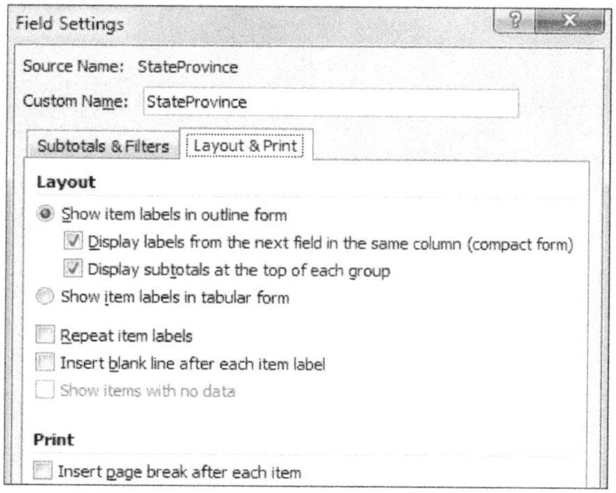

Figure 11-9 Layout & Print tab options

Design Tab

The options shown in Figure 11-10 are used to change the appearance of the pivot table. Selecting the **BANDED ROWS** option will change the background color of every other row in the pivot table, as shown in Figure 11-11. Enabling this option may make it easier to read the data in a pivot table that has a lot of rows.

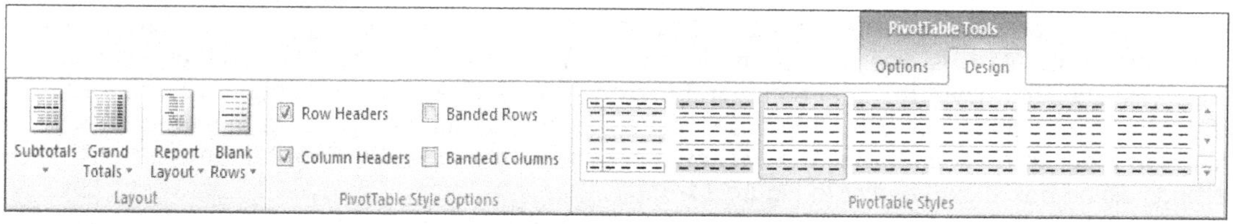

Figure 11-10 Pivot table Design tab options

Count of ID	Column Labels									
Row Labels	CA	CO	FL	HI	IL	NV	TN	UT	WI	Grand Total
Axen	1									1
Edwards						1				1
Eggerer	1									1
Goldschmidt	1									1
Grilo		1								1
Hasselberg								1		1

Figure 11-11 Pivot table with Banded Rows option applied

Using One Pivot Chart

Select this option when you only need to create one pivot chart without a pivot table displayed on the same worksheet. Figure 11-12 shows the options when the pivot chart option is selected. Notice that the instruction in the chart area on the left tells you to select fields from the PivotTable Field List instead of the PowerPivot Field List, just like you saw earlier in Figure 11-4 for pivot tables.

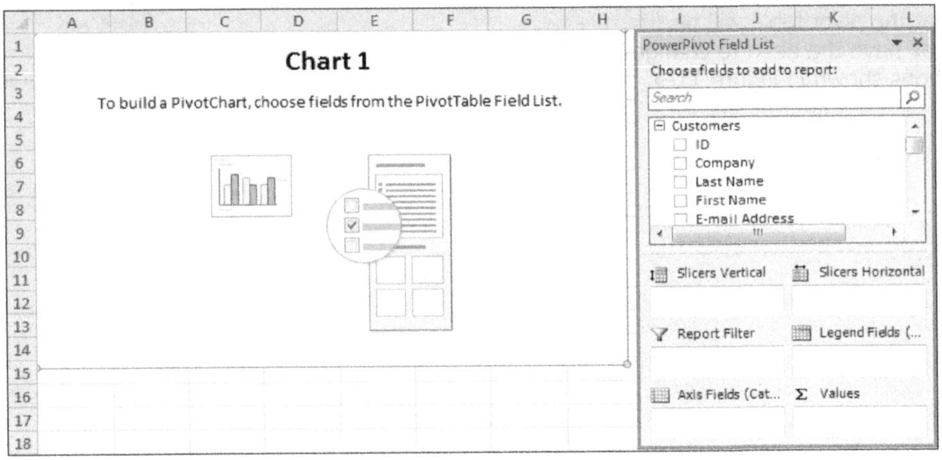

Figure 11-12 PowerPivot pivot chart layout

Using A Flattened Pivot Table

Flattened pivot tables are designed to be more print friendly. They are only available for PowerPivot data. As shown in Figure 11-13, notice that some of the column headings are easier to understand in the Flattened pivot table and that each row displays the filter group name. To me, a flattened pivot table looks similar to a spreadsheet because of the repetition of data in columns.

Compare the pivot table shown in Figure 11-13 to the one shown later in Figure 11-14. While they display different data sets, you can see the features that a flattened pivot table has that a standard pivot table does not have. It would be great if there was a way to turn an existing pivot table into a flattened pivot table, if needed. The closet that I was able to get was to select the **SHOW ITEM LABELS IN TABULAR FORM** and **REPEAT ITEM LABELS** options on the Layout & Print tab on the Field Settings dialog box shown earlier in Figure 11-9.

G	H	I	J	K
StoreType	Online			
Sum of SalesAmount		CalendarYear		
StoreName	ProductCategoryName	2007	2008	2009
Contoso Asia Online Store	Audio	1392089.651	3845074.381	6291990.679
Contoso Asia Online Store	Cameras and camcorders	53105292.45	58530245.16	58853219.11
Contoso Asia Online Store	Cell phones	17463766.24	18727338.05	25224586.92
Contoso Asia Online Store	Computers	61730570.51	69293994.96	77309017.96
Contoso Asia Online Store	Music, Movies and Audio Books	3678032.351	3803581.908	3302814.112
Contoso Asia Online Store	TV and Video	19514108.38	34227110.08	41869086.99
Contoso Asia Online Store Total		156883859.6	188427344.5	212850715.8
Contoso Europe Online Store	Audio	1671060.3	3349933.152	5007450.127
Contoso Europe Online Store	Cameras and camcorders	57331963.15	53269536.98	46157400.89
Contoso Europe Online Store	Cell phones	18198798.43	16433105.71	19823942.39
Contoso Europe Online Store	Computers	64859018.44	64252887.1	68548449.65
Contoso Europe Online Store	Music, Movies and Audio Books	3607160.158	3358547.241	2796927.117
Contoso Europe Online Store	TV and Video	22011515.96	29780126.03	32905552.27
Contoso Europe Online Store Total		167679516.4	170444136.2	175239722.4

Figure 11-13 Flattened pivot table layout

PowerPivot Field List Options For A Pivot Table

Chapter 3 introduced you to the PowerPivot Field List shown earlier on the right side of Figure 11-4 and the PivotTable Field List. The options at the top of the PowerPivot Field List are used to search for and select fields to add to the pivot table. While the field lists look similar and both are used to create pivot tables, there are some differences, as discussed below.

① Only the PowerPivot Field List can be used to create pivot tables and pivot charts that are based on PowerPivot data.
② The PowerPivot Field List displays all of the tables from the PowerPivot window. This means that you can select fields from any of the tables in the list. The PivotTable Field List does not have this functionality.
③ The PowerPivot Field List makes it easier to use the slicer feature because the bottom section of the list has horizontal and vertical slicer options.
④ The PivotTable Field List has the **FIELDS SECTION** and **AREAS SECTION** options that the PowerPivot Field List does not have.
⑤ The PivotTable Field List has a **DEFER LAYOUT UPDATE** option, which is used to enable manual updating of the pivot table, instead of the default automatic update option.

Drop Zones

The options at the bottom of the PowerPivot Field List are called **DROP ZONES**. They are used to add, move and remove rows and columns from the pivot table. These options are explained in Table 11-1. Figure 11-14 illustrates the last four drop zones in Table 11-1.

Drop Zone	Fields Added To This Drop Zone . . .
Slicers Vertical	Display all of the values in the field vertically, as shown on the left side of Figure 11-15. Clicking on an option in the slicer displays the corresponding values in the pivot table, as shown in Figure 11-16. (1)
Slicers Horizontal	Display all of the values in the field horizontally. (1)
Report Filter	Are automatically placed above the column labels in the pivot table. The fields in this drop zone are used to filter the data in the pivot table.
Column Labels	Are placed across the top of the pivot table. This list of values should be shorter then the list in the Row Labels drop zone.
Row Labels	Will appear down the left side of the pivot table. They are usually fields that you imported into a PowerPivot table, instead of calculated fields. Often, they are text fields. Fields placed in this drop zone usually are the longer list of values, just like it would be in a cross-tab report.
Values	Contain a numeric value the majority of the time. A total calculation is automatically created for fields that are added to this drop zone. You can also create a field to place in this drop zone by clicking the New Measure button on the PowerPivot tab. Fields in this drop zone are called **MEASURES** because they have a formula.

Table 11-1 PowerPivot Field List drop zone options for pivot tables explained

(1) This option is covered in Chapter 14.

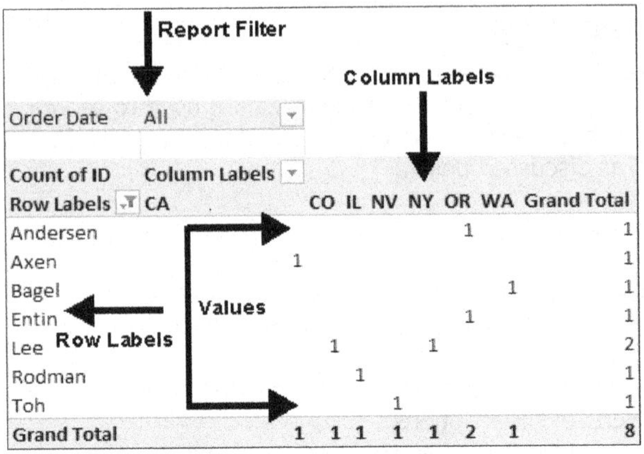

Figure 11-14 Parts of a pivot table illustrated

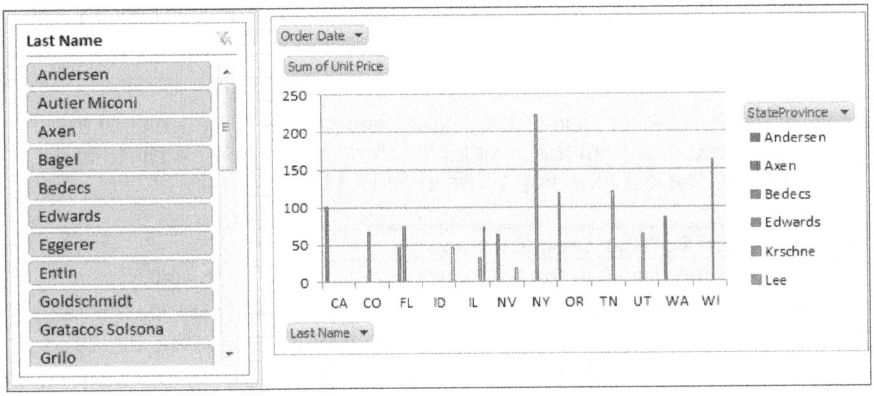

Figure 11-15 Vertical slicers

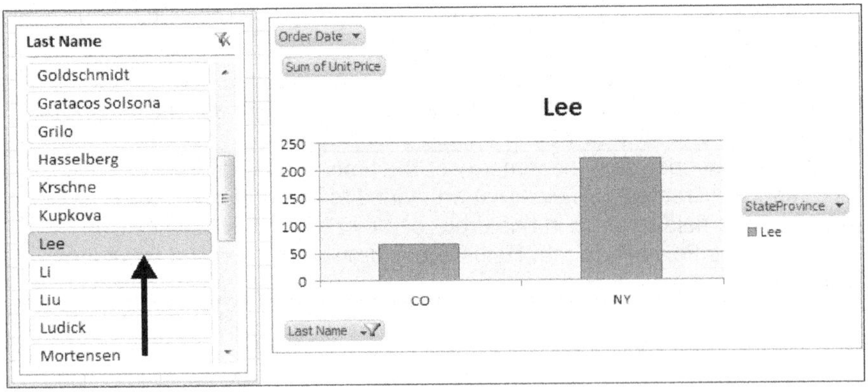

Figure 11-16 Option selected in slicer section of the report illustrated

PowerPivot Field List Check Box Functionality
The check boxes next to each field in the top section of the PowerPivot Field List are used to automatically add fields to a drop zone in the PowerPivot Field List based on the field type, as explained below.

① Numeric fields are added to the Values drop zone with a Sum calculation.
② Text and date fields are added to the Row Labels drop zone.

Pivot Table Creation Tip
In the pivot table exercises in this chapter, you will see the dialog box shown in Figure 11-17 after you select a pivot table option from the PivotTable button on the PowerPivot tab. Unless the exercise states otherwise, select the Existing Worksheet option, then click OK.

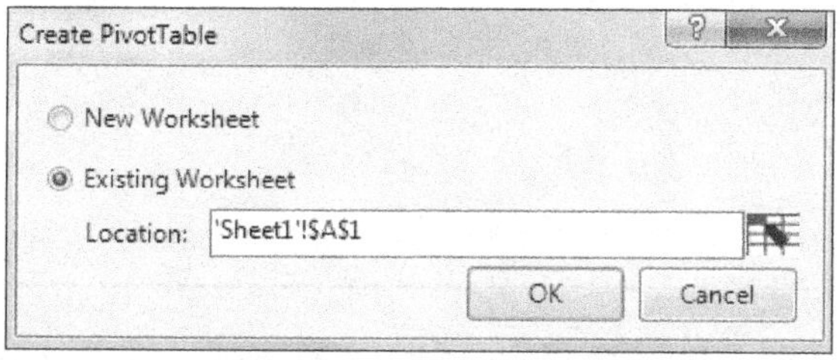

Figure 11-17 Create PivotTable dialog box

Exercise 11.1: Use The Check Boxes To Create A Pivot Table

In this exercise you will create a basic pivot table by using the check boxes in the PowerPivot Field List. The pivot table will display customers and their order subtotal.

1. Save the E9.2 workbook as `E11.1 Use check boxes to create a pivot table`.

2. PowerPivot tab ⇒ Report group ⇒ PivotTable button ⇒ PivotTable.

3. In the Orders table in the PowerPivot Field List, check the box for the Ship Name field.

4. In the Order Subtotals table, check the box for the Subtotal field.

   The bottom of the PowerPivot Field List should look like the one shown in Figure 11-18.

   The pivot table should look like the one shown in Figure 11-19.

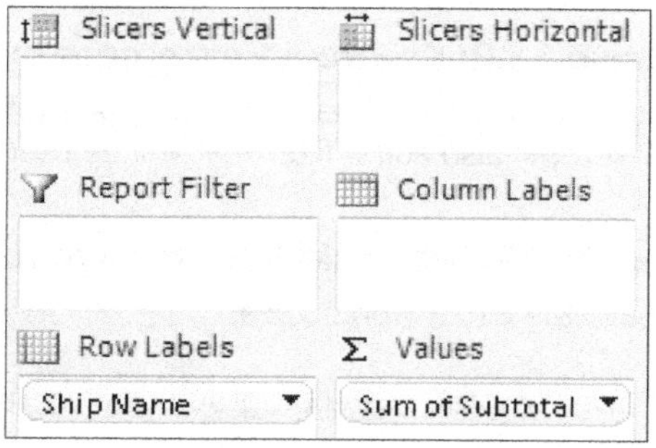

Figure 11-18 PowerPivot Field List drop zone options

	A	B
1	**Row Labels**	**Sum of Subtotal**
2	Amritansh Raghav	15432.5
3	Anna Bedecs	2410.75
4	Christina Lee	4949
5	Elizabeth Andersen	4683
6	Francisco Pérez-Olaeta	8007.5
7	John Edwards	1190
8	John Rodman	860
9	Karen Toh	1505
10	Ming-Yang Xie	13800
11	Peter Krschne	1019.5
12	Roland Wacker	1412.5
13	Run Liu	3625.25
14	Soo Jung Lee	2905.5
15	Sven Mortensen	3786.5
16	Thomas Axen	2550
17	**Grand Total**	**68137**

Figure 11-19 Order subtotal pivot table

5. Save the changes.

> **OLAP Database**
> In Chapter 1, I mentioned that PowerPivot imports the data into an Online Analytical Processing database (OLAP). If you look towards the right side of the status bar in the Excel window, right after you select a field to add to the Values drop zone, you will see the messages shown in Figures 11-20 and 11-21. This is the OLAP database that is attached to a PowerPivot workbook. It stores the data in all of the tables in the PowerPivot window.

Refreshing the OLAP Cube ... (Press Esc to cancel)

Figure 11-20 OLAP Cube processing message

Running OLAP query ... (Press Esc to cancel)

Figure 11-21 OLAP query processing message

Exercise 11.2: Create A Customers By State Pivot Table

In this exercise you will learn how to create a pivot table that displays a count of customers per state. You will also add a filter that will be used to select order dates to filter the pivot table by.

Select The Pivot Table Report Layout

1. Save the E10.2 workbook as `E11.2 Customers by state pivot table.`
2. PowerPivot tab ⇒ Report group ⇒ PivotTable button ⇒ PivotTable.
3. Select the Existing Worksheet option on the Create PivotTable dialog box, then click the button at the end of the Location field.

4. Click in cell B3. You should see in the dialog box shown in Figure 11-22.

   Click OK twice to close both dialog boxes.

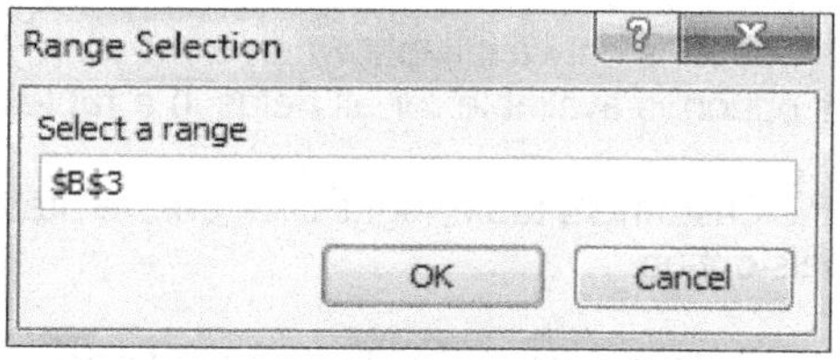

Figure 11-22 Range Selection dialog box

Select The Fields For The Pivot Table

In this part of the exercise you will select the fields for the Column Labels, Row Labels and Report Filter drop zones.

1. Display the fields in the Customers table, if they are not already displayed.
2. Right-click on the Customer Full Name field and select Add to Row Labels on the shortcut menu shown in Figure 11-23.

   The options on this shortcut menu are explained in Table 11-2.

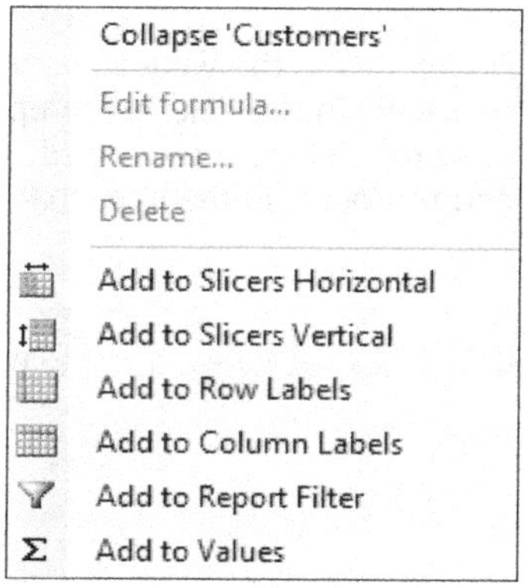

Figure 11-23 PowerPivot Field List shortcut menu (for pivot tables)

PowerPivot Field List Shortcut Menu Options

Option	Description
Collapse "Table Name"	Hides the fields in the table.
Edit formula	Opens the Measure Settings dialog box so that the formula can be modified. (2)
Rename	Opens the Measure Settings dialog box so that the Measure Name field can be changed. (2)
Delete	Deletes the selected measure.
Show Error	Opens the Measure Settings dialog box to view the error that the formula has. This option is not shown in Figure 11-23. (2)
Add to Slicers Horizontal	Adds the field to the Slicers Horizontal drop zone. (3)
Add to Slicers Vertical	Adds the field to the Slicers Vertical drop zone. (3)
Add to Row Labels	Adds the field to the Row Labels drop zone. (3)
Add to Column Labels	Adds the field to the Column Labels drop zone. (3)
Add to Report Filter	Adds the field to the Report Filter drop zone. (3)
Add to Values	Adds the field to the Values drop zone. (3)

Table 11-2 PowerPivot Field List shortcut menu options (for pivot tables) explained

(2) This option is only available when a measure field is selected.
(3) This option is available for all fields in a table except measure fields.

3. In the Customers table, right-click on the State Province field, then select the Add to Column Labels option.

4. In the Orders table, right-click on the Order Date field, then select the Add to Report Filter option.

Add A Field To The Values Drop Zone

In this part of the exercise you will add the fields that will be summarized to the Values drop zone. In this exercise the goal is to get a count of customers by state. That means that you need to select a customer field that has a unique value for each customer.

1. In the Customers table, right-click on the ID field, then select the Add to Values option.

If you look at the pivot table shown in Figure 11-24, the values in each state column are not a count, they are the actual Customer ID number. In the field in the upper left corner of Figure 11-24 you see the Values drop zone field and how the field is summarized. To get a count, the ID field in the Values drop zone needs to be changed to Count. Remember that the default aggregation is Sum.

Sum of ID	Column Labels															
Row Labels	CA	CO	FL	HI	ID	IL	MA	MN	NV	NY	OR	TN	UT	WA	WI	Grand Total
Alexander Eggerer	19															19
Amritansh Raghav												28				28
Andre Ludick												13				13
Anna Bedecs														1		1
Antonio Gratacos Solsona							2									2
Bernard Tham								21								21

Figure 11-24 Pivot table with incorrect values

2. Click on the Sum of ID field in the Values drop zone.

   You will see the shortcut menu shown in Figure 11-25.

   Select the **SUMMARIZE BY** option, then select Count.

   The options on the shortcut menu are explained in Table 11-3.

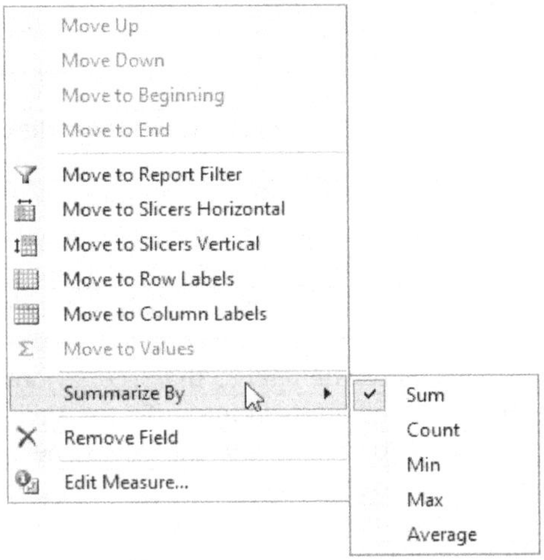

Figure 11-25 PowerPivot Field List drop zone shortcut menu

PowerPivot Field List Drop Zone Shortcut Menu Options

Option	Description
Move Up	Moves the selected field up one in the drop zone.
Move Down	Moves the selected field down one in the drop zone.
Move to Beginning	Moves the selected field to the top of the drop zone.
Move to End	Moves the selected field to the bottom of the drop zone.
Move to Report Filter	Moves the selected field to the Report Filter drop zone.
Move to Slicers Horizontal	Moves the selected field to the Slicers Horizontal drop zone.
Move to Slicers Vertical	Moves the selected field to the Slicers Vertical drop zone.
Move to Row Labels	Moves the selected field to the Row Labels drop zone.
Move to Column Labels	Moves the selected field to the Column Labels drop zone.
Move to Values	Moves the selected field to the Values drop zone.
Summarize By	The options on this submenu are used to change how the field is calculated. (4)
Remove Field	Deletes the field from the drop zone.
Edit Measure	Opens the Measure Settings dialog. (4)
Field Settings	Opens the dialog box shown in Figure 11-26. This option is available for all drop zones except the Values drop zone.

Table 11-3 PowerPivot Field List drop zone shortcut menu options explained

(4) This option is only available for fields in the Values drop zone.

This dialog box is used to change the field name that is displayed in the pivot table.

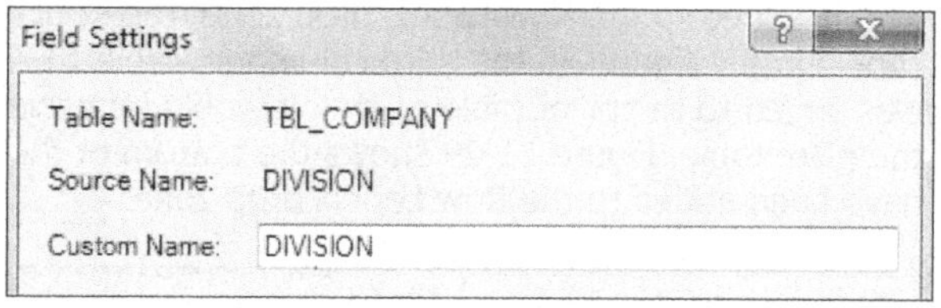

Figure 11-26 Field Settings dialog box

3. Your pivot table should look like the one shown in Figure 11-27. Save the changes.

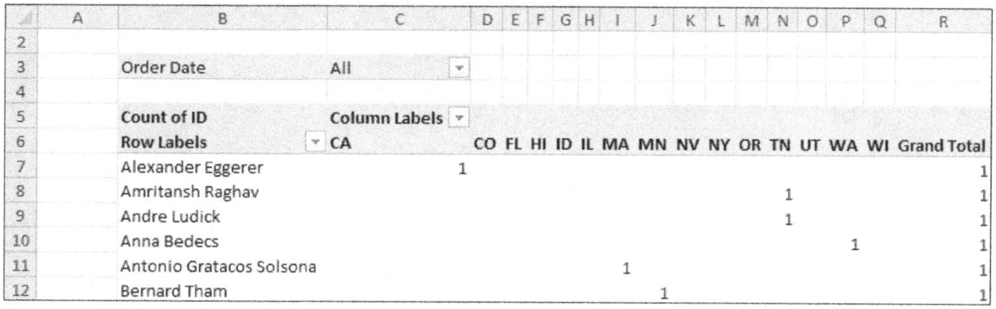

Order Date: All

Count of ID — Column Labels

Row Labels	CA	CO	FL	HI	ID	IL	MA	MN	NV	NY	OR	TN	UT	WA	WI	Grand Total
Alexander Eggerer	1															1
Amritansh Raghav												1				1
Andre Ludick												1				1
Anna Bedecs														1		1
Antonio Gratacos Solsona							1									1
Bernard Tham								1								1

Figure 11-27 Customers by state pivot table report

Exercise 11.3: Create A Yearly Sales By Country Pivot Table

In this exercise you will create a pivot table that displays the yearly sales for each country.

1. Save the E9.3 workbook as `E11.3 Yearly sales by country pivot table.`

2. Add a pivot table to the worksheet.

3. Add the Calendar Year field in the DimDate table to the Column Labels drop zone.

4. Add the Channel Name field in the DimChannel table to the Report Filter drop zone.

5. Add the Sales Amount field in the FactSales table to the Values drop zone. The pivot table should look like the one shown in Figure 11-28.

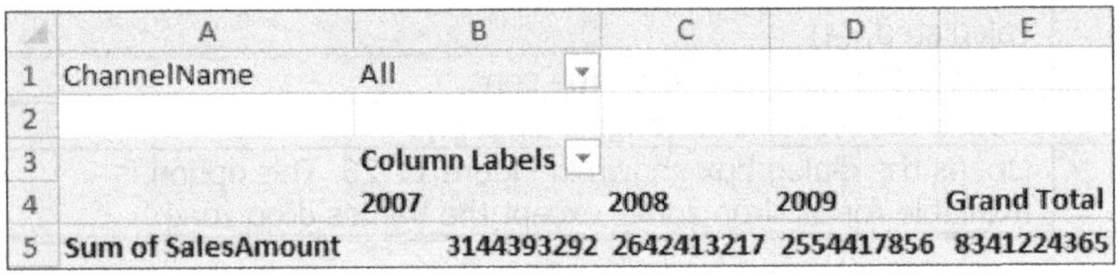

	A	B	C	D	E
1	ChannelName	All			
2					
3		Column Labels			
4		2007	2008	2009	Grand Total
5	Sum of SalesAmount	3144393292	2642413217	2554417856	8341224365

Figure 11-28 Yearly sales by country pivot table

6. Add the fields in Table 11-4 to the Row Labels drop zone, then save the changes. After each field is added to the Row Labels drop zone, the structure of the pivot table will change, as shown in the figures in the third column in Table 11-4. I included a screen shot after each field was added to the pivot table so that it would be easier for you to know what each field adds to the pivot table. Figure 11-29 shows the bottom of the PowerPivot Field List after all of the fields have been added to the Row Labels drop zone.

Table	Field	Figure
DimGeography	Region Country Name	Figure 11-30
Stores	Store Name	Figure 11-31
DimProductCategory	Product Category Name	Figure 11-32
DimProductSubcategory	Product Subcategory Name	Figure 11-33

Table 11-4 Fields to add to the Row Labels drop zone

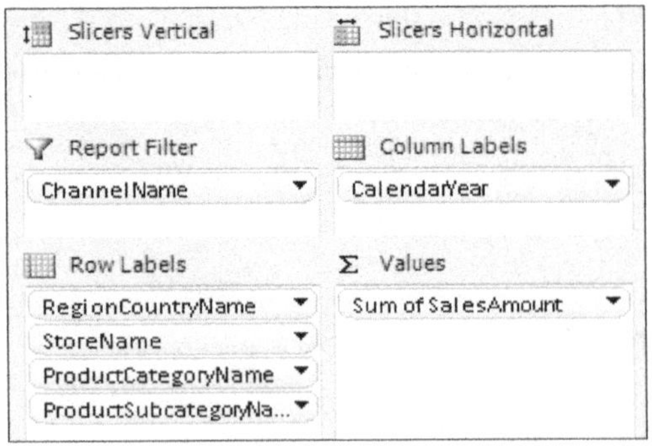

Figure 11-29 Drop zone section of the PowerPivot Field List

	A	B	C	D	E
3	**Sum of SalesAmount**	**Column Labels**			
4	**Row Labels**	**2007**	**2008**	**2009**	**Grand Total**
5	Armenia	7940032.42	8662141.736	9482761.087	26084935.24
6	Australia	23168631.98	26881924.55	29116033.12	79166589.65
7	Bhutan	7837852.029	8628060.29	13570713.85	30036626.16
8	Canada	77067627.45	53160435.69	45714689.59	175942752.7
9	China	308391585.3	358389358.1	397075325.6	1063856269

Figure 11-30 Region Country Name field added to the Row Labels drop zone

	A	B	C	D	E
3	**Sum of SalesAmount**	**Column Labels**			
4	**Row Labels**	**2007**	**2008**	**2009**	**Grand Total**
5	**Armenia**	**7940032.42**	**8662141.736**	**9482761.087**	**26084935.24**
6	Contoso Yerevan Store	7940032.42	8662141.736	9482761.087	26084935.24
7	**Australia**	**23168631.98**	**26881924.55**	**29116033.12**	**79166589.65**
8	Contoso Canberra Store	7167499.39	8836086.69	9798438.882	25802024.96
9	Contoso Sydney No.2 Store	8306886.651	8920073.264	9487219.845	26714179.76
10	Contoso Sydney No.1 Store	7694245.939	9125764.601	9830374.39	26650384.93
11	**Bhutan**	**7837852.029**	**8628060.29**	**13570713.85**	**30036626.16**
12	Contoso Thimphu No.1 Store	364257.4875		4575478.112	4939735.6
13	Contoso Thimphu No.2 Store	7473594.541	8628060.29	8995235.734	25096890.56
14	**Canada**	**77067627.45**	**53160435.69**	**45714689.59**	**175942752.7**
15	Contoso Calgary Store	7344666.61	4805380.377	4407697.753	16557744.74
16	Contoso Montreal No.1 Store	6783333.57	5009971.002	4082012.037	15875316.61

Figure 11-31 Store Name field added to the Row Labels drop zone

	A	B	C	D	E
3	**Sum of SalesAmount**	**Column Labels**			
4	**Row Labels**	**2007**	**2008**	**2009**	**Grand Total**
5	**Armenia**	**7940032.42**	**8662141.736**	**9482761.087**	**26084935.24**
6	**Contoso Yerevan Store**	**7940032.42**	**8662141.736**	**9482761.087**	**26084935.24**
7	Audio	52884.9945	180801.195	250527.2515	484213.441
8	Cameras and camcorders	2785514.395	2727453.277	2512621.3	8025588.972
9	Cell phones	829705.4025	899327.8635	1095869.603	2824902.869
10	Computers	3079107.409	3203311.879	3774741.016	10057160.3
11	Music, Movies and Audio Books	178498.462	165105.07	132000.2655	475603.7975
12	TV and Video	1014321.757	1486142.452	1717001.652	4217465.86
13	**Australia**	**23168631.98**	**26881924.55**	**29116033.12**	**79166589.65**
14	**Contoso Canberra Store**	**7167499.39**	**8836086.69**	**9798438.882**	**25802024.96**
15	Audio	86781.126	143315.8575	324926.376	555023.3595
16	Cameras and camcorders	2454620.865	2812380.54	2667839.262	7934840.666
17	Cell phones	813624.1955	786757.777	1124706.939	2725088.911
18	Computers	2750508.393	3377157.91	3642935.033	9770601.335
19	Music, Movies and Audio Books	151915.7975	212148.49	157278.586	521342.8735
20	TV and Video	910049.014	1504326.115	1880752.688	4295127.817
21	**Contoso Sydney No.2 Store**	**8306886.651**	**8920073.264**	**9487219.845**	**26714179.76**
22	Audio	65652.227	146496.093	292657.352	504805.672
23	Cameras and camcorders	2667837.58	2830525.637	2768488.283	8266851.499
24	Cell phones	939330.6445	787205.089	1175428.399	2901964.132

Figure 11-32 Product Category Name field added to the Row Labels drop zone

	A	B	C	D	E
3	**Sum of SalesAmount**	**Column Labels**			
4	**Row Labels**	**2007**	**2008**	**2009**	**Grand Total**
5	**Armenia**	**7940032.42**	**8662141.736**	**9482761.087**	**26084935.24**
6	**Contoso Yerevan Store**	**7940032.42**	**8662141.736**	**9482761.087**	**26084935.24**
7	Audio	52884.9945	180801.195	250527.2515	484213.441
8	Bluetooth Headphones	9148.382	40768.109	106332.3185	156248.8095
9	MP4&MP3	30147.82	68799.3985	79658.038	178605.2565
10	Recording Pen	13588.7925	71233.6875	64536.895	149359.375
11	Cameras and camcorders	2785514.395	2727453.277	2512621.3	8025588.972
12	Camcorders	1634654.5	1581742.35	1230821.1	4447217.95
13	Cameras & Camcorders Accessories	24799.725	45675.097	109827.31	180302.132
14	Digital Cameras	392388.91	369581.62	346682.815	1108653.345

Figure 11-33 Product Subcategory Name field added to the Row Labels drop zone

Exercise 11.4: Create A Customer Orders By Year Pivot Table

In this exercise you will create a pivot table that displays customer orders by year. The Year field that you will use is from the formula that you created in Exercise 10.4. You will also add three report filters to the pivot table.

1. Save the E10.4 workbook as `E11.4 Customer orders by year pivot table.`
2. Add a pivot table to the worksheet.
3. Add the fields in Table 11-5 to create the pivot table. When prompted to create a relationship, do so.

Table	Field	Add To Drop Zone	Rename To
Sales_SalesOrderHeader	Total Due	Values	
Sales_SalesTerritory	Name	Report Filter	Select A Territory
Production_Product	Name	Report Filter	Select A Product
Purchasing_ShipMethod	Name	Report Filter	Shipping Method
Sales_SalesOrderHeader	Order Year	Column Labels	
Person_Contact	Last Name	Row Labels	
Person_Contact	First Name	Row Labels	

Table 11-5 Fields to create the pivot table

4. The pivot table should look like the one shown in Figure 11-34. Save the changes.

	A	B	C	D	E	F
1	SelectTerritory	All				
2	SelectAProduct	All				
3	SelectAShippingMethod	All				
4						
5	**Sum of TotalDue**	**Column Labels**				
6	**Row Labels**	**2001**	**2002**	**2003**	**2004**	**Grand Total**
7	**⊟Abel**			**79447.5981**	**73054.246**	**152501.8441**
8	Catherine			79447.5981	73054.246	152501.8441
9	**⊟Abercrombie**	**111519.1132**	**306635.7003**	**200671.0143**	**70881.2252**	**689707.053**
10	Kim	111519.1132	306635.7003	200671.0143	70881.2252	689707.053
11	**⊟Acevedo**	**49873.5599**	**40573.306**	**9793.1668**	**1251.6049**	**101491.6376**
12	Humberto	49873.5599	40573.306	9793.1668	1251.6049	101491.6376
13	**⊟Achong**	**5370.284**	**88472.2984**	**81925.44**		**175768.0224**
14	Gustavo	5370.284	88472.2984	81925.44		175768.0224
15	**⊟Ackerman**			**150384.0443**	**150966.1133**	**301350.1576**
16	Pilar			150384.0443	150966.1133	301350.1576
17	**⊟Adams**	**122054.2101**	**169275.4384**	**344830.635**	**291599.1534**	**927759.4369**
18	Aaron			130.3458		130.3458
19	Adam				156.8879	156.8879

Figure 11-34 Customer orders by year pivot table report

Custom Lists

Custom lists are used to sort data. By default, PowerPivot sorts in alphabetical order because it does not know about the custom list functionality in Excel. Often, sorting in alphabetical order is just what you need. Other times, sorting alphabetically products unexpected results, as you will see in Exercise 11.5. Excel provides default custom lists and allows you to create your own. If you are not familiar with custom lists, follow the steps below to view the default lists that come with Excel.

1. File tab ⇒ Options ⇒ Advanced. You will see the dialog box and options shown in Figure 11-35.

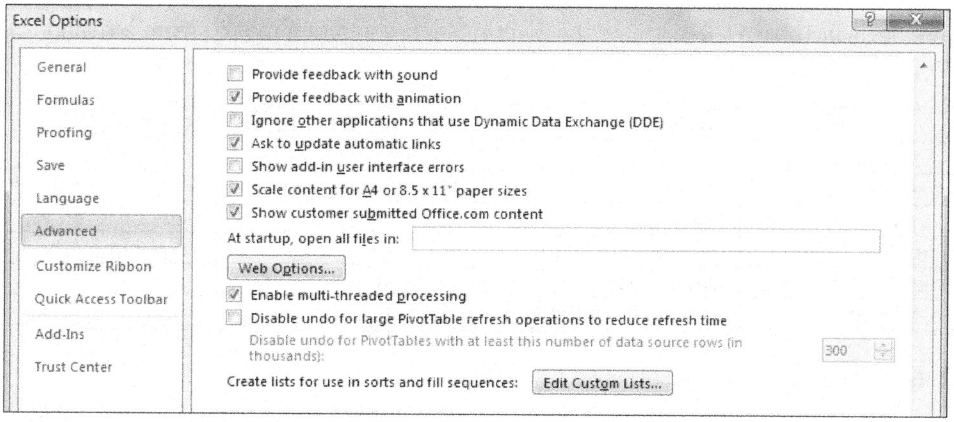

Figure 11-35 Excel Options dialog box

2. Click the **EDIT CUSTOM LISTS** button shown above in Figure 11-35.

   You will see the dialog box shown in Figure 11-36.

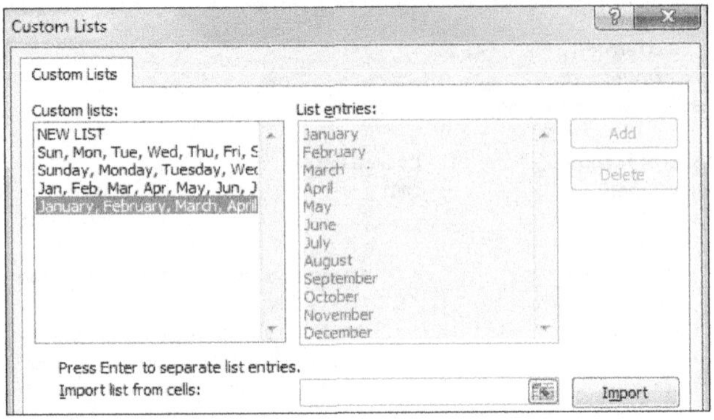

Figure 11-36 Custom Lists dialog box

3. Click on a custom list to view all of the entries. As shown above in Figure 11-36, a default custom list exists to sort the months in what I call calendar month order. You will learn how to apply this custom list in Exercise 11.5.

Exercise 11.5: Create A Customer Orders By Month And Year Pivot Table

The pivot table that you will create in this exercise is similar to the one that you created in Exercise 11.4. The difference is that the month names will be displayed in the left column instead of the customers name. In Exercise 10.4 you created a formula that formatted the order date field to display the full month name.

1. Save the E10.4 workbook as `E11.5 Customer orders by month and year.`

2. Add a pivot table to the worksheet.

3. Add the fields in Table 11-6 to create the pivot table. When prompted to create a relationship, do so.

Table	Field	Add To Drop Zone	Rename To
Sales_SalesOrderHeader	Total Due	Values	
Sales_SalesTerritory	Name	Report Filter	Select A Territory
Production_Product	Name	Report Filter	Select A Product
Purchasing_ShipMethod	Name	Report Filter	Shipping Method
Sales_SalesOrderHeader	Order Year	Column Labels	
Sales_SalesOrderHeader	OrderFullMonthName	Row Labels	

Table 11-6 Fields to create the pivot table

4. Save the changes. The pivot table should look like the one shown in Figure 11-37. As you can see, the month names are not in the order that you expected.

	A	B	C	D	E	F
1	Select A Territory	All				
2	Shipping Method	All				
3	Name	All				
4						
5	**Sum of TotalDue**	**Column Labels**				
6	**Row Labels**	**2001**	**2002**	**2003**	**2004**	**Grand Total**
7	April		1905833.909	3041865.441	4722890.735	9670590.085
8	August	2605514.981	5433609.343	6775857.075		14814981.4
9	December	3097637.338	3545522.738	6582833.044		13225993.12
10	February		3130823.038	3705635.498	5207182.512	12043641.05
11	January		1605782.192	2233575.113	3691013.223	7530370.527
12	July	1172359.429	3781879.071	4681520.64	56178.9223	9691938.062
13	June		2546121.962	3257517.701	6728034.987	12531674.65
14	March		2643081.08	2611621.26	5272786.811	10527489.15
15	May		3758329.295	4449886.232	6518825.226	14727040.75
16	November	3690018.665	4427598.001	5961182.676		14078799.34
17	October	1688963.274	2854206.752	4243366.594		8786536.62
18	September	2073058.539	4242717.717	6762753.814		13078530.07
19	**Grand Total**	**14327552.23**	**39875505.1**	**54307615.09**	**32196912.42**	**140707584.8**

Figure 11-37 Customer orders by month and year pivot table report

How To Change The Sort Order Of Month Names

As you can see above in Figure 11-35, the month names are in alphabetical order. The pivot table would be easier to read if the month names were displayed in calendar month order. The steps below will show you how to change the sort order of the month names.

1. In the pivot table, open the Row Labels drop-down list, then select the option **MORE SORT OPTIONS**, as shown in Figure 11-38.

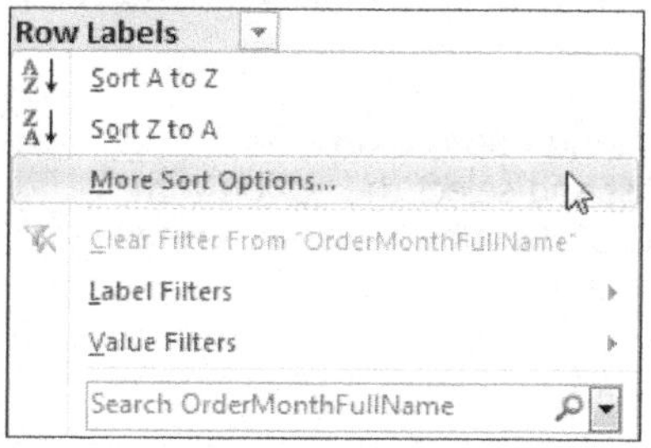

Figure 11-38 Row Labels drop-down list options

2. Select the **ASCENDING (A TO Z) BY** option, then select the OrderMonthFullName field from the drop-down list if necessary.

   You should have the options selected that are shown in Figure 11-39.

Figure 11-39 Sort dialog box

3. Click the **MORE OPTIONS** button at the bottom of the Sort dialog box, shown above in Figure 11-39.

4. Clear the check mark for the **SORT AUTOMATICALLY** option at the top of the More Sort Options dialog box.

5. Open the **FIRST KEY SORT ORDER** field drop-down list and select the option with the full name of the months, as illustrated in Figure 11-40.

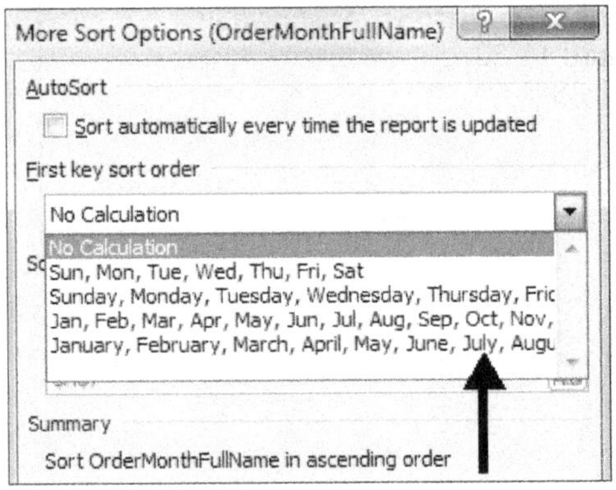

Figure 11-40 Sort option illustrated

6. Click OK twice to close both dialog boxes.

7. Save the changes.

   The pivot table should look like the one shown in Figure 11-41.

Sum of TotalDue	Column Labels				
Row Labels	2001	2002	2003	2004	Grand Total
January		1605782.192	2233575.113	3691013.223	7530370.527
February		3130823.038	3705635.498	5207182.512	12043641.05
March		2643081.08	2611621.26	5272786.811	10527489.15
April		1905833.909	3041865.441	4722890.735	9670590.085
May		3758329.295	4449886.232	6518825.226	14727040.75
June		2546121.962	3257517.701	6728034.987	12531674.65
July	1172359.429	3781879.071	4681520.64	56178.9223	9691938.062
August	2605514.981	5433609.343	6775857.075		14814981.4
September	2073058.539	4242717.717	6762753.814		13078530.07
October	1688963.274	2854206.752	4243366.594		8786536.62
November	3690018.665	4427598.001	5961182.676		14078799.34
December	3097637.338	3545522.738	6582833.044		13225993.12
Grand Total	14327552.23	39875505.1	54307615.09	32196912.42	140707584.8

Figure 11-41 Months sorted in calendar order

Top N Reports

Top and Bottom N reports, commonly known as Top N reports, are used to display the first N or bottom N records in a group. N is a number that you select. In previous exercises in this chapter you created reports that grouped data. By default, the groups are sorted on the value in the group field. For example, in Exercise 11.4 the orders were grouped by year.

There is another way to sort groups on a report. Just like you can filter detail records, you can filter groups. One way to explain Top N reports is that this sort method is sorting the groups on the value of a group summary field instead of the values in the group by field. Top N reports do not display all of the groups. They only display the number of groups that N has. Top N reports rank the groups based on the summary field values. For example, if N=7, only the seven highest groups based on the value of the summary field would be displayed in the pivot table.

Exercise 11.6: Create A Top 10 Pivot Table

In this exercise you will learn how to create a Top 10 pivot table that shows the top 10 stores and their yearly sales amounts.

1. Save the E11.3 workbook as `E11.6 Top 10 pivot table`.

2. Remove all of the fields in the Row Labels drop zone except for the Store Name field. You should see a list of stores, their sales amounts for three years and the grand totals in the pivot table.

Select The Top 10 Options

1. Open the Row Labels drop-down list in cell A4.

2. Select the Value Filters option, then select **TOP 10**, as shown in Figure 11-42.

   You will see the dialog box shown in Figure 11-43.

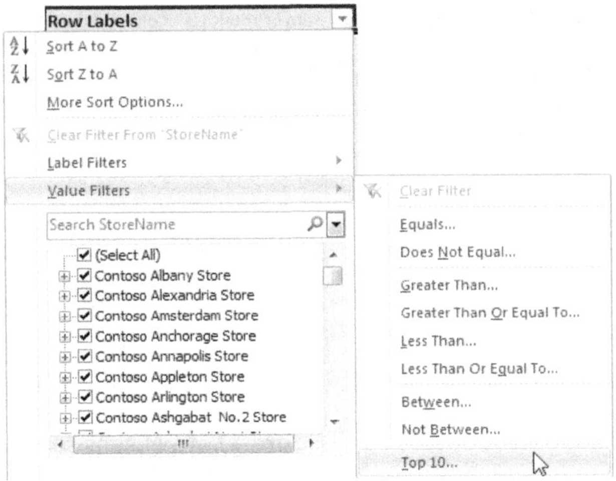

Figure 11-42 Value Filters Top 10 option selected

Top 10 Filter Dialog Box

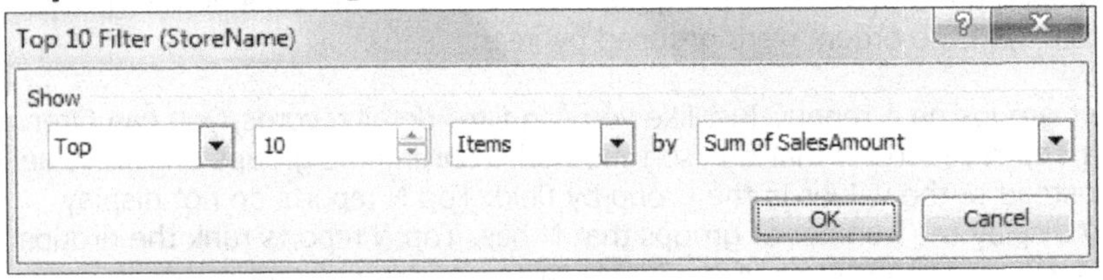

Figure 11-43 Top 10 Filter dialog box

The options on the Top 10 Filter dialog box are primarily used to select a specific number of rows (the N value) to display in the pivot table. The options are explained in Table 11-7.

Option	Description
Show	Is used to select and display the top (highest or largest) values or the bottom (the lowest or smallest) values in the pivot table.
Spinner button	Is used to select how many the N value (the number of items, the percent or sum) to display in the pivot table. Click the Up or Down arrow button at the end of the field to select the number that you want.
Third field	The options in this drop-down list are used to select how you want to filter. The **ITEMS** option is used with the spinner button. It only allows a specific number of rows to be displayed in the pivot table. The **PERCENT** option retrieves the rows that equal the percent that you select. The **SUM** option is used for What-If analysis. It lets you find out how many of something is needed to get to a certain amount. (5)
Fourth field	Displays a list of the value fields in the pivot table, including the fields in the Values drop zone. PowerPivot adds a count field for every table listed at the top of the PowerPivot Field List, as shown in Figure 11-44. (5)

Table 11-7 Top 10 Filter dialog box options explained

(5) I could not find an official name for this field.

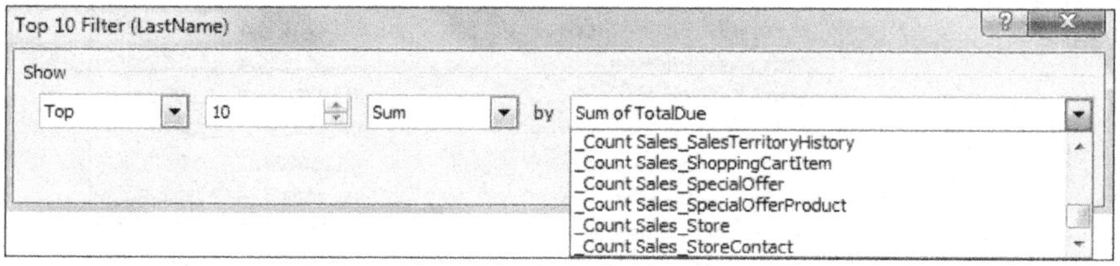

Figure 11-44 Fourth field options

3. For this exercise, accept the default options shown earlier in Figure 11-43. Click OK, then save the changes. The pivot table should look like the one shown in Figure 11-45. This Top 10 report is based on three years of sales data.

Sum of SalesAmount	**Column Labels**			
Row Labels	**2007**	**2008**	**2009**	**Grand Total**
Contoso Asia Online Store	156883859.6	188427344.5	212850715.8	558161919.9
Contoso Asia Reseller	114185396.5	122563956.4	125585967.9	362335320.8
Contoso Catalog Store	273924905.9	211973099.7	210006950.2	695904955.8
Contoso Europe Online Store	167679516.4	170444136.2	175239722.4	513363375.1
Contoso Europe Reseller	122337430.5	111492927	104077933.7	337908291.1
Contoso North America Online Store	189940381.4	208983212.7	215622220.8	614545814.9
Contoso North America Reseller	139379974.1	135938379.3	128986735.5	404305088.9
Contoso Sydney No.2 Store	8306886.651	8920073.264	9487219.845	26714179.76
Contoso Sydney No.1 Store	7694245.939	9125764.601	9830374.39	26650384.93
Contoso Taipei Store	7728609.191	9090492.564	9621821.554	26440923.31
Grand Total	**1188061206**	**1176959386**	**1201309662**	**3566330255**

Figure 11-45 Top 10 stores by sales amount

If you wanted to see the Top 10 stores in terms of sales for a specific year, open the Column Labels drop-down list shown in Figure 11-46 and select the year that you want to see the Top 10 store sales for.

If you select the year 2008, the pivot table would look like the one shown in Figure 11-47.

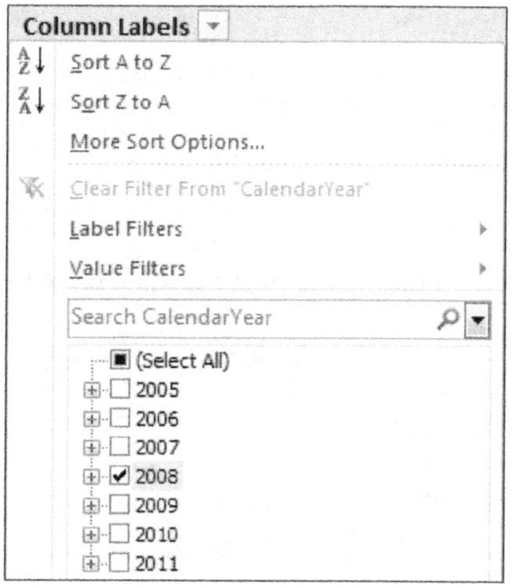

Figure 11-46 Column Labels filter options

It would be a good idea to remove the grand total column because the values are the same as the yearly values.

Sum of SalesAmount	Column Labels	
Row Labels	2008	Grand Total
Contoso Asia Online Store	188427344.5	188427344.5
Contoso Asia Reseller	122563956.4	122563956.4
Contoso Catalog Store	211973099.7	211973099.7
Contoso Europe Online Store	170444136.2	170444136.2
Contoso Europe Reseller	111492927	111492927
Contoso Kolkata Store	9137428.476	9137428.476
Contoso North America Online Store	208983212.7	208983212.7
Contoso North America Reseller	135938379.3	135938379.3
Contoso Sydney No.1 Store	9125764.601	9125764.601
Contoso Tehran No.1 Store	9247336.393	9247336.393
Grand Total	**1177333585**	**1177333585**

Figure 11-47 Top 10 stores in 2008 pivot table

If you wanted to see the stores in the lowest 5% of sales, select the options shown in Figure 11-48. You will see the pivot table shown in Figure 11-49. If you can't remember the Top 10 Filter options that are currently applied to the pivot table, hold the mouse pointer over the filter button, as shown in Figure 11-50, to display the filter options. Only part of the pivot table is displayed in the figure.

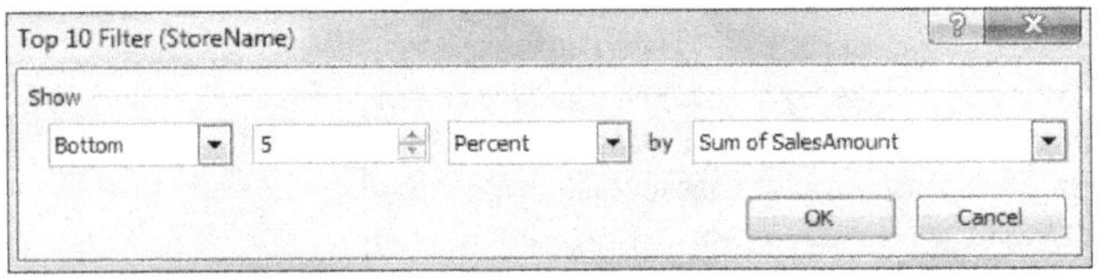

Figure 11-48 Options for the Bottom 5% of stores based on the sales amount

Sum of SalesAmount	Column Labels			
Row Labels	2007	2008	2009	Grand Total
Contoso Venezia Store	158812.43		1056569.072	1215381.502
Contoso Racine No.2 Store	156462.16		1647448.511	1803910.671
Contoso Kyoto Store	262519.1975		2986907.5	3249426.698
Contoso Berlin Store	218948.212	717511.994	2603316.819	3539777.025
Contoso Dallas Store	277258.685	414425.76	2987313.636	3678998.081
Contoso Paterson Store	215552.155	454932.438	3012963.561	3683448.154
Contoso Guangzhou Store	292283.91		4153204.666	4445488.576
Contoso Thimphu No.1 Store	364257.4875		4575478.112	4939735.6
Contoso Marseille Store	273691.894	2456794.119	2414010.286	5144496.299

Figure 11-49 Bottom 5% of store sales pivot table

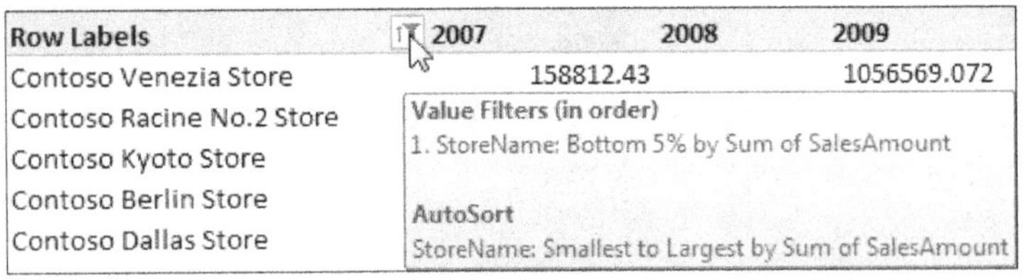

Figure 11-50 Row Labels filter options

CREATING PIVOT CHARTS

In addition to learning how to create pivot charts, you will also learn about the following:

- ☑ Pivot Chart Tools contextual tab options
- ☑ PowerPivot Field List options for pivot charts
- ☑ Pivot chart components
- ☑ Top N pivot charts
- ☑ Selecting a different chart type

CHAPTER 12

Pivot Charts Overview

A pivot chart is a graphical representation of data in a pivot table. This visual representation often makes it easier to understand and summarize the data. Because of the various chart types, it is often easier to see trends and patterns in the data, as well as make comparisons in one chart type then another.

What Is A Pivot Chart Report?

A pivot chart report is like a pivot table report, because they have filters and slicers. Keep in mind that changes made to the pivot table that the pivot chart is linked to, are automatically made to the pivot chart. Pivot charts can be interactive and display data the same way that standard charts do because they display data series, data markers, axis and categories.

PivotChart Tools Contextual Tabs

Like pivot tables, there are tools in Excel specifically for pivot charts. Figures 12-1 to 12-4 show the pivot chart tools. If you have created standard charts in Excel, you may have already used some of these options.

Design Tab

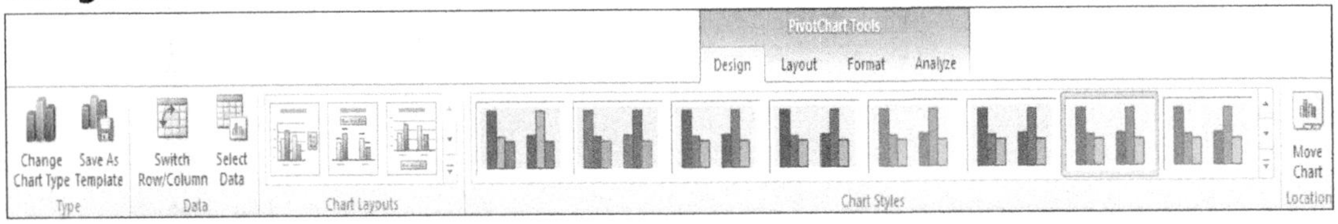

Figure 12-1 Design tab options

Layout Tab

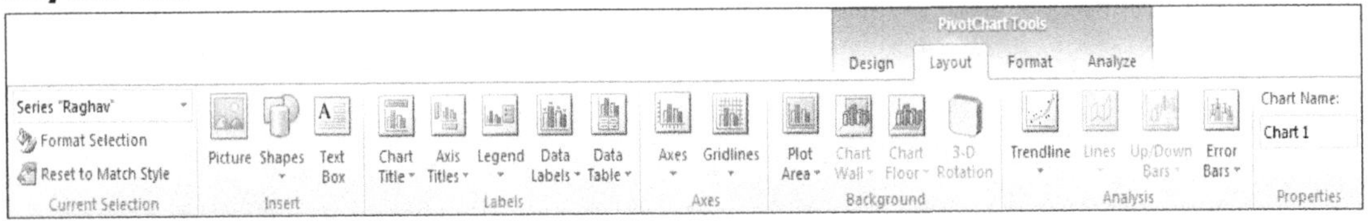

Figure 12-2 Layout tab options

Format Tab

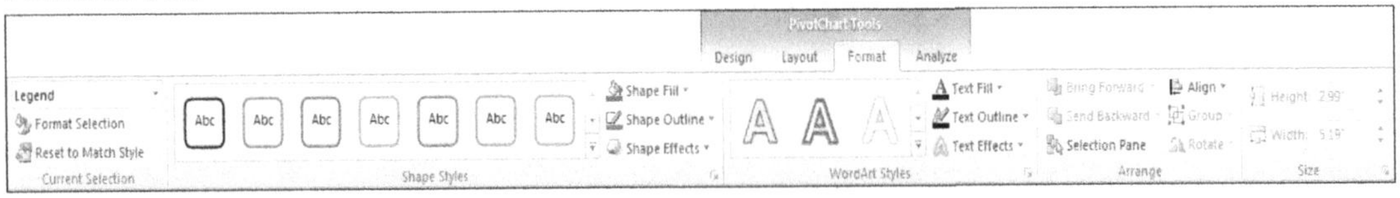

Figure 12-3 Format tab options

Analyze Tab

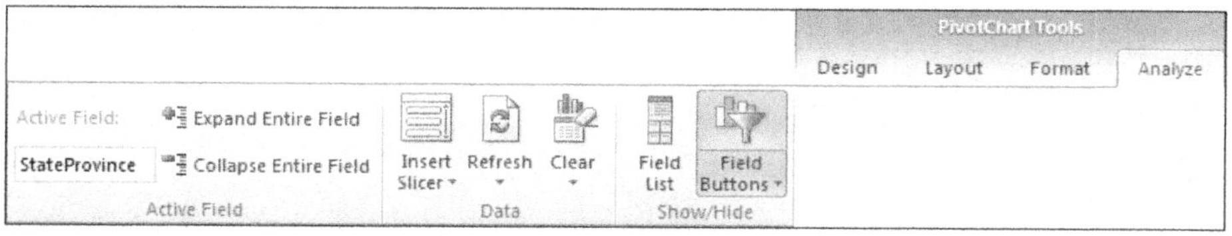

Figure 12-4 Analyze tab options

Pivot Chart Tools That You May Find Helpful

Below are a few options that you may find helpful to enhance your pivot charts.

The **CHART LAYOUTS** options on the Design tab shown in Figure 12-5 are used to rearrange chart objects like the position and style of the legend and the grid style.

The **DATA LABELS** options on the Layout tab shown in Figure 12-6 are used to display the actual value that the slice of a pie chart, a bar or line represents. Figure 12-7 shows the **OUTSIDE END** option applied to the chart.

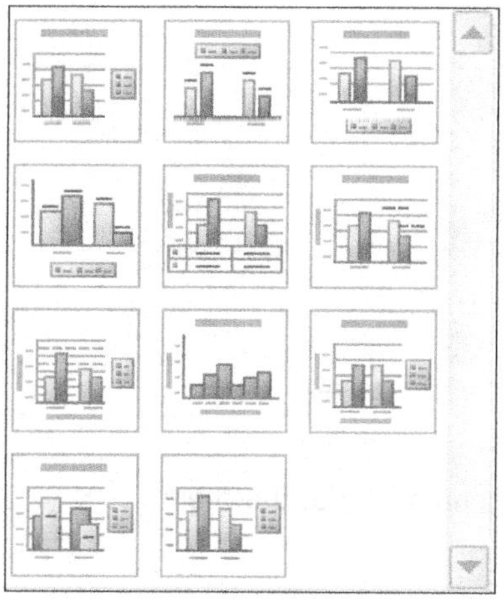

Figure 12-5 Chart Layouts options

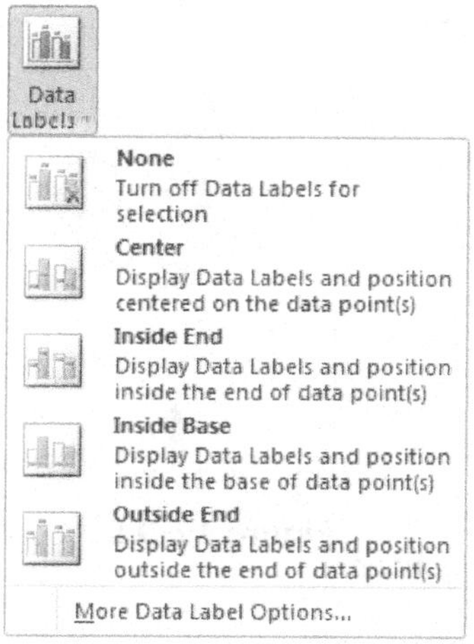

Figure 12-6 Data Labels options

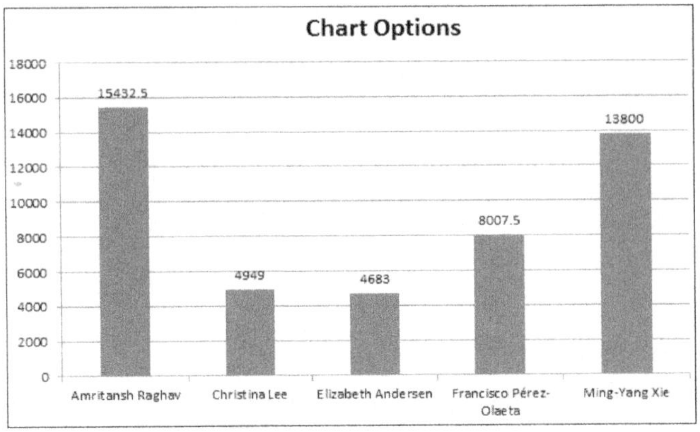

Figure 12-7 Outside End data labels option applied to a chart

The **DATA TABLE** options on the Layout tab shown in Figure 12-8 are used to add a table to the bottom of a chart. The values in the table are the values displayed in the chart. Figure 12-9 shows the pivot chart with a data table and legend keys at the bottom of the chart. If the chart displays a lot of data, this option can be used instead of placing the actual values on the chart, which would keep the chart easy to read.

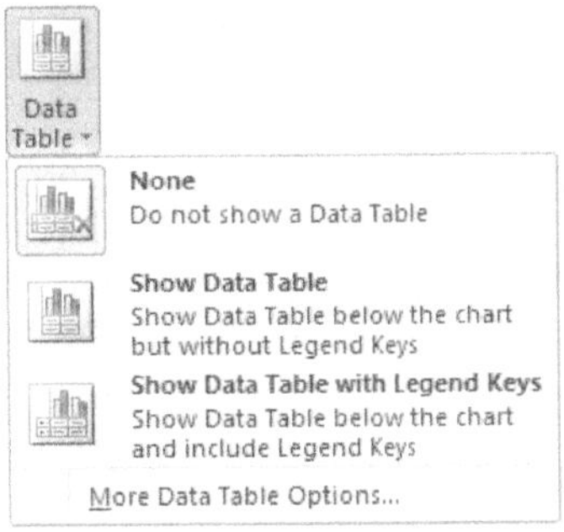

Figure 12-8 Data Table options

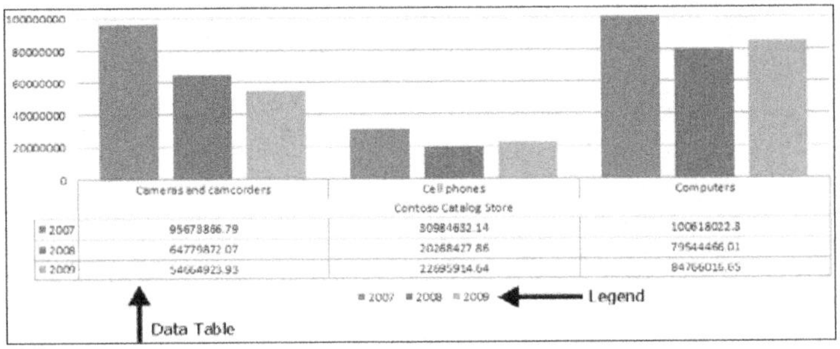

Figure 12-9 Data Table and legend added to the chart

The **CHART WALL** and **CHART FLOOR** options on the Layout tab are used to add a solid color or fill pattern color to the background of certain areas of a 3D chart.

Figure 12-10 shows a 3D bar chart without any background formatting.

Figure 12-11 shows the Format Walls fill pattern options that can be applied to the chart.

Figure 12-12 shows the chart with the fill pattern for the chart walls applied.

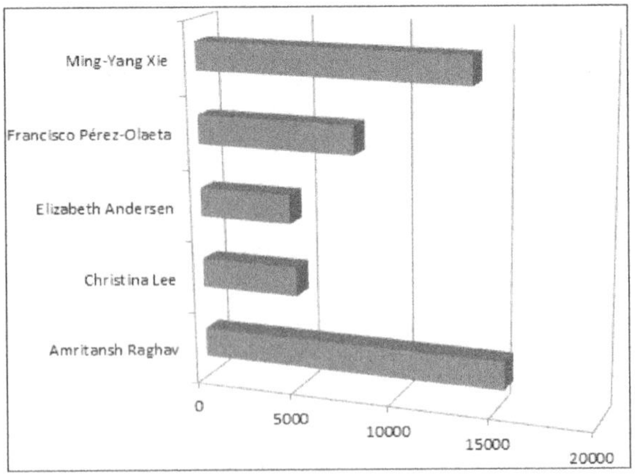

Figure 12-10 3D bar chart

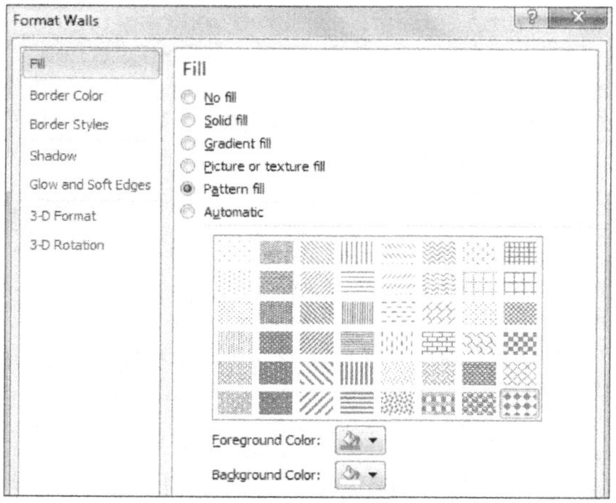

Figure 12-11 Format Walls dialog box

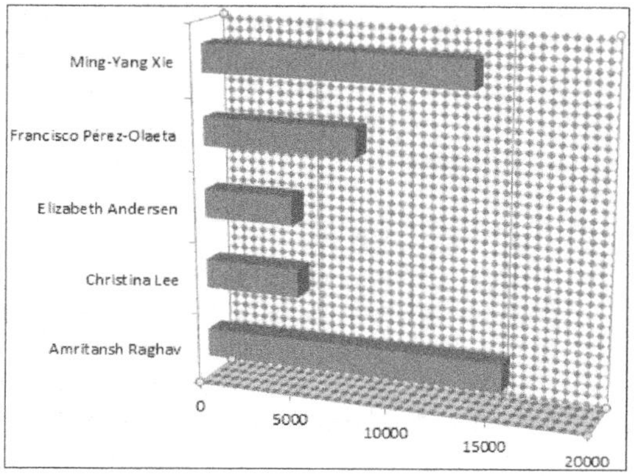

Figure 12-12 Fill pattern applied to the chart

Differences On The PowerPivot Field List For Pivot Charts

In Chapter 11 you learned about the options on the PowerPivot Field List.

Figure 12-13 shows the PowerPivot Field List when a pivot chart is selected.

The Row Labels and Column Labels drop zones shown in Chapter 11 Figure 11-12, are not available for pivot charts.

Instead, pivot charts have the drop zones explained below. You can refer back to Chapter 11, Table 11-1 [PowerPivot Field List drop zone options] for an explanation of the drop zones that pivot tables and pivot charts have in common.

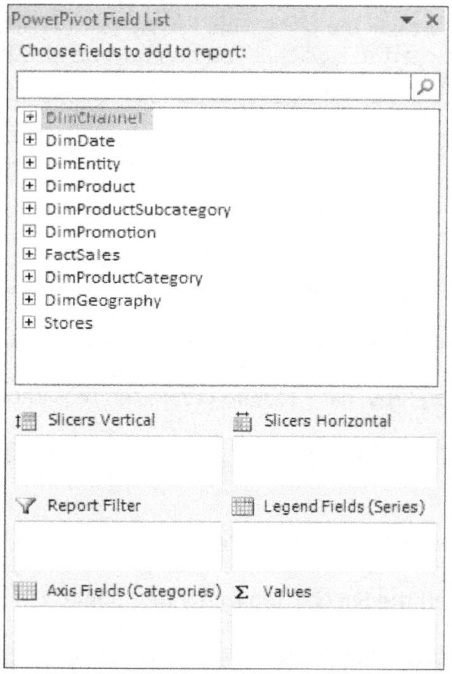

Figure 12-13 PowerPivot Field List for pivot charts

① **AXIS FIELDS (CATEGORIES)** The fields placed in this drop zone are displayed across the bottom of the chart. If a text field is checked at the top of the PowerPivot Field List, by default it is placed in this drop zone. This drop zone replaces the Row Labels drop zone that pivot tables have.

② **LEGEND FIELDS (SERIES)** The fields placed in this drop zone are displayed vertically on the left side of the chart. If a text field is added to this drop zone, each item becomes a new series in the chart. This drop zone replaces the Column Labels drop zone that pivot tables have. Like the Column Labels drop zone, the Legend Fields drop zone can be used to filter the data.

Pivot Chart Data
If you are only creating a pivot chart, PowerPivot needs a place to store the data for a pivot chart, just like Excel does. The difference is that creating a pivot chart from PowerPivot data does not require you to select a range of cells. PowerPivot will automatically create the pivot table for the pivot chart, based on the options that you select in the PowerPivot Field List to create the pivot chart.

When the PivotChart option is selected, PowerPivot will automatically create a worksheet and place a pivot table on it. This is the data that the pivot chart will be created from. The syntax for the name of the tab that the pivot chart will be placed on is **DATA FOR <SHEET NAME> CHART <NUMBER>**, as illustrated in Figure 12-14. The name of the tab lets you know which chart the pivot table is for. Why the new (pivot table) worksheets are inserted to the left of the worksheet that it is connected to is a mystery to me because new worksheets are added to the right in Excel, by default. If you do not plan to hide the tab that has the pivot table for the pivot chart, rename the Sheet 1 tab before you add a pivot chart to it so that you and anyone else that uses the workbook will understand what the pivot table is for.

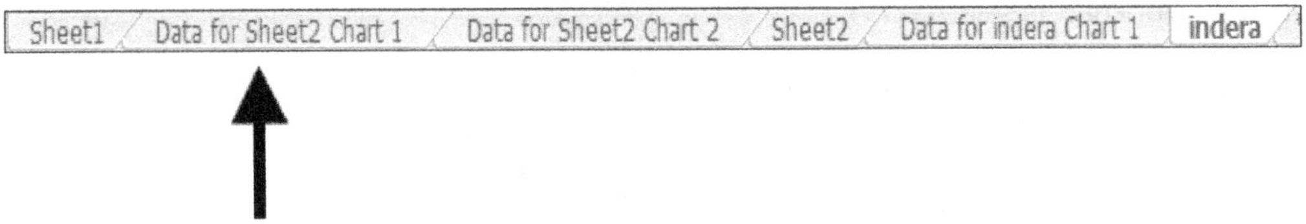

Figure 12-14 Data for pivot chart tab illustrated

Below are the steps that I took to create the tabs shown above in Figure 12-14.

1. On the Sheet 2 tab, I added a pivot chart, the Data for Sheet 2 Chart 1 tab was automatically created.

2. I added a second chart to Sheet 2. That created the Data for Sheet 2 Chart 2 tab.

3. I renamed the Sheet 3 tab to my first name.

4. I added a pivot chart to the tab with my name. The Data for indera Chart 1 tab was created.

Pivot Chart Components

Pivot charts have features that pivot tables do not have. These features are explained below.

① **DATA SERIES** are related points of data that are plotted on a chart. More than one data series can be plotted on a chart, except for pie charts. Each color on a chart represents a different series of data. For example, the chart shown in Figure 12-15 has three series of data. The easiest way to tell how many series of data a chart has is to count the number of items in the legend. The legend contains one item for each series of data.

② A **LEGEND** displays the color of each data series in the chart.

③ **DATA MARKERS** are a symbol on the chart that represents a single value on the chart. Data markers that are related, create a data series.

④ A **DATA LABEL** provides more information about the data point that the data marker represents in the chart. Usually, this is the value of the data point because it can be difficult to tell what the exact value of the data point is.

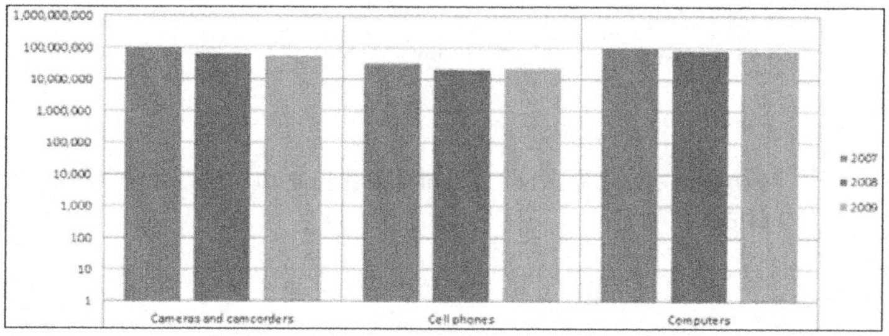

Figure 12-15 Data series

Pivot Chart Creation Tips

① In the pivot chart exercises that you will create, you will see the dialog box shown in Figure 12-16 after you select a pivot chart option from the PivotTable button on the PowerPivot tab. Unless the exercise states otherwise, select the Existing Worksheet option, then click OK.

② Often, the default size of charts is small. You can make them larger as needed.

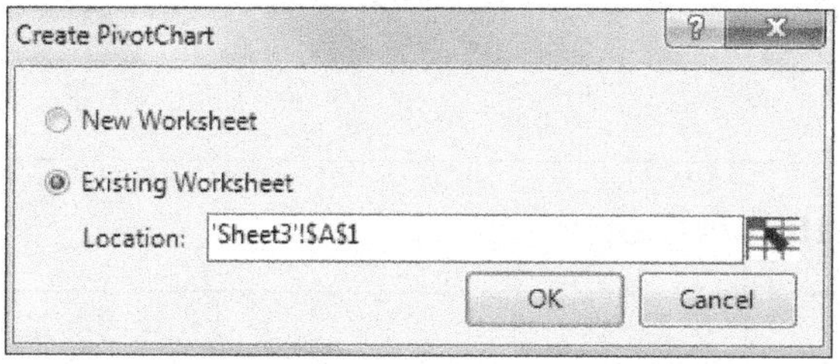

Figure 12-16 Create PivotChart dialog box

Exercise 12.1: Create A Customer Order Subtotal Pivot Chart

In this exercise you will create a pivot chart that displays customer order subtotal information.

1. Save the E9.2 workbook as `E12.1 Customer order subtotal pivot chart.`

2. PowerPivot tab ⇒ Report group ⇒ PivotTable button ⇒ PivotChart.

3. Add the Ship Name field in the Orders table to the Axis Fields drop zone.

4. Add the Subtotal field in the Order Subtotals table to the Values drop zone.

   The bottom of the PowerPivot Field List should look like the one shown in Figure 12-17.

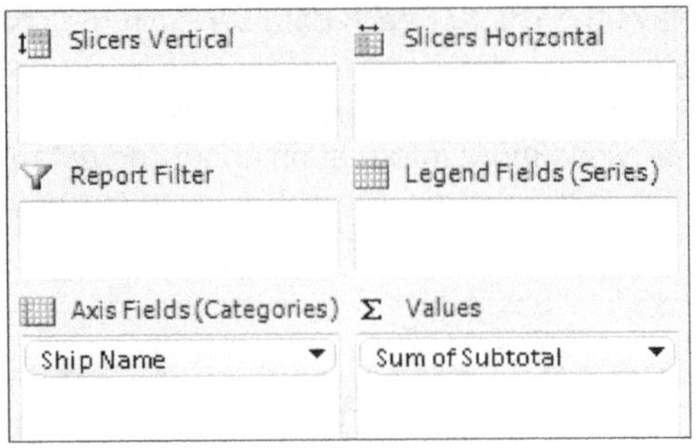

Figure 12-17 PowerPivot Field List drop zone options for a pivot chart

5. Save the changes.

   The pivot chart should look like the one shown in Figure 12-18.

   This chart layout works because there are not a lot of customers.

   If there were thousands of customers, the pivot chart would need filters and/or slicers to reduce the number of customers displayed in the chart.

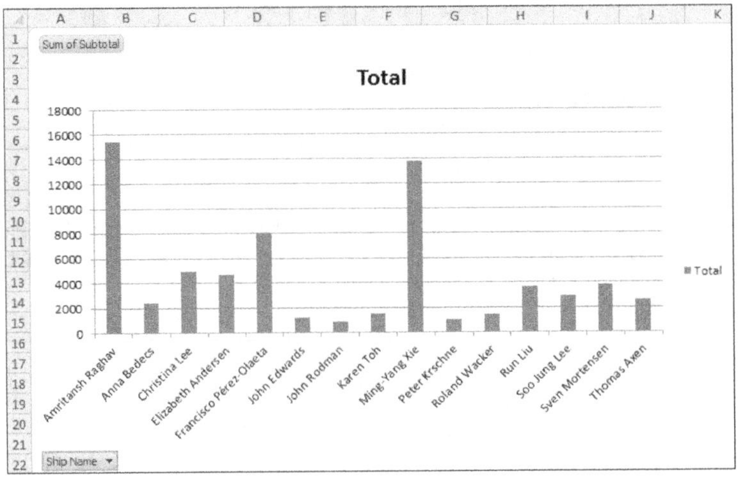

Figure 12-18 Pivot chart

Selecting fewer names in the Ship Name filter would cause the chart to look like the one shown in Figure 12-19.

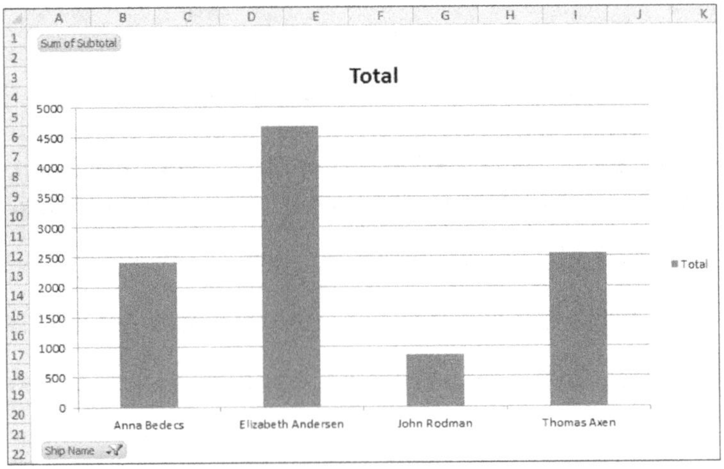

Figure 12-19 Fewer ship names selected

If the Employee ID field was added to the Report Filter drop zone, sales reps could be selected to only display their orders on the pivot chart. Selecting the Employee ID filter options shown in the upper left corner of Figure 12-20 would display the chart shown in the figure.

If the Employee ID field was added to the Legend Fields drop zone, the pivot chart would look like the one shown in Figure 12-21.

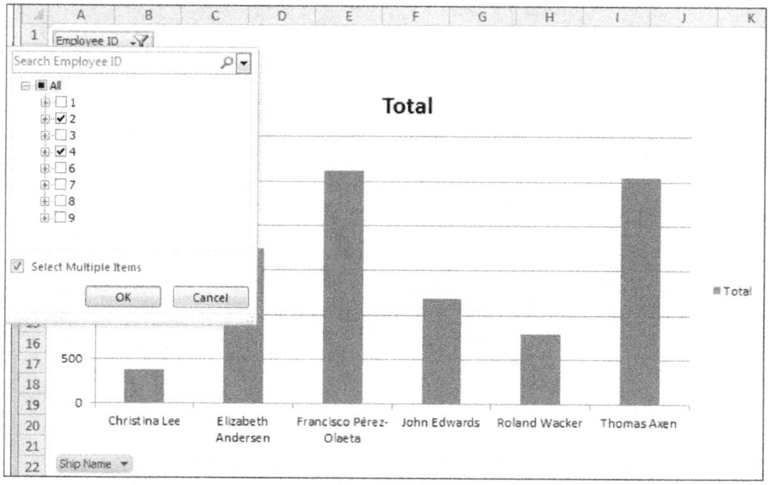

Figure 12-20 Report Filter added to a report

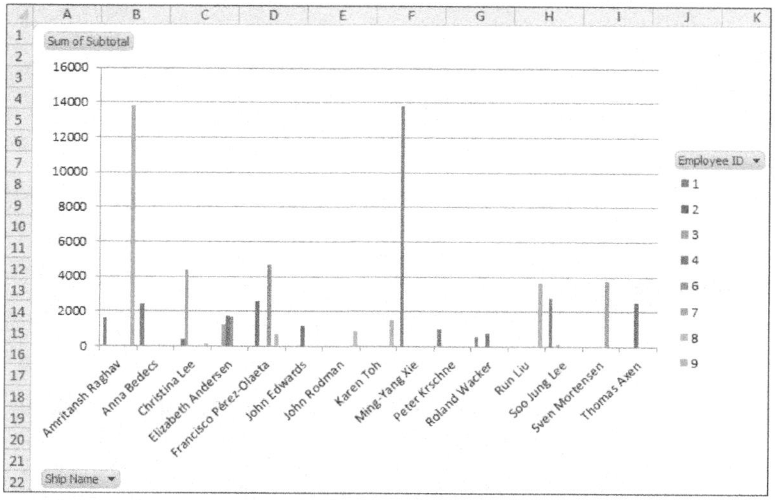

Figure 12-21 Employee ID field added to the Legend Fields drop zone

If you click on the Data for Sheet 1 Chart 1 tab, you will see the pivot table that was automatically created when you created the pivot chart in this exercise. This pivot table is linked to the pivot chart.

Exercise 12.2: Create A Customers By State Pivot Chart

In this exercise you will learn how to create a pivot chart that displays a count of customers per state. You will also add a filter that will be used to select order dates to filter the pivot chart by.

Select The Pivot Chart Report Layout

1. Save the E10.2 workbook as `E12.2 Customers by state pivot chart.`

2. Add a pivot chart to the worksheet.

3. Click in cell B3. You should see in the dialog box shown in Figure 12-22.

   Click OK twice to close both dialog boxes.

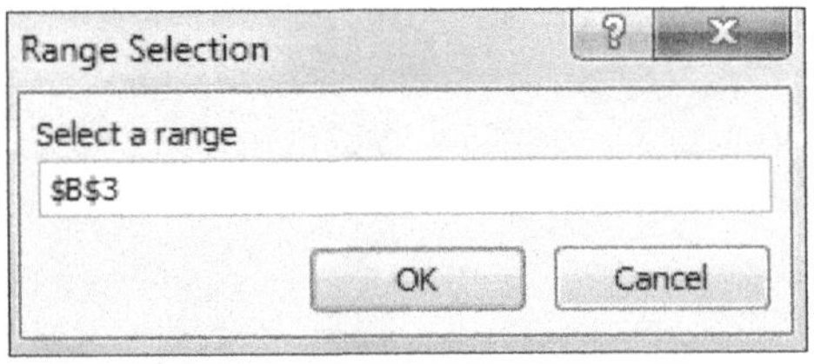

Figure 12-22 Range Selection dialog box

Select The Fields For The Pivot Chart

In this part of the exercise you will select the fields for the Legend Fields, Axis Fields and Report Filter drop zones.

1. Display the fields in the Customers table, if they are not already displayed.

2. Right-click on the Customer Full Name field and select Add to Legend Fields, as shown in Figure 12-23.

   The majority of options on this shortcut menu were explained in Chapter 11, Table 11-2.

   The remaining options are explained in Table 12-1.

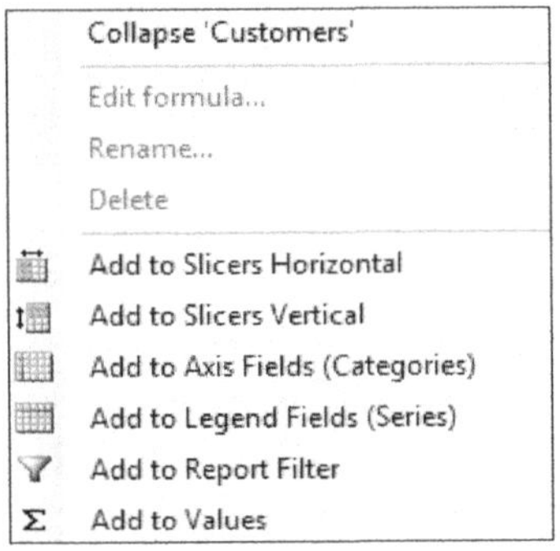

Figure 12-23 PowerPivot Field List shortcut menu (for pivot charts)

PowerPivot Field List Shortcut Menu Options For Pivot Charts

Option	Adds The Field To The . . .
Add to Axis Fields (Categories)	Axis Fields drop zone. (1)
Add to Legend Fields (Series)	Legend Fields drop zone. (1)

Table 12-1 PowerPivot Field List shortcut menu options (for pivot charts) explained

(1) This option is available for all fields in a PowerPivot table except measure fields.

3. In the Customers table, right-click on the State Province field, then select the Add to Legend Fields option.

Add A Field To The Values Drop Zone

In this part of the exercise you will add the fields that will be summarized to the Values drop zone. In this exercise the goal is to get a count of customers by state. That means that you need to select a customer field that has a unique value for each customer.

1. In the Customers table, right-click on the ID field, then select the Add to Values option.

2. Click on the Sum of ID field in the Values drop zone.

   You will see the shortcut menu shown in Figure 12-24.

   Select the **SUMMARIZE BY** option, then select Count.

   The majority of options on this shortcut menu were explained in Chapter 11, Table 11-3.

   The remaining options are explained in Table 12-2.

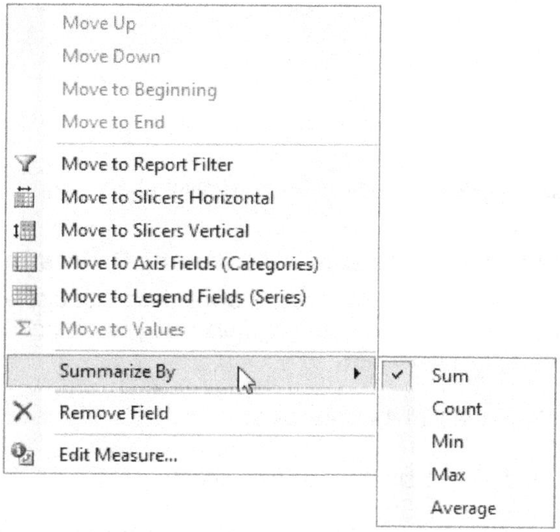

Figure 12-24 PowerPivot Field List drop zone shortcut menu (for pivot charts)

PowerPivot Field List Drop Zone Shortcut Menu Options For Pivot Charts

Option	Description
Move to Axis Fields (Categories)	Moves the selected field to the Axis Fields drop zone.
Move to Legend Fields (Series)	Moves the selected field to the Legend Fields drop zone.

Table 12-2 PowerPivot Field List drop zone shortcut menu options (for pivot charts) explained

3. Save the changes. Your pivot chart should look like the one shown in Figure 12-25.

   As you can see, the customer by state pivot chart does not look like what you expected. The values on the vertical axis need to be changed to only display whole numbers because the pivot chart is suppose to display a count of customers by state. If the customers table had more records, the chart would be of more value. In Chapter 13 you will learn how to modify the values on the vertical axis.

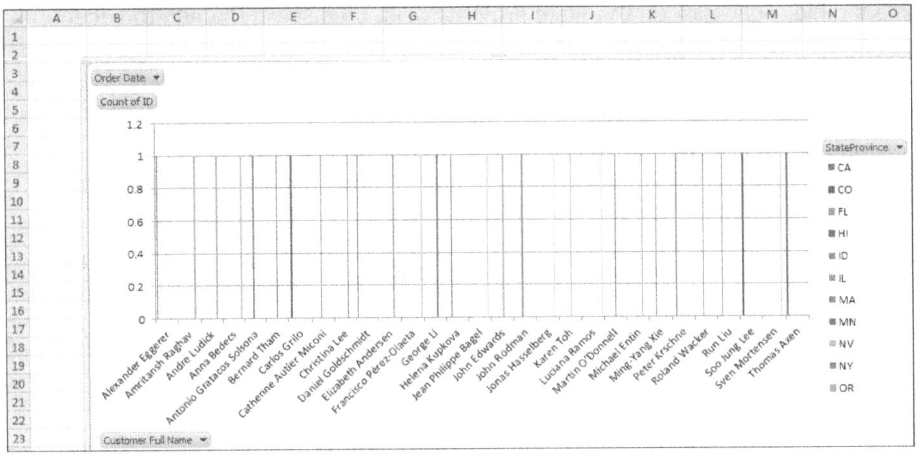

Figure 12-25 Customers by state pivot chart

Exercise 12.3: Create A Customer Orders By Year Pivot Chart

In this exercise you will create a pivot chart that displays customer orders by year. The Year field that you will use is from the formula that you created in Exercise 10.4. You will also add three filters to the pivot chart.

1. Save the E10.4 workbook as `E12.3 Customer orders by year pivot chart.`

2. Add a pivot chart to the worksheet.

3. Add the fields in Table 12-3 to create the pivot chart. When prompted to create a relationship, do so.

Table	Field	Add To Drop Zone	Rename To
Sales_SalesOrderHeader	Total Due	Values	
Sales_SalesTerritory	Name	Report Filter	Select A Territory
Production_Product	Name	Report Filter	Select A Product
Purchasing_ShipMethod	Name	Report Filter	Shipping Method
Sales_SalesOrderHeader	Order Year	Legend Fields	
Person_Contact	Last Name	Axis Fields	

Table 12-3 Fields to create the pivot chart

4. Select the filter options in Table 12-4 for the pivot chart.

Filter	Option
Order Year	2002 and 2004
Select A Territory	NorthEast
Select A Product	See Figure 12-26
Shipping Method	Cargo Transport 5

Table 12-4 Filter options for the pivot chart

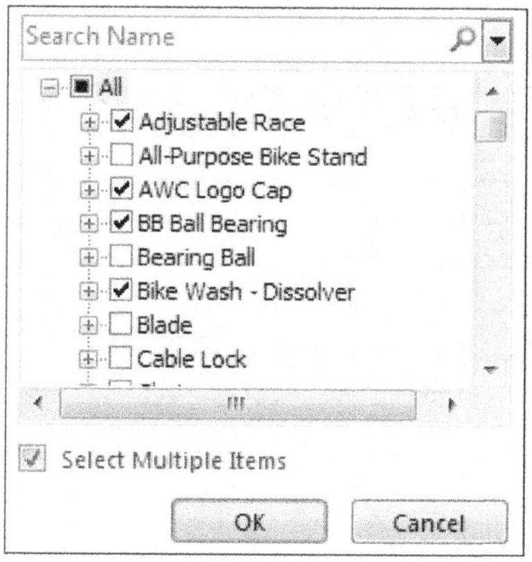

Figure 12-26 Product filter options to select

5. Save the changes. Your pivot chart should look like the one shown in Figure 12-27.

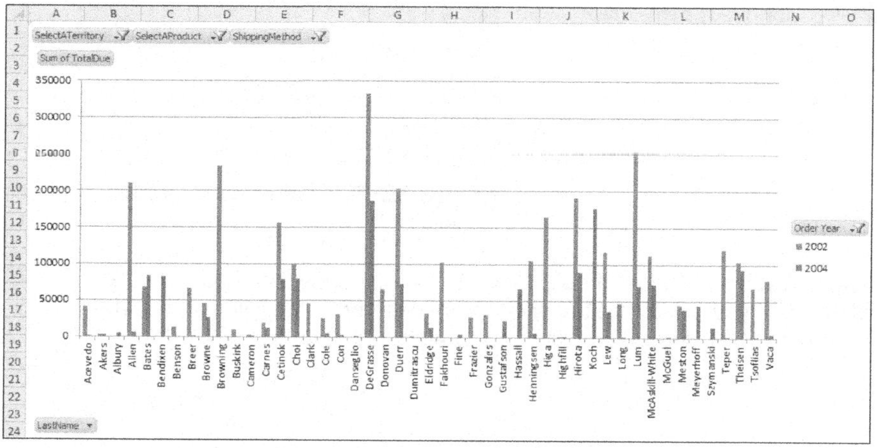

Figure 12-27 Customer orders by year pivot chart

Exercise 12.4: Create A Yearly Sales By Country Pivot Chart

In Exercise 11.3 you created a pivot table based on the data in the Contoso database. If you recall, the pivot table had a lot of data [See Chapter 11, Figure 11-32]. Sometimes, displaying that amount of data in a pivot chart does not look good. It is also difficult to see the trends or patterns in the data. When you have that much data, it is sometimes a good idea to create a few pivot charts on the same worksheet.

In this exercise you will create a pivot chart that has fewer Axis Fields, then there were Row Labels in the pivot table that was created from the same data.

1. Save the E11.3 workbook as `E12.4 Yearly sales by country pivot chart.`

2. Add a pivot chart to a new worksheet.

3. Add the fields in Table 12-5 to create the pivot chart.

Table	Field	Add To Drop Zone	Rename To
FactSales	Sales Amount	Values	
Stores	Store Type	Report Filter	
DimDate	Calendar Year	Legend Fields	
Stores	Store Name	Axis Fields	
DimProductCategory	ProductCategoryName	Axis Fields	Product Category

Table 12-5 Fields to create the pivot chart

4. Select the filter options in Table 12-6 for the pivot chart.

Filter	Option
Store Type	Online
Product Category	See Figure 12-28

Table 12-6 Filter options for the pivot chart

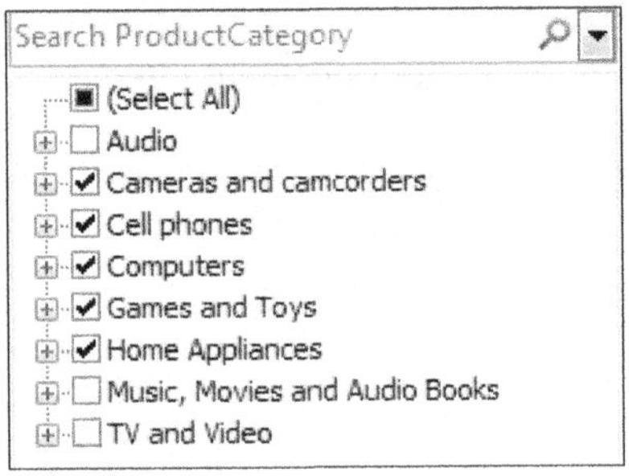

Figure 12-28 Product Category filter options to select

5. Save the changes. Your pivot chart should look like the one shown in Figure 12-29. This chart is legible. If you selected all of the store types, the chart will look like the one shown in Figure 12-30. As you can see, this chart is not legible.

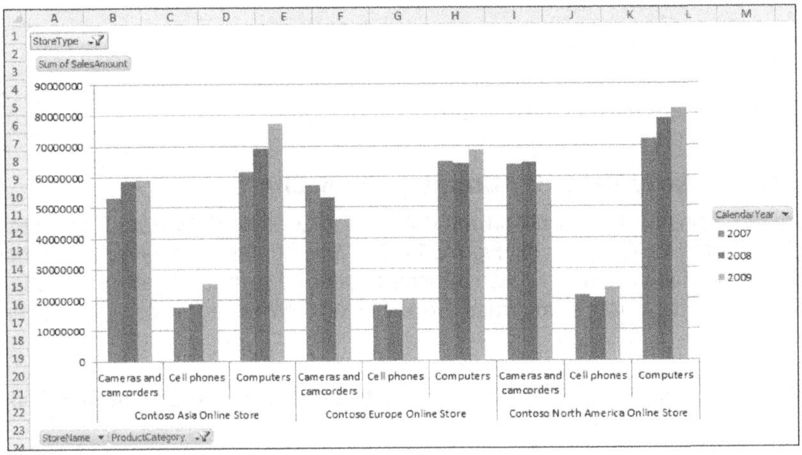

Figure 12-29 Sales by country pivot chart

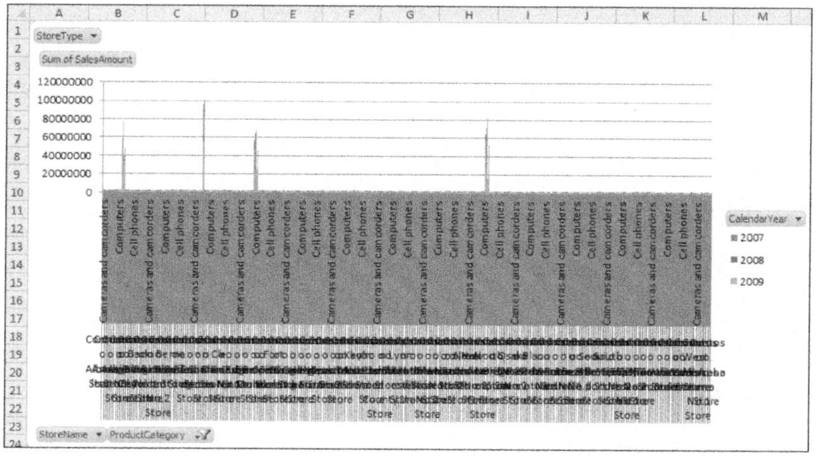

Figure 12-30 Pivot chart with all of the store type filter options selected

Exercise 12.5: Create A Top 10 Pivot Chart

In this exercise you will learn how to create a Top 10 pivot chart that shows the top 10 stores and their yearly sales amounts.

1. Save the E9.3 workbook as `E12.5 Top 10 pivot chart.`
2. Add a pivot chart to the worksheet.
3. Add the fields in Table 12-7 to create the pivot chart.

Table	Field	Add To Drop Zone
FactSales	Sales Amount	Values
DimChannel	Channel Name	Report Filter
DimDate	Calendar Year	Legend Fields
Stores	Store Name	Axis Fields

Table 12-7 Fields to create the pivot chart

4. Open the Store Name filter on the pivot chart and select the stores shown in Figure 12-31.

Figure 12-31 Store Name filter options

5. Save the changes. The pivot chart should look like the one shown in Figure 12-32.

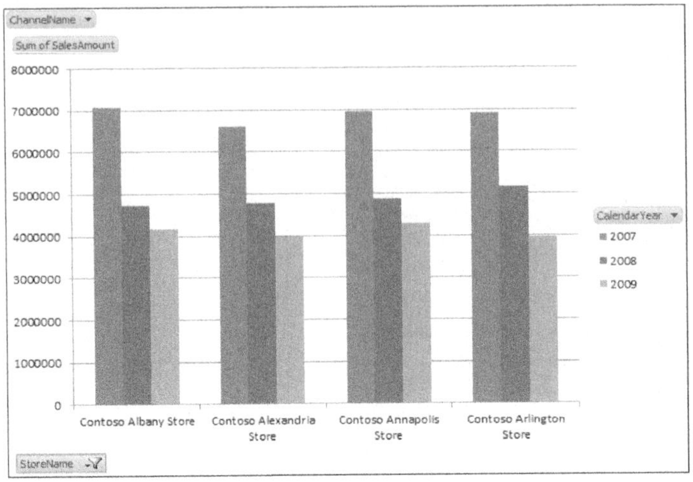

Figure 12-32 Pivot chart without the Top 10 filter

Apply The Top 10 Filter To The Pivot Chart

In this part of the exercise you will add the Top 10 filter functionality to the pivot chart.

1. Open the Store Name filter shortcut menu, then select all of the stores.
2. Select the Value Filters option on the Store Name filter shortcut menu, then select the Top 10 option, shown in Figure 12-33.

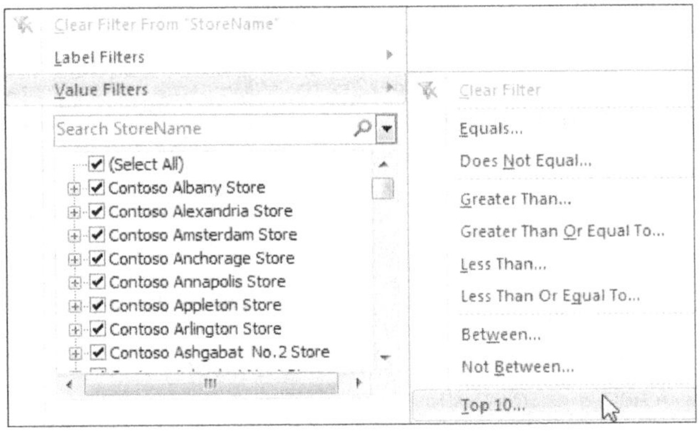

Figure 12-33 Value Filters Top 10 option selected

3. Accept the default Top 10 options, then click OK. The pivot chart should look like the one shown in Figure 12-34.

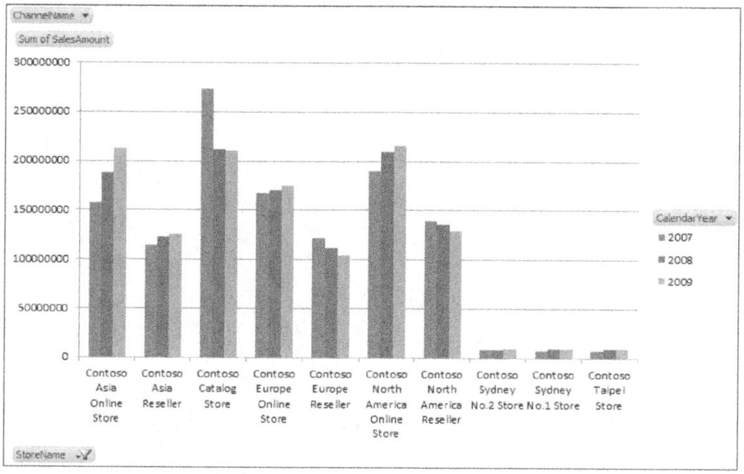

Figure 12-34 Top 10 filter options applied to the pivot chart

4. Open the Channel Name filter and clear all of the options except Store, then click OK.
5. Save the changes.

   The Top 10 pivot chart should look like the one shown in Figure 12-35.

   This pivot chart displays the top 10 stores for all three years.

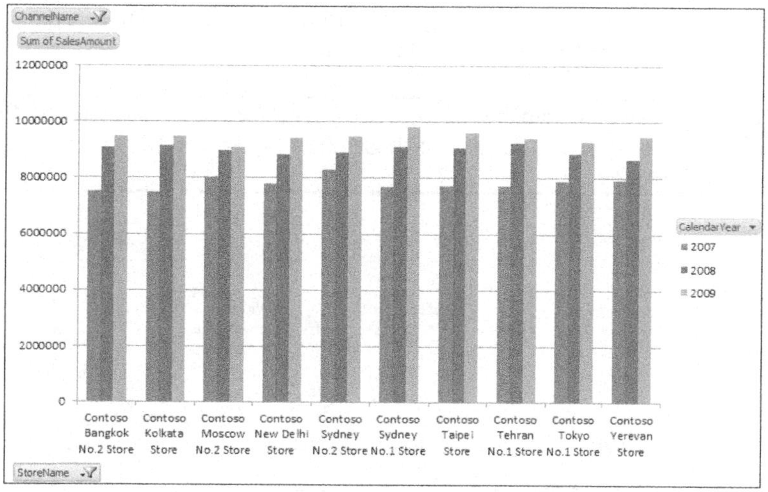

Figure 12-35 Top 10 pivot chart for (retail) stores only

Figure 12-36 shows the top 10 stores just for 2008.

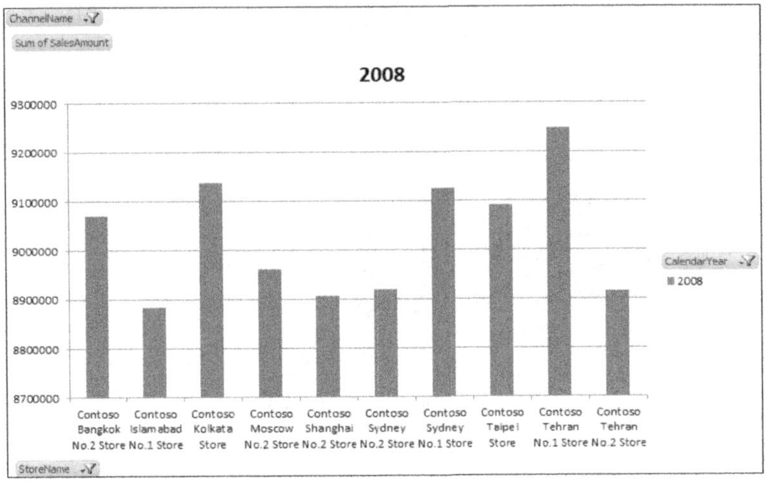

Figure 12-36 Top 10 stores by sales in 2008

Chart Types

The default chart type for pivot charts is a Clustered Column chart. The good thing is that you can use the majority of chart types that Excel has.

The only chart types that cannot be used for pivot charts are **XY (SCATTER)**, **STOCK** and **BUBBLE**. If you select one of these chart types, you will see the message shown in Figure 12-37.

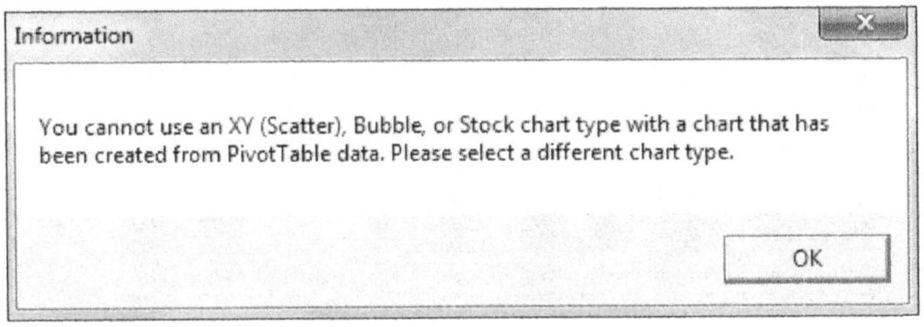

Figure 12-37 Chart type warning message

Once you have created a pivot chart you can change the chart type by right-clicking on the chart and selecting **CHANGE CHART TYPE**, as shown in Figure 12-38.

Depending on where in the chart that you right-click, you will see additional options on the shortcut menu.

This will open the dialog box shown in Figure 12-39.

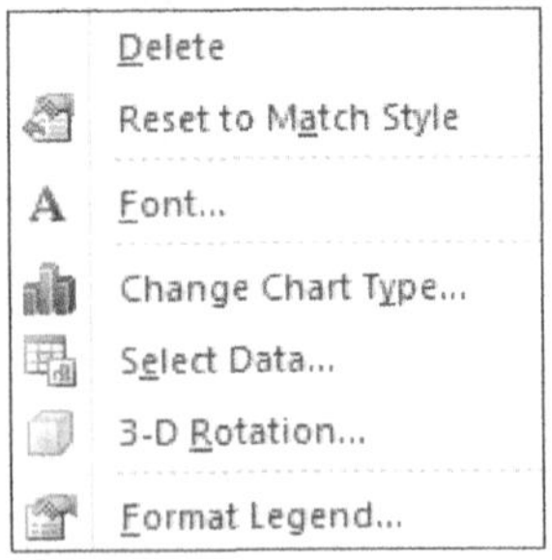

Figure 12-38 Pivot chart shortcut menu

Change Chart Type Dialog Box

This dialog box is used to select a chart type. The chart types that are available for pivot charts are explained in Table 12-8.

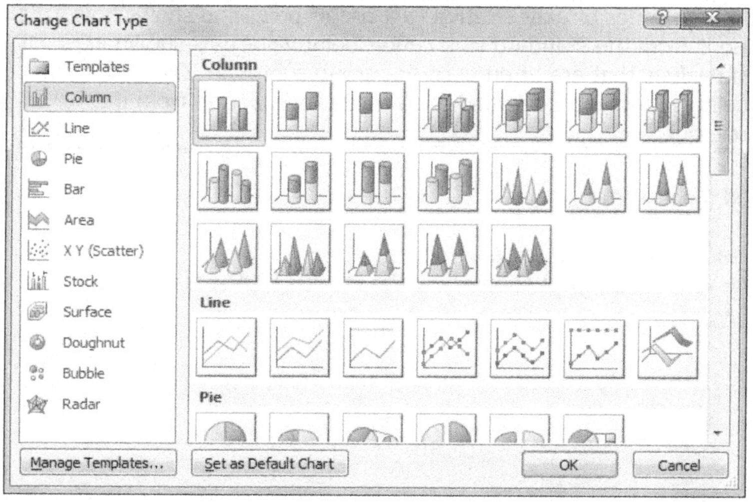

Figure 12-39 Change Chart Type dialog box

Chart Types

Chart Type	Description
Column	Column charts, as shown in Figure 12-40 show differences between items and relationships between grouped data. This is probably the most used chart type. Stacked column charts show each item as a percent of the total.
Line	Line charts, as shown in Figure 12-41 show trends and changes over a period of time. A good use of **3D LINE CHARTS** is when the data lines cross each other often. This makes a line chart easier to read. (2)
Pie	Pie charts only show data for one point in time. Figure 12-42 shows the store sales for 2007. Each slice of the pie represents the percent of sales for a different store. (3)
Bar	They have the same functionality as a column chart. The only difference is the direction that the bars face, as shown in Figure 12-43.
Area	Area charts show how the data has changed over a period of time. Figure 12-44 shows how the revenue of five stores has changed from year to year. Area charts are almost identical to stacked line charts. The difference is that area charts are filled in below the trendline. Area charts are probably best suited for a few groups of data. (2)
Surface	This is the 3D version of area charts. Figure 12-45 shows a surface chart. This chart type uses three series of data. The surface of the chart has a curve and shows trends in relation to time.

Table 12-8 Chart types explained

Chart Type	Description
Doughnut	This chart type is similar to pie charts, as shown in Figure 12-46. The difference is that there is a hole in the center, which contains the grand total of the data presented in the chart, if selected. (3)
Radar	Radar charts compare series of data relative to a center point and shows how far the data value is from the standard (the center point value), as shown in Figure 12-47. The values that are often used are group subtotals. The data from the X axis is usually plotted in a circle and the Y values are plotted from the center of the circle out.

Table 12-8 Chart types explained (Continued)

(2) This chart type requires at least two series of data.
(3) This chart type only uses one value because it shows how the whole (100%) is divided.

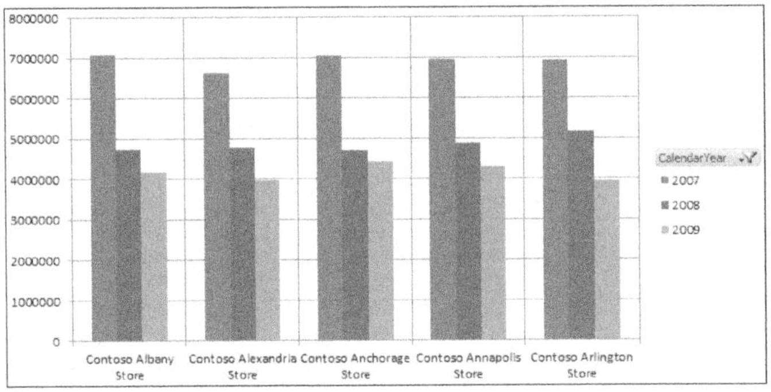

Figure 12-40 Column chart

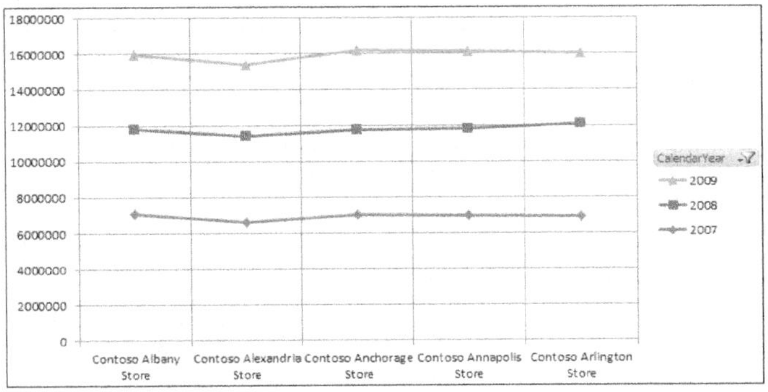

Figure 12-41 Line chart

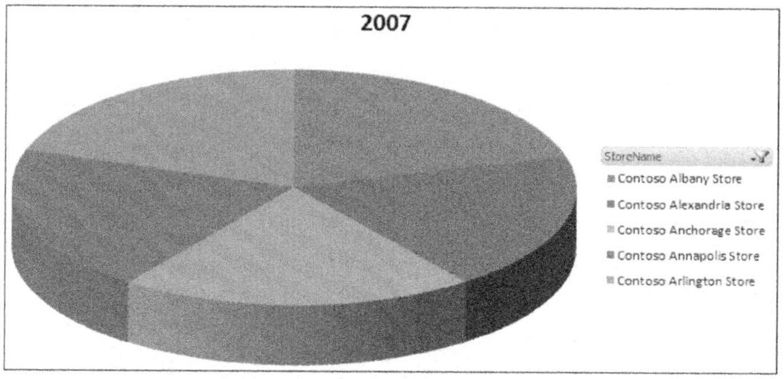

Figure 12-42 Pie chart

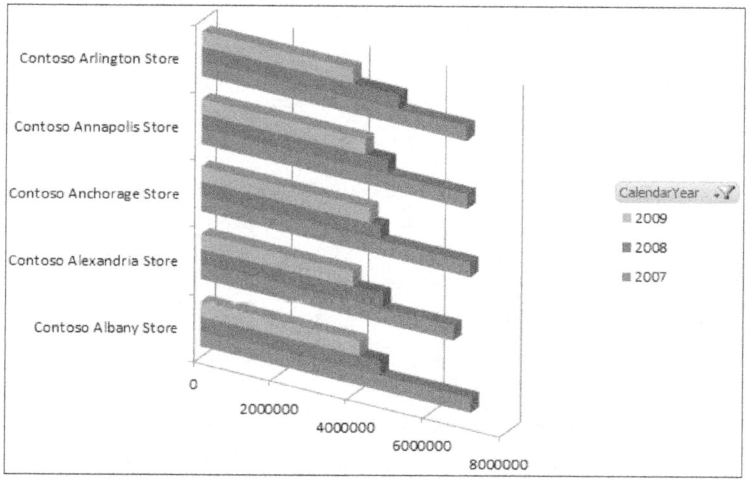

Figure 12-43 Bar chart

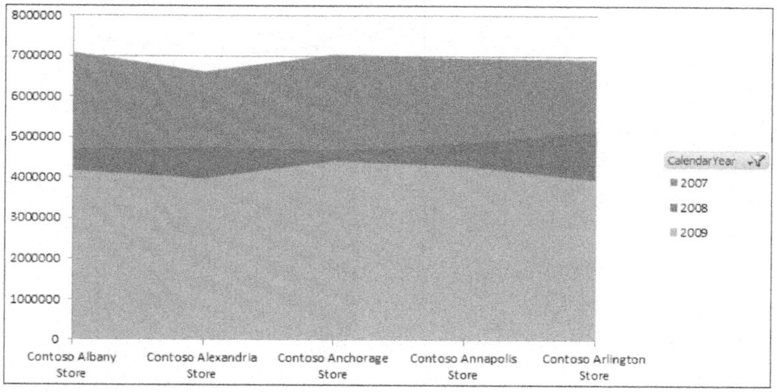

Figure 12-44 Area chart

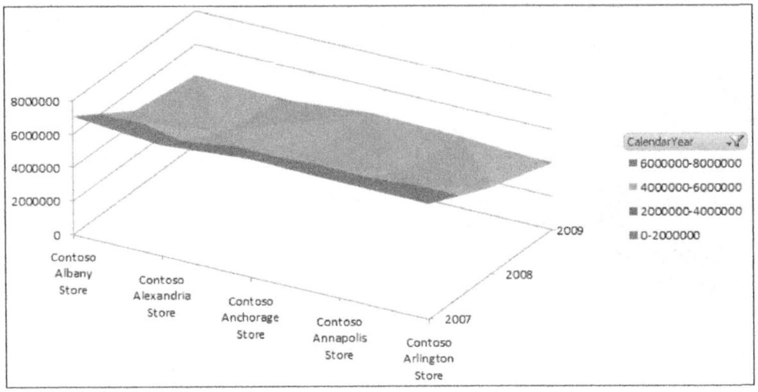

Figure 12-45 Surface chart

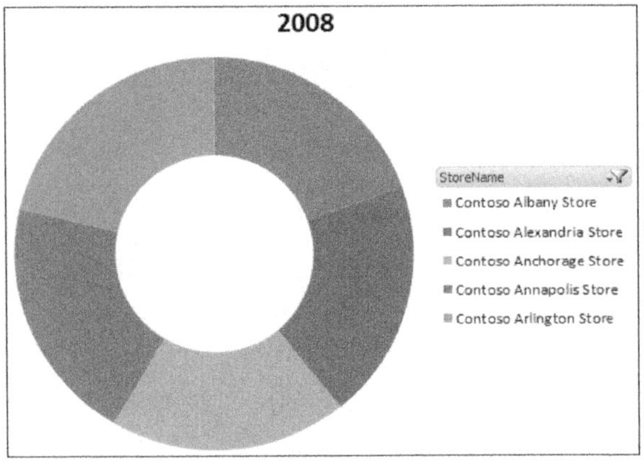

Figure 12-46 Doughnut chart

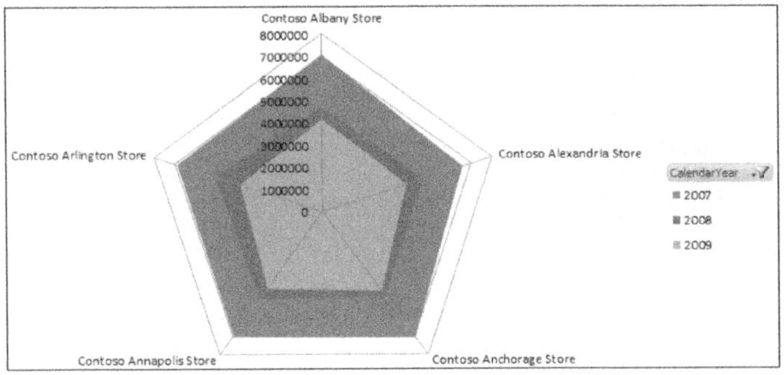

Figure 12-47 Radar chart

Exercise 12.6: Change The Chart Type

In this exercise you will change the chart type of the Top 10 pivot chart.

1. Save the E12.5 workbook as `E12.6 Top 10 with a different chart type.`

2. PivotChart Tools Design tab ⇒ Type group ⇒ Change Chart Type button.

3. Select the Line with Markers chart. The pivot chart should look like the one shown in Figure 12-48. Save the changes. Compare this chart to the one shown earlier in Figure 12-35.

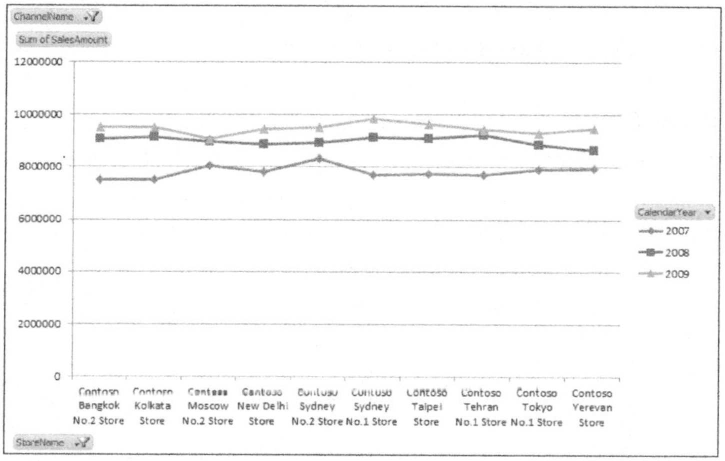

Figure 12-48 Chart type changed

Exercise 12.7: Create A Total Cost By Product Category Pivot Chart

In this exercise you will create a pivot chart that displays the total cost by product category.

1. Save the E9.3 workbook as `E12.7 Total cost by product category.`

2. Add a pivot chart to the Existing Worksheet.

3. Add the fields in Table 12-9 to create the pivot chart.

Table	Field	Add To Drop Zone
FactSales	Sales Amount	Values
DimProductCategory	Total Cost	Axis Fields

Table 12-9 Fields to create the pivot chart

4. Change the chart title to Total Cost By Product Category.

Change The Chart Type And Chart Style

1. Change the chart type to Pie.

2. Open the Chart Style list, then select one of the styles in the last row that has a black background, as shown in Figure 12-49.

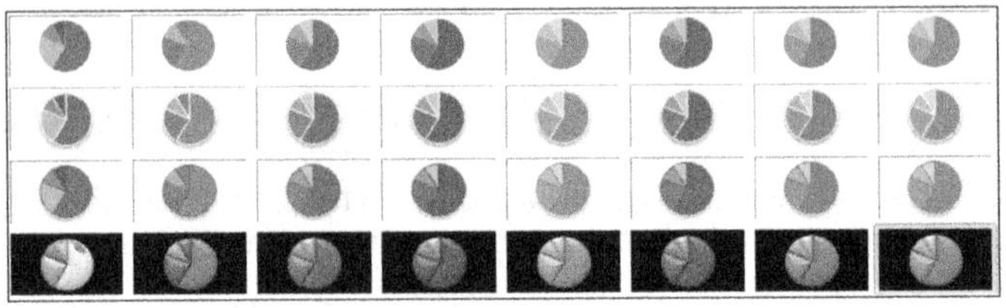

Figure 12-49 Chart Style options

Add Data Labels To The Pivot Chart

1. PivotChart Tools Layout tab ⇒ Labels group ⇒ Data Labels button ⇒ More Data Label Options.

2. Select the Category Name, Percentage and Outside End options, as shown in Figure 12-50.

   Click the Close button.

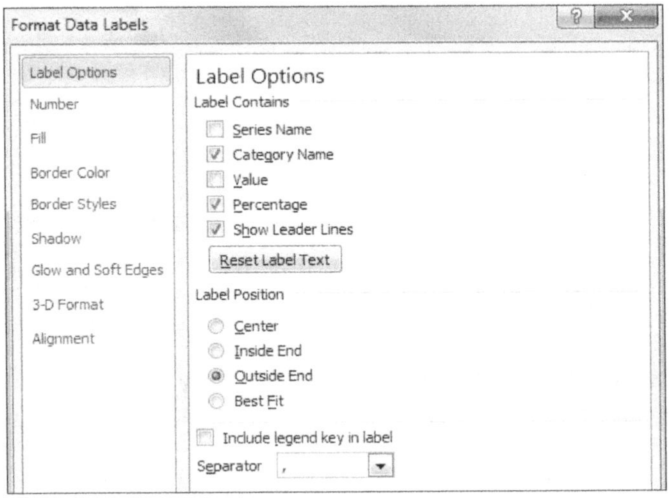

Figure 12-50 Format Data Labels dialog box

3. Hide the Value Field button.

4. Save the changes.

   The pivot chart should look like the one shown in Figure 12-51.

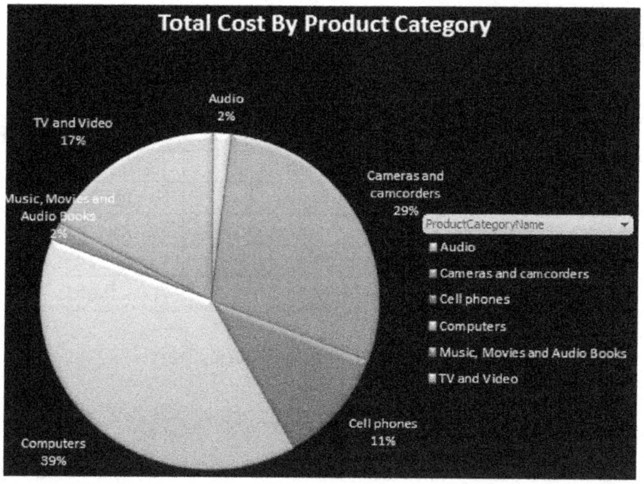

Figure 12-51 Total Cost By Product Category pivot chart

Exercise 12.8: Create A Pivot Chart And Pivot Table

So far, all of the pivot tables and pivot charts that you have created in this book were one or the other, but not both on the same worksheet. In this exercise you will create both on the same worksheet.

1. Save the E9.3 workbook as `E12.8 Chart and Table (Horizontal)`.

2. Select the Chart and Table (Horizontal) option on the PivotTable button drop-down list.

Create The Pivot Table

1. Add the fields in Table 12-10 to create the pivot table.

Table	Field	Add To Drop Zone
FactSales	Sales Amount	Values
DimChannel	Channel Name	Report Filter
DimGeography	State Province Name	Report Filter
DimDate	Calendar Year	Column Labels
Stores	Store Name	Row Labels

Table 12-10 Fields to create the pivot table

2. Open the Channel Name filter drop-down list and select the Store option.

3. Open the State Province Name filter drop-down list and select the states: Colorado, Ohio and Texas.

4. Open the Column Labels filter and select the years 2007 and 2009.

Create The Pivot Chart

1. Add the fields in Table 12-11 to create the pivot chart.

Table	Field	Add To Drop Zone
FactSales	Sales Amount	Values
DimChannel	Channel Name	Report Filter
DimGeography	State Province Name	Report Filter
DimDate	Calendar Year	Legend Fields
Stores	Store Name	Axis Fields

Table 12-11 Fields to create the pivot chart

2. Open the Channel Name filter drop-down list and select the Store option.

3. Open the State Province Name filter drop-down list and select Colorado.

4. Open the Calendar Year filter and select the years 2007 and 2009.

5. Save the changes. The pivot chart and pivot table should look like the ones shown in Figure 12-52. If you are like me, you were hoping that there was an option where you could add the same fields to the pivot table and pivot chart at the same time. Maybe in the next version of PowerPivot if enough people request this feature.

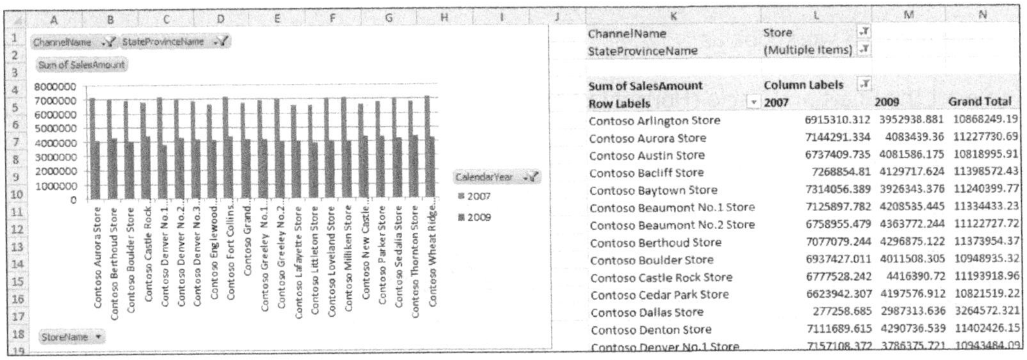

Figure 12-52 Pivot table and pivot chart

ENHANCING PIVOT TABLES AND PIVOT CHARTS

In this chapter you will learn about the following options that can be used to enhance pivot tables and pivot charts.

- ☑ Formatting cells
- ☑ Customizing the values displayed on the vertical axis of a pivot chart
- ☑ Named Sets
- ☑ Measures

CHAPTER 13

Overview

In the previous two chapters you learned how to create pivot tables and pivot charts using data in a PowerPivot workbook. The topics covered in those chapters may handle all of your pivot table and pivot chart needs. If you need more functionality, hopefully, the topics covered in this chapter will help.

Customizing A Pivot Table Or Pivot Chart

As you read in Chapter 11, pivot tables and pivot charts created from data in PowerPivot tables can be customized, just like pivot tables and pivot charts can be customized that are created from data on an Excel worksheet. The first two exercises in this chapter will you how to customize pivot tables and pivot charts created from data in PowerPivot tables.

Formatting Cells

Just like you can format cells in a spreadsheet or pivot table created in Excel, you can format cells in a pivot table created with PowerPivot data. Remember that any formatting that you add to the data in the PowerPivot window is not brought over to the pivot tables and pivot charts that you create. To format cells, right-click on the cells in the pivot table. You will see a shortcut menu with all or some of the options shown in Figure 13-1 when the cell is not from the Values drop zone. Select the Format Cells option. You will see the dialog box shown in Figure 13-2. You can format the cells as needed.

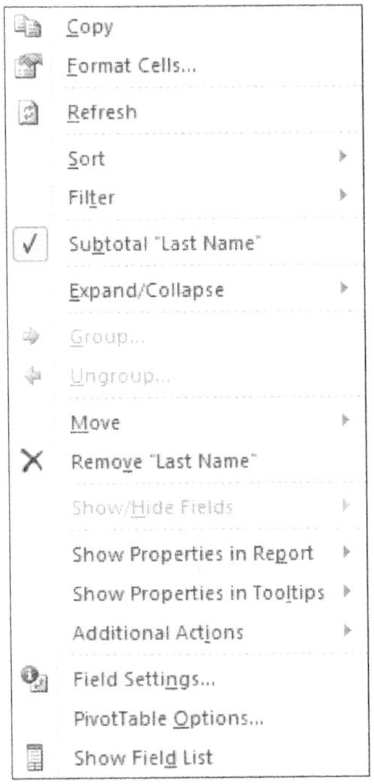

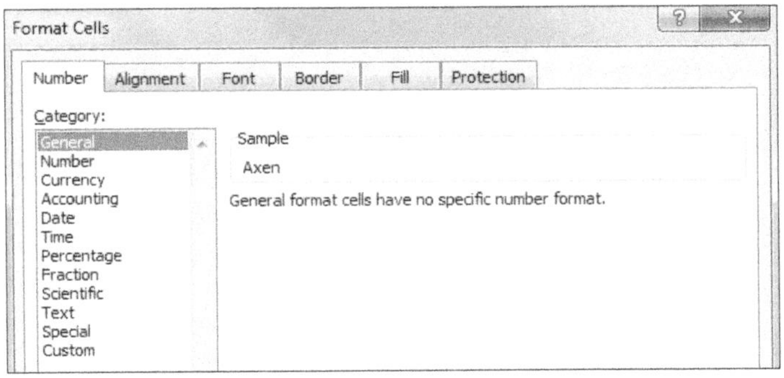

Figure 13-2 Format Cells dialog box

Figure 13-1 Pivot table shortcut menu for cells not in the Values drop zone

When you right-click on a cell from the Values drop zone, you will see the shortcut menu shown in Figure 13-3. Instead of the Field Settings option shown earlier in Figure 13-1, the **VALUE FIELD SETTINGS** option is available. Selecting this option opens the dialog box shown in Figure 13-4.

The options on this dialog box are used to customize the fields in the Values drop zone on the PowerPivot Field List.

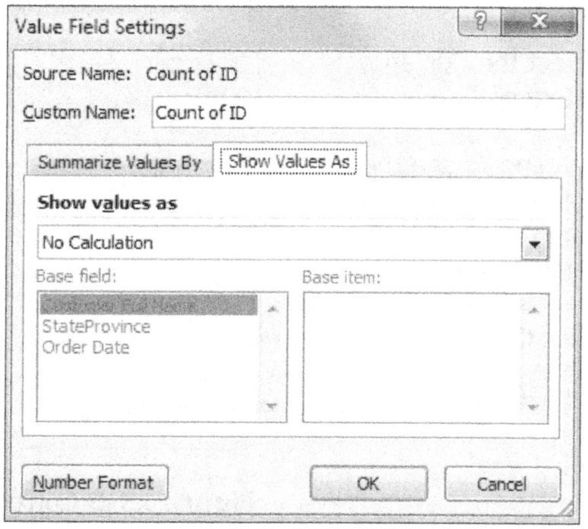

Figure 13-4 Value Field Settings dialog box

Figure 13-3 Pivot table shortcut menu for cells from the Values drop zone

> **Number Format Button**
> Clicking the Number Format button on the Value Field Settings dialog box shown above in Figure 13-4 opens the Format Cells dialog box shown earlier in Figure 13-2. This is the same as selecting the **FORMAT CELLS** option on the shortcut menu shown earlier in Figure 13-1 and Figure 13-3. Selecting the **NUMBER FORMAT** option on the shortcut menu shown earlier in Figure 13-3 also opens the Format Cells dialog box.

> **Data List Not Valid Message**
> It is possible that after importing more data into the PowerPivot window after you have created a pivot table, you may see an error message that says that the data list is no longer valid. If that is the case, right-click on the table and select the **REFRESH** option shown earlier in Figure 13-1 and Figure 13-3.

Exercise 13.1: Customize A Pivot Table

Some of the names generated by the fields in the drop zones could be changed to make the pivot tables easier to read.

In this exercise you will customize a pivot table by changing the Row Labels name, adding currency formatting and changing the custom name of a measure. One of the best things that you can do for fields that are added to the Values drop zone is to change the name. This will make it easier to understand the name in the pivot table or pivot chart.

1. Save the E11.1 workbook as `E13.1 Customize a pivot table`.

   If you look at the field in the Row Labels drop zone, you see that the name of the field is Ship Name. If you look at the pivot table, you don't see "Ship Name". Instead, you see the generic name "Row Labels". I find it easier to understand the pivot table when it has row and column names that represent the data.

2. Click in cell A1 in the pivot table. Type `Ship To Name` in the formula bar, then press Enter.

3. Right-click on Column B and select Format Cells.

4. Select the Currency category.

   You should see the options shown in Figure 13-5. If not, select them now.

   Click OK.

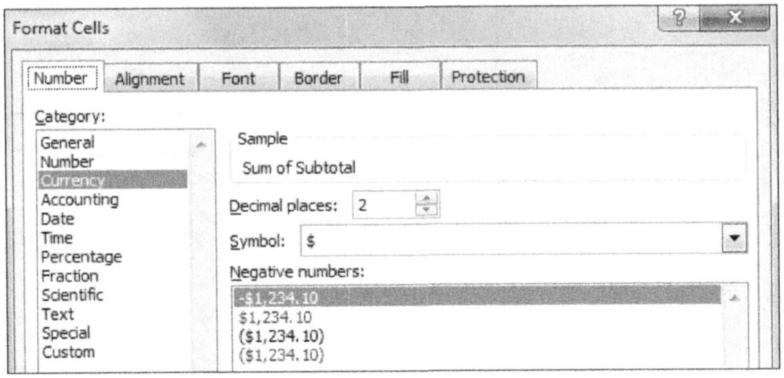

Figure 13-5 Currency formatting options

5. Click on the Sum of Subtotal field in the Values drop zone and select Edit Measure.

6. In the Custom Name field type `Order Subtotal`, then click OK.

7. Save the changes.

   The pivot table should look like the one shown in Figure 13-6.

	A	B
1	**Ship To Name**	**Order Subtotal**
2	Amritansh Raghav	$15,432.50
3	Anna Bedecs	$2,410.75
4	Christina Lee	$4,949.00
5	Elizabeth Andersen	$4,683.00
6	Francisco Pérez-Olaeta	$8,007.50
7	John Edwards	$1,190.00
8	John Rodman	$860.00
9	Karen Toh	$1,505.00
10	Ming-Yang Xie	$13,800.00
11	Peter Krschne	$1,019.50
12	Roland Wacker	$1,412.50
13	Run Liu	$3,625.25
14	Soo Jung Lee	$2,905.50
15	Sven Mortensen	$3,786.50
16	Thomas Axen	$2,550.00
17	**Grand Total**	**$68,137.00**

Figure 13-6 Modified pivot table

Exercise 13.2: Customize A Pivot Chart

In this exercise you will learn how to modify the values displayed on the vertical axis of a pivot chart.

1. Save the E12.1 workbook as `E13.2 Modify vertical axis values.`
   The values on the vertical axis on the pivot chart are currency values. The pivot chart would be easier to understand if these values were displayed with currency formatting.

2. Right-click on the values on the vertical axis and select **FORMAT AXIS**, as shown in Figure 13-7.

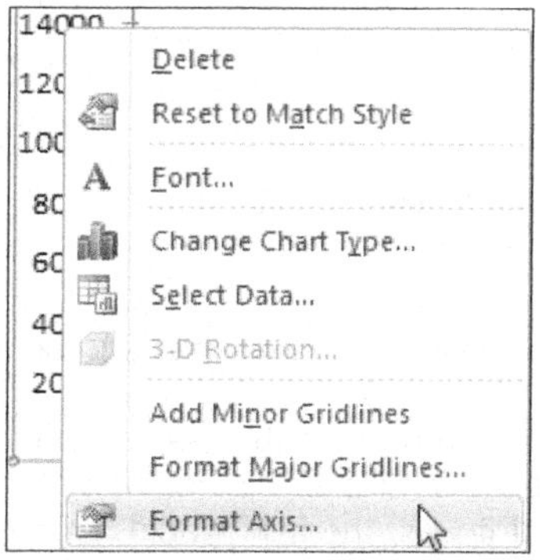

Figure 13-7 Chart object shortcut menu

3. On the Format Axis dialog box, click on the Number button, then click on the **CURRENCY** category.

4. Click in the Format Code field. Delete the decimal point and the two zeros after it.

5. Click the Add button.

   You should have the options shown in Figure 13-8.

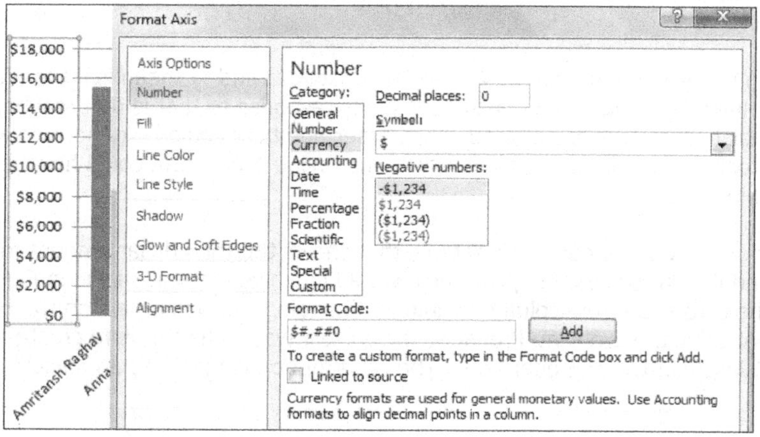

Figure 13-8 Currency formatting options

If you look on the left side of Figure 13-8, you will see that the values on the vertical axis have changed to the format that you selected. This is a good way to make sure that you selected the formatting that you want before closing the dialog box.

6. Click the Close button, then save the changes.

Exercise 13.3: Customizing Data To Display In A Pivot Table

There are times when you may have the need to display data in a pivot table or pivot chart differently then it is stored in the PowerPivot table.

An example that I saw is shown in Figure 13-9. It is the Online Order Flag column, which is in the Sales_SalesOrderHeader table in the E5.5 workbook. I hid some columns so that the ones needed for this discussion would be large enough.

OnlineOrderFlag	PurchaseOrderNumber	SalesPersonID
-1		
-1		
0	PO18444137892	285
0	PO18473177913	285

Figure 13-9 Field with data that needs to be converted

From experience, I know that this was meant to be a Yes/No or True/False field. The problem in this case is that the data that this field is saved in has the data type as Number, when it should be a Yes/No field. If it was, the field would have Yes or No in it instead of zero and -1.

To non programmers the values zero and -1 probably have no meaning. -1 is Yes or True and zero is No or False. That means that this field indicates whether or not the order was placed online. -1 means that the order was placed online.

One way to confirm this is to look at the Sales Person ID column in the table. If you look in this column for orders that have -1 in the Online Order Flag column, you will see that the Sales Person ID field is empty. That makes sense because online orders are automated and do not have a sales person.

You may say that another way to tell what zero and -1 mean is if the Purchase Order Number column is blank, it is an online order. My response to that is that maybe, maybe not. The reason that I say that is because purchase order numbers could be generated automatically during the process of creating an online order. The online order form could have a purchase order number field.

If you need to create a pivot table that shows the total dollar amount for each product for online and regular orders, the pivot table would look like the one shown in Figure 13-10. As you can see, the zero and -1 are column headings. Changing the Name field on the Field Settings dialog box will not solve the problem. Probably, the easiest way to fix this is to create a calculated column in the Sales_SalesOrderHeader table. The other option is to create a measure.

	A	B	C	D
1	**Sum of LineTotal**	**Column Labels**		
2	**Row Labels**	**-1**	**0**	**Grand Total**
3	All-Purpose Bike Stand	39591		39591
4	AWC Logo Cap	19688.1	31541.34562	51229.44562
5	Bike Wash - Dissolver	7218.6	11188.37208	18406.97208
6	Cable Lock		16240.22	16240.22
7	Chain		9377.710144	9377.710144

Figure 13-10 Pivot table with non informative column headings

In this exercise you will create a calculated column to save one of two values in the column: Ordered Online or All Other.

Convert The Data

1. Save the E5.5 workbook as `E13.3 Customize the data to display in a pivot table.`

2. Create a calculated column in the Sales_SalesOrderHeader table with this formula.
```
=IF(Sales_SalesOrderHeader[OnlineOrderFlag]=-1,"Ordered
Online", "All Other")
```

3. Rename the column to `HowOrdered`, then save the changes.

Create The Pivot Table

1. Add a pivot table to the existing worksheet, then add the fields in Table 13-1.

Table	Field	Add To Drop Zone
Sales_SalesOrderDetail	Line Total	Values
Sales_SalesOrderHeader	HowOrdered	Column Labels
Production_Product	Name	Row Labels

Table 13-1 Fields to create the pivot table

2. Save the changes. The pivot table should look like the one shown in Figure 13-11. Compare this pivot table to the one shown above in Figure 13-10.

	A	B	C	D
1	Sum of LineTotal	Column Labels		
2	Row Labels	All Other	Ordered Online	Grand Total
3	All-Purpose Bike Stand		39591	39591
4	AWC Logo Cap	31541.34562	19688.1	51229.44562
5	Bike Wash - Dissolver	11188.37208	7218.6	18406.97208
6	Cable Lock	16240.22		16240.22
7	Chain	9377.710144		9377.710144

Figure 13-11 Modified column headings

Named Sets

This is a new feature in Excel 2010, that also works with pivot tables that are created from PowerPivot data. Named sets are used to define a group of columns or a group of rows to display in a pivot table. Named sets were created to make using MDX named sets easier to use in Excel. Because PowerPivot can use the Named Sets feature in Excel, you can use MDX data without learning MDX.

A Named Set is a Multidimensional Expression (MDX) that returns a set of dimension members. Named sets are used to create OLAP pivot table reports that show different metrics for different areas of a business.

Relationships are not automatically created between fields in a PowerPivot table and Names Sets. Instead of importing the Named Set, add the individual fields from the Named Set to a PowerPivot table.

Named sets can be created from the data in a pivot table. They are a subset of the data displayed in the pivot table. They allow you to easily display a particular view of the data, like only displaying orders from two particular countries.

Figure 13-12 shows the E11.3 Yearly sales by country pivot table without the Store Name and Products Subcategory fields in the Row Labels drop zone.

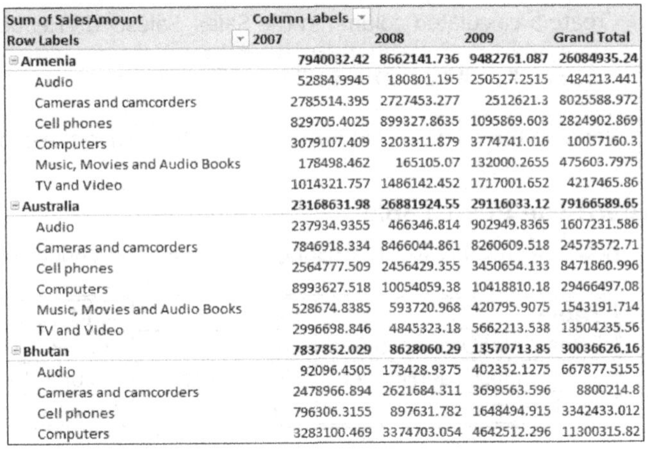

Sum of SalesAmount	Column Labels			
Row Labels	2007	2008	2009	Grand Total
Armenia	**7940032.42**	**8662141.736**	**9482761.087**	**26084935.24**
Audio	52884.9945	180801.195	250527.2515	484213.441
Cameras and camcorders	2785514.395	2727453.277	2512621.3	8025588.972
Cell phones	829705.4025	899327.8635	1095869.603	2824902.869
Computers	3079107.409	3203311.879	3774741.016	10057160.3
Music, Movies and Audio Books	178498.462	165105.07	132000.2655	475603.7975
TV and Video	1014321.757	1486142.452	1717001.652	4217465.86
Australia	**23168631.98**	**26881924.55**	**29116033.12**	**79166589.65**
Audio	237934.9355	466346.814	902949.8365	1607231.586
Cameras and camcorders	7846918.334	8466044.861	8260609.518	24573572.71
Cell phones	2564777.509	2456429.355	3450654.133	8471860.996
Computers	8993627.518	10054059.38	10418810.18	29466497.08
Music, Movies and Audio Books	528674.8385	593720.968	420795.9075	1543191.714
TV and Video	2996698.846	4845323.18	5662213.538	13504235.56
Bhutan	**7837852.029**	**8628060.29**	**13570713.85**	**30036626.16**
Audio	92096.4505	173428.9375	402352.1275	667877.5155
Cameras and camcorders	2478966.894	2621684.311	3699563.596	8800214.8
Cell phones	796306.3155	897631.782	1648494.915	3342433.012
Computers	3283100.469	3374703.054	4642512.296	11300315.82

Figure 13-12 Yearly sales by country pivot table

You could define a set for computer sales in 2009 for Australia, audio sales in 2009 for Australia and Armenia and cell phone sales in 2007 for Armenia.

Pivot Table Tools Options tab ⇒ Calculations ⇒ Fields, Items & Sets button, displays the options shown in Figure 13-13.

The options are explained in Table 13-2.

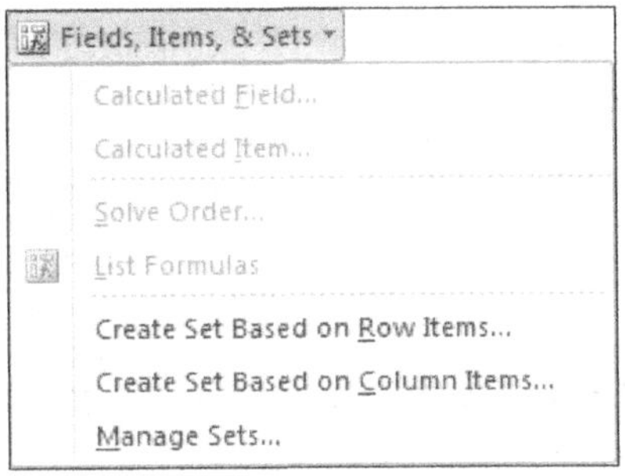

Figure 13-13 Named Sets options

Option	Description
Create Set Based on Row Items	Is used to create sets for fields in the Row Labels zone.
Create Set Based on Column Items	Is used to create sets for fields in the Column Labels zone.
Manage Sets	Opens the dialog box shown in Figure 13-14. The options are used to create, edit and delete named sets.

Table 13-2 Named Sets options explained

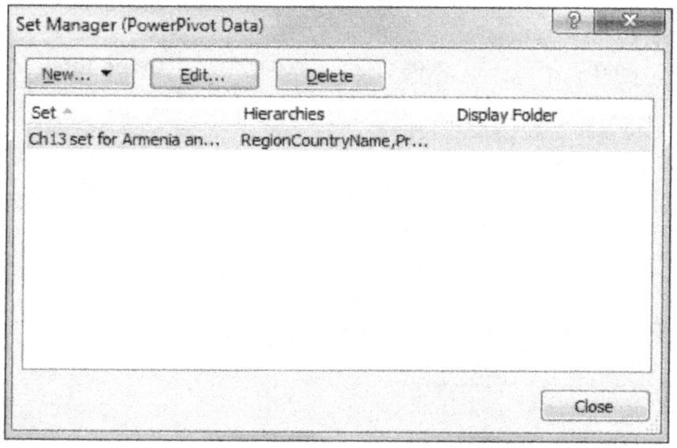

Figure 13-14 Set Manager dialog box

Selecting the Row Items option displays the dialog box shown in Figure 13-15.

To create a set, type in a name for it in the **SET NAME** field. As you can see, there are two columns, which correspond to the fields in the Row Labels drop zone.

By default, all of the named set combinations are displayed on the dialog box. If you only wanted to include a few of them, you would have to delete all of the combinations that you did not want to use. That can be time consuming.

Figure 13-16 shows the items mentioned above that could be used to create a named set.

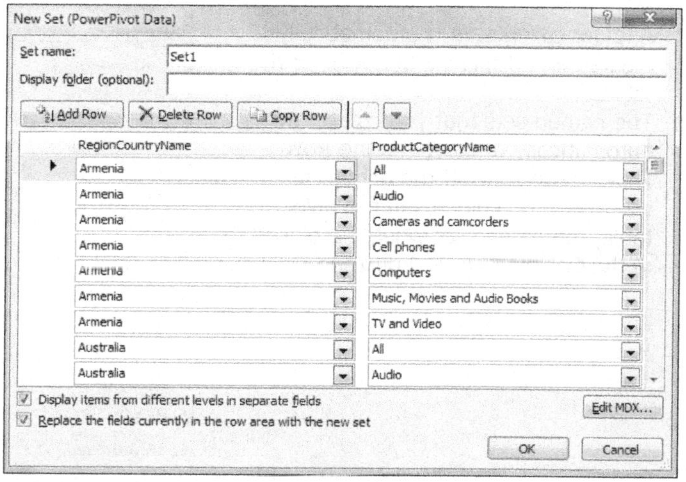

Figure 13-15 New Set dialog box

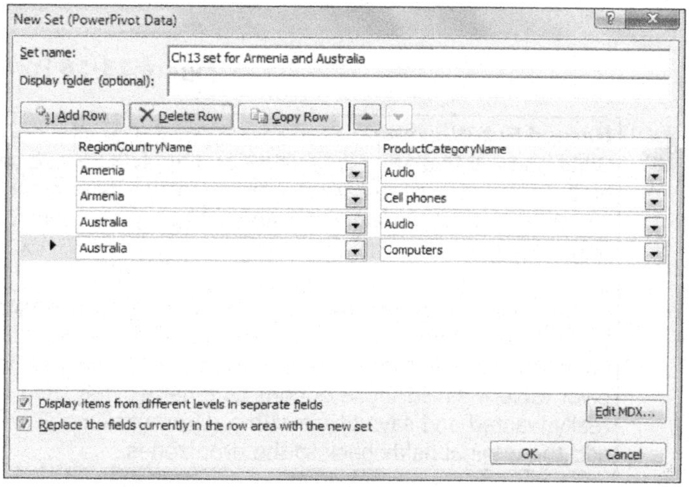

Figure 13-16 Items for a named set

When you select a named set to be displayed, the data in the pivot table will be changed accordingly, as shown in Figure 13-17.

Sum of SalesAmount	Column Labels			
Row Labels	2007	2008	2009	Grand Total
Armenia				
Audio	52884.9945	180801.195	250527.2515	484213.441
Cell phones	829705.4025	899327.8635	1095869.603	2824902.869
Australia				
Audio	237934.9355	466346.814	902949.8365	1607231.586
Computers	8993627.518	10054059.38	10418810.18	29466497.08

Figure 13-17 Pivot table with a named set applied

You will also notice changes in the PowerPivot Field List, as shown in Figure 13-18. The changes are discussed below.

① A folder called **SETS** is automatically created and displayed below all of the tables.

② The named sets that you create are automatically displayed in the Row Labels drop zone. If the named set was based on columns in the pivot table, the named set would be placed in the Column Labels drop zone.

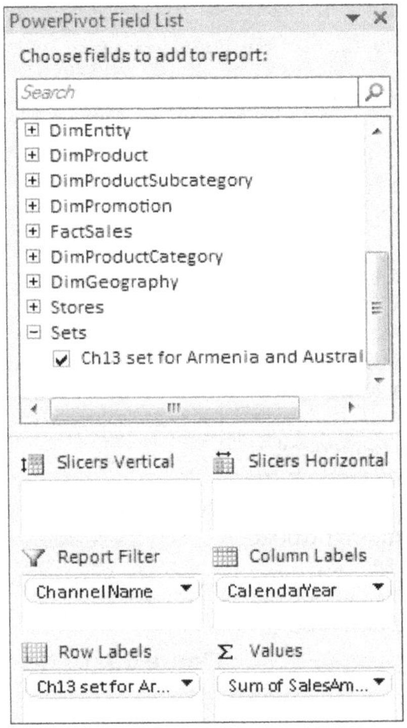

Figure 13-18 PowerPivot Field List with a named set

Named Set Warning
What you will find after you create and apply a named set to a pivot table is that there is no built in option to restore the pivot table to its original state. For example, Figure 13-17 shown earlier has a named set applied to a pivot table. Figure 13-12 shown earlier is the original pivot table.

There is no way to redisplay the pivot table shown earlier in Figure 13-12. The work around that I came up with is that when the New Set dialog box (see Figure 13-15) is opened for the first time in the current pivot table, the items displayed are for the full pivot table. I saved those options as a named set, then I created the named set that I really wanted and saved that with a different name. That seemed easier then having to add the original fields back to the drop zones.

Named Set Warning (Continued)
The other piece of advice that I would give is that it may bring you some peace of mind if you save the workbook with a new name before creating a named set. That way, if you really get yourself into trouble and do not want to learn MDX to be able to make the changes on the dialog box shown in Figure 13-19 to restore the pivot table, you can open the original pivot table workbook, save it with a new name again and start over.

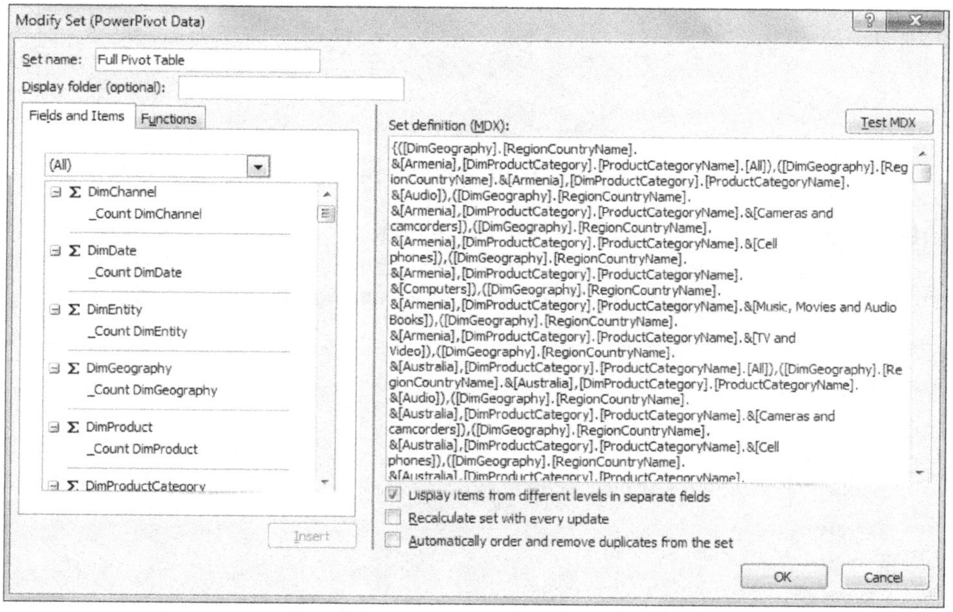

Figure 13-19 Modify Set dialog box (MDX)

DAX Measures

In Chapter 10 you learned how to create calculated columns. These formulas are at the row level of a PowerPivot table, meaning that the formula is calculated for every row in a table. In Chapter 11 you added fields with numeric values to the Values drop zone, which by default created a Sum measure. You also learned that you could change how the numeric field could be aggregated with a few mouse clicks. This provides a lot of options for the totals that can be created in pivot tables and pivot charts. It is possible that between calculated column formulas and the aggregate measures, all of your formula needs are met.

There is one more option available to create formulas. Unlike the calculated column formulas that are for rows in a PowerPivot table, measures are formulas that are calculated only when displayed in the pivot tables and are often based on a report filter or slicer selection. The dialog box shown in Figure 13-20 is used to create measures.

Fields placed in the Values drop zone of the PowerPivot Field List create DAX measures, which are expressions that return values. These values are displayed in the pivot table.

How To Open The Measure Settings Dialog Box

There are two ways to open the dialog box shown in Figure 13-20, as explained below.

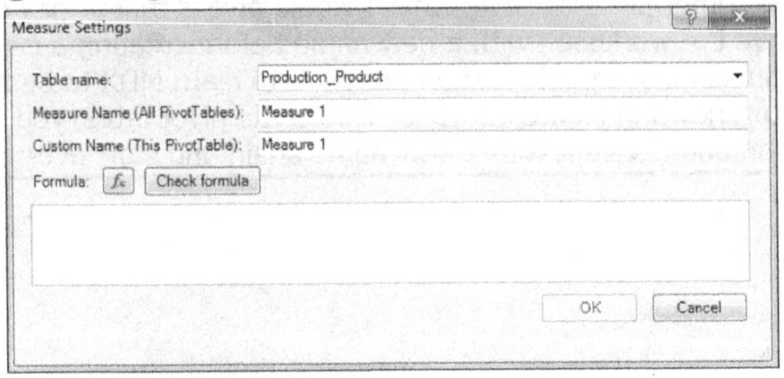

Figure 13-20 Measure Settings dialog box

① PowerPivot tab ⇒ Measures group ⇒ New Measure button.

② Right-click on the table name in the PowerPivot Field List that you want to create the measure field in and select Add New Measure, as shown in Figure 13-21.

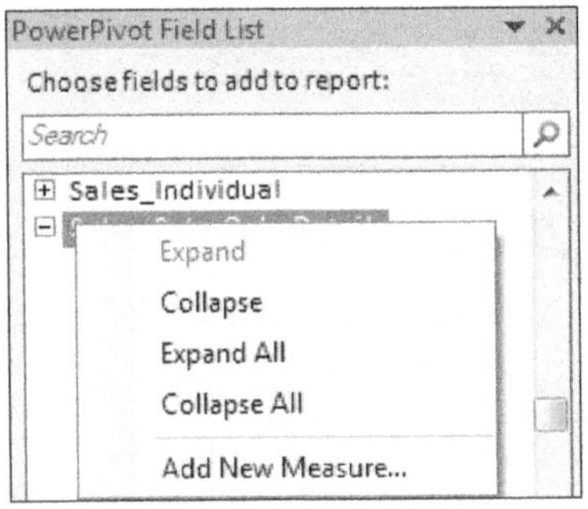

Figure 13-21 Table shortcut menu

How To Edit Or View A Measure

Right-click on the field in the Values drop zone and select **EDIT MEASURE**.

You will see the dialog box shown in Figure 13-22 for aggregate measures or the dialog box shown earlier in Figure 13-20.

If you want to view the measure that has been created for a field, right-click on the field in the Values drop zone. Select **EDIT MEASURE**. You will see the dialog box shown in Figure 13-22.

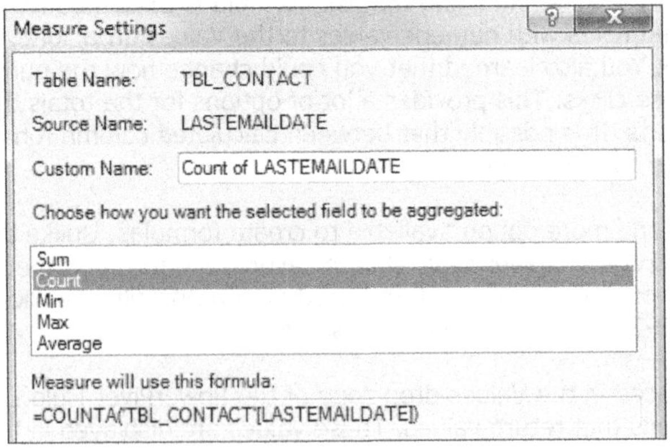

Figure 13-22 Measure Settings dialog box (for aggregations)

While calculated columns and measures both use DAX to create expressions, measures are calculated when the cells that they are for need to be displayed in the pivot table or pivot chart. Measures are evaluated once for each cell in the middle of the pivot table. The measure values are not saved in the PowerPivot table like the values in calculated columns are.

Measures used in pivot tables are created from data in a PowerPivot table. DAX measures are created in the Excel window, either from the PowerPivot Field List or by clicking the **NEW MEASURE** button on the PowerPivot tab. They are only calculated once per cell in the pivot table.

Measures appear at the bottom of a table in the PowerPivot Field List and have an icon next to them, as illustrated in Figure 13-23.

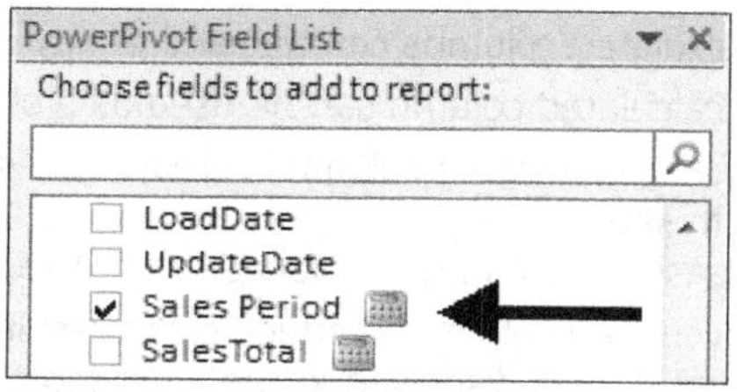

Figure 13-23 Measure icon in the PowerPivot Field List illustrated

Measures are automatically added to the Values drop zone in the PowerPivot Field List, if you click on the check box in front of the field. A pivot table or pivot chart has to be selected before creating a measure. Figure 13-24 shows a measure from the PowerPivot Healthcare Audit workbook. [See Chapter 1, Additional Sample Databases, to download this sample file]

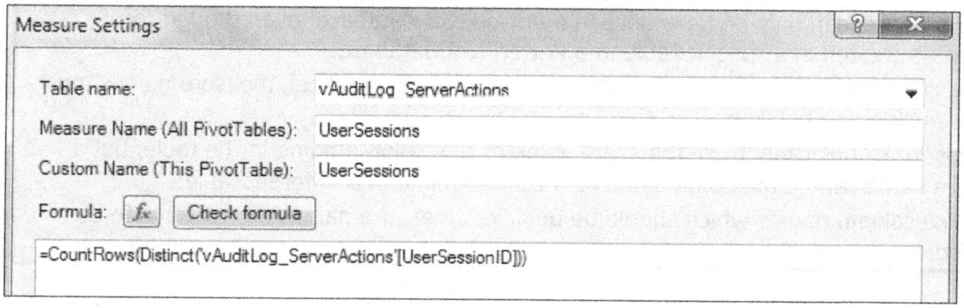

Figure 13-24 Measure Settings dialog box (for DAX measures)

In addition to the calculated columns and measures that you just read about, there is another way to create a measure. You actually already used the option in Chapter 2 during the quick tour. This option has less functionality than the measure option that you just read about, but it may handle a lot of your needs.

You can use this second way to create a measure when all you need to do for a column of data is aggregate it by using one of the **FIVE BUILT IN AGGREGATIONS**: SUM, COUNT, MIN, MAX or AVERAGE, shown earlier in Figure 13-22. The default aggregation that PowerPivot uses is SUM.

To create this type of measure, at the top of the PowerPivot Field List, click in the box in front of the numeric field that you want to aggregate or right-click on the field in the PowerPivot Field List and select Add to Values. You used this option in Chapter 11 to create pivot tables and in Chapter 12 to create pivot charts.

Calculated Columns vs Measures

There are some differences between calculated columns and measures that you need to be aware of. They are explained below.

① Calculated columns can be used in any of the drop zones in the PowerPivot Field List.

② A calculated column can be used as a slicer, measures cannot.

③ After a calculated column is created, it is only recalculated when the data in the table is refreshed.

④ Measures can only be placed in the Values drop zone.

⑤ Calculated columns produce static results, meaning that there are no options to select what data is displayed in the pivot table. Measures produce dynamic (every changing) results because the formulas are only executed for the rows of data that are displayed in the pivot table or pivot chart. The rows displayed in a pivot table or pivot chart change based on the filter, group or sorting that is applied to the pivot table or pivot chart.

DAX Measure Names
Below are conventions for DAX measure names that you should be aware of.

① Unlike column names, which can be used once per table in a PowerPivot database, measure names can only be used once in a PowerPivot database, even though the measure is created in a specific table in a PowerPivot database.

② Like column names in expressions must be enclosed in brackets, measure names must also be enclosed in brackets.

③ Measure names cannot use the same name as any column name in the table, but a measure name can be the same name as a column name in a different table.

④ Unlike column names which should be qualified, measure names do not have to be qualified.

Exercise 13.4: Use A Measure To Create A Sales By Country By Period Pivot Table

In Chapter 10 you learned about Filter context and Query context and how they effect how measures are evaluated. For example, in this exercise you will create two measures; one to calculate the sales total amount and one to add the sales total amount to a specific column in the pivot table.

This is a popular pivot table style that is used to track sales. This pivot table will display total sales amounts for three periods: Current, Month to date and Year to date. To accomplish this type of grouping, the Bucket column in the WhichPeriod table is used. (This is a table that I created for this exercise.) The measure that you will create and add to the pivot table is a nested IF statement.

The DimDate Table

This table is in the ContosoSales database. This table is a collection of fields that is used to filter data in other tables. The data in this table is used to help create measures and pivot tables. There is a row in the Date Key column in this table, for every day of the year. Each column in the DimDate table provides a unique way of being able to display the date or part of the date.

For example, the Calendar Week Label column contains the week of the year that each date falls into. The Date Key field in the FactSales table in the Contoso Sales database is the Order Date. There is a relationship between these tables based on the value of the Date Key field.

Import The Data

In this part of the exercise you will import the table that has the periods that you want to use across the top of the pivot table.

1. Save the E9.3 workbook as `E13.4 Sales by country by period pivot table.`

2. Import the worksheet in the Buckets workbook into a PowerPivot table.

3. Click on the WhichPeriod tab in the PowerPivot window.

   You should see the data shown in Figure 13-25.

   Save the changes.

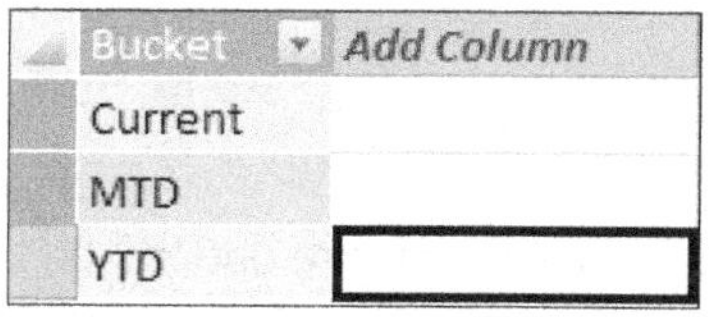

Figure 13-25 Periods for the pivot table

MTD stands for Month to date. This bucket will contain the sum of all orders from the first date of the current month to today.

YTD stands for Year to date. This bucket will contain the sum of all orders from the first day of the current year to today.

The current month and year is based on the date selected in the report filter. This means that if you select a date from two years ago in the report filter, the current month and year values displayed are based on that date, not today.

Create The Measures

In this part of the exercise you will create two measures for the pivot table.

Create The Sales Total Amount Measure

In this part of the exercise you will create a measure that calculates the sales total amount. This measure will not be added to the pivot table. It will be used as part of another measure, which will be added to the pivot table.

1. Add a pivot table to the worksheet.

2. PowerPivot tab ⇒ Measures group ⇒ New Measure button.

3. Open the Table name drop-down list and select FactSales.

4. Type `Sales Total` in the Measure Name field.

5. Type `=SUM(FactSales[Sales Amount])` in the formula field.

6. Check the formula. You should have the options shown in Figure 13-26. Click OK.

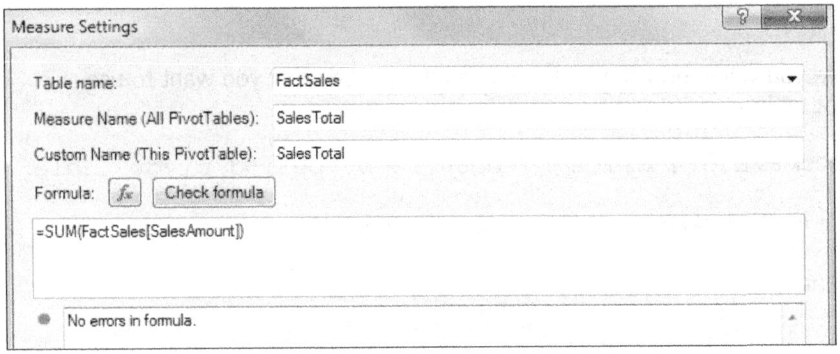

Figure 13-26 Sales Total measure options

7. Clear the check mark in front of the Sales Total measure field in the top section of the PowerPivot Field List.

Create The Sales Period Measure

In this part of the exercise you will create the measure that will add the sales total for each row of data to the correct bucket.

1. Click the New Measure button.
2. Open the Table name drop-down list and select FactSales if it is not already selected.
3. Type `Sales Period` in the Measure Name field.
4. Type the formula shown in Figure 13-27 at the bottom of the Measure Settings dialog box, as shown in Figure 13-28. This formula adds the sales total amount to one of three buckets; Current, MTD or YTD, based on the order date that is selected in the report filter.

```
=IF( COUNTROWS( VALUES( WhichPeriod[Bucket]))=1,
  IF( VALUES( WhichPeriod[Bucket]) = "Current", [Sales Total],
  IF( VALUES( WhichPeriod[Bucket]) = "MTD", [Sales Total](DATESMTD(DimDate[Datekey])),
  IF( VALUES( WhichPeriod[Bucket]) = "YTD", [Sales Total](DATESYTD(DimDate[Datekey])),
  BLANK()))),[Sales Total])
```

Figure 13-27 Formula to create the sales period

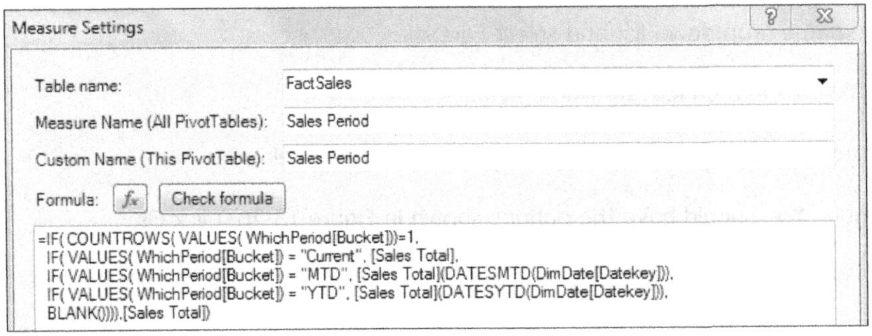

Figure 13-28 Sales Period measure formula

5. Check the formula. Click OK, then save the changes.

Create The Pivot Table

1. Add the Full Date Label field in the DimDate table to the Report Filter drop zone.

2. Add the Bucket field in the WhichPeriod table to the Column Labels drop zone.

3. Add the Region Country Name field in the DimGeography field to the Row Labels drop zone.

4. The Grand Total column in the pivot table is not needed. PivotTable Tools Options tab ⇒ Pivot Table group ⇒ Options button ⇒ Options. On the Totals & Filters tab, clear the Show grand totals for rows option, then click OK.

Use The Pivot Table

1. Open the Full Date Label drop-down list report filter and select the date 6-24-2009.

2. Open the Row Labels drop-down list, then clear the option that does not have a name, as illustrated in Figure 13-29.

The option that does not have a value means that there is at least one record in the DimGeography table that does not have data in the RegionCountryName field.

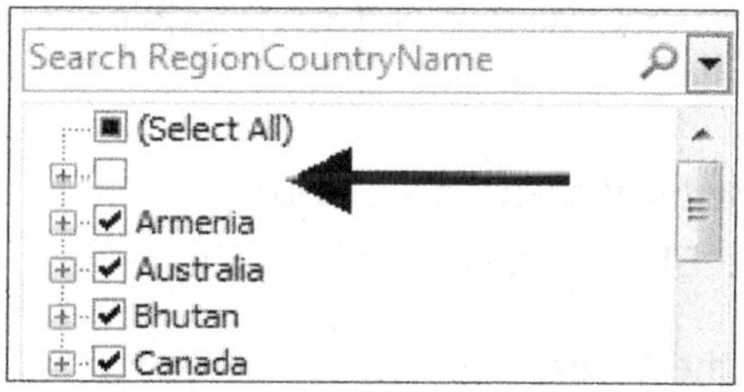

Figure 13-29 Row Labels drop-down list options

3. Format the cells that have a currency value to have a dollar sign and two digits after the decimal point.

4. Save the changes.

   Your pivot table should look like the one shown in Figure 13-30.

	A	B	C	D
1	FullDateLabel	2009-06-24		
2				
3	**Sales Period**	**Column Labels**		
4	**Row Labels**	**Current**	**MTD**	**YTD**
5	Armenia	$19,966.02	$575,832.63	$4,309,629.54
6	Australia	$60,751.65	$1,997,588.61	$13,617,449.14
7	Bhutan	$19,016.94	$638,264.76	$4,168,192.06
8	Canada	$134,287.70	$3,552,896.90	$21,331,141.77
9	China	$1,035,643.68	$27,608,267.40	$177,671,551.46
10	Denmark	$9,533.60	$217,565.80	$1,886,057.89

Figure 13-30 Sales by country by period pivot table

Handling Null Values

As you saw earlier in Figure 13-29, there are some rows of data in a table that do not have a value in a column that is displayed in a pivot table. By clearing the check mark illustrated earlier in Figure 13-29, the rows without a value will not be displayed in the pivot table.

Figure 13-31 shows another pivot table that has missing data. The person that creates the pivot table from this data may know what the blank cell represents. Others that view or use the pivot table may not.

The table may look better if that cell (in this case, the Payment Type) was filled in with a generic phrase to indicate that data is missing.

Ship To Name	Order Subtotal
Amritansh Raghav	**$15,432.50**
Check	$13,800.00
Credit Card	$1,632.50
Anna Bedecs	**$2,410.75**
	$2,410.75
Christina Lee	**$4,949.00**
	$380.00
Check	$184.00
Credit Card	$4,385.00

Figure 13-31 Pivot table with missing data

Exercise 13.5: Filling In Null Values On A Pivot Table

In this exercise you will modify the pivot table shown above in Figure 13-31 so that it displays a message for the empty cells in the pivot table.

Create The Null Values Formula

1. Save the E13.1 workbook as `E13.5 Fill in pivot table null values.`
2. Display the Orders table.
3. Add a calculated column with this formula. This formula will display text in the pivot table to let the user know that data is missing.
   `=IF(Orders[Payment Type]="", "*No Pymt Type*", [Payment Type])`
4. Rename the column to `New Pymt Type`, then save the changes.

Modify The Pivot Table

1. Display the pivot table, then refresh the data.
2. Add the New Pymt Type field in the Orders table to the Row Labels zone.
3. Save the changes.

   The pivot table should look like the one shown in Figure 13-32.

Ship To Name	Order Subtotal
Amritansh Raghav	**$15,432.50**
Check	$13,800.00
Credit Card	$1,632.50
Anna Bedecs	**$2,410.75**
No Pymt Type	$2,410.75
Christina Lee	**$4,949.00**
No Pymt Type	$380.00
Check	$184.00
Credit Card	$4,385.00

Figure 13-32 Null values filled in

Similar Style Reports

The same functionality that you used earlier in Exercise 13.4, can be used to group other types of data. Based on where the value in a field falls within the range of values for all of the buckets, determines which bucket the record will be placed in. In the pivot table that you created in Exercise 13.4, there are three buckets if you will: Current, Month to date (MTD) and Year to date (YTD).

For example, if you wanted to know how many customers bought specific items, you would replace the periods (the options in the buckets table) with the names of the products.

An example that you are familiar with is converting numeric grades into letter grades. The letter grades (A, A-, B+, C, etc) is what would be in the Buckets table. The range of numeric grades is 0-100, with 96-100 going into the "A" bucket and numeric grades 70-75 going into the "C" bucket.

Exercise 13.6: Create A Sales By Country Pivot Table With Percents

In Exercise 13.4 you created measures that would display the current monthly sales amount, the month to date sales amount and the year to date sales amount. Often, you may also need to know what percent of the total, each sales amount represents.

In this exercise you will modify the E13.4 pivot table to add a column that displays the percent that the sales amount for the country represents for each period.

If you used the Convert to percent option in Excel, that would replace the actual dollar amounts currently in the pivot table. Pivot tables do not allow columns or rows to be inserted, which means that you can't manually insert the percent columns. Fortunately, you can create a measure that will calculate the percent of sales by column.

1. Save the E13.4 report as `E13.6 Sales by country with percents.`
2. Click the New Measure button, then open the Table name drop-down list and select FactSales.
3. Type `Percent of Period` in the Measure Name field.
4. Type the formula shown in Figure 13-33.

```
=[Sales Period]/CALCULATE([Sales Period], ALL(DimGeography[RegionCountryName]))
```

Figure 13-33 Formula to create a percent column of data

5. Check the formula.

   The dialog box should look like the one shown in Figure 13-34.

   Click OK.

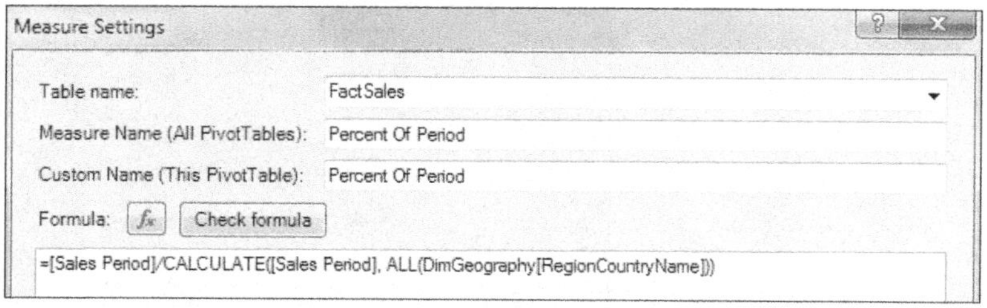

Figure 13-34 Percent of period measure formula

Add The Measure To The Pivot Table

In this part of the exercise you will add the measure to the pivot table, then format the value.

1. Add the Percent of Period measure in the FactSales table to the Values drop zone.

2. Select all of the numeric values including the Grand Total in the first Percent of Period column.

3. Right-click on the selected cells and select the Format Cells option.

4. Click on the Percentage category.

   The decimal places option should be set to 2, as shown in Figure 3-35.

   Click OK.

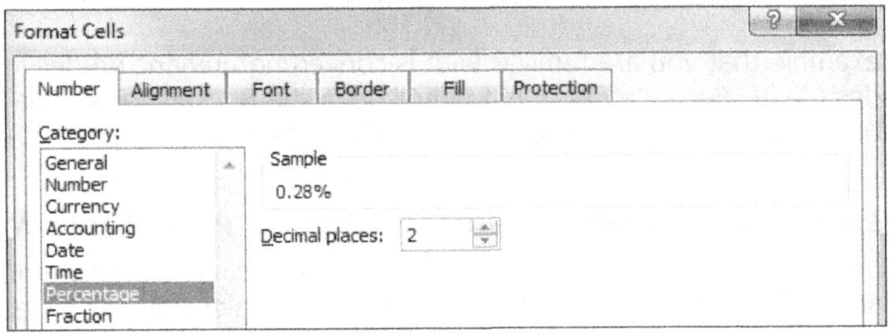

Figure 13-35 Percent format options

5. If necessary, repeat steps 2 through 4 for the other two columns.

6. To make it easier to visually know which Percent of Period goes with each sales period, you may want to add a vertical line.

7. Save the changes.

   The pivot table should look like the one shown in Figure 13-36.

	A	B	C	D	E	F	G
1	FullDateLabel	2009-06-24					
2							
3		Column Labels					
4		Current		MTD		YTD	
5	Row Labels	Sales Period	Percent Of Period	Sales Period	Percent Of Period	Sales Period	Percent Of Period
6	Armenia	$19,966.02	0.28%	$575,832.63	0.32%	$4,309,629.54	0.37%
7	Australia	$60,751.65	0.84%	$1,997,588.61	1.09%	$13,617,449.14	1.16%
8	Bhutan	$19,016.94	0.26%	$638,264.76	0.35%	$4,168,192.06	0.35%
9	Canada	$134,287.70	1.86%	$3,552,896.90	1.95%	$21,331,141.77	1.82%
10	China	$1,035,643.68	14.33%	$27,608,267.40	15.12%	$177,671,551.46	15.13%
11	Denmark	$9,533.60	0.13%	$217,565.80	0.12%	$1,886,057.89	0.16%
12	France	$379,196.10	5.25%	$9,735,006.10	5.33%	$62,678,377.33	5.34%
13	Germany	$562,760.80	7.79%	$16,658,190.70	9.12%	$105,454,133.58	8.98%
14	Greece	$7,978.00	0.11%	$260,622.20	0.14%	$1,919,387.86	0.16%
15	India	$78,528.17	1.09%	$2,110,895.75	1.16%	$12,896,337.85	1.10%
16	Iran	$75,868.25	1.05%	$1,345,036.19	0.74%	$8,725,764.59	0.74%
17	Ireland	$8,749.80	0.12%	$278,045.60	0.15%	$1,681,503.12	0.14%
18	Italy	$45,494.00	0.63%	$1,099,325.90	0.60%	$6,871,536.07	0.58%
19	Japan	$177,890.87	2.46%	$4,501,285.89	2.47%	$28,638,235.87	2.44%
20	Kyrgyzstan	$46,154.02	0.64%	$651,120.26	0.36%	$4,356,733.34	0.37%
21	Malta	$21,479.90	0.30%	$272,726.60	0.15%	$1,803,019.84	0.15%
22	Pakistan	$37,075.65	0.51%	$1,188,789.30	0.65%	$8,243,868.69	0.70%
23	Poland	$11,491.00	0.16%	$272,892.10	0.15%	$1,649,803.35	0.14%
24	Portugal	$939.80	0.01%	$239,062.30	0.13%	$1,840,088.23	0.16%
25	Romania	$1,960.00	0.03%	$253,880.30	0.14%	$1,889,376.30	0.16%
26	Russia	$52,957.36	0.73%	$1,609,911.10	0.88%	$10,055,564.31	0.86%
27	Singapore	$15,448.46	0.21%	$504,475.25	0.28%	$4,222,135.21	0.36%
28	Slovenia			$252,343.30	0.14%	$1,739,029.42	0.15%
29	South Korea	$45,651.66	0.63%	$1,191,133.98	0.65%	$8,066,882.72	0.69%
30	Spain	$3,219.90	0.04%	$278,385.10	0.15%	$1,985,264.69	0.17%
31	Sweden	$7,748.90	0.11%	$196,811.10	0.11%	$1,806,397.59	0.15%
32	Switzerland	$2,900.00	0.04%	$323,998.10	0.18%	$1,830,474.36	0.16%
33	Syria	$75,994.75	1.05%	$1,193,859.56	0.65%	$7,787,080.03	0.66%
34	Taiwan	$46,700.93	0.65%	$713,112.59	0.39%	$4,489,443.48	0.38%
35	Thailand	$69,227.15	0.96%	$1,163,809.64	0.64%	$8,073,671.65	0.69%
36	the Netherlands	$6,286.00	0.09%	$284,685.90	0.16%	$1,629,315.87	0.14%
37	Turkmenistan	$82,420.21	1.14%	$1,233,687.86	0.68%	$8,621,957.56	0.73%
38	United Kingdom	$165,616.80	2.29%	$3,941,514.40	2.16%	$26,466,813.02	2.25%
39	United States	$3,916,043.00	54.20%	$96,222,994.30	52.71%	$616,236,890.04	52.46%
40	Grand Total	$7,224,981.05	100.00%	$182,568,017.48	100.00%	$1,174,643,107.81	100.00%

Figure 13-36 Pivot table with percents added

Using Percents

In the previous exercise you created a measure to display percents in a pivot table next to the values. If you do not need to see values and percents in the same pivot table, you can right-click on a value in the pivot table and select **SHOW VALUES AS**, then select one of the options shown on the right of Figure 13-37.

Selecting one of the percent options **REPLACES** the values in the pivot table with percents. It is not uncommon to have one pivot table display the values and another pivot table display the percents of the values on the same worksheet.

Figure 13-38 is the sales by country by period pivot table that you created in Exercise 13.4. It shows the same data on both pivot tables. The pivot table on the left contains the values. The pivot table on the right shows the same values with the **% OF COLUMN TOTAL** percent option applied.

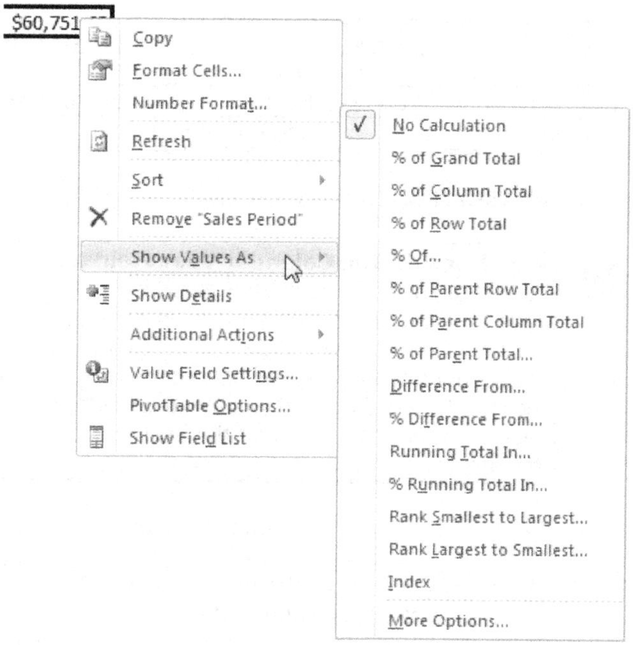

Figure 13-37 Percent options on the shortcut menu

Sales Period	Column Labels		
Row Labels	Current	MTD	YTD
Armenia	$19,966.02	$575,832.63	$4,309,629.54
Australia	$60,751.65	$1,997,588.61	$13,617,449.14
Bhutan	$19,016.94	$638,264.76	$4,168,192.06
Canada	$134,287.70	$3,552,896.90	$21,331,141.77
China	$1,035,643.68	$27,608,267.40	$177,671,551.46
Denmark	$9,533.60	$217,565.80	$1,886,057.89
France	$379,196.10	$9,735,006.10	$62,678,377.33

Sales Period	Column Labels		
Row Labels	Current	MTD	YTD
Armenia	0.28%	0.32%	0.37%
Australia	0.84%	1.09%	1.16%
Bhutan	0.26%	0.35%	0.35%
Canada	1.86%	1.95%	1.82%
China	14.33%	15.12%	15.13%
Denmark	0.13%	0.12%	0.16%
France	5.25%	5.33%	5.34%

Figure 13-38 Same data displayed as a percent

Exercise 13.7: Create A Summary Pivot Table

In Exercise 11.3, you learned how to create a yearly sales pivot table. That pivot table contained a lot of data. In this exercise you will create a yearly sales pivot table. The difference is that the totals will be displayed by year and by month.

1. Save the E9.3 workbook as `E13.7 Sales summary by year and month pivot table.`

2. Add a pivot table to the worksheet.

3. Add the fields in Table 13-3 to create the pivot table.

Table	Field	Add To Drop Zone
FactSales	Sales Amount	Values
DimChannel	Channel Name	Report Filter
DimDate	Calendar Month Label	Row Labels

Table 13-3 Fields to create the pivot table

> **Why Not Add The Calendar Year Field Now**
> As you can see, the months in the pivot table are not in the order that you want. If you added the Year field now, you would not be able to sort the months because the Row Labels sort options would be applied to the year field. The sort options only work for the first field in the Row Labels drop zone. This means if you are going to add several fields to the Row Labels drop zone and need to sort one or all of them, add one field, use the Row Labels sort options, then add the next field to the Row Labels drop zone and use the sort options.

4. Format the Sales Amount column to currency with two decimal places.

5. As shown in Figure 13-39, the months need to be sorted in calendar month order.

   Follow the steps in Exercise 11.5 to sort the months.

ChannelName All

Row Labels	Sum of SalesAmount
January	$561,216,897.49
February	$581,500,422.48
March	$568,366,355.56
April	$712,634,825.41
May	$743,555,624.44
June	$725,464,132.48
July	$746,564,685.77
August	$716,846,199.59
September	$700,042,513.20
October	$721,896,133.34
November	$777,311,657.31
December	$785,824,917.76
Grand Total	**$8,341,224,364.83**

Figure 13-39 Sales summary pivot table

6. Add the Calendar Year field in the DimDate table to the Row Labels drop zone, then move it up.

7. Save the changes. The pivot table should look like the one shown in Figure 13-40.

Row Labels	Sum of SalesAmount
2007	**$3,144,393,292.13**
January	$193,305,554.64
February	$209,439,067.93
March	$203,991,979.69
April	$276,891,048.16
May	$288,749,508.61
June	$283,186,644.54
July	$272,818,635.11
August	$263,780,279.28
September	$257,282,781.95
October	$288,853,903.92
November	$308,752,784.65
December	$297,341,103.65
2008	**$2,642,413,217.03**
January	$183,970,020.28
February	$191,106,948.30
March	$183,393,312.89

Figure 13-40 Summary sales pivot table grouped by the year

Add The Quarter Field To The Pivot Table

In this part of the exercise you will add another dimension if you will, to the pivot table. To be able to see the differences with and without the new dimension, you will make a copy of the current pivot table on the same worksheet.

1. Select Columns A and B, then right-click on the column heading and select Copy.

2. Right-click on Column D and select Paste.

3. Click in the second pivot table. Add the Calendar Quarter Label field in the DimDate table to the Row Labels drop zone, then move it up above the Calendar Month Label field.

4. Save the changes.

   The second pivot table should look like the one shown in Figure 13-41.

   As you can see, you can minimize a quarter (See 2007 Q3) or a year.

Row Labels	Sum of SalesAmount
⊟2007	**$3,144,393,292.13**
⊟Q1	**$606,736,602.25**
January	$193,305,554.64
February	$209,439,067.93
March	$203,991,979.69
⊟Q2	**$848,827,201.31**
April	$276,891,048.16
June	$283,186,644.54
May	$288,749,508.61
⊞Q3	**$793,881,696.34**
⊟Q4	**$894,947,792.23**
October	$288,853,903.92
November	$308,752,784.65
December	$297,341,103.65
⊟2008	**$2,642,413,217.03**
⊟Q1	**$558,470,281.47**
January	$183,970,020.28
February	$191,106,948.30
March	$183,393,312.89
⊟Q2	**$658,806,976.11**
April	$223,849,292.33
June	$214,455,381.54
May	$220,502,302.24

Figure 13-41 Sales summary by year, quarter and month

USING SLICERS

In this chapter you will learn how to use slicers to enhance pivot tables and pivot charts. You will also learn how to create dashboard reports.

CHAPTER 14

Slicers

Slicers are new to Excel 2010. They are an interactive tool that is used to reduce the amount of data that is displayed in pivot tables and pivot charts that are connected to the slicers. They are also used to analyze data and create some types of What If scenarios. This is possible because slicers allow the data in the PowerPivot table to be filtered, grouped and sorted. One set of slicers can control multiple pivot tables and pivot charts that are created with PowerPivot data. Slicers are useful when creating dashboards.

There are two versions of slicers; one in Excel (without PowerPivot being installed) and one in PowerPivot. Slicers are similar to report filters in terms of functionality. In some respects, I think that slicers are easier to use then report filters.

Slicers In Excel

Because Excel slicers can be used with PowerPivot data, an overview of their functionality is warranted.

A slicer can control more than one pivot table or pivot chart on the worksheet. Slicers in Excel are placed on the worksheet, as illustrated in Figure 14-1.

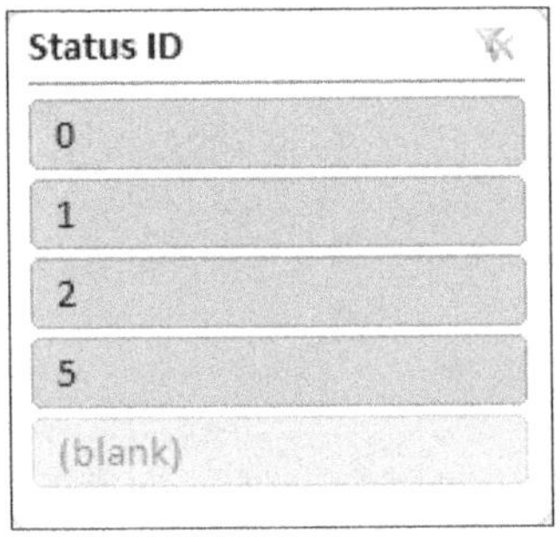

Figure 14-1 Excel slicers illustrated

Clicking on a button on the slicer filters the data that is displayed in the pivot table or pivot chart. For example, in Figure 14-1 above, no button on the slicer is selected. If you click on the third button on the slicer, the pivot table would display the data shown in Figure 14-2.

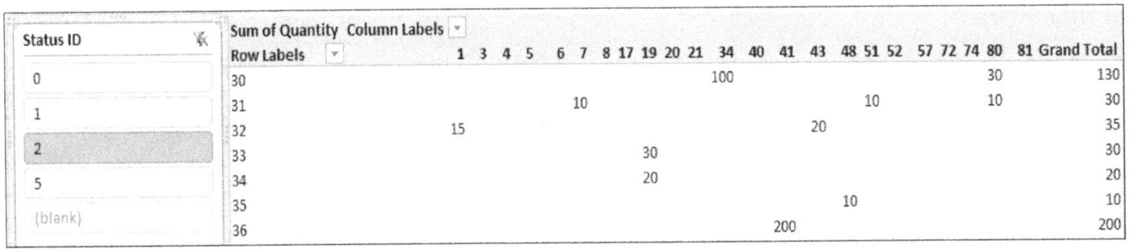

Sum of Quantity	Column Labels																						
Row Labels	1	3	4	5	6	7	8	17	19	20	21	34	40	41	43	48	51	52	57	72	74	80	81	Grand Total
30												100										30		130
31						10											10					10		30
32	15														20									35
33									30															30
34									20															20
35																10								10
36														200										200

Figure 14-2 Pivot table data filtered by an option on the slicer

Excel Slicers vs Report Filters

In Excel, the Report filter drop-down list, shown in Figure 14-3 is used to select all values or specific values that will filter the data by. The **SELECT MULTIPLE ITEMS** option must be checked before you can select more than one item in the list.

The Report Filter feature can be used with data on a spreadsheet, as well as, data in a table or pivot table. Slicers can only be used with pivot tables or pivot charts. If you only need to select one item from the Report Filter list to filter a pivot table on, you can probably continue to use the Report Filter for pivot tables.

If you need to select more than one item from the list to filter on, it is probably better to create a slicer because slicers make it easier to know which items are selected, because all of the items are visible in a slicer.

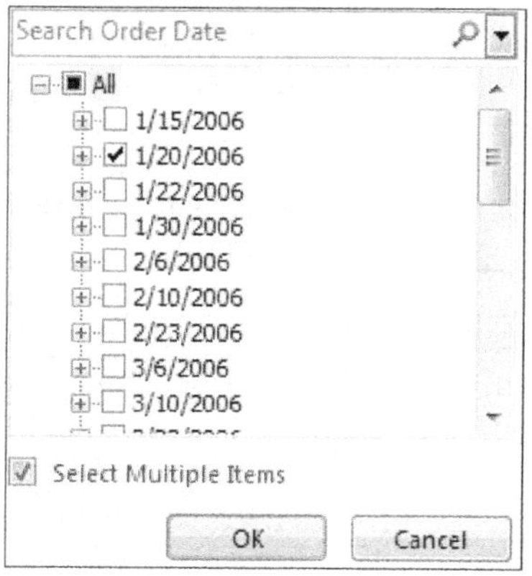

Figure 14-3 Report Filter drop-down list

Slicer Tools Options Contextual Tab

The options on the tab shown in Figure 14-4 are part of Excel, but can be used with slicers created in PowerPivot. They are used to change the size and orientation of the entire slicer or its buttons. The alignment of slicers can also be set. The options are explained in Table 14-1.

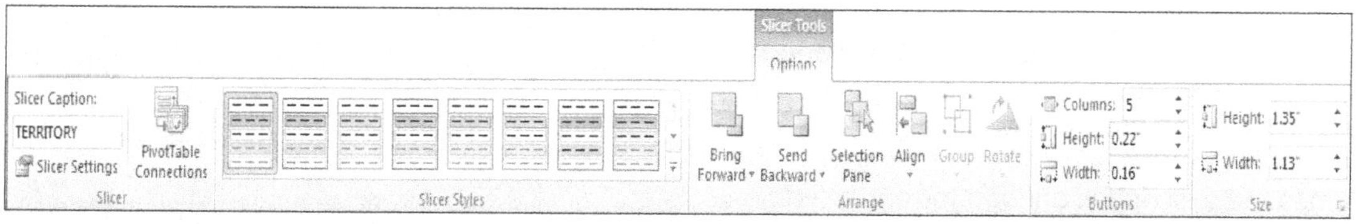

Figure 14-4 Slicer Tools Options tab

Option	Description
Slicer Caption	This is the name displayed above the slicer. By default, the field name (the field that the slicer is attached to) is displayed. If you want to change the name, type over the name in this field.
Slicer Settings	Opens the dialog box shown in Figure 14-5.
Pivot Table Connections	Opens the dialog box shown in Figure 14-6.
Slicer Styles	The options in this section are used to change the color scheme of the slicer.
Bring Forward	Is used to move the selected object forward one level or to the front of all objects.
Send Backward	Is used to move the selected object back one level or all the way to the back.
Selection Pane	Will display the Selection and Visibility pane, shown in Figure 14-7. The feature is helpful if you have trouble selecting an object on the worksheet.
Align	Is used to line up the selected objects.

Table 14-1 Slicer Tools Options tab options explained

Option	Description
Group	Treats two or more objects as one, so that they can be used as one object. This is helpful when you need to apply the same formatting to several objects. If the objects are grouped, you only have to apply the formatting options once and they will be applied to all objects in the group.
Rotate	Is used to flip or rotate the selected object.
Columns (Buttons)	Is used to change the number of columns in the slicer.
Height (Buttons)	Is used to change the height of the slicer buttons.
Width (Buttons)	Is used to change the width of the slicer buttons.
Height	Is used to change the height of the shape or picture.
Width	Is used to change the width of the shape or picture.

Table 14-1 Slicer Tools Options tab options explained (Continued)

Clicking the **SLICER SETTINGS** button on the Options tab opens the dialog box shown in Figure 14-5.

The options are used to change the display settings of the selected slicer.

The one option that you may want to change is the **CAPTION** option because it is displayed on the slicer. As you can see, the default caption is the field name and not all field names are descriptive enough for end-users.

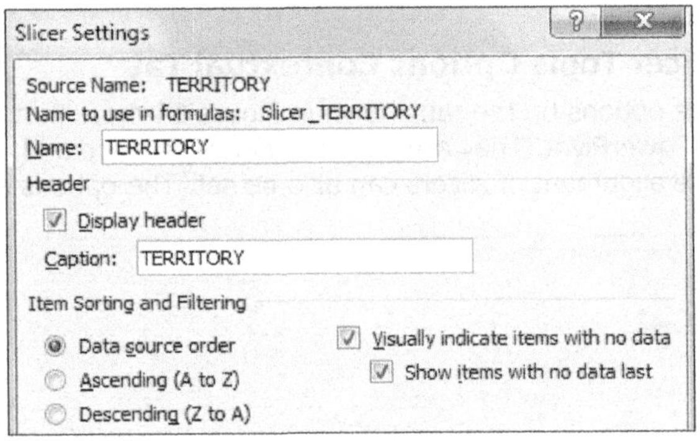

Figure 14-5 Slicer Settings dialog box

Clicking the **PIVOTTABLE CONNECTIONS** button on the Options tab opens the dialog box shown in Figure 14-6.

The list contains all of the pivot tables in the workbook.

The options are used to manage the pivot tables that the slicer is connected to.

You can select pivot tables to connect to the slicer or remove the connection of pivot tables from the slicers.

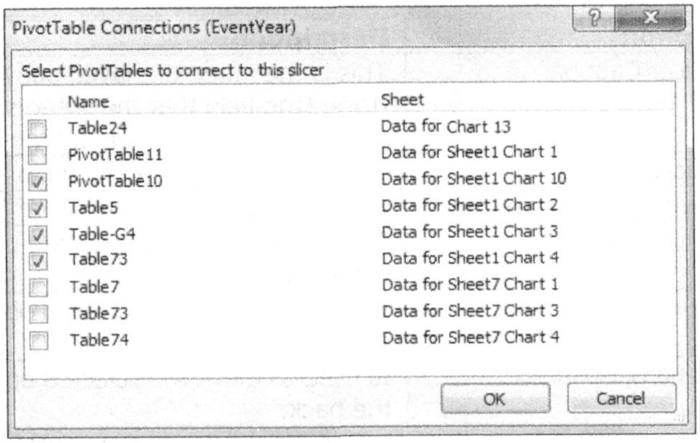

Figure 14-6 PivotTable Connections dialog box

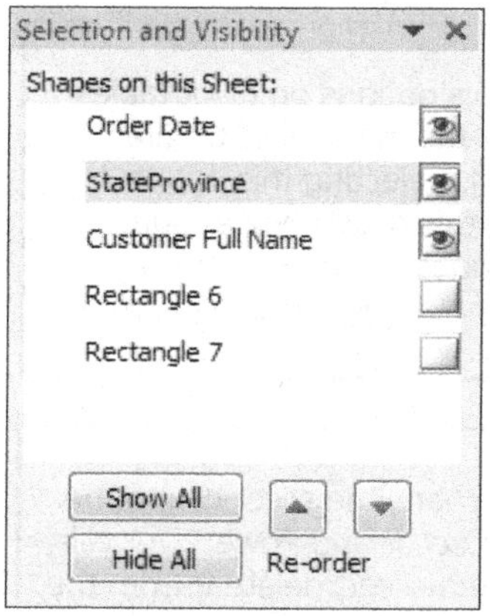

Figure 14-7 Selection and Visibility pane

Insert Slicer Options

The options shown in Figure 14-8 are on the PivotTable tools Options tab for pivot tables and the Pivot Chart Tools Analyze tab for pivot charts. The options are explained below.

Figure 14-8 Insert slicer button options

① **INSERT SLICER** opens the dialog box shown in Figure 14-9.

② **SLICER CONNECTIONS** opens the dialog box shown in Figure 14-10.

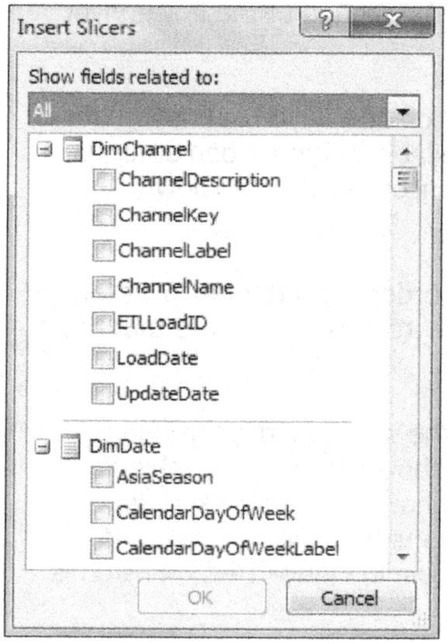

Figure 14-9 Insert Slicers dialog box in a PowerPivot workbook

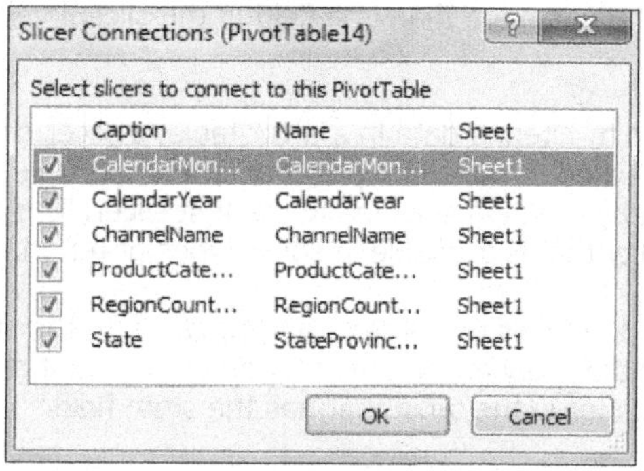

Figure 14-10 Slicer Connections dialog box

Options Tab Slicer Options
In Chapter 11 you learned that you can use the Pivot Table Tools options on pivot tables created with PowerPivot data. On the Pivot Table Tools Options tab in the Sort & Filter group, is an **INSERT SLICER** option [See Chapter 11, Figure 11-5]. Selecting this option opens the dialog box shown above in Figure 14-9. You can use this dialog box to add slicers to the pivot table, just like you can use the Slicer drop zones on the PowerPivot Field List. The difference is that this dialog box does not have the automatic slicer layout functionality that the PowerPivot Field List provides.

Disconnecting Slicers
When a PowerPivot slicer is connected to a pivot table or pivot chart, the slicer cannot be disconnected later. If disconnected, unpredictable behavior can occur and PowerPivot will automatically reconnect the slicer. If you want to totally remove a slicer, delete it from the slicer drop zone in the PowerPivot Field List.

Excel Slicers
Excel slicers can be used with pivot tables and pivot charts created with PowerPivot data. A difference that I noticed between Excel slicers and PowerPivot slicers is that Excel slicers seem to provide more control in terms of resizing them, but PowerPivot slicers are a little easier to use.

Slicers In PowerPivot

The biggest difference that PowerPivot slicers have that slicers in Excel do not have is that the PowerPivot Field List has drop zones for slicers. This lets you add fields to the slicer drop zones by using the shortcut menus, as shown in Chapter 11, Figure 11-23 for pivot tables and Chapter 12, Figure 12-23 for pivot charts. You can also drag the fields from the top of the PowerPivot Field List to the appropriate slicer section. What PowerPivot adds to pivot tables and pivot charts is that one set of slicers can be used to control multiple pivot tables and pivot charts.

You can also resize the slicers, move the slicers to a different place, rearrange the order of the slicers if there is more than one field in the slicers vertical or horizontal section of the PowerPivot Field List.

In addition to filtering data in a pivot table, a slicer can filter the options displayed in another slicer that is attached to the same pivot table. For example, the items available in the second slicer are controlled by the item selected in the first slicer. This is the same concept as the drill-down functionality that is available in some types of reports.

Figure 14-11 shows two slicers. As you can see, the slicers have a border around them. This lets you know that they are grouped together. The first slicer displays an item for each state that there are records for in the table that has the state field.

When an item is selected in this slicer, the corresponding cities for the state are displayed in the second slicer. Clicking on a state in the first slicer displays the data shown in the pivot table in Figure 14-12. When a city is selected in the second slicer, the data shown in Figure 14-13 is displayed. The options in the second slicer that are not enabled, means that they are not part of the group selected in the first slicer. For example, in the options shown in Figure 14-13, Boston is not enabled because it is not a city in California.

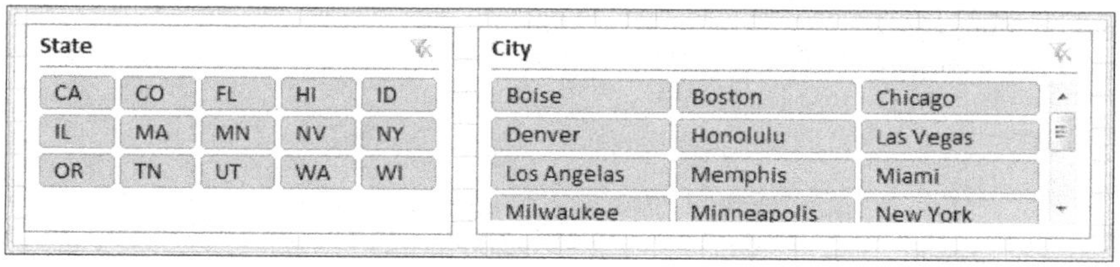

Figure 14-11 Two slicers connected to the same pivot table

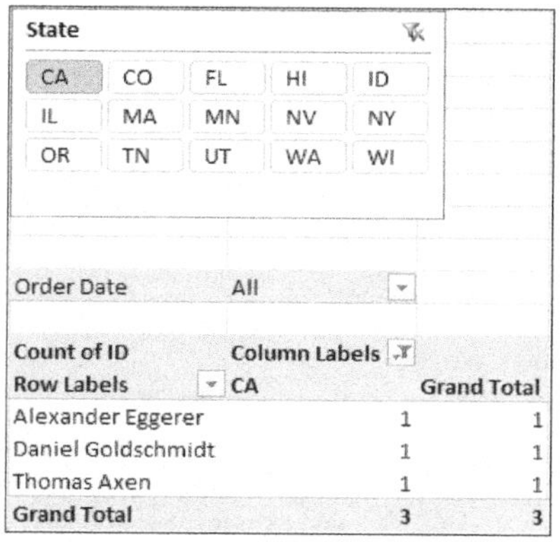

Figure 14-12 Data from the first slicer

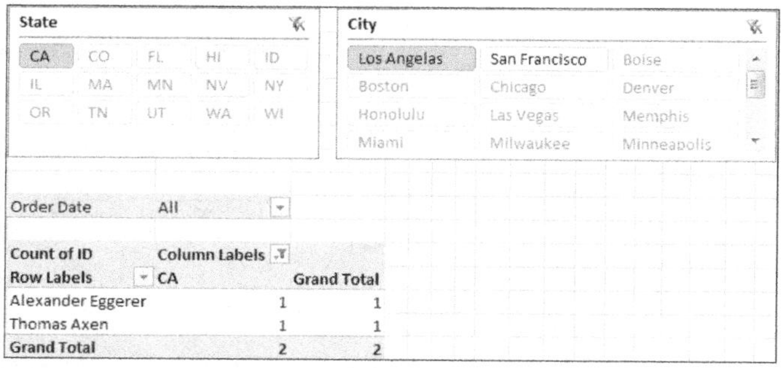

Figure 14-13 Data from the second slicer

Slicers in Excel appear as individual objects, as shown in Figure 14-14. This means that they can be placed anywhere on the worksheet. In PowerPivot, all slicers that are added to the vertical or horizontal slicer drop zone are grouped together.

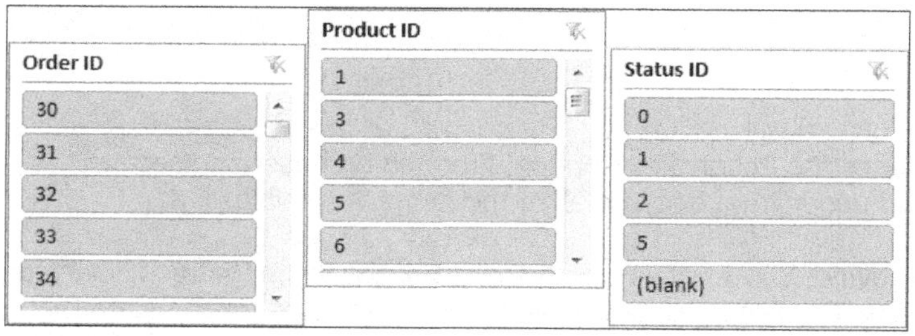

Figure 14-14 Three slicers in Excel

Exercise 14.1: Add Slicers To The Customers By State Pivot Table

In Exercise 11.2 you created a pivot table that displayed customers by state. In this exercise you will modify that pivot table by adding slicers for the customers, state and city.

1. Save the E11.2 workbook as `E14.1 Customers by state slicers`.

2. Add the State Province field in the Customers table to the Slicers Horizontal drop zone. Add the City field in the Customers table to the Slicers Horizontal drop zone.

3. The bottom of the PowerPivot Field List should have the options shown in Figure 14-15.

   Save the changes.

   The pivot table and slicers should look like the ones shown in Figure 14-16.

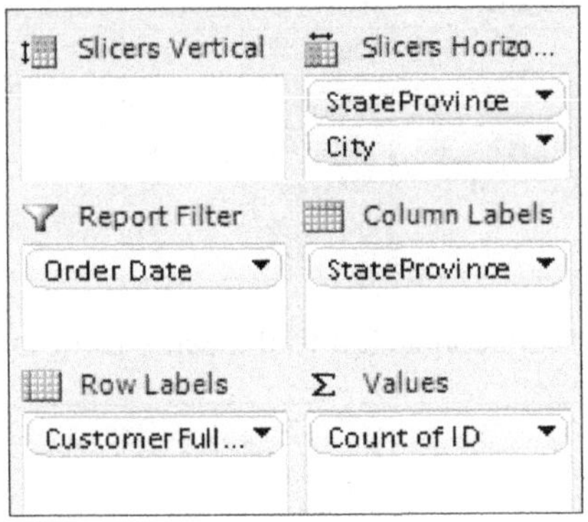

Figure 14-15 PowerPivot Field List drop zone options

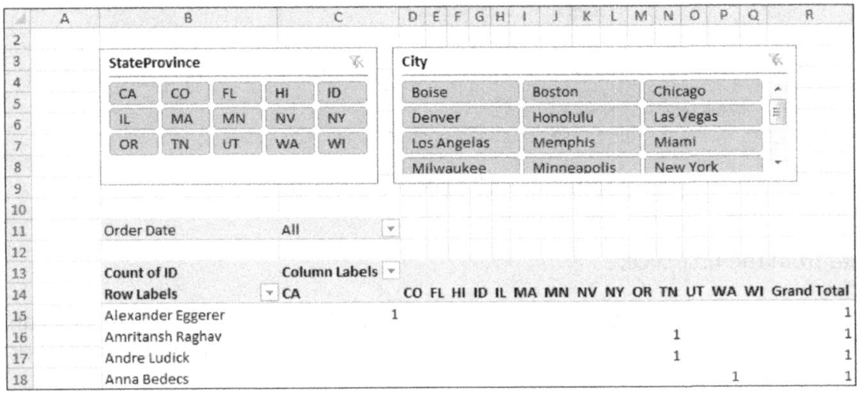

Figure 14-16 Pivot table with slicers

Using Slicers

As you read earlier, slicers are similar to the Report Filter option. From an end-user perspective, slicers are probably easier to use and understand because all of the items are visible.

If you click on a state in the State Province slicer, only records that have the value that you selected will be displayed in the pivot table. The City slicer will only have the cities enabled for the state that is selected. As you select an option in the first slicer, the corresponding items in the second slicer will automatically be rearranged and the available options will be moved to the beginning of the slicer section. The pivot table displays all customers in CA, as shown earlier n Figure 14-12.

Notice that the filter icon in the upper right corner of the State slicer has a red x through it. That lets you visually know that the data displayed in the pivot table has been filtered by that slicer. If you want to remove a filter, click on the red x.

If you select an option in the City field, the pivot table will change to only display rows of data that match both filter options, as shown earlier in Figure 14-13. In this scenario, you do not have to select a state first and then select a city.

Exercise 14.2: Create Slicers For A Pivot Table And Pivot Chart

In the previous exercise you created two slicers for a pivot table. As you have read, slicers can control more than one pivot table or pivot chart. In this exercise you will create year and month slicers that will be used to control a pivot table and pivot chart.

Add Slicers To The Pivot Table

1. Save the E12.7 workbook as `E14.2 Mini dashboard report.`
2. Add the Calendar Year field in the DimDate table to the Slicers Horizontal drop zone.
3. Add the Calendar Month Label field in the DimDate table to the Slicers Horizontal drop zone.

Add Slicers To The Pivot Chart

1. If you click on the chart, you should see the slicers that you added to the pivot table are in the PowerPivot Field List for the chart. If so, go to the next section. If not, complete the remaining steps in this section.
2. Add the Calendar Year field in the DimDate table to the Slicers Horizontal drop zone.
3. Add the Calendar Month Label field in the DimDate table to the Slicers Horizontal drop zone.

Modify The Report

In this part of the exercise you will resize parts of the report.

1. Make the pivot chart smaller.
2. Make the slicers frame smaller.
3. Format the numbers on the vertical axis of the pivot chart to display in currency format without a decimal point.
4. Format the numeric values in the pivot table to display in currency format with 2 decimal places.

Move The Pivot Table

You should see a few blank columns between the pivot chart and the pivot table. The report would look better without the blank columns. There are two options for moving a pivot table, as discussed below.

① **DELETE THE COLUMNS OR ROWS**. If there are columns or rows around the pivot table that are not needed and are not being used by another object on the report, you can delete them, just like you would in a spreadsheet.

② Use the **MOVE PIVOT TABLE DIALOG BOX**. This dialog box is used to select a new worksheet in the workbook or a specific place on the current worksheet, as shown in Figure 14-17.

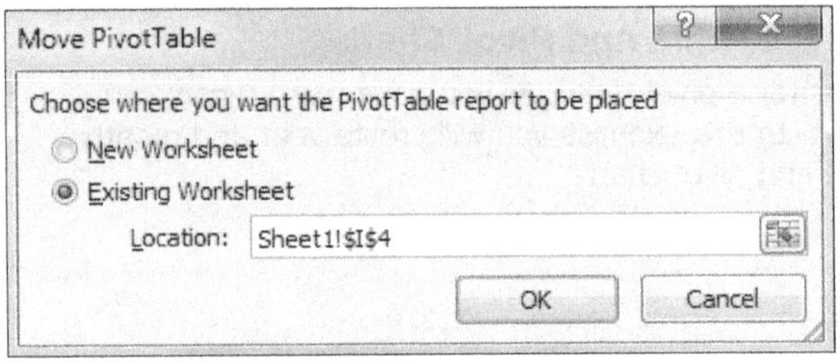

Figure 14-17 Move PivotTable dialog box

1. Click in the pivot table.

2. PivotTable Tools Options tab ⇒ Actions group ⇒ Move Pivot Table button.

3. Select the Existing Worksheet option, then click the button at the end of the Location field.

4. Click in the cell where you want the upper left corner of the pivot table to be placed. Make sure that there is room above the cell that you select for the Report Filters. Figure 14-17 above, shows the cell that I selected, but select the cell that works best for your pivot table. Once you have selected the cell that you want, click the button at the end of the field.

5. Click OK, then save the changes. My report looks like the one shown in Figure 14-18.

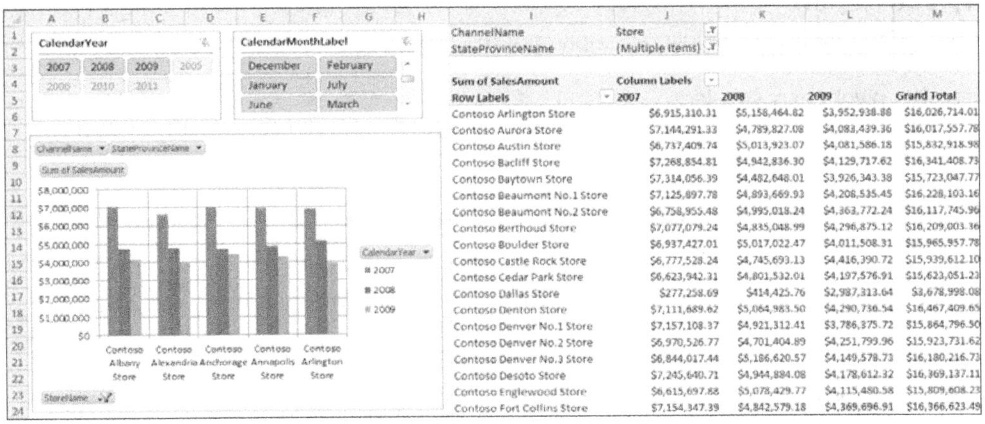

Figure 14-18 E14.2 Mini dashboard report

Not surprising, but the months in the slicer are not in calendar month order. There are currently no options that can be used to sort the items in a slicer like you can in a report filter for the pivot table. Hopefully, this is something that will be worked on for the next release.

As you can see, the pivot table and pivot chart have two other filters in common; the Channel Name and the State Province Name filters. You can leave them as individual filters or you can create slicers for them.

Moving A Chart
Just like you can move a pivot table using a dialog box, you can move a chart. PivotChart Tools Design tab ⇒ Location group ⇒ Move chart button, opens the dialog box shown in Figure 14-19. As you see, moving a chart to a different location on the same worksheet using the dialog box does not have the same precision that pivot tables have. Because pivot charts have a frame, it is easier to manually drag the chart to where you need it to be.

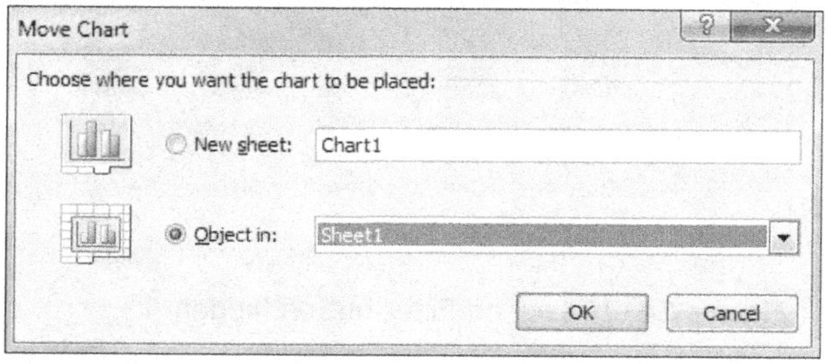

Figure 14-19 Move Chart dialog box

Using Filters And Slicers

The pivot table and pivot chart in Exercise 14.2 both have a Calendar Year filter. What you will notice is that if you select an option on the Calendar Year filter on the pivot chart, the same option will be applied to the pivot table automatically. The Calendar Year slicer will also change to what you selected in the calendar year filter.

Hiding Filter Buttons On Pivot Tables And Pivot Charts

When a report has slicers, some of the Report Filter buttons may not be needed. An example of this is the Calendar Year Legend Field button shown earlier in Figure 14-18.

I suspect that out of habit many people will leave this field button visible because slicers do not appear to have the functionality to allow more than one option to be selected at the same time. At the end of this chapter you will learn how to use the CTRL key to select more than one option in a slicer.

You can hide any field button on a pivot table or pivot chart that there is a slicer for. You can also hide the buttons if there are no slicer for the same field. The filters that do not have a slicer can stay visible because they are specific to the pivot table or pivot chart.

You can hide the Calendar Year button and still display the legend, as illustrated in Figure 14-20.

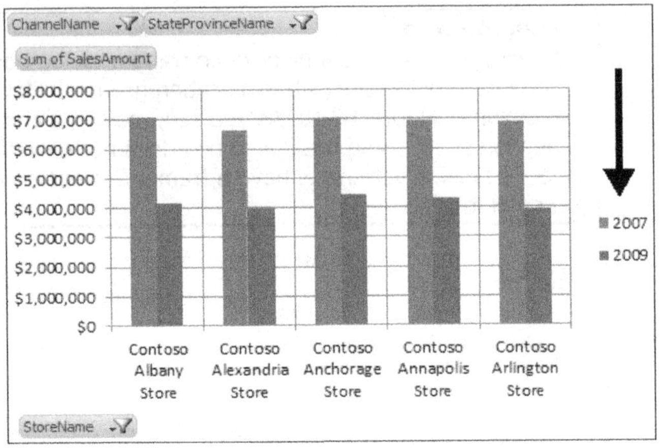

Figure 14-20 Legend Filter button hidden

How To Show And Hide Filter Buttons On Pivot Charts

There are two ways to show and hide filter buttons, as explained below. The options below use the Legend button shown earlier on the pivot chart in Figure 14-18, but the steps and process is the same for all filter buttons on a pivot chart.

① Right-click on the Filter button in the pivot chart. You will see the shortcut menu shown in Figure 14-21. Select the first "Hide" option to hide the selected filter button. Select the second "Hide" option to hide all of the filter buttons on the pivot chart.

② Use the **FIELD BUTTONS** button. This button is on the Pivot Chart Tools Analyze tab. Click the button to display the options shown in Figure 14-22.

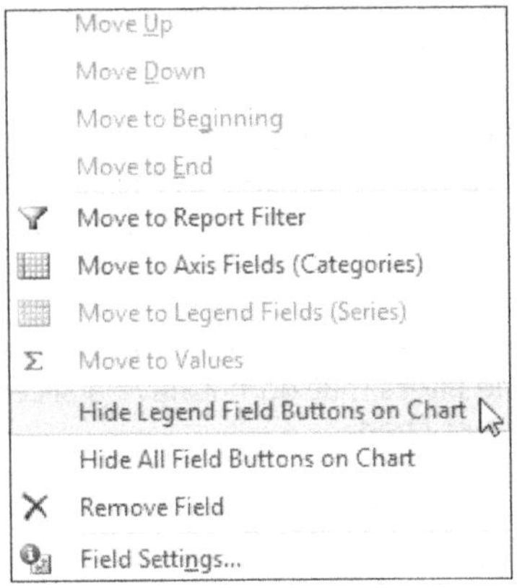

Figure 14-21 Legend filter button shortcut menu

Filter Buttons
In Excel, filter buttons are called **FIELD BUTTONS**.

Clearing the check mark for a button will hide it on the pivot chart.

Selecting an option that is not checked, will display the button on the pivot chart.

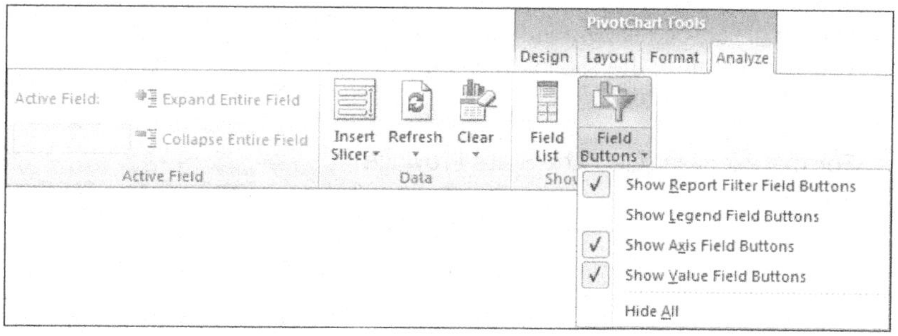

Figure 14-22 Field Buttons options

Exercise 14.3: Add A Pivot Chart And Attach Slicers To An Existing Report

In Exercise 14.1 you added slicers to a pivot table. In this exercise you will modify that report by adding a pivot chart and then attach the existing slicers to the pivot chart.

Add The Chart To The Report

1. Save the E14.1 workbook as `E14.3 Attach slicers`.

2. Add a pivot chart to the right of the pivot table.

3. Add the fields from the Customers table in Table 14-2 to create the pivot chart.

Field	Add To Drop Zone
ID	Values
State Province	Legend Fields
Customer Full Name	Axis Fields

Table 14-2 Fields to create the pivot chart

Attach The Slicers

When you add a pivot table or pivot chart to an existing report it is not a requirement to attach it to the existing slicers. You can attach the new pivot table or pivot chart to some slicers and not others. You can also create slicers just for the new pivot table or pivot chart by adding the field to one of the slicer drop zones on the PowerPivot Field List. Fortunately, there is a way to attach a pivot table or pivot chart that was added to a report that already has slicers.

1. Click on the pivot chart.

2. Pivot Chart Tools Analyze tab ⇒ Data group ⇒ Insert Slicer button ⇒ Slicer Connections, as shown earlier in Figure 14-8.

3. On the dialog box shown in Figure 14-23, you will see all of the slicers that are currently in the report.

   For this exercise select the State Province slicer.

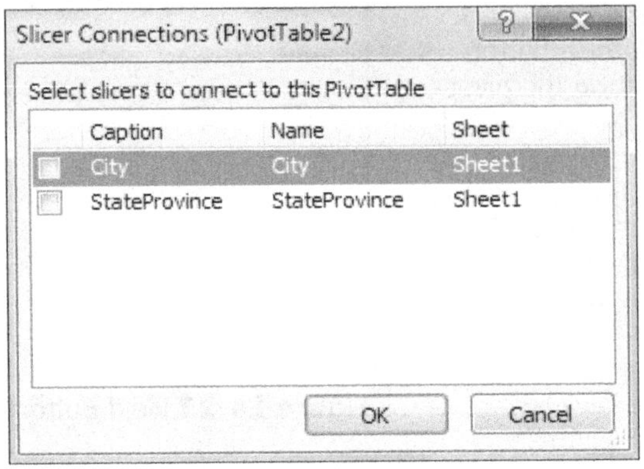

Figure 14-23 Slicer Connections dialog box

4. Click OK. Save the changes. Now when you use the slicers, the data in the pivot chart will be filtered.

Test The Slicers

1. Click on the CA button in the State Province slicer.
2. Click on the San Francisco button in the City slicer. Notice that the pivot chart values did not change, which is what is expected in this exercise.

Dashboard Reports

You have probably heard this term before and wondered what makes a report in Excel a dashboard report. In all honesty, a dashboard report can consist of whatever the report designer can dream up. Typically though, for an Excel report to be considered a dashboard report, at a minimum, it has to meet the following criteria:

① There are at least two slicers.

② There are two or more pivot charts. Usually, dashboard reports do not display pivot tables. Probably because pivot tables can require varying amounts of space, depending on the filter or slicer options that are selected. Pivot charts do not have this issue because they are self contained and resize automatically in the frame to accommodate the amount of data that needs to be displayed.

I called the report in Exercise 14.2 a mini dashboard because it has the smallest number of objects that some people consider a requirement to be called a dashboard. Most of the time, dashboards have at least four pivot tables and three or more slicers, some of which are placed horizontally and some placed vertically.

Another reason that pivot tables generally are not displayed on a dashboard report is because they do not display the data visually, like pivot charts do. By design, pivot charts display the same amount of data as a pivot table that has the same filters and slicers, in less space on the worksheet. This means that more pivot charts can fit in the same amount of space then pivot tables.

What Each Chart Needs
As you will read in Exercise 14.4, you will be creating four pivot charts. Some of the requirements for all four charts are the same. Rather then type the same thing four times, the functionality that every chart needs is listed below. Complete the tasks below for each chart after you have added the fields to the drop zones at the bottom of the PowerPivot Field List.

1. Add the Region Country Name field in the DimGeography table to the Report Filter drop zone.

   Modify the filter list to only display records in the United States, as shown in Figure 14-24.

Figure 14-24 Region Country Name field filter list option

2. Hide all of the Field buttons on the chart.

3. **Create A Chart Title**
   By default, pivot charts do not have a chart title. Chart 1, Chart 2 etc. that you will see at the top of charts is the chart name. The steps below show you how to create a chart title.

   1. PivotChart Tools Layout tab ⇒ Labels group ⇒ Chart Title button ⇒ Above Chart option, as shown in Figure 14-25.
   2. Type in the title for the chart in the formula bar, then press Enter.

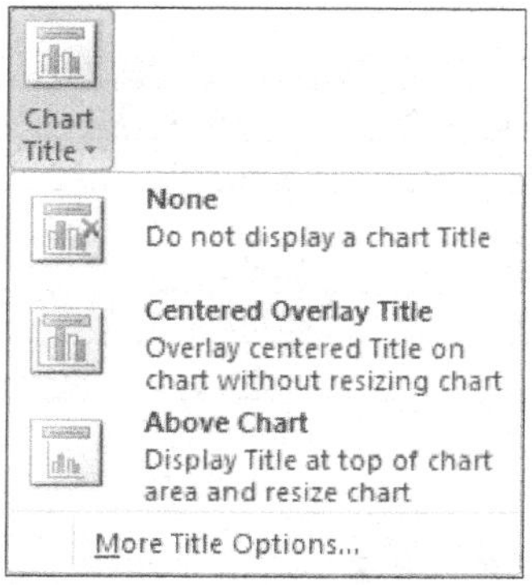

Figure 14-25 Chart Title button options

4. Resize the chart as needed.

Exercise 14.4: Create A Dashboard Report

In this exercise you will create a dashboard report that has four pivot charts and four slicers. The pivot charts will display the top 5 stores by sales, top 5 stores and top 5 products, sales by product and top 5 products. All of the charts will only display data for stores in the United States. The vertical slicers will allow all of the charts to be filtered by year and month. The horizontal slicers will allow the charts to be filtered by state, product category and channel.

1. Save the E9.3 workbook as `E14.4 Dashboard with 4 charts.`

2. Add the **FOUR CHARTS** PivotTable layout to the existing worksheet.

Create Pivot Chart 1: Top 5 Stores

This pivot chart will display the top 5 stores based on sales.

1. Click on Chart 1, then add the fields in Table 14-3 to create the pivot chart.

Table	Field	Add To Drop Zone
FactSales	Sales Amount	Values
DimDate	Calendar Year	Legend Fields
DimChannel	Channel Name	Report Filter
Stores	Store Name	Axis Fields

Table 14-3 Fields to create pivot chart 1

2. Open the Store Name filter list ⇒ Value Filters ⇒ Top 10.

3. On the Top 10 Filter dialog box, change the second field to 5, then click OK.

4. Change the format of the values on the vertical axis to currency with no decimal places.

5. Create the chart title `Top 5 Stores.`

6. Create the slicers in Table 14-4 for the pivot chart.

Table	Field	Slicer Drop Zone	Rename To
DimDate	Calendar Year	Vertical	
DimDate	Calendar Month Label	Vertical	
DimGeography	StateProvinceName	Horizontal	State (1)
DimProductCategory	ProductCategoryName	Horizontal	Product Category
DimChannel	Channel Name	Horizontal	

Table 14-4 Fields to create the slicers for the pivot charts

(1) Right-click on the State slicer in the pivot chart and **SELECT SORT A TO Z**.

How Slicers Work
The good thing is that once you create the slicers above in Table 14-4, you do not have to create them for the remaining pivot charts because they are automatically applied to the other three pivot charts on the worksheet. If there is a pivot chart that does not need a slicer, it can be removed for that particular pivot chart by removing it from the slicer drop zone.

7. Save the changes.

   The chart should look like the one shown in Figure 14-26.

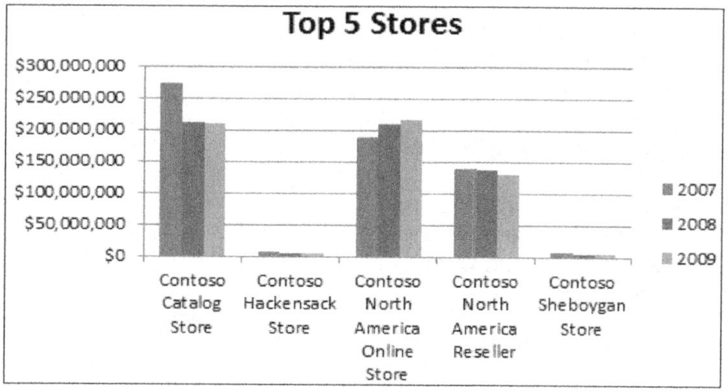

Figure 14-26 Top 5 Stores pivot chart

Create Pivot Chart 2: Top 5 Products And Top 5 Stores

This pivot chart will display the sales amounts for the top 5 products and the top 5 stores that sold these products.

1. Click on Chart 2, then add the fields in Table 14-5 to create the pivot chart.

Table	Field	Add To Drop Zone
FactSales	Sales Amount	Values
DimProduct	Product Name	Legend Fields
Stores	Store Name	Axis Fields

Table 14-5 Fields to create pivot chart 2

2. Open the Product Name filter list ⇒ Value Filters ⇒ Top 10.
3. On the Top 10 Filter dialog box, change the second field to 5, then click OK.
4. Open the Store Name filter list ⇒ Value Filters ⇒ Top 10.
5. On the Top 10 Filter dialog box, change the second field to 5, then click OK.

> **Viewing The Filter Order**
> If you hold the mouse pointer over the Product Name or Store name filter you will see the order that the filters have been applied to the pivot chart, as shown in Figure 14-27. This order is based on the order that you created the filter criteria.

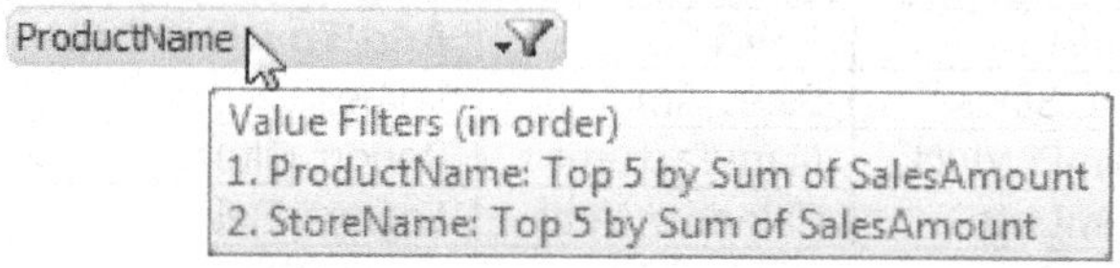

Figure 14-27 Filter order for the pivot chart

6. Create the chart title `Top 5 Products By Top 5 Stores.`

7. Right-click on the Store Name at the bottom of the chart and select **FORMAT AXIS.**

   Click the Alignment button.

   Open the Text direction drop-down list and select the **ROTATE ALL TEXT 270°** option, as shown in Figure 14-28.

   Click the Close button.

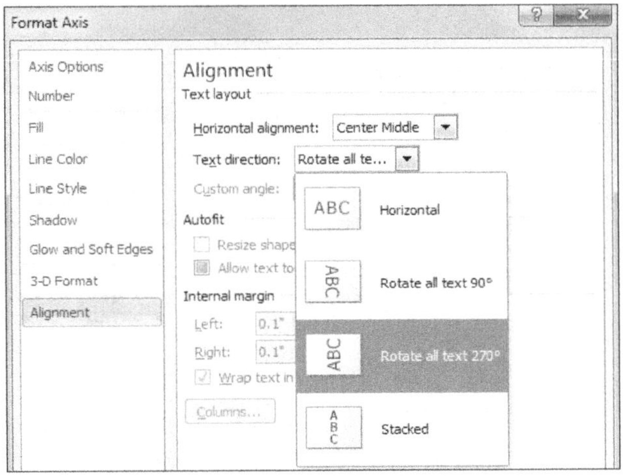

Figure 14-28 Format Axis dialog box options

8. Save the changes.

   The chart should look like the one shown in Figure 14-29.

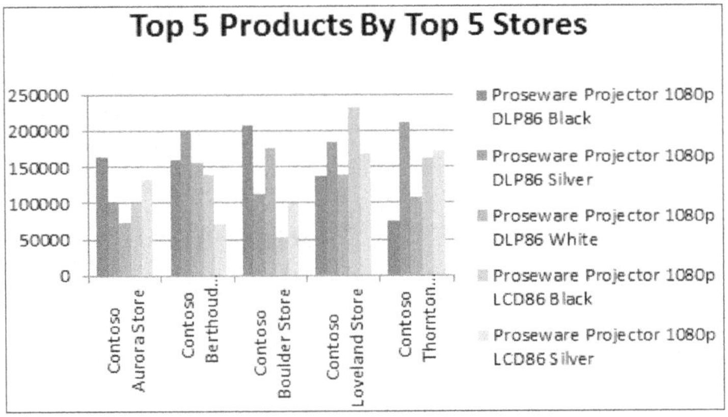

Figure 14-29 Top 5 Products By Top 5 Stores pivot chart

Create Pivot Chart 3: Sales By Product Manufacturer

This pivot chart will display the products of a specific manufacturer. The Product Name will be shown on the pivot chart, but will be filtered by the manufacturer field in addition to the country filter.

1. Click on Chart 3, then add the fields in Table 14-6 to create the pivot chart.

Table	Field	Add To Drop Zone
FactSales	Sales Amount	Values
DimProduct	Manufacturer	Report Filter
DimDate	Calendar Year	Legend Fields
DimProduct	Product Name	Axis Fields
Stores	Store Name	Axis Fields

Table 14-6 Fields to create pivot chart 3

2. Select Northwind Traders in the manufacturer report filter.

3. Create the chart title `Sales By Product Manufacturer`.

4. Rotate the text on the horizontal axis to 270°.

5. Format the values on the vertical axis to currency with no decimal places.

6. Save the changes.

   The chart should look like the one shown in Figure 14-30.

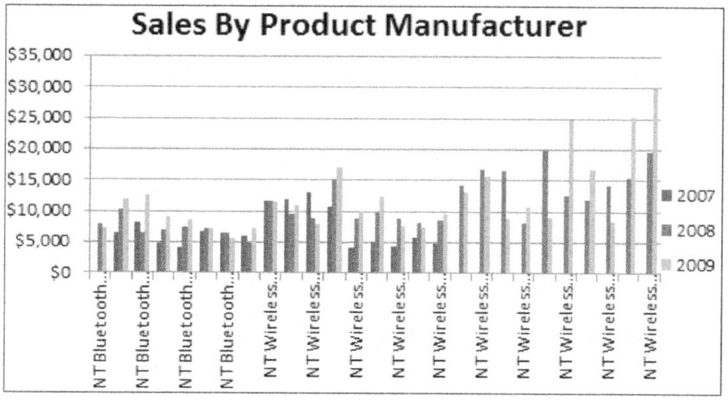

Figure 14-30 Sales By Product Manufacturer pivot chart

Create Pivot Chart 4: Top 5 Products

This pivot chart will display the top 5 products for the calendar years that are selected.

1. Click on Chart 4, then add the fields in Table 14-7 to create the pivot chart.

Table	Field	Add To Drop Zone
FactSales	Sales Amount	Values
DimProduct	Manufacturer	Report Filter
DimDate	Calendar Year	Legend Fields
DimProduct	Product Name	Axis Fields
Stores	Store Name	Axis Fields

Table 14-7 Fields to create pivot chart 4

2. Create a Top 5 filter for the Product Name field.

3. Create the chart title `Top 5 Products`.

Change The Chart Type

1. Change the chart type to **BAR OF PIE**.

2. Open the Chart Styles drop-down list and select a color that you like.

3. On the Layout tab, click on the Data Labels button, then select the option **MORE DATA LABEL OPTIONS**.

4. Select the Percentage and Outside End options, then select the **(NEW LINE)** Separator option, as shown in Figure 14-31.

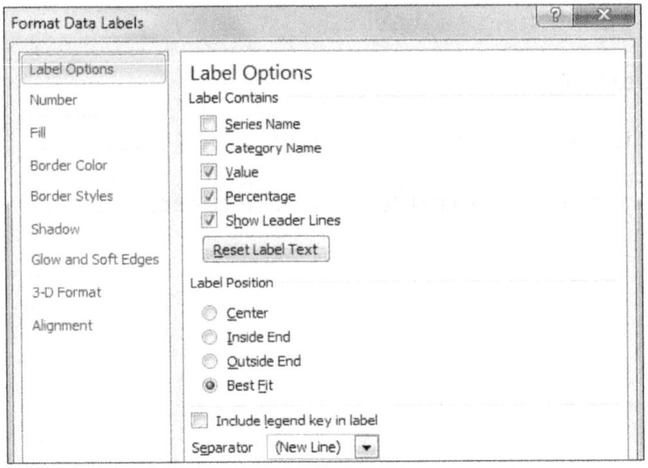

Figure 14-31 Data Label options

5. Click on the Number button on the Format Data Labels dialog box shown above in Figure 14-31. Select the Number category and remove the Decimal places option in the **FORMAT CODE** field, then click the Add button.

6. Click the Close button.

7. Move the legend to the bottom of the chart.

8. Save the changes.

   The chart should look like the one in Figure 14-32.

   Figure 14-33 shows the entire dashboard report.

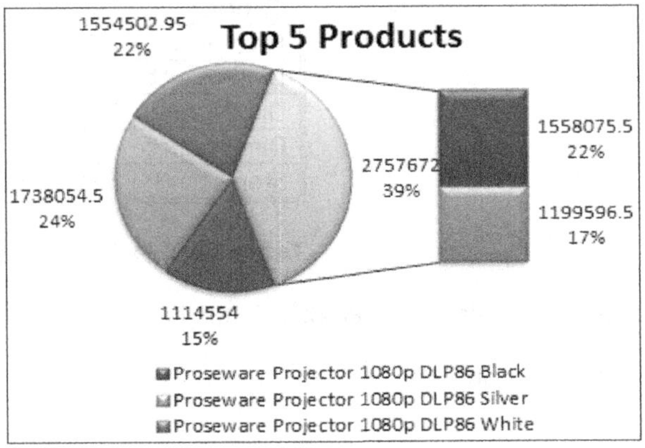

Figure 14-32 Top 5 Products pivot chart

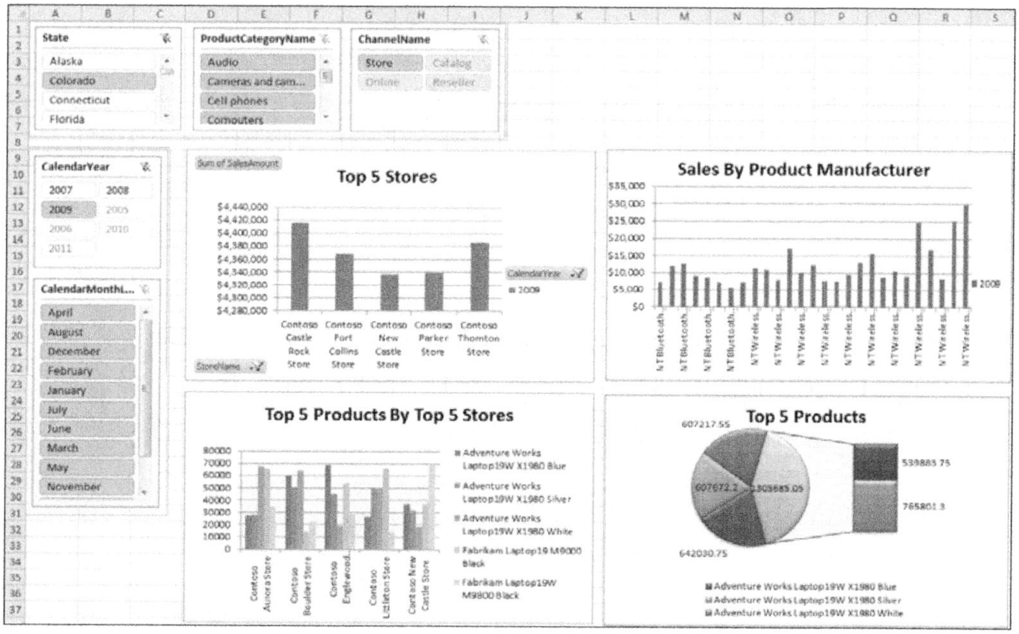

Figure 14-33 Dashboard report

Using The CTRL + Click Keys With Slicers

This key combination will allow you to clear multiple options in a slicer while leaving other options selected. For example, the Product Category slicer has several options selected, as shown in Figure 14-34. If you hold the CTRL key down, then click on the Audio, Cell Phone and Computers options, they will be cleared, as shown in Figure 14-35. The pivot charts will be filtered by the remaining options.

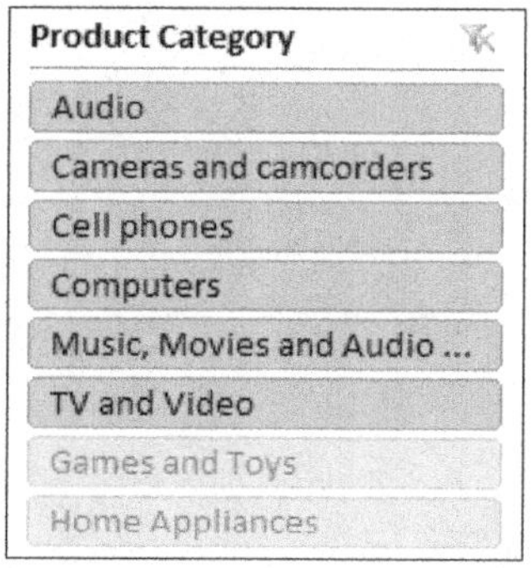

Figure 14-34 Product Category slicer

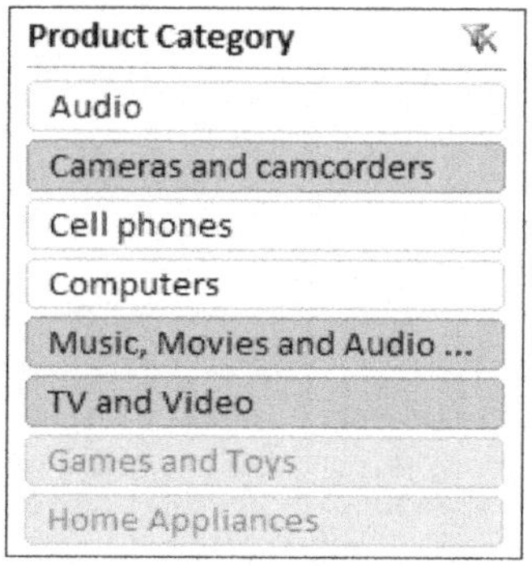

Figure 14-35 Product Category slicer after using the CTRL + Click keys

INDEX

D

E

Q

R

S

T

U

V

W

X

Y

Made in the USA
Monee, IL
05 November 2026

67810730R00171